About Island Press

Since 1984, the nonprofit organization Island Press has been stimulating, shaping, and communicating ideas that are essential for solving environmental problems worldwide. With more than 1,000 titles in print and some 30 new releases each year, we are the nation's leading publisher on environmental issues. We identify innovative thinkers and emerging trends in the environmental field. We work with world-renowned experts and authors to develop cross-disciplinary solutions to environmental challenges.

Island Press designs and executes educational campaigns, in conjunction with our authors, to communicate their critical messages in print, in person, and online using the latest technologies, innovative programs, and the media. Our goal is to reach targeted audiences—scientists, policy makers, environmental advocates, urban planners, the media, and concerned citizens—with information that can be used to create the framework for long-term ecological health and human well-being.

Island Press gratefully acknowledges major support from The Bobolink Foundation, Caldera Foundation, The Curtis and Edith Munson Foundation, The Forrest C. and Frances H. Lattner Foundation, The JPB Foundation, The Kresge Foundation, The Summit Charitable Foundation, Inc., and many other generous organizations and individuals.

The opinions expressed in this book are those of the author(s) and do not necessarily reflect the views of our supporters.

TRAINS, BUSES, PEOPLE

SECOND EDITION

TRAINS, BUSES, PEOPLE

AN OPINIONATED ATLAS
OF US AND CANADIAN TRANSIT

SECOND EDITION

CHRISTOF SPIELER

ISLANDPRESS | Washington | Covelo

Library of Congress Control Number: 2021935870

All Island Press books are printed on environmentally responsible materials.

Manufactured in the United States of America

10 9 8 7 6 5 4 3 2 1

Keywords: Activity, Albuquerque, Atlanta, Austin, Boston, Buffalo, Bus Rapid Transit (BRT), Charlotte, Chicago, Cincinnati, Cleveland, commuter rail, Dallas, density, Denver, Detroit, El Paso, Eugene, Fort Collins, Hartford, heavy rail, Honolulu, Houston, Jacksonville, Kansas City, Las Vegas, light rail, Little Rock, Los Angeles, Memphis, Miami, Milwaukee, Minneapolis–St. Paul, modal equality, monorail, Nashville, New Orleans, New York, Norfolk, Oklahoma City, Orlando, peoplemover, Philadelphia, Phoenix, Pittsburgh, Portland, Richmond, Sacramento, Salt Lake City, San Diego, San Francisco, Seattle, streetcars, St. Louis, Tampa, transit connectivity, transit frequency, travel time, Tucson, Washington, DC, Toronto, Montreal, Vancouver, Ottawa, Edmonton, Calgary

FOR KIMBERLY,

without whose encouragement this book would not exist,
and also in memory of Al, who loved urbanity.

CONTENTS

Metro Areas by Population

ACKNOWLEDGMENTS

All photographs by Christof Spieler. Graphics for "Modes," "Guideways," "Stations," Fares, and "Capacity," as well the maps under "What transit does well," bus drawing under "Funding" and the trip diagram under "Activity" by David Copeland Loredo. Ridership graph by Mandi Chapa. Jacki Schaefer at Water Oak Studio (wateroakstudio.com) processed RAW files for photos.

All other maps and graphics by Christof Spieler, except for the card under "connectivity," the bus rendering, signage, and system map under "legibility," the USGC map for New York City, the OC Streetcar rendering, the rendering for Arrow commuter rail, the rendering for the Maryland Purple Line, the Boston route map, the Boston Silver Line route diagram, the Dallas route diagram, the Dallas Silver Line rendering, the Miami busway rendering, the Miami Metromover route diagram, the Toronto Hurontario rendering, the Toronto Finch West rendering, the Tempe Streetcar rendering, the Montreal metro map, the Monteal REM rendering, the Montreal Pie-X rendering, the Charlotte regional plan map, the Daybreak plan in Salt Lake City, the Austin downtown route map, the Milwaukee Streetcar expansion diagram, the Oklahoma City route map and rendering, the Edmonton campus map, the Richmond map, and the Honolulu renderings. The race dot map of New Orleans is Image Copyright, 2013, Weldon Cooper Center for Public Service, Rector and Visitors of the University of Virginia (Dustin A. Cable, creator.) Transit agency logos, maps, and renderings are © the transit agencies and are used under fair use.

Map data for the metropolitan area-wide maps is from the United States Census Bureau. Map data for the detail maps © OpenStreetMap contributors. Most ridership data is from the American Public Transportation Association's quarterly ridership report and from 2019 Federal Transit Administration data, with some additional data from other sources; it reflects pre-COVID ridership data. Construction status of new routes is as of January 2021; systems in deign but not yet under construction by then are not included. Employment center data is from "Downtown Rebirth: Documenting the Live-Work Dynamic in 21st-century US Cities," prepared for the International Downtown Association by the Philadelphia Center City District, Paul R. Levy and Lauren M. Gilchrist, 2013, http://de finingdown town.org.

The best source of transit news is Jeff Wood's *Overhead Wire* compilation (https://theoverheadwire. com), and the best information on new projects is Yonah Freemark's *Transport Politic* blog and Transport Explorer database at www.thetransportpolitic.com.

This book reflects my views only, and not those of my employer. I have served on the board of one of the agencies in the book (Houston METRO) and done consulting work for several (MBTA, Trinity Metro, Sound Transit, METRO) but I have done my best to treat those systems no differently than any others.

Thanks to Heather Boyer at Island Press, to Jeff Wood, Lucy Galbraith, and Darryl Young for encouraging me to write this book, to Lisa Gray who edited the *Cite Magazine* article that ultimately resulted in this book, to Mandi Chapa for graphic advice, to David Brag- don, Stephanie Lotshaw, and Angelique Siy for input on text, to the great staff and board at Metro, to my team at Huitt-Zollars, who make me excited to come to work nearly every day, to all the transit advocates and agency staff across the United States whom I've learned from, to everyone on Transit Twitter, to Annise Parker and Sylvester Turner, who thought it was a good idea to put a blogger on a transit board, to John Sedlak, whose class at Rice inspired my interest in transit, to my parents, and above all to my wife, Kimberly Carter, who is somehow okay with planning vacations around transit photography.

Frequent route networks were identified, and the data on population accessible by frequent transit calculated, using the Remix Transit platform, https://www.remix.com.

Find updates on the transit systems in the book and more on what makes good transit at http://trainsbusespeople.com.

INTRODUCTION

TRANSIT WHERE THE PEOPLE ARE

In 2020, COVID hit the transit industry hard. Thousands of train operators, bus drivers, mechanics, and other staff were infected; at the MTA in New York alone 136 transit employees died. With office employees working from home, restaurants, bars, and shops closed, events cancelled, and many of the ordinary parts of life paused, US transit ridership in April 2020 was 80% lower than April 2019. That triggered a financial crisis as fare revenue dropped and tax revenue decreased. COVID almost instantly, became another talking point for the regular cast of anti-transit pundits. But transit continued to prove its value. Essential workers such as nurses, grocery store employees, and distribution workers kept riding, and transit kept cities functioning.

COVID doesn't change the fundamentals of transit. Over thousands years of history, epidemics have not killed cities. Our human urge to gather is not going away. There will surely be some changes, but the basic travel patterns will still be there. And what makes transit successful will still be the same.

I live in Houston, Texas, a famously car-oriented city. I work at an urban planning practice and teach at Rice University. During the pandemic I have been fortunate enough to be able to work from home. But in normal tmes, I would walk out my door, go three blocks down the street, and get on a train. It would take me to work, to meetings, to lunch with friends, to medical appointments, to lectures, to museums, to the park, dropping me off right in the middle of things at all those places. Transit makes my life better.

This is possible because the transit I live next to is high quality. The train runs every six minutes, so my wait is short. It has its own lane, so it's not slowed down by congestion. It has nice stations that shelter me from the rain, and good passenger information.

But, most importantly, I can take the train for most of my travel because it goes to the right places. It runs by lots of apartments and condos and houses. It runs by lots of office buildings. It also runs by many of the other things I want to do in my life—socialize, learn, have fun. More people ought to have the choice to live like this. I'm on the train with lots of different people, who live in different places and work in different kinds of jobs. This transit line works for them, too. Good transit offers access, opportunity, and freedom.

People who don't ride transit benefit from transit, too. People who use transit—be they downtown professionals or minimum-wage service workers—are essential to the economy. Everybody on a bus or a train represents one less car on the road. Public transit significantly reduces the environmental impacts of cities, reducing energy use and preventing sprawl that eats up natural habitat. All of these benefits scale with ridership—as people use transit more, its societal benefits increase.

Some cities have built transit that has transformed the experience of living there. Some have simply built a lot of transit. Some have built very little. It is worth comparing them and drawing lessons. That's what this book is about. It looks at every metro area in the United States and Canada that has built rail or bus rapid transit (or currently has a line under construction), considers why they made the decisions that they did, and looks at how well those lines have worked.

This edition is expanded to include Canada, where there are many lessons for the US. Two new US cities have been added: Indianapolis and San Juan, Puerto Rico. The cities have been updated to include changes since 2018 and the introductory material has been revised and expanded. I hope this new edition will help anyone who is working to offer more people great transit.

WHAT TRANSIT DOES WELL

Transit is not the primary mode of transportation in the United States. Seventy-seven percent of Americans commute in a single-occupant car, and only 5 percent by train, bus, or ferry (the rest carpool, walk, or bike). Improving transit options and ridership is essential for two reasons.

The first reason is that transit is available to almost anyone, regardless of age, ability, or income. We tend to consider cars as universal, but a significant portion of Americans are not able to drive because they are too young, because they have physical or mental disabilities (which get more common with age), or because they cannot afford a car.

This alone is reason to have transit. Transit allows everyone to get around, to have interesting and fulfilling lives, to be full and productive members of society. Countries like Switzerland and Japan, as a matter of national policy, provide transit everywhere, regardless of how many people will ride it. This is what transportation expert Jarrett Walker calls "coverage service." In the United States, we take this approach to roads. Cities generally pave every street, regardless of how many houses it has on it. They don't do cost-effectiveness calculations to see if the property taxes collected on the adjoining properties will cover the cost of pavement, or project traffic figures to see if the use of the road will meet minimum standards. They simply pave a street to every house. State highway departments do the same. Every town, no matter how small, is on a network of highways. Transit is not as universal, but it is still widespread; nearly every town of meaningful size has some bus routes, and even rural areas have "dial a ride" services for seniors and the disabled.

But if transit is only a lifeline service, it will be limited in quality. Even in Switzerland, rural bus service is hourly or less. There is simply not enough travel demand in small alpine villages to justify running a bus any more often. In areas with a low level of transit service, from an Alpine village to a US suburb, people who can use and afford a car are likely to drive. In these low-density places, roads are less congested and every building has a parking space in front if it. Someone driving can park right in front of their destination in plentiful and free parking spaces, but someone arriving on a bus must navigate that parking lot on foot to get to their destination. Lifeline transit is a necessity for some people, but it is never as good as driving.

But the majority of the global population lives in cities, which makes transit essential for a second reason: it moves a lot of people in very little space. A transit bus seats 40 people (and can handle another 40 people standing) and takes up about as much space on the street as two to three cars. Thus, 80 people can travel in the space it takes to move three people in single-occupant vehicles. Transit also requires no parking space at the destination—the vehicle simply keeps going and makes another trip. Consider Manhattan: 2.4 million people work on the island. Getting them all to work in cars would require several hundred lanes of bridges and tunnels and 2.4 million parking spaces, which, built as surface parking, would cover the entire 30-square-mile island, leaving no space for the workplaces those commuters are traveling to. This space advantage is a matter of geometry, not technology. Taxis, whether hailed at the curb or summoned via an app, still take up as much space as a car. In fact they take more, since they circle empty as they wait for a rider. Autonomous cars may be able to travel closer together than cars, but they still cannot approach the space efficiency of an ordinary bus, let alone a subway.

Space efficiency is vital because cities succeed by crowding things together. A company works by bringing together its employees, with their various skills and functions, into one place. It also depends on other businesses, from lawyers to reprographics services, and benefits from having them nearby. Moreover, it benefits from being near its competitors, so it can draw from a larger talent pool, and from being near restaurants and stores and cultural institutions that will make its lo-

The Swiss Post bus system (above) is classic coverage transit. The 213 bus (like the Salginatobel Bridge it is crossing) links a village of fewer than 30 houses to Schiers, a town of only 2,600 people, and its train station.

cation desirable to talented employees. Even the tech industry—which actually makes its money by allowing people to communicate, shop, and entertain themselves anywhere—is highly concentrated not just in the San Francisco Bay Area but in specific neighborhoods. Cities work by physically bringing people together, and that generates commerce, ideas, and culture. Cities are vital to the nation as a whole. The ten largest US metropolitan areas, all of which have large transit networks, represent a third of the US economy. Some of the most economically productive places in the United States, from Midtown Manhattan to the Las Vegas Strip to Harvard University, are utterly dependent on transit. Around the world, every major economic center has a large and busy transit network.

Transit can be the mode of choice in a city. In Manhattan, getting around on the subway is faster and more convenient than driving. Even in famously car-oriented Houston, half of the suburban commuters to downtown take the bus because it is often faster, generally less expensive, and always less stressful than driving. But it is not just affluent riders who benefit from the high-quality transit that cities can support; time often matters even more to low-income riders.

But for transit to be a mode of choice, it has to be integrated into a walkable, mixed-use place. Every transit rider is either a pedestrian or a bicyclist for some part of their transit trip. Even people who drive to a park-and-ride lot have to walk to their job at the other end of the ride. Transit is only convenient if walking is convenient. And, once a rider is at their destination, they want to be able to do other things a well—get a coffee, eat lunch with their coworkers, shop, and run an errand. If they need a car to do any of those things, they will use a car for their entire trip.

Successful transit systems work because they serve places where many people want to go: commuting destinations like employment centers and universities; gathering places like sports stadiums, convention centers, and entertainment districts; and dense, walkable, mixed-use neighborhoods. Transit is not the best mode for everything, and there are many places where it will never play a large role. But there are some places where it not only works well, but becomes essential. In those places, transit still mattered after cars became widespread and the government invested billions in highways, and it will still matter no matter what future technologies come along.

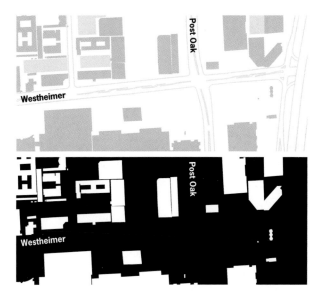

At Westheimer and Post Oak in Uptown Houston (top), a car-oriented retail, office, and residential area, roads and parking (above, shaded in black) take up over half the land.

In cities of all sizes, big employment centers have the highest transit use. Forty-seven percent of downtown Seattle (above) employees take transit, even though many of them have cars at home. Only 30% commute in a car alone. From 2010 to 2016, downtown added 45,000 jobs, but only 2,000 more car trips. In dense, walkable neighborhoods with a mix of uses, people can depend on transit for all trips. In central Toronto neighborhoods (below), a third of households have no cars.

WHY WE GET IT WRONG

To build good public transit, which is transit that is useful to lots of people, we need to have the right conversations about transit. We need to talk about what matters—to focus on the quality of service, not the technology that delivers it; to talk about all kinds of transit riders, not just about a narrow target market; to understand that the transit experience depends on buildings and streets and sidewalks as much as it does on stations and trains; and, above all, to talk about getting transit in the right places. We also need to be willing to talk about where transit is falling short.

It is remarkable how much of the public transit we build in the United States and Canada doesn't go where people want to go or when they want to go there. Many cities have invested in transit that doesn't maximize the zone of access—rail or bus-rapid-transit lines that miss the city's densest residential areas, ignore major employment centers, or don't serve major hospitals or universities.

When we get transit wrong, it's usually not because transit planners don't know what they're doing; it's because of the larger political context within which transit agencies are operating. Each transit line represents a decision made by elected officials, agency staff, and the public. Some were good decisions, and some were bad decisions. All are lessons we can learn from.

The measure of success in transit is not miles of track or ribbon cuttings, it is whether transit makes people's lives better. Transit isn't really about trains and buses; it's about people. ∎

We tend to talk too much about modes of transit and not enough about where we build that transit. Statements such as "This city needs light rail" are not useful. Statements that identify the specific goal, such as "We need better transit connecting downtown, the hospitals, and the university," are much more helpful. One example of where this went wrong is Cincinnati, where a plan to connect five employment centers became a plan to build a streetcar. When politics and funding constrained the project, the "streetcar" part of the project was kept but the "connect centers" part was dropped.

We hurry through system planning. Once a transit agency decides to build a transit project in a specific corridor, it does detailed analysis, following federal guidelines, of the exact alignment, the station locations, and what parts of the line will be elevated or at grade. But the earlier, and more important, decision to focus on that corridor often gets much less analysis.

We don't think about networks. No rail transit or BRT line exists in isolation; it is part of a network of multiple routes, both bus and rail. Many riders will use more than one of those lines. An effective line makes the whole network more useful. A good rail corridor will add ridership to connecting bus routes, and vice versa.

We talk about infrastructure, not service. Tracks, bus lanes, and stations are easy to see and easy for elected officials to get excited about. But what transit riders actually need is service. It's notable how much frequency and span is an afterthought in transit planning discussions.

We plan single-purpose transit. Transit that does only one thing will never be as useful—or draw as many riders—as transit that meets multiple needs. Yet we tend to talk about really specific types of trips, such as 9-to-5 commutes to downtown or trips to the airport. Those alone won't fill trains or buses all day long, every day. In places like New Jersey (below), for example, commuter rail has

frequent service only at peak hours, and neither schedules nor fares are coordinated with local busses. Those tracks could be carrying people all day long, but single-purpose thinking means they're underused except at rush hour.

We focus on "choice riders." Many transit projects are aimed specifically at attracting new riders. Many of the highest ridership transit projects, though, succeeded because they also made trips better for existing transit riders. Moreover, the idea of "choice riders" often gets decision makers thinking about very specific target audiences, and caught up in false perceptions of what riders want, leading to a focus on "sexiness" rather than usefulness.

We don't use data. Often transit is planned based on people's mental image of the city. Assumptions are made that everyone works downtown and lives in the suburbs, that close-in neighborhoods are dense and suburban neighborhoods are not, and that low-income residents all live in certain places. The people—whether agency staff or elected officials—who are drawing lines are rarely looking at population or employment data. When public meetings are held, the people who show up are usually not representative of the population as a whole. Some of the people who need transit most—like low-income families juggling multiple jobs—do not have time to come to an open house. But they do show up in the data.

We think at too large a scale. Regional planning exercises draw regional maps. On those maps, long lines look impressive. But that is not what determines usefulness. At a large scale, a regional system can appear to cover everything, but a rider getting off a train is likely willing to walk no more than half a mile. Anything that is farther away is essentially out of reach. A short line that serves many destinations is far more useful than a long one through low-density development. In San Francisco, for example, the Geary bus (left) carries more people than SMART, eBART, and the Pleasanton BART line combined (right).

We think about right of way, not destinations. Many, perhaps most, of US rail lines were conceived because some sort of right of way already existed. It is easy to look at a freight rail line and imagine running trains there. But the purpose of transit isn't to run trains; it is to get people to destinations. If an existing corridor happens to do that, it is useful. If it doesn't, how easy it is to acquire or construct is irrelevant.

We avoid opposition. When we build transit through areas that have lots of transit demand, there are many "stakeholders"—residents, businesses owners, and property owners. Many will welcome better transportation options, but many will have concerns about the impacts of a transit project. Some will be very angry. That opposition is an inevitable part of building a transit project. A good project has to take the concerns seriously, and will be designed to minimize the impact and maximize the benefits. Neighbors understand their neighborhood, and their concerns are usually valid. But the fact that somebody opposes a project should not be reason enough to stop it. In fact, if nobody opposes a project, that is a sign that it is a bad project, since it doesn't go anywhere crowded enough to justify good transit. The fear of opposition often leads to bad projects. New York's Port Authority, for example, is planning an airport train (solid line, below) that requires a transfer and will actually take riders in the wrong direction rather than a subway expansion (dashed line) or dedicated bus lane that would be more useful but might draw neighborhood opposition.

We build on past injustice and add to it. Transit agencies are still managing and operating systems that have racism embedded in them. They have inherited past decisions, entrenched systems and ways of thinking. They have operated in a world full of racist policy — such as deed restrictions, zoning, and mortgage-lending policies designed to keep the suburbs white. Planning processes that are based on what we already have, and policies that take past policy decisions for granted, only perpetuate that injustice.

We don't share power. Transit will always reflect the priority of the people who make decisions on what to build and what service to operate. Those decision makers often don't reflect the regions that represent or the people who ride transit. Across the United States and Canada, transit boards still tend to be disproportionately white and male, and include few transit riders. Moreover, decision-making structures are often inequitable, over-representing suburban interests, and some people (like business leaders) are invited into discussions while others are not. This often leads to transit that serves fewer people.

In the 1960s, rail transit was a rarity in the United States, confined to the Northeast and a few scattered cities elsewhere. Today, it's normal. All of the top 25 metropolitan areas have at least one rail transit line. This is the result of decades of construction. In 2018, the United States will have gone 50 years with at least a mile of new rail transit opening every year.

But this expansion is not uniform. Some cities have built more than others, and few have built steadily. We've also seen more rail shut down. In Boston, Chicago, and Pittsburgh, much of the new construction was actually replacements for older lines that were shut down. Philadelphia's heavy rail, light rail, and streetcar system is actually 35% smaller in 2016 than in 1960.

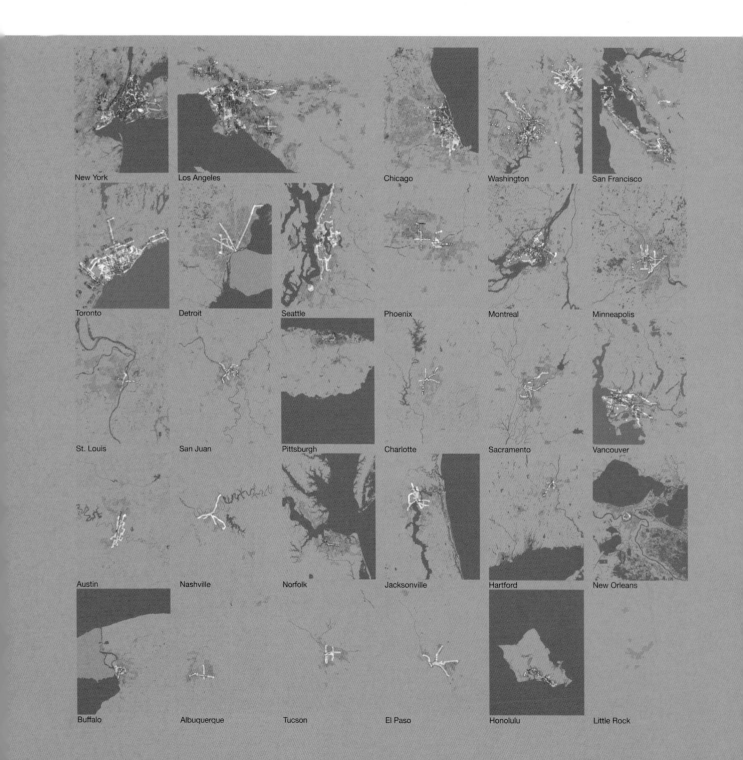

New York

Los Angeles

Chicago

Washington

San Francisco

Toronto

Detroit

Seattle

Phoenix

Montreal

Minneapolis

St. Louis

San Juan

Pittsburgh

Charlotte

Sacramento

Vancouver

Austin

Nashville

Norfolk

Jacksonville

Hartford

New Orleans

Buffalo

Albuquerque

Tucson

El Paso

Honolulu

Little Rock

PART 1
HOW TRANSIT WORKS

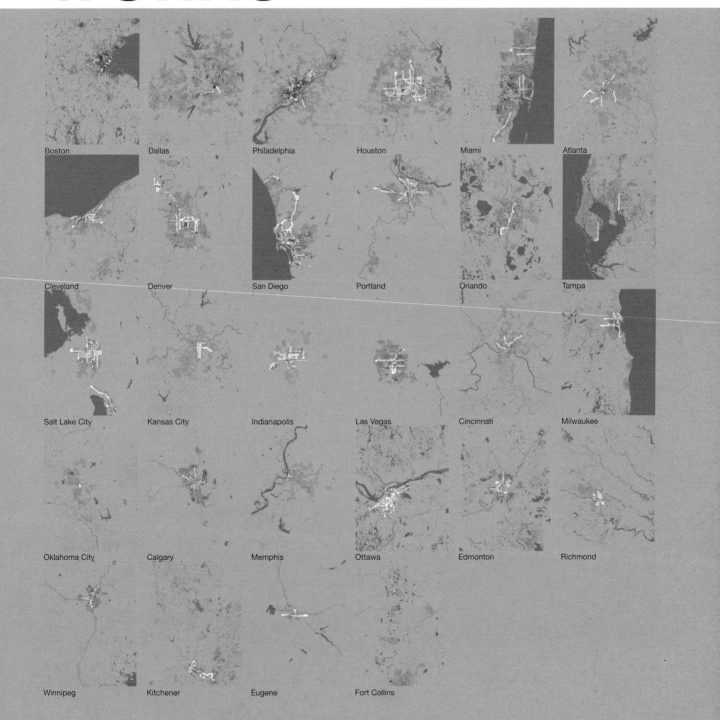

Boston

Dallas

Philadelphia

Houston

Miami

Atlanta

Cleveland

Denver

San Diego

Portland

Orlando

Tampa

Salt Lake City

Kansas City

Indianapolis

Las Vegas

Cincinnati

Milwaukee

Oklahoma City

Calgary

Memphis

Ottawa

Edmonton

Richmond

Winnipeg

Kitchener

Eugene

Fort Collins

THE HISTORY OF TRANSIT

The history of transit in the United States and Canada goes back to the 1800s, but since the 1970s, transit has been reinvented and reinvigorated. Today's networks reflect over 150 years of evolution. ■

In the 1920s, transit operated in a different world. Cars had been introduced, but only a quarter of households owned one. In urban areas, horses and carriages had always been for the rich. Most Americans and Canadians were dependent on walking.

Transit was a profit-making venture. Nearly all transit was privately owned. Some transit lines were owned by developers to support new neighborhoods, some by utilities who held city franchises to operate transit and provide electricity, and some by pure transit companies. Most were able to cover the costs of operating and building transit with fares. In fact, many cities depended on transit companies, with these fares, to provide additional services like street paving and cleaning and to pay franchise fees to the city.

Streetcars, invented in the 1880s, were the most common transit technology in the United States. Nearly every city—not just big ones like New York and Vancouver, but small ones like Missoula, Biloxi, and Lethbridge—once had streetcars. These provided the same kind of transit service that buses do today. They typically shared lanes with other vehicles and stopped at every corner. While some routes ran every few minutes, many ran only every 20 minutes or even just once an hour. Railroads were still the dominant means of long-distance travel, and virtually every town had a railroad station. Only a few cities, though, had train service specifically targeted to daily commuters.

In a few big cities like Boston, New York, Philadelphia, and Chicago, congestion caused by streetcars, carriages, and delivery wagons got intolerable, and elevated rail lines and subways were built. These lines (Like Philadelphia's, below, opened 1907-1938) were generally confined to the city limits, and stops were close together: these were systems built for walking to the stations or transferring from streetcars.

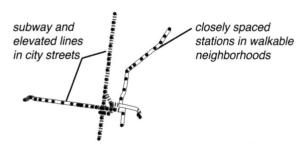

subway and elevated lines in city streets

closely spaced stations in walkable neighborhoods

Philadelphia Heavy Rail as of 1945

Across the world, the advent of mass-produced cars in the 1940s and 1950s changed the role of transit. In the United States, though, due to government policy, this change was particularly dramatic.

Starting in the early 1900s, government at all levels began to invest heavily in roadways. Prior to this, only cities had made major investments in road infrastructure. Rural roads were often maintained (to very low standards) by local farmers. In 1916, the US federal government began funding roads and encouraged all states to create highway departments. The Federal Aid Highway Act of 1956, which created the interstate system, cemented the idea that all levels of government would fund roads and that most highways would not be tolled.

In Canada, while the federal government committed funding for the Trans-Canada Highway in 1949, the primary planning and funding has always been controlled by the provinces. Ontario started building provincial highways in 1920; in the 1950s and 1960s Ontario and Quebec both started building extensive freeway systems. Government set up an unequal situation: roadways were subsidized by the government, but transit was provided by the private sector and expected to pay its own way. For obvious reasons, that did not work, and transit companies started to lose money.

In the United States, government began to require or incentivize new land-development forms that were inherently transit-hostile. Using new powers to regulate land uses and density through zoning, as granted by the US Supreme Court in 1926, cities required single-family homes and separate uses, lowering density and making it harder to do everyday chores without a car. Through the GI bill and home mortgage deduction, the US federal government explicitly favored home ownership, and that usually meant a home in a car-oriented suburb.

The shift to suburbanization and homeownership was not as strong in Canada as it was in the United States. But the population growth—Canada grew by 44% between 1945 and 1960—led to cities spreading outward beyond the reach of existing transit, and most of the new growth was car-oriented.

Transit companies started converting streetcar lines to buses in the 1920s. This made economic sense for the companies, since it reduced maintenance costs. It was also encouraged by civic leadership, who saw streetcars as obstructions to automobiles and as fundamentally old-fashioned. After a peak during World War II rationing, transit ridership started dropping precipitously. The construction of new roads encouraged people to shift to cars, which reduced ridership, which caused companies to cut service, which drove more people to buy cars. This was not inevitable. The same decline was not seen in either Japan, where major roadways were tolled, or Europe, where government subsidized transit (as well as cars). The US and Canada saw a real divergence in this period—Canadian transit ridership did not drop as much as US ridership did, and Canadian transit systems remained generally healthier.

US and Canadian transit, 1960-1969

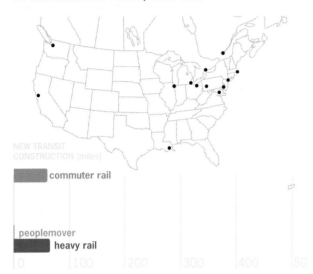

US and Canadian transit, 1970-1979

The 1960s marked the low point of North American transit. Most cities had replaced their streetcars with buses in the Great Depression or just after World War II; even systems that had modernized were now abandoned. Small portions of the San Francisco, New Orleans, Cleveland, Pittsburgh, Philadelphia, and Boston networks remained. Only Toronto kept its system largely intact. Buses cut costs, but ridership continued to fall, and service and equipment deteriorated. Major railroads in the Northeastern United States, approaching bankruptcy, cut commuter-rail service. Even in large cities that continued to be reliant on transit, expansion largely stopped. The last major new line of the New York Subway was in 1956. The notable exceptions were Chicago expanding the "L" in new freeway corridors, and Toronto opening a brand new subway system in 1954.

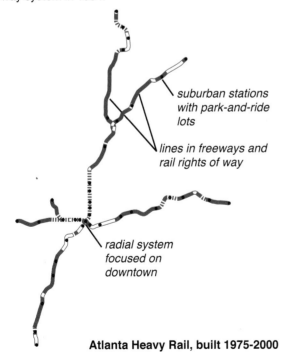

suburban stations with park-and-ride lots

lines in freeways and rail rights of way

radial system focused on downtown

Atlanta Heavy Rail, built 1975-2000

By the 1970s, cities faced two different crises. Transit systems, no longer as central as they had been, but still critical lifelines for some of the population, were going bankrupt. Meanwhile, the idea that more highways would alleviate traffic jams was proving false. Transit agencies were formed to solve these problems. The first solution was relatively straightforward: government funds were needed for operating costs and new buses. The second required something more ambitious: new rail systems.

With new freeways, and in counterreaction to the Civil Rights Movement, US cities segregated along economic and racial lines. The middle class moved outward and left the inner cities to the poor. This left most cities with a relatively prosperous, car-oriented suburban fringe, a belt of declining poor areas inside the fringe, and a vestigial downtown—still a major employment center but no longer a retail or entertainment destination. The 1970s rail systems were intended primarily to sustain those central business districts. Business interests worried that congestion would drive white-collar jobs out of the city and promoted rail as a way to make life easier for suburbanites coming to work.

But rail transit was still widely seen as old-fashioned, and the major prewar systems were falling apart. Thus, the new systems were marketed as something altogether new: open, minimalist stations, shiny trains with carpeting inside, mission-control-inspired computerized control systems, and big, free parking lots off suburban highways. These new networks introduced not only new technology but a new planning philosophy. Generally, these systems were explicitly targeted at suburban (and white) "choice riders." That meant lines heading farther out from the city, and stations further apart to allow for fast trips. These systems (like Atlanta's MARTA, left, Philadelphia's PATCO, San Francisco's BART, and Washington DC's Metrorail) were built to be driven to (or maybe take the bus to), not to be walked to. In Canada, Montreal also opened a shiny new space-aged system, but its underground lines in densely populated neighborhoods more closely resembled prewar subways.

US and Canadian transit, 1980-1989

US and Canadian transit, 1990-1999

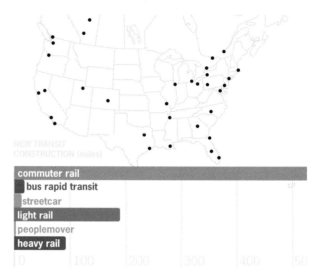

In the 1980s, new technologies and funding sources allowed rail transit to spread beyond a few big cities.

In 1964, the US Congress and President Johnson created the Urban Mass Transit Administration, today's FTA. Federal laws enacted in 1979 and 1983 established long-term funding for transit projects and formalized the program for awarding grants, today known as "New Starts." By covering up to 50% of the cost of transit projects, it put rail within the reach of more cities, but it also set up funding requirements and processes that extend the planning process and sometimes lead to odd choices. The federal government also created "formula" funds that would go to every metropolitan area, paying for new buses and transit centers and greatly improving the experience of riding transit, and promoted the development of new transit technologies like peoplemovers. In Canada, similar efforts happened on a provincial level. Ontario funded development of new transit technologies through the Urban Transportation Development Corporation.

The federal governments rescued what was left of long-distance trains with the creation of Amtrak in the US in 1971 and VIA Rail in Canada 1997, but neither provided for local trains. Thus states and provinces were forced to take over the remaining commuter-rail service or let it disappear. New equipment began appearing on the service that remained, sometimes replacing 50-year-old trains.

Light-rail systems in Edmonton (1978), Calgary (1981), San Diego (1981), Portland (1986), and Sacramento (1987) became a new model for rail transit. Cheaper than heavy rail, but still attractive enough for the desired "choice riders," light rail was an appealing option for many places. The new transit systems of the 1980s largely continued the 1970s planning philosophy, building lines far into the suburbs, with widely spaced stations. Sacramento (right) was typical in using railroad lines combined with short street-running segments in downtown.

In the 1990s, rail transit once again became a normal part of American cities. Transit advocates, agency staff, and consultants worked to spread expertise, technology, ideas, and political strategies from city to city.

Increasingly, transit became a tool for livability. Cities tried to revitalize downtowns with convention centers and boutique hotels, museums, ballparks, restaurants, lofts, and condos. Meanwhile, inner-city neighborhoods gentrified as the children of suburbia looked for shorter commutes and places with character. Even suburbs wanted walkable places and saw rail as a way to get them; Vancouver built a regional growth strategy around dense development at Skytrain stations. "Transit-oriented development" became a major theme of industry conferences.

With increased political support, cities got more ambitious. Early light-rail systems were generally expanded one line at a time; now cities began going to voters with master plans covering many lines. Dallas, Salt Lake City, and Denver embarked on multi-decade rail expansions. Along with light rail, cities started building commuter rail, with six new systems in the 1990s.

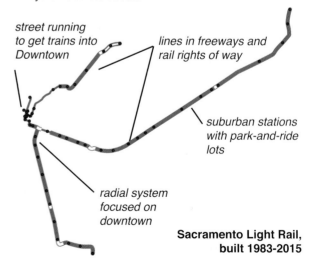

street running
to get trains into
Downtown

lines in freeways and
rail rights of way

suburban stations
with park-and-ride
lots

radial system
focused on
downtown

**Sacramento Light Rail,
built 1983-2015**

US and Canadian transit, 2000-2009

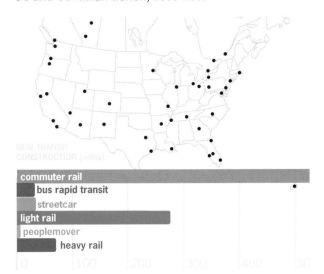

NEW TRANSIT
CONSTRUCTION (miles)

commuter rail	
bus rapid transit	
streetcar	
light rail	
peoplemover	
heavy rail	

0   100   200   300   400   500

US and Canadian transit, 2010-2019

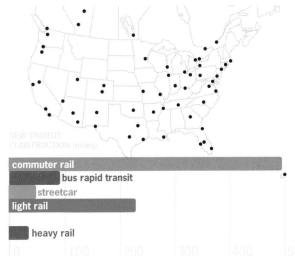

NEW TRANSIT
CONSTRUCTION (miles)

commuter rail	
bus rapid transit	
streetcar	
light rail	
heavy rail	

0   100   200   300   400   500

In the 2000s, the transit toolbox expanded further. The Bush administration pushed hard for bus rapid transit as an alternative to rail, pointing to successes in Pittsburgh and Ottawa. This resulted in some high-quality dedicated-lane systems, and in multiple cities investing in multi-corridor rapid bus lines that still shared lanes with traffic but improved speed, frequency, and passenger amenities. Meanwhile, the modern streetcar line that Portland opened in 2001 inspired dozens of other cities to study streetcars, several of which got funding under the Obama administration's stimulus in 2009 and the TIGER program that followed.

US transit is as diverse as it has ever been, and major transit infrastructure—rail and BRT—is now a normal part of American cities. Big cities like Phoenix and Houston (below) that had rejected rail expansion in the 1980s opened new BRT systems. So did cities like Norfolk (1.8 million), Albuquerque (1.2 million), Tucson (1 million) and Eugene (360,000) that had been considered too small for anything but local bus.

In the 2010s, massive transit expansion in large cities continued. In 2016, Seattle voters approved $53.8 billion in new transit and LA voters approved $120 billion. So did the expansion of rail and BRT into smaller cities, with new streetcars in Milwaukee, El Paso, and Tucson and BRT in Richmond, Albuquerque, and Fort Collins. But merely building a lot of transit doesn't make a good transit network. Many rail lines had been planned as separate overlays on existing bus networks. Now more cities, like Portland, Houston, Minneapolis (below), and Seattle, are starting to see rail and bus as one network, improving the quality of bus service and redesigning bus networks in conjunction with rail and BRT projects. Boston and New York, cities where the transit discussion had focused mainly on rail, are making bus service faster and more reliable with new bus lanes. The focus on bus came in part from a focus on equity, with networks explicitly designed to connect people to jobs and education and offer current bus riders faster and more-reliable trips. Portland, Minneapolis, Houston, and Toronto all deliberately built rail to benefit low-income neighborhoods where transit ridership was already high.

branded bus route with upgraded stops and traffic signal priority

rail connecting multiple employment centers and universities

light rail on city streets through low income neighborhoods

Minneapolis-St. Paul, 2020

DRAWING A LINE

The first, most important, act in the building of transit is drawing a line. Across hundreds of square miles, a metropolitan area has to decide which corridor is most worthy of investment because it will serve the most people or best improve access. No region has an unlimited transit budget, so prioritization is key.

That decision creates a zone of access—a line of stations or stops that each serve whatever is within half a mile. Everything in that zone should be easier to get to. If there are enough useful destinations in that area, transit becomes a viable option for many people.

On a large scale, transit planning is simple. It takes real expertise to schedule buses or to compare the cost effectiveness of different possible rail corridors, but anyone can look at a city and see where transit will serve the most people, and thus where investing in bus and rail will do the most good.

Governments generally require formal planning processes for major transit projects. But simply mandating a process will not ensure good planning. Planning is a process of deciding what matters to us. Having these planning discussions publicly will make for better transit. We often disguise policy issues as if they are technical issues, but transit planning is really about what kinds of cities we want to build. That's a discussion for everyone. ■

Step 0: Agree on goals. Transit lines can be designed to accomplish different things. Different lines may try to increase transit ridership, or add capacity, or speed up existing transit trips, or serve visitors, or support new development. Those are policy decisions, and they will guide how corridors are prioritized. Being explicit about what the goals are will lead to more open discussions and better decisions.

Step 1: Identify density. Some cities have a higher population density than others, but just about every city with a medium or large population in the United States has some clusters of density. These high-density areas are places where a transit stop is likely to serve many residents within walking distance.

Step 2: Identify centers. Every city has a downtown, which is generally a significant travel destination. Most cities have other centers as well. These can be other prewar downtowns where multiple cities grew together into one metropolitan area: postwar "edge city" employment centers, government complexes, universities, hospitals, or cultural districts. New development can create new centers in old industrial neighborhoods or on greenfield sites. These places are major destinations for commuters going to school or to work, and they often drive other kinds of ridership, such as people going to appointments, to shop, eat, visit museums, or attend events.

Step 3: Identify bottlenecks. Many cities have natural barriers that restrict travel. The most common are bodies of water with only a few crossing points, but mountain ranges can have the same impact. These bottlenecks tend to funnel lots of trips through the same corridor, and tend to be congestion points on both roadways and transit.

Step 4: Identify corridors. A good transit corridor is one with high density where multiple centers line up, perhaps resulting in a bottleneck. Most cities have at least one strong potential transit corridor like this. Often, it is already a transit corridor. Simply looking for a city's busiest bus route is good way to identify a strong transit corridor. A good corridor must be reasonably straight: people do not want to move in "U"s or circles or zig-zags. It is critical when identifying corridors to think about land use, not existing transportation infrastructure. A congested freeway might be a sign that transit is needed, but that doesn't mean that freeway is a strong transit corridor. We need to think about where people are going, not what path they are currently taking.

Step 5: Decide what level of service, capacity, and travel time is appropriate.

A transit corridor will be useful only if the transit is there when people need it. That means a reliable frequency, total travel time, and span of service (five days a week, or seven? all day, or rush hour only?). If it is a good transit corridor, it should justify service seven days a week, from early morning to late at night, at least every 15 minutes for most of the day. That is what makes the investment in tracks, busways, and stations worthwhile.

Step 6: Pick a mode. The technological decisions— light rail or heavy rail, street level or elevated—should be made last, based on what will provide the best service in that corridor. Sometimes the decision may be driven by capacity. For example, heavy rail can carry more people than light rail, which can carry more than BRT. Sometimes, it is driven by speed. Sometimes, it relates to what exists already. If an existing line can be extended, that is usually preferable to building a separate line that requires passengers to transfer, and if existing infrastructure can be repurposed, that is better than starting from scratch. Sometimes the decision to use a specific mode is driven purely by cost—either the capital cost to build it or the operating cost when it is open.

Frequent Transit in US and Canadian Metropolitan Areas with Rail or BRT

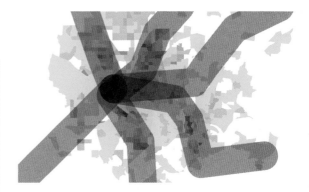

	total population	within 1/2 mile of frequent transit
Vancouver, BC	2,463,431	66%
Toronto, ON	5,928,040	59%
Ottawa–Gatineau, ON/QC	1,323,783	46%
New York-Newark, NY-NJ-CT-PA	22,589,036	43%
Kitchener–Cambridge–Waterloo, ON	523,894	43%
Montreal, QC	4,098,927	43%
San Diego-Chula Vista-Carlsbad, CA	3,338,330	37%
Chicago-Naperville, IL-IN-WI	9,825,325	29%
Urban Honolulu, HI	974,563	29%
Salt Lake City-Provo-Orem, UT	2,641,048	28%
Portland-Vancouver-Salem, OR-WA	3,259,710	26%
Edmonton, AB	1,321,426	25%
Winnipeg, MB	778,489	24%
Seattle-Tacoma, WA	4,903,675	23%
Las Vegas-Henderson, NV	2,313,238	23%
Los Angeles-Long Beach, CA	18,711,436	22%
Denver-Aurora, CO	3,617,927	22%
Tucson-Nogales, AZ	1,093,777	22%
Philadelphia-Reading-Camden, PA-NJ-DE-MD	7,209,620	22%
Austin-Round Rock-Georgetown, TX	2,227,083	22%
Calgary, AB	1,392,609	20%
Eugene-Springfield, OR	382,067	20%
Buffalo-Cheektowaga-Olean, NY	1,204,100	19%
San Jose-San Francisco-Oakland, CA	9,665,887	17%
Washington-Baltimore-Arlington, DC-MD-VA-WV-PA	9,814,928	17%
Houston-The Woodlands, TX	7,253,193	16%
Milwaukee-Racine-Waukesha, WI	2,047,966	16%
Boston-Worcester-Providence, MA-RI-NH-CT	8,287,710	14%
Phoenix-Mesa, AZ	5,002,221	14%
El Paso-Las Cruces, TX-NM	1,062,319	13%
Minneapolis-St. Paul, MN-WI	4,027,861	12%
Miami-Port St. Lucie-Fort Lauderdale, FL	6,889,936	12%
Fort Collins, CO	356,899	12%
Richmond, VA	1,291,900	10%
Sacramento-Roseville, CA	2,639,124	10%
Jacksonville-St. Marys-Palatka, FL-GA	1,688,701	8%
Detroit-Warren-Ann Arbor, MI	5,341,994	8%
Pittsburgh-New Castle-Weirton, PA-OH-WV	2,603,259	8%
Indianapolis-Carmel-Muncie, IN	2,457,286	8%
Cincinnati-Wilmington-Maysville, OH-KY-IN	2,280,246	7%
Hartford-East Hartford, CT	1,470,083	7%
Albuquerque-Santa Fe-Las Vegas, NM	1,158,464	7%
Nashville-Davidson–Murfreesboro, TN	2,062,547	6%
Tampa-St. Petersburg-Clearwater, FL	3,194,831	6%
Kansas City-Overland Park-Kansas City, MO-KS	2,501,151	6%
Cleveland-Akron-Canton, OH	3,586,918	5%
Atlanta–Athens-Clarke County–Sandy Springs, GA-AL	6,853,392	5%
New Orleans-Metairie-Hammond, LA-MS	1,507,017	5%
Charlotte-Concord, NC-SC	2,797,636	5%
St. Louis-St. Charles-Farmington, MO-IL	2,907,648	4%
San Juan-Carolina, PR	2,297,875	3%
Dallas-Fort Worth, TX-OK	8,057,796	3%
Orlando-Lakeland-Deltona, FL	4,160,646	2%
Virginia Beach-Norfolk, VA-NC	1,857,626	1%
Memphis-Forrest City, TN-MS-AR	1,371,039	1%
Oklahoma City-Shawnee, OK	1,481,542	1%
Little Rock-North Little Rock, AR	908,941	0%

Generally speaking, transit planning happens in two steps. First, we decide what corridors to serve. A city might adopt a master plan with multiple corridors, or it might pick a single corridor to prioritize. Then, within a corridor, we pick a precise alignment—which actual streets or other rights-of-way to follow, whether the line will be at grade, elevated or tunneled, and where the stations will be. The second step often gets much more public discussion, but the first does far more to determine ridership.

Top to bottom: The population density of Houston, employment centers in Houston, and the Houston frequent-bus network. Understanding the structure of a city is key to creating good transit. Sometimes, as with Houston's multicentric skyline (left), that is obvious; sometimes it is counterintuitive, and data can help us reset our incorrect mental maps.

NETWORKS

The basic structures of transit networks—how routes connect, where they overlap, which places they focus on—are shaped by local geography, history, and the philosophies of transit planners. While there are some commonalities, there are notable differences from city to city. In the Northeast, for example, Boston has a strong radial bus-to-rail feeder structure, New York overlaps bus with radial rail, and Philadelphia has a bus/rail grid within the city and a feeder network outside it. Once these patterns are set, they shape networks and determine which trips are easy and which are not, for decades. ■

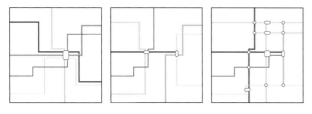

Some networks are radial (left), with routes radiating out from downtown. Some radiate out from multiple hubs (center). Some are grids (right), with parallel routes that intersect in many places. The radial networks work best for downtown-bound trips; grids offer quicker and more direct trips to many places outside downtown.

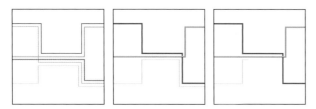

Some networks provide as many one-seat rides as possible (left). Others focus service on fewer routes, providing more frequency but requiring more transfers (right).

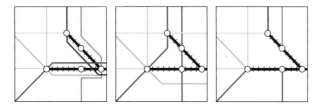

Some cities have overlapping networks where some trips can be made on bus or rail (left). Some have crosstown bus routes that intersect rail lines (center). Others terminate bus routes at rail stations (right). Overlapping networks can reduce transfers and lighten the load on crowded rail lines. Feeder networks require transfers, but free up resources to increase frequency on the bus routes.

MBTA's bus network in Boston (above) is designed to feed rail. In this map, thick lines are rail. Thin colored lines are bus routes that connect to only one rail line outside downtown Boston. Black routes go directly downtown; gray routes connect to more than one rail line. Each rail line has its set of feeder routes, like a transit watershed: the Red Line to the northwest and south, the Orange Line to the north and southwest, the Blue Line to the northeast. The Green Line—which, like the bus routes, is descended from streetcars—has fewer feeders.

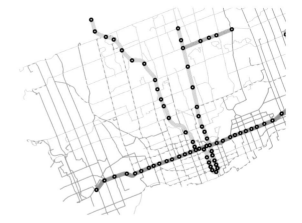

TTC's network in Toronto (above) is a grid. The routes shown in yellow connect to the Yonge-University subway line. The green routes connect to the Bloor-Danforth subway line. Unlike in Boston, lines don't converge, and they often continue across the subway instead of ending there.

Network structures often have long historical roots. In central St. Paul (below), bus routes (black) still make the same turns that streetcars (yellow) did 100 years ago. While it's often said that buses are more flexible than rail, physical infrastructure is not the biggest impediment to change. Transit agencies have institutional inertia and elected officials are reluctant to make changes that could negatively impact anyone. As a result, networks tend to evolve through piecemeal changes that gradually add complexity. Where agencies have leadership buy-in and political support, network redesigns can dramatically improve networks. In Houston, a radial network with 11 frequent routes (top right) was replaced in 2015 by a grid with twice as many frequent routes (bottom right).

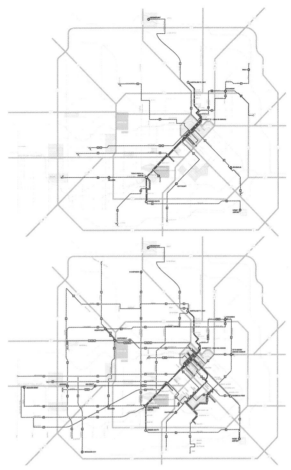

The track layouts of rail networks determine how service can—and can't—be provided. Branches, in particular, complicate operations. Additional outward spokes let networks serve more places, but add load on the core. DC's Metrorail (below left) was designed so that two lines share the tracks through the core. The Silver Line added a third. The capacity of the central tunnel limits the frequency of all three routes, and a delay on any of the lines can ripple to the other two. Denver (below right) has the opposite problem: the radial lines feed into two different downtown lines that don't intersect. Therefore, RTD has to run two rail lines on the spokes, which means the frequency of each connection is cut in half.

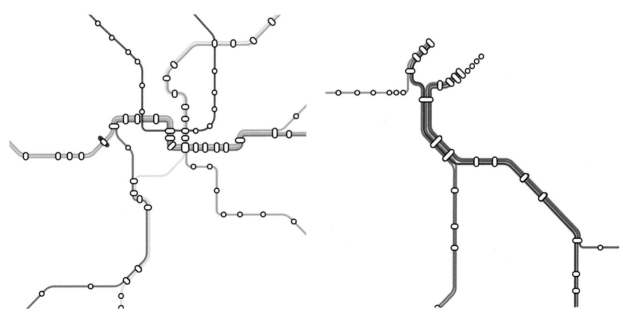

MODES

Many transit discussions focus on modes. There are people who advocate specifically for light rail, commuter rail, streetcars, or monorails, and it is easy to have a debate about any of these. But mode is not the most important aspect of transit. What riders care about most is where transit goes, how fast it is, and how reliable it is. It is better to think of modes as tools, so that once a transit corridor is selected, one mode or another may be a better fit in terms of capacity, cost, or capability. ∎

Streetcars are the least-expensive, lowest-capacity, and least reliable form of rail transit. The vehicles are not much bigger than a bus—50 to 100 feet long—and generally powered by overhead electric wires, so they can mix freely with cars, pedestrians, and bicycles. Some new systems use battery power to allow wireless segments, one is powered by diesel engines, and San Francisco's cable cars are pulled along by underground cables. While streetcars (like buses) can have their own lanes for speed and reliability, most US streetcar lines share lanes with regular traffic.

Before the 1930s, streetcars were the most common transit technology in the United States, providing the same kind of transit service that buses do today. They were almost all replaced by buses.

In the 1970s and 1980s, a few US cities revived streetcars as nostalgic circulators, using historic cars or replicas of historic cars. In 2001, the Portland Streetcar, the first in the United States to use modern vehicles with level boarding, kicked off a boom in streetcar lines. These new systems (below top) are designed as much (or more) to drive development as to provide transportation.

The term "**peoplemover**" was coined in the 1960s at Disneyland and became adopted for grade-separated automated systems using small vehicles, around 40 feet long. A 1970s federal program attempted to popularize these as circulators in downtown areas but largely proved a failure, with only four systems built. However, the technology has been used widely, and successfully, in airports, resorts, and large institutional complexes. Monorails have been the technology of the future for over 100 years now and still have not been widely used. Some monorail systems in Asia resemble heavy rail in vehicle size and capacity, but the US systems in Seattle and Las Vegas resemble peoplemovers.

Like streetcars, **light-rail** trains are powered by overhead wires and can mix with cars, pedestrians, and bicycles. However, light rail differs in that the trains are longer—cars 70–130 feet long in one-to four-car trains—and have significant separation from other traffic through dedicated lanes, separate rights of way, and grade separation.

Modern light rail evolved in Germany as an upgrade of existing streetcar networks, and the first light-rail lines in the United States were created the same way. In the 1980s, US cities started building new light-rail lines, and it has now become the most common rail-transit technology in the United States.

Initially, light-rail vehicles were "high floor," with the floors about three feet above the rail. Some systems built high station platforms to match these floors. Other systems used low platforms, requiring riders to climb up steps to board. Around 2000, vehicle manufacturers started making "low floor" cars, where the floors inside most of the car were 14 inches above the rails. This makes it easy to build platforms that match floor height, and every new system since has used these cars.

Light-rail lines and networks differ considerably in their degree of separation from traffic. Some have a lot of track in city streets, with frequent intersections with surface traffic (left bottom). Others make extensive use of overpasses, elevated segments, and even subways.

The concept of **bus rapid transit** (BRT) is fundamentally simple: separating buses from traffic makes them faster and more reliable. "BRT" can include many different things. At the high end, buses can run in subways or other completely grade-separated guideways. At the low end, some cities call painted buses and nice shelters "BRT."

For the purposes of this book, BRT has three characteristics: (1) extensive use of dedicated lanes that are not shared with any cars, (2) high-quality stations, and (3) branding that treats the service as distinct from local bus service.

BRT can be as good as, or even better than, rail. But it does have two very specific technological disadvantages. While level boarding is possible, the gap between the vehicle and the platform is not as predictable as it is on rail. Also, BRT vehicles are smaller than light-rail vehicles and can't be coupled into multi-vehicle trains. A lane of light rail can carry more people than a lane of BRT.

BRT systems can be "open" or "closed." Open systems have multiple routes that extend beyond the end of the dedicated lanes. Routes on closed systems are confined to the lanes. The capacity of BRT systems is dependent on how many lanes there are at stations. Where stations have one lane in each direction, buses cannot pass each other and the time it takes people to board limits capacity. Where stations have two lanes in each direction, buses can pass, allowing multiple buses to stop at once, and express buses to bypass the station entirely.

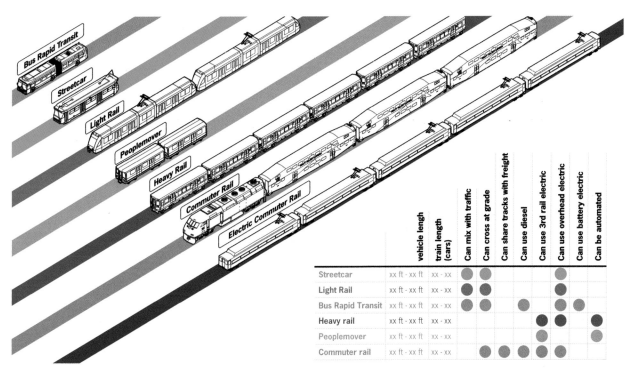

	vehicle length	train length (cars)	Can mix with traffic	Can cross at grade	Can share tracks with freight	Can use diesel	Can use 3rd rail electric	Can use overhead electric	Can use battery electric	Can be automated
Streetcar	xx ft - xx ft	xx - xx	●	●				●		
Light Rail	xx ft - xx ft	xx - xx	●	●				●		
Bus Rapid Transit	xx ft - xx ft	xx - xx	●	●		●		●	●	
Heavy rail	xx ft - xx ft	xx - xx					●	●		●
Peoplemover	xx ft - xx ft	xx - xx						●		●
Commuter rail	xx ft - xx ft	xx - xx			●	●	●	●		

Heavy rail is the highest capacity form of rail transit, with the most elaborate infrastructure. Heavy-rail trains are 4–10 cars long and are powered by electric third rails. Because those trains can't fit in a city block, and because the third rail will electrocute anyone who touches it, heavy rail requires full-grade separation in a subway, on an elevated structure, or in a sealed right of way at ground level. Station platforms are at the same level as the railcar floors for easy loading. All of this infrastructure makes heavy rail by far the costliest form of rail transit to build.

Before World War II, only a few large, very dense cities— Boston, New York, Philadelphia, and Chicago—built heavy rail. All of these systems survived. These generally have smaller cars and shorter trains than postwar systems, but they carry some of the highest loads of any rail system.

In the 1960s and 1970s, heavy rail was the preferred technology for new rail systems. Philadelphia, San Francisco, Washington, Atlanta (above), Miami, and Baltimore have systems that date from this era. Compared to the older systems, these networks have longer cars and longer trains. From the 1980s onwards, greater competition for federal funding and limited local resources favored light rail over heavy rail.

The most modern heavy-rail systems are fully automated. Driverless systems have lower operating costs, which allows for very high-frequency service. This in turn allows trains to be shorter and stations smaller. This type of small-scale, automated heavy rail was pioneered in London with Docklands Light Railway, and the best North America example is Vancouver's Skytrain. San Juan opened such a system in 2004 and Honolulu is now building one.

Commuter rail differs from all other forms of rail transit in that it is part of a connected, national railroad network that also carries freight and Amtrak. This distinction between "transit" and "railroads" is strongly held in the United States, and it has many implications in terms of regulation, design, operating practices, and attitudes. The term "commuter rail" is a misnomer. All forms of rail transit carry commuters, and commuter rail can be used to go to the beach or a game. However, due more to attitudes than to the technology, most US commuter-rail systems focus strongly on 9-to-5 commuters.

The most common commuter-rail technology in the United States is trains made up of 3 to 10 85-foot long passenger cars powered by a single diesel locomotive. Some commuter lines are electrified, which reduces operating costs but requires larger upfront investment. These use either locomotive-hauled trains like the diesel lines or self-propelled cars ("Electric Mutliple Units," or EMUs) with no locomotive. While commuter-rail trains can share tracks with freight trains, not all do. Some commuter-rail lines operate on busy mainlines with dozens of freight trains a day; others operate on lines that carry no freight trains at all, but once did, or they are simply connected somewhere to lines that do.

In Europe, self-propelled diesel cars the size of light-rail cars are common, operating sometimes as a single car and sometimes as trains of 2 or more. These "Diesel Multiple Units" (or DMUs) have now been brought to the United States, and half a dozen systems use them. Some of these trains are not compatible with freight rail and are sometimes called "diesel light rail," but that distinction is a relic of outdated US regulations. In the rest of the world, these trains are seen as commuter-rail trains, and they are treated that way in this book.

GUIDEWAYS

Every transit system has to fit into an existing city. How that's done affects where transit can go, what technology it can use, how fast and reliable it is, how much it costs, how safe it is, and what impacts it will have on the surrounding streets, businesses, and homes. ■

At Grade (All Modes)

Mainline railroads are generally built at grade, in so-called "private right-of-way" on strips of railroad-owned land. Trains only interact with cars and pedestrians at cross streets. The same approach can be used for any kind of transit. The degree of separation in at-grade rights-of-way varies dramatically. Some have cross streets with crossing gates every block. Others are in embankments or in cuts or have overpasses at cross streets (below). There are limitations to operating BRT, light rail, or heavy rail alongside mainline freight rail. Federal Railroad Administration rules encourage a 25-foot separation, and some railroads have asked for more. Many segments of light rail, though, are immediately alongside active freight tracks.

An at-grade right-of-way is possible only where the land is available. Railroads (including today's commuter-rail systems) were largely built through undeveloped land; cities grew around them. New at-grade rail-transit lines almost always use rights-of-way that already exist: abandoned railroad lines, active freight rail, or power line corridors ("hydro corridors" in Canadian parlance). Thus, while at-grade rights –of-way are reliable to operate in and relatively inexpensive to build, they are not often available where there is transit demand.

The safety of an at-grade right-of-way depends on the number of at-grade crossings. Up to 300 people a year die at railroad crossings in the United States; around 10 of those are in collisions with transit vehicles.

Street Running (Streetcar, Light Rail, Bus Rapid Transit)

The vast majority of transit operates in city streets. For local bus routes, that generally means buses are in the same lanes as cars, and bus stops are located in the sidewalk. Those same buses can be faster and more reliable if they get their own lanes. The same applies to rail transit: streetcars and light rail can both operate in the same lanes as cars, but they are far better in their own lanes. Either a rail track or a bus lane takes up the same space as a traffic lane; station platforms take up an additional lane. A typical 80-foot urban street right-of-way (not to mention a 100-foot-plus suburban arterial) can easily accommodate two tracks, traffic lanes, and good sidewalks with room to spare for station platforms. Where the lanes are matters—curbside lanes generally allow cars to cross or use the lane for right turns, to access driveways, and get into parking. Median lanes (below) can be designed so the only conflicts with cars are signal-designed left turns at intersections. Streets are generally dangerous places, and transit in streets has the same risk of car, pedestrian, and bike collisions that cars do. Intersection design (such as signalized left-turn lanes) can reduce the risk.

The major constraint on putting transit in the street is limited right or, rather, political unwillingness to covert traffic or parking lanes into transit lanes. Street-running transit, while relatively inexpensive to build, is often the most controversial.

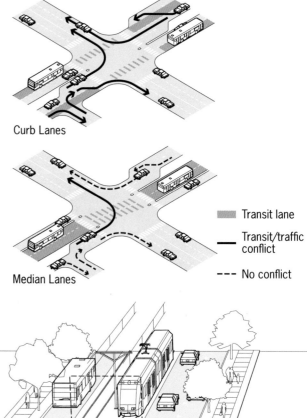

Curb Lanes

Median Lanes

| Transit lane |
| Transit/traffic conflict |
| No conflict |

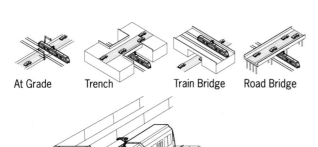

At Grade Trench Train Bridge Road Bridge

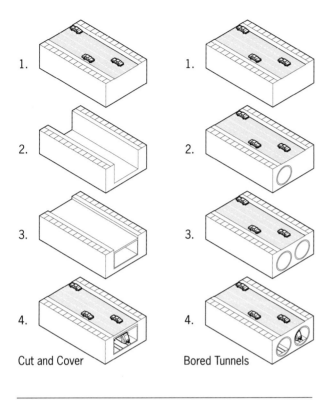

1.

2.

3.

4.

Cut and Cover

1.

2.

3.

4.

Bored Tunnels

Elevated (All Modes)

Since the 1830s, elevated structures have been an effective way to get transit out of the congestion at surface level. Early viaducts were built of brick, but steel was the dominant material for pre-WWII US systems. Postwar systems usually use concrete structures.

The major downside to elevated is visual impact—in an urban context, they are big objects that cast significant shadows. The elevated structures built above city streets in New York, Chicago, and Philadelphia are generally politically unacceptable today. Some cities have built elevated structures above wide suburban streets, but most modern elevated structures are above freeways or along railroad right-of-ways.

Transitioning from at grade to elevated or tunnel requires about 600 feet (right), longer than a typical city block. That limits the locations were transition is possible.

Freeway (All Modes)

Freeways are a relatively easy way to build grade-separated rights-of-way, either in the median or along one side. In some cases, transit has been fit into existing freeways, but it's more common for transit to be part of a freeway reconstruction or widening. Some bus-rapid-transit projects use HOV lanes—shared with carpools and vanpools. While freeway alignments are fast and reliable, it is difficult to make freeway stations welcoming to pedestrians.

Subway (All Modes)

Putting transit in a tunnel allows for complete separation from traffic and pedestrians with minimal impact on the surface, but at a considerable cost. Subways can cost 10 times as much as building elevated or at grade. Because of that, tunnels are mostly used only in dense urban cores, in special conditions like university campuses or airports, or to cross mountain ranges and rivers.

Before World War II, most subways were built using "cut and cover" construction (left), digging a large trench in a street, building the tunnel structure, then filling in the dirt above the tunnel and rebuilding the street. Since the 1970s, though, it has become much more common to use tunnel-boring machines that can cut a tunnel through the earth for miles from an access shaft. While this is often more expensive, it's not restricted by the locations of streets above and is less disruptive during construction.

In some ways, a subway tunnel is the perfect place to put transit. The high cost, though, represents an unavoidable tradeoff: a city that has the money to build 10 miles of subway could build 100 miles of surface rail instead.

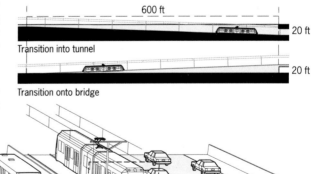

600 ft

20 ft

Transition into tunnel

20 ft

Transition onto bridge

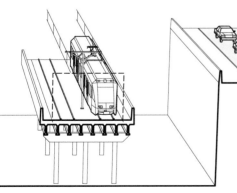

STATIONS

Transit stations are the interface between the human scale of pedestrians and the infrastructural scale of transit vehicles. They vary in scale and complexity based on vehicle size, degree of grade separation, and passenger volumes. ■

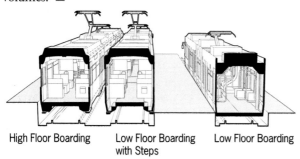

High Floor Boarding   Low Floor Boarding   Low Floor Boarding
               with Steps

Station platforms have to work with vehicles. High platforms (left) match the floors of trains, making it easy for large numbers of passengers to board at once and allowing people in wheelchairs to roll on board easily. These are typical for heavy rail (heights vary by system, generally around 40"–45"), but are also used by light-rail systems (LA Metro uses 39" platforms), and commuter-rail systems (48" in the Northeast). But high platforms are expensive to build, require ramps to get passengers up to train level (difficult to fit into a station built in a street), and interfere with freight cars (commuter-rail stations that also have freight service require bypass tracks).

Low platforms (center) also work with high-floor cars if the cars have built-in steps. This is common on commuter rail and on many pre-2000 light-rail lines; platforms are typically 8" above the rail, but are sometimes just pavement at rail level. Platforms are simpler, but boarding is slower and wheelchair boarding requires lifts or short sections of high platform. Some light-rail and many commuter-rail vehicles are designed with retractable steps or plates, which drop over the steps to work with either high or low platforms. Low-floor vehicles (right) combine level boarding with the simplicity of low platforms. All new light-rail and streetcar systems since 2000 have been built this way, with platforms and car floors at around 14". That is too low to fit wheels under, though, so trains often have these floors for 3/4 of the car, with higher-floor sections at the end, with internal steps up to them. The same approach also works for commuter rail, typically with 20"–15" platforms. Low-floor buses have become standard for most US local bus service, with floor heights around 14". Some BRT systems use this to have level boarding, but buses do not align with platforms as precisely as trains, so a short plate that extends from the bus when the door opens is used to bridge the gap. Other BRT systems use lower platforms—one step down from the bus—with a short ramps for wheelchairs.

In street (light rail, streetcar, BRT)

An in-street station is quite simple: a platform (8' to 12' wide) with a shelter, benches, and ticket vending machines. Turnstiles are not practical—they take too much space, and passengers could easily walk around them. Passengers show fare tickets from the vending machine as proof of payment or pay the driver. At each end the platform slopes down to street level where a crosswalk allows passengers to cross the traffic lanes.

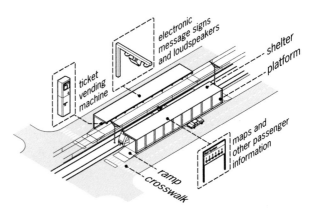

One of the challenges of street-running-station design is fitting a station into the limited space of a street (below). A platform takes up the width of one traffic lane. For curb-running transit, the platform can be integrated into the sidewalk. For median transit lanes, a single center station can serve both directions, but that requires vehicles with doors on both sides, like light-rail trains, streetcars, and some specialized BRT buses. Typical buses have doors only on the right, so require double outside platforms, which also allow more room for passengers at crowded stations then center platforms. Outside platforms can also be arranged to alternate with turn lanes, taking less space.

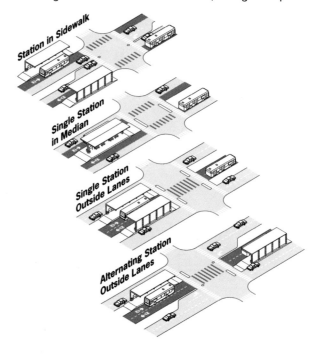

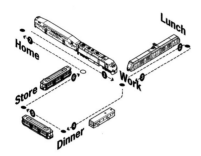

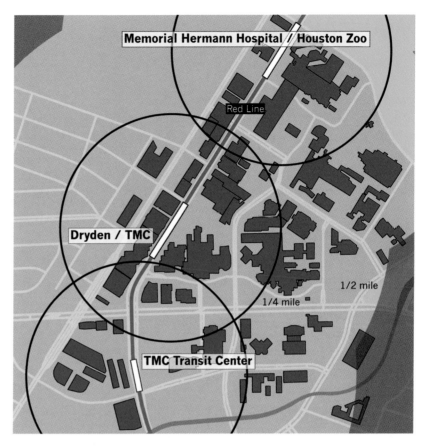

Surprisingly, many rail networks do not serve secondary centers as well as Houston's. Dallas's medical center, anchored by UT Southwestern, employs as many people as Houston's, but rather than running through the center, DART light rail skirts one edge (right), and TRE commuter rail (which does not have frequent service) skirts the other edge. These lines account for only 2,500 light-rail riders and 600 commuter-rail riders—only a quarter as many as in Houston.

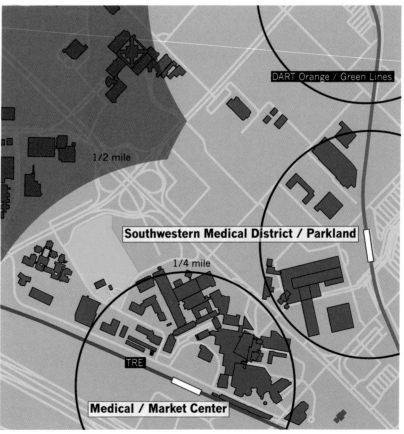

WALKABILITY

Nearly every transit trip begins or ends on foot or on a bike. Across the country, most local bus passengers walk to the bus stop. Passengers have been walking to the busy rail systems in Boston, New York, Philadelphia, and Chicago for a century. Even rail networks that serve auto-oriented suburbs and provide lots of parking get many of their riders on foot. San Francisco's BART has a total of 45,984 parking spaces at 34 of its 45 stations, but only half of passengers get from home to the train by car. Moreover, those passengers arriving in a car don't have a second car waiting on the other end of their trip; once they arrive, they, too, become pedestrians. Making walking convenient, comfortable, and safe builds ridership.

Walkability requires partnerships. Only some pieces of the pedestrian experience are shaped by the transit agency: public works departments build sidewalks, planning departments enforce building regulations, and developers build buildings. ∎

Optimize the quarter mile. Every transit station creates a zone of pedestrian access. Most people will walk approximately a quarter of a mile to transit. Many will walk up to half a mile, particularly if pedestrian conditions are good. That walkable zone is the key to successful transit: whatever is in it is within the reach of a transit rider, whatever is outside is not. Putting station in the right place; where there are as many destinations as possible, maximizes the usefulness of transit and thus transit ridership. More development around that station adds more destinations.

Create complete networks. Passengers can walk only if there is a path for them to take. Traditional streets grids do that very well by providing a closely spaced interconnected network that never requires pedestrians to go out of their way. Suburban street patterns, with long blocks and cul-de-sacs, can force pedestrians onto long, roundabout paths. Making transit effective in such areas can require retrofitting streets, pedestrian paths, and bridges. The same strategy can be useful in older neighborhoods too, when rivers, railroad lines, and old industrial sites break up the grid.

Create a great pedestrian environment. People will walk if walking is safe, comfortable, and enjoyable. Pedestrians, especially those in wheelchairs, or with strollers, need smooth surfaces. They need to be protected from cars when they walk along a street and when they cross. They need shade during the day, light at night, and protection from wind and rain. They want a sense of enclosure, and active buildings to keep them interested as they walk.

Turn front doors to the pedestrian. Transit riders are coming to or from buildings. If those buildings have front doors that face onto the sidewalk, arriving or departing on transit is easy. If the building is surrounded by a vast parking lot, it isn't.

Pedestrian connections are cheap, but they're often forgotten. When Houston's light-rail line opened in 2004, the sidewalk leading to Ensemble/HCC station (top left) was crumbling. In 2017, a rebuilt sidewalk and a new residential and retail development transformed the experience (bottom left). Elsewhere, the City of Houston retrofitted new sidewalks into existing neighborhoods.

Sometimes, transit agencies themselves work against walkability. At Little Tokyo/Arts District station (above), potential passengers are greeted by security fencing and a series of "pedestrians prohibited" signs.

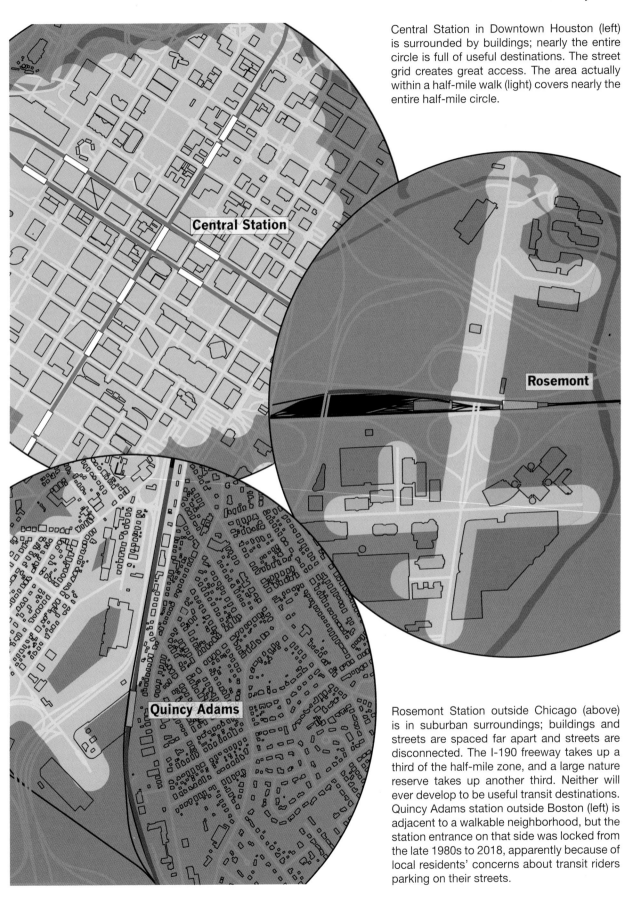

Central Station in Downtown Houston (left) is surrounded by buildings; nearly the entire circle is full of useful destinations. The street grid creates great access. The area actually within a half-mile walk (light) covers nearly the entire half-mile circle.

Central Station

Rosemont

Quincy Adams

Rosemont Station outside Chicago (above) is in suburban surroundings; buildings and streets are spaced far apart and streets are disconnected. The I-190 freeway takes up a third of the half-mile zone, and a large nature reserve takes up another third. Neither will ever develop to be useful transit destinations. Quincy Adams station outside Boston (left) is adjacent to a walkable neighborhood, but the station entrance on that side was locked from the late 1980s to 2018, apparently because of local residents' concerns about transit riders parking on their streets.

CONNECTIVITY

Every transit network depends on connection. On DC's Metrorail, a relatively simple system where every train goes downtown, a third of passengers use more than one of the six lines on their trip. Connections are what make transit useful, turning a line that goes to a limited number of places into a network that covers a whole region. But connections can be where a trip goes wrong: they are often sources of delay, confusion, and hassle. Good connections offer freedom; bad ones offer frustration. ■

Design networks to create connections. A connection is only possible if two transit routes intersect. That doesn't always happen; US transit networks have many near misses where two routes come close but don't connect.

Some connections require that major infrastructure be built. In New Jersey, the Secaucus Junction transfer hub, opened in 2003, connects commuter-rail lines that run into Hoboken Station with commuter-rail lines that run into Penn Station. It cost $450 million, but it is now the third-busiest rail station on the network, with 27,000 connections made a day.

Other connections simply require better route design. Across many US cities, the structure of bus networks is essentially unrelated to the rail systems they overlay. Bus–rail connections are created incidentally, but the network is not designed to take advantage of these connections. Sometimes this is due to bus and rail networks having been inherited from different operators. Sometimes it is because rail networks have expanded rapidly and the bus network hasn't been redesigned. Sometimes it is because agency staff thinks of bus riders and rail riders as two different groups of people. If bus networks and rail networks are integrated well, rail can become a fast, reliable spine of the network, giving all riders faster trips to major activity centers, and bus routes can connect to places rail doesn't serve.

One of the keys to connections is overall network structure. Many cities have radial transit networks. That made sense when all major activities—work, shopping, and entertainment—happened downtown. Today, though, many people are heading elsewhere, and radial networks take them out of their way. This makes downtown, which is often the place where transit moves most slowly, the major regional transfer hub. Grid networks can make trips between any two points on a network reasonably direct, preserving easy trips to downtown, though a connection may now be required. They can also greatly simplify trips to other destinations. Grids aren't a one-size-fits-all solution, though; the right network structure for a city depends highly on local geography. But many cities would benefit from the exercise of rethinking their networks.

Build hubs. Where routes and modes meet, good architecture and good urban design make a good experience. Short walks, shelter, good signage, and general visibility are key.

Unify fares. Fare networks are one of the biggest barriers to connections. Free transfers are essential to well-connected networks. Consider two transit riders. One takes a single bus for 10 miles; the other takes a bus for five miles and connects to a second bus for five miles. Both get the same amount of transportation, both cost the agency the same to transport. The first rider actually has a more convenient trip. But, while most agencies now have free transfers, some agencies would charge the second rider more. Furthermore, many agencies have different fares by mode. Bus is sometimes less expensive than light rail or heavy rail. Commuter rail almost always has a different fare structure. One might cynically conclude that its riders pay a premium fare so that they can ride with fellow members of the middle class rather than the low-income (and minority) riders they may encounter on the bus.

Complex fare structures not only make life hard for riders, they also limit agencies. When an agency charges for transfers, there is a strong incentive to keep current networks intact and focus on one-seat rides rather than frequent riders so that a network-design change doesn't impose new transfer costs on riders. When an agency charges more for rail than bus, it is essentially forced to provide bus service that parallels rail, since eliminating that redundant service would effectively be a fare increase for those riders. Many Northeastern cities have commuter-rail infrastructure and trains that are underused at off-peak hours, while they spend lots of money providing parallel bus service on congested streets.

Where multiple agencies meet, fares get messier. Few cities have free transfers between agencies, and many cities have different fare media.

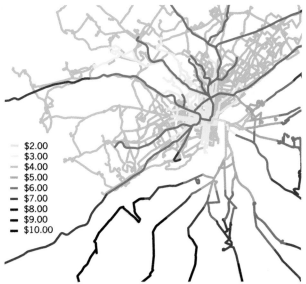

— $2.00
— $3.00
— $4.00
— $5.00
— $6.00
— $7.00
— $8.00
— $9.00
— $10.00

At Radnor, SEPTA's Norristown Station, a high-speed line (opposite bottom) and regional rail (opposite top) cross. The closest stations are one-half mile apart—a 10-minute walk. Otherwise the two networks don't meet until downtown Philadelphia, more than 30 minutes away. Moreover, the two lines, which have been owned and operated by the same agency since 1983, don't use the same fare system. From Radnor, the high-speed-line fare to downtown is $2.50. On regional rail it varies between $5.25 and $7.00, depending on payment method and time of day. The map to the top right shows the transit cost to downtown Philadelphia in 2018. It varied based on what mode is used (bus/streetcar/heavy rail or commuter rail), whether a connection is needed (SEPTA is one of the few agencies that charges for transfers) and agency (SEPTA, New Jersey Transit, and PATCO all operate into the city). Unlike in Seattle, where one card (above) works on multiple transit agencies, all three Philadelphia systems have different fares and fare media.

When new connection hubs are built, Grand Central Terminal is often held up as a model. But it was built for long-distance trains. The beautiful waiting hall (right, 2nd from top) doesn't help commuter rail riders, who are hurrying from the sidewalk or subway straight to their train. Hubs do not need to be large or monumental. Salt Lake Central, with its simple platforms and short distances, actually gets riders where they want to go more quickly (right, 3rd from top).

Houston's bus network was redesigned in 2015 to take advantage of new rail lines; many of the bus routes in the North Side now run east–west (right bottom), connecting to the north–south rail line that goes downtown while making crosstown trips easier.

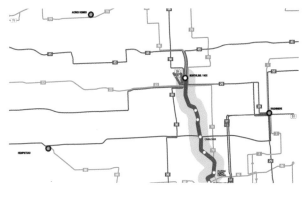

FREQUENCY

At the intersection of Jeffery and 71st in Chicago (below), rail meets bus. Metra Electric and the Jeffery Jump bus both stop here, and both take about 20 minutes to go downtown. But the bus runs every five to 16 minutes during the day, and the train runs every 20 minutes at best, and once an hour for much of the day. Approximately 100 people a day board the train here; nearly 1,000 board the bus. Riders care more about frequency than they do about mode.

Frequency, as transportation planner Jarrett Walker says, is freedom. How frequently a transit route operates makes the difference between a rider being able to depend on transit to be there when they need it, and a rider needing to plan their life around transit. ■

Provide all-day frequent service. Much of American transit is infrequent. The country is full of bus routes that run once an hour, or at rush hour only, or once a day. Even rail lines, which are said to offer passengers an assurance of service, offer dramatically different levels of service. At 7:30 a.m. on a weekday, some lines operate every 30 minutes, and some every five. That difference is huge for a passenger. In the transit industry, 15 minutes is generally considered "frequent." At that level of service, a passenger can just show up to a station without consulting a schedule. Baltimore and Sacramento have light-rail stations that don't even get that level of service at rush hour on a weekday. On a Sunday morning at 7:30, more than two-thirds of US light-rail systems have segments that aren't frequent, and three systems don't offer service at all.

Invariably, the most successful systems have the highest frequencies. That is a reflection of two things. The first is that, as ridership goes up, higher frequency is needed to carry the loads. Every system has a limit on train length. If a system can accommodate only three car trains, and a three-car train every 15 minutes is crammed full, the way to fit more people is to run three cars trains every 10 minutes. The second is that more-frequent services are more convenient and will thus draw more passengers. Therefore, increasing frequency will actually increase total ridership.

Ultimately, frequency is as much a reflection of philosophy as of raw numbers. Some cities treat frequency as a basic promise, running trains every 15 minutes or less even if they are not full. Some cities—notably Los Angeles and Minneapolis—extend this philosophy to bus as well as rail, specifically promoting frequent networks. Other cities try to minimize operating costs by running longer trains less often, thus reducing labor costs. In other words, some cities start by providing all-day service and building on that for the peaks. Others focus on peak service and provide some minimal service off-peak.

Sunday-morning frequencies on US light-rail systems vary widely (right), from every two minutes under Market Street in San Francisco to no service at all in Norfolk. The sections outlined in red have service less than every 15 minutes. The contrast reflects the type of destinations that systems serve. Many of the newer rail systems, such as Denver, Salt Lake, Sacramento, and Dallas, are designed to accommodate home-to-work trips for office workers, so ridership on these systems peaks heavily at rush hour. Low off-peak demand leads to lower frequencies. Older systems in Boston and San Francisco and new systems in Houston, Buffalo, and Jersey City connect walkable neighborhoods to a variety of destinations. These systems attract riders all day, every day, increasing overall ridership and justifying more off-peak frequency.

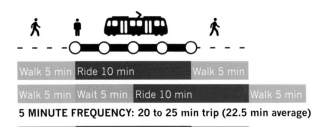

5 MINUTE FREQUENCY: 20 to 25 min trip (22.5 min average)

30 MINUTE FREQUENCY: 20 to 50 min trip (35 min average)

Frequency determines wait time, which is a big part of transit trips. At a five-minute frequency, the average wait for a train is only two and a half minutes, and waiting will be an insignificant part of the trip. At a 30-minute frequency, a passenger's day can be ruined if they miss a train.

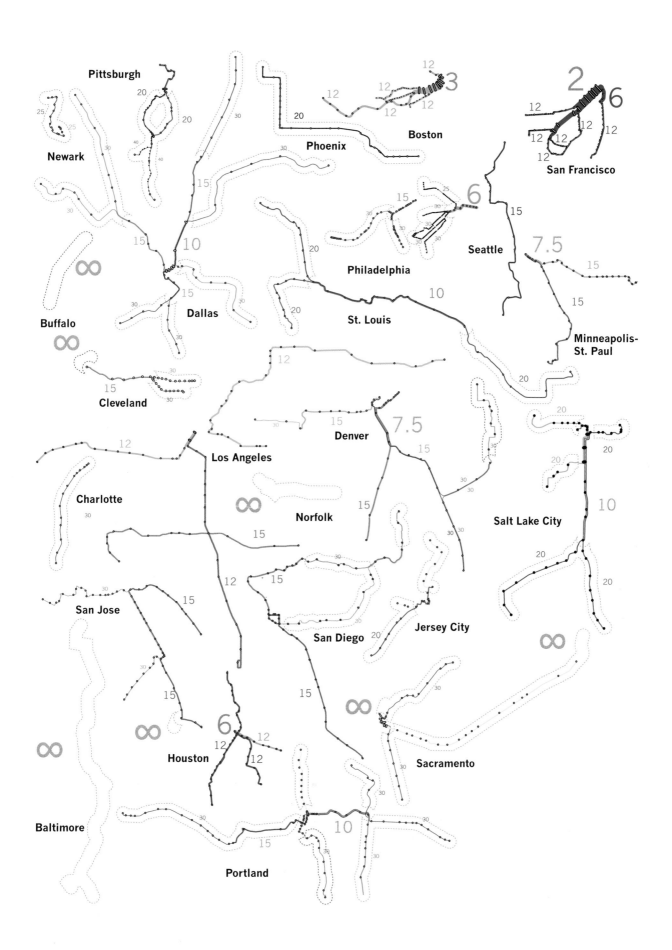

TRAVEL TIME

Travel time matters. It matters to people who have access to a car and will simply choose to drive if transit offers an hour-long commute in place of a 30-minute drive. It may matter even more to a low-income or fixed-income person working multiple jobs and juggling childcare. ■

Measure access, not distance. People do not travel to cover distance; they travel to get somewhere. The measure of how useful transit is to riders is not how far transit goes in half an hour, but how many destinations (jobs, homes, education, retail, culture) transit can reach in half an hour. The New York subway averages only about 17 mph, including stops, but few transit systems enable a rider to reach as many destinations in 30 minutes. Nashville's Music City Star is twice as fast at 38 mph, but it reaches far less.

Optimize trip time, not speed. A transit trip is not from station to station; it is from door to door. That trip time includes walking, waiting, riding, and walking again. It is not unusual for a quarter or even half a trip to consist of walking and waiting. Even the time spent on transit, though, is not all moving. For every stop, a train slows down, pauses, then speeds up again. Thus, the maximum speed of a vehicle is only a small part of trip time. Increasing frequency, and thus reducing average wait time, will speed up trips. Putting stations in the right places, and thus reducing walking time, will speed up trips. Decreasing the number of stops will speed up trips. The right balance of these factors depends a lot on distance. For longer trips, speed matters more; for shorter trips, station location and frequency matters more. At one extreme, intercity rail stops only occasionally and goes up to 200 mph. At the other, urban light-rail lines stop frequently and go up to 35 mph.

Provide express service. One of the fundamental conundrums of transit is the stop/distance tradeoff. Reducing stops speeds up service but serves fewer places. At the extremes, it is fairly easy: there is no need to have stops less than one half mile or so apart, since many people are willing to walk that far. Beyond a half-mile spacing, though, you begin to have places that are next to the transit line but not really accessible by it. Even with a half-mile spacing, though, it is hard to get average speeds over 25 mph.

But there is a solution: run express service parallel to the local service. The New York subway is a classic example. From Queens Plaza and Forest Hills, just under six miles, the M and R lines make all local stops, 11 between those two stations, averaging a stop every half mile. That takes 20 minutes. The E runs express between those two stations, with only one intermediate stop. It takes 13 minutes.

At Church and Market Streets in San Francisco (above), a J Church light-rail train (at left) meets an F Market and Wharves streetcar (at right). Both go downtown; the J takes a subway and gets there in 11 minutes, while the F stays on the surface and takes 20. This pattern (below) repeats itself at the south end of the J Church. Thirty-five minutes from downtown it meets BART heavy rail, which also goes to downtown, with fewer stops, in 15 minutes. At the south end of BART it meets Caltrain, which also goes downtown. Market Street is the only street in the United States with three different rail transit systems along it—fast, slow, and medium. All four run standing-room-only during rush hour: the F carries 19,000 trips a day, the J carries 18,000, BART carries 59,000 within San Francisco, and Caltrain carries 33,000. The four systems are designed for trips of different distances: the shorter a trip, the more close station-spacing matters to minimize walks; the longer a trip, the more speed matters. All these systems are optimizing trip time, just for different trips.

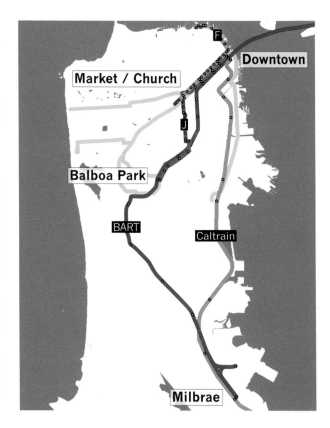

Making trains faster doesn't necessarily make trips faster; in fact it can do the reverse. In one hypothetical example (below) we can speed up trains by moving them onto a faster right of way, likely a freeway or a railroad corridor rather than a street, or by reducing the number of stations, but both of those increase walk distance, making the trip longer. In Houston, planners considered a former rail line or a busy street for the University light-rail corridor (above). The rail line would let trains run faster, but the street goes into the heart of Greenway Plaza, a major employment center. For people headed there, faster trains would mean longer trips.

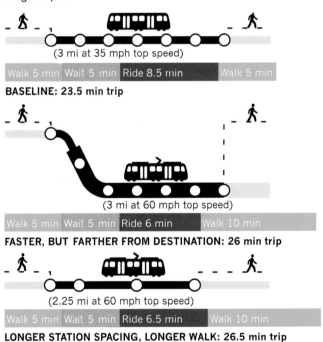

(3 mi at 35 mph top speed)

| Walk 5 min | Wait 5 min | Ride 8.5 min | Walk 5 min |

BASELINE: 23.5 min trip

(3 mi at 60 mph top speed)

| Walk 5 min | Wait 5 min | Ride 6 min | Walk 10 min |

FASTER, BUT FARTHER FROM DESTINATION: 26 min trip

(2.25 mi at 60 mph top speed)

| Walk 5 min | Wait 5 min | Ride 6.5 min | Walk 10 min |

LONGER STATION SPACING, LONGER WALK: 26.5 min trip

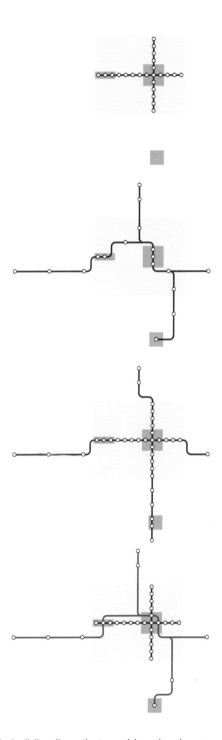

Different cities use different strategies to balance speed and access. Some rail networks, like the New York subway and Houston's light-rail lines, are confined to the urban core (right, top, with the core in yellow), with closely spaced station to maximize access and good travel times for close-in destinations. Some, like BART or MARTA, are focused more on regional trips, with long lines with few stations that provide quick trips to the suburbs but don't serve the core well (2nd from top). Some, like Portland, try to do both, building lines that combine closely spaced stations in the core with long suburban lines (3rd from top), but that leads to long, slow regional trips. Ultimately, the best way to get both urban access and regional trip times is to build parallel systems with different purposes (4th from top): a local system for the core and an express system for the region, connecting at hubs in major activity centers.

RELIABILITY

Reliability is nearly as important to transit users as travel time. A 2014 TransitCenter survey ranked it as the second-most important factor in what mode people chose. Being late can mean disappointing friends, missing an important appointment, or losing a job. For transit trips that involve connections, delays further compound with every connection that gets missed. It is possible for a rider to try to compensate by leaving early, but that increases travel time.

Reliability on US transit in general isn't great. Bus networks typically have on time performance around 70–80 percent, but some are under 60 percent. Some rail systems achieve 98 percent, but the New York subway is now under 80 percent on weekdays. ■

Minimize unreliability due to traffic. By far the biggest source of unreliability is sharing space with cars. The vast majority of bus routes in the United States travel in regular car lanes. When traffic jams up at rush hour, or queues at a light, or comes to a stop as someone waits to make a turn, transit riders are delayed. This is made worse because buses need to operate in the curb lane, most subject to delay from driveways and parking. Furthermore, unlike cars, buses are not allowed to be early, since that could lead to riders who showed up to stops on time being stranded. Transit planners can compensate for delay by adding time to trips, but if traffic is better than average, that means buses will run early and will need to slow down or wait at stops until they are in schedule again.

There are several solutions to the unreliability of traffic.

Dedicated lanes pull transit out of traffic. Transit vehicles can move at full speed regardless of the speed of traffic and at a traffic signal transit will always be at the front of the line. Semi-dedicated lanes, shared with right turns, or "floating" lanes that cars can cross to access parking space, are helpful, but not nearly as much as fully dedicated lanes separated so that cars can cross only at signalized intersections.

Traffic-signal priority minimizes the time transit vehicles spend waiting for cross traffic. Absolute priority means that transit vehicles always get a green light, but there are also conditional-priority schemes that extend green lights, shorten red lights, or give preference to transit vehicles that are running late. Transit-signal priority works best with dedicated lanes, but can also be implemented, and have significant benefits, in mixed traffic.

Grade separation eliminates interaction between transit and other traffic entirely, eliminating delays due to traffic

and also greatly reducing the risk of collisions due to car drivers not following traffic laws.

While grade separation is the most effective approach to achieving reliability, it is also the most expensive. Dedicated lanes can achieve most of the benefit at a fraction of the cost.

Minimize unreliability due to boarding. The second source of unreliability is boarding. On a typical bus, every rider boards through the front door and pays the driver. The more people board, the longer the bus waits at the stop. If someone fumbles for cash, folds a stroller, or has to wrestle a big bag, everyone else waits behind them, and the bus waits longer. If a rider is in a wheelchair, the driver has to deploy a ramp, wait for the rider to roll on, and then get up to buckle them in. The time spent at a stop can range from nothing (if no one is waiting or getting off) to several minutes.

There are several solutions to boarding unreliability.

Off-board fare collection separates the process of buying fares from the process of boarding. Ticket machines at the station allow riders to pay, then simply board whenever the vehicle shows up.

All-door boarding allows riders to board at any door, not just the front door. This is usually combined with off-board fare collection, but it doesn't have to be. A ticket machine can be on board, or readers can be installed on all doors so that riders who have electronic fare cards can board at any door while riders paying cash board at the front. All-door boarding requires a "proof of payment" fare system, in which randomly roaming inspectors enforce fares, instead of the driver.

Level boarding puts the stop or station platform at the same level as the vehicle floor. Passengers do not need to negotiate a step to board. This speeds things up for everyone, but especially for people with luggage or strollers and for people in wheelchairs.

Besides traffic and boarding, reliability also depends on agency culture. Many sources of delays are within a transit agency's control through maintenance, handling of disruptions, and the actions of staff. San Francisco MUNI discovered that 30% of their light-rail trains were running late when they first left the yard in the morning, before they encountered any passengers or traffic. Elsewhere, operators are committed to on-time performance. In Japan (opposite, top left), train delays are measured in seconds, and the Tsukuba Express issued a public apology for a train departing 20 seconds early. But ultimately, as long as transit vehicles mix with cars and board one at a time, they will be unreliable. Good infrastructure isn't enough, but reliable transit is impossible without it.

A study of Route 84 in Minneapolis–St. Paul (upper right) found that buses spent half their time boarding passengers or waiting at red lights. Delays in both of these have major impacts on travel times. This finding prompted

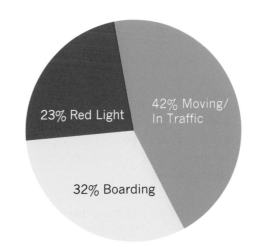

Metro Transit to upgrade the corridor with limited stops and traffic signal priority for buses, increasing speed and reliability. In Grand Rapids, stations on the Silver Line have ticket machines and elevated platforms for level boarding, and passengers can board at any door. Buses have priority at traffic signals, and a special bus-only light at the intersection of Fulton Street and Ransom Avenue (right) lets buses turn left without delay.

In Toronto, Viva buses bypass traffic delays in transit lanes (right bottom). With dedicated lanes, almost all of the causes of delay can be eliminated. But the United States is still spending hundreds of millions on rail transit that shares lanes with cars. The majority of US streetcar systems, most of which were opened in the last 10 years, have extensive shared lanes (red in figure at bottom) and minimal dedicated lanes (green.)

The ultimate in reliability comes with full-grade separation, but at a high cost. Often the motivation for grade separation is not transit reliability but minimizing impacts on cars. That may be the case at West Portal (below) in San Francisco, where light-rail trains emerge from a 1970s subway onto a surface street where the first traffic-control device is a four-way stop. A traffic signal and dedicated lanes here could do as much for reliability as the $100-million signal system inside the subway.

CAPACITY

All modes of transit have high capacity. Even an ordinary city bus route, running in mixed traffic, can carry thousands of people per hour. Any transit technology can carry more people than single-occupant vehicles in the same space. Often, then, capacity is not the driver; the drivers are speed, reliability, and quality of service. ■

Provide enough capacity to meet demand. On some heavily used transit routes, though, capacity is key. Houston's Main Street Line is one of the busiest light-rail lines in the country. Fifteen thousand riders pass through downtown (right) daily. Two-car trains, standing-room-only at rush hour, run every six minutes. At the same frequency, a bus-rapid-transit line, using single 60-foot buses, would have a quarter of the capacity, inadequate to handle the load. But light rail is limited, too. Trains can't run much more often without giving up traffic-signal priority (and thus slowing trains down); the intersections are already handling a train every three minutes. Trains can't be longer, either: because of the block lengths laid out by the Allen Brothers in 1836, they're limited to two cars. The only way to significantly increase capacity would be to grade separate. A subway could carry longer trains more frequently. But a subway would also be considerably more expensive.

Thus, capacity can determine what mode might make sense for a corridor. The table below shows the range of capacity, from a typical US line of that mode to the highest capacity possible through major infrastructure. Most US transit lines have reserve capacity; upgrading is easily achieved by buying more trains or buses. "Maximum" requires considerably more investment and space. It may make sense to invest to allow for future growth in ridership, but it may make more sense to use those dollars to build more transit elsewhere.

		local bus	BRT	light rail	heavy rail	commuter rail
typical	people/vehicle	80	120	225	200	162
	train	40 ft. (1 bus)	95 ft. (1 bus)	190 ft. (2 car)	450 ft. (6 car)	400 ft. (4 car)
	people/train	80	120	450	1200	648
	trains/hour	4	6	6	6	2
	hourly capacity	320	720	2,700	7,200	1,296
	daily capacity	**5,120**	**11,520**	**43,200**	**115,200**	**20,736**

		bus-only lane, multiple routes	full grade separation, passing lanes at stations	private right of way outside city streets, grade separation at major intersections	express and local tracks	full grade separation, multiple tracks at stations
maximum	people/vehicle	80	120	225	200	162
	train	40 ft. (1 bus)	95 ft. (1 bus)	380 ft. (4 car)	750 ft. (10 car)	910 ft. (10 car)
	people/train	80	120	900	2000	1620
	trains/hour	120	120	24	48	24
	hourly capacity	9,600	14,400	21,600	96,000	38,880
	daily capacity	**153,600**	**230,400**	**345,600**	**1,536,000**	**622,080**

Infrastructure limits frequency, which limits capacity. Some light-rail and many commuter-rail lines have single track. Here, trains can only pass where a short second track is built for that purpose, often at stations (right). The length of single-track segments determines how often trains can run. If a segment takes five minutes for a train to pass through, a southbound train will tie up that track for five minutes, followed by a northbound tying it up for five minutes, so the next southbound can't leave until 10 minutes after the first. On multiple track lines, additional tracks can increase capacity, allowing one train to pass another. That works for BRT, too. On a typical two-lane busway (below left), only one bus can stop at a time, and the time spent in stations limits frequency. If the busway widens at stations (below right), buses can pass, and capacity goes up dramatically. But that requires more space to widen the station busway—65 feet instead of 45.

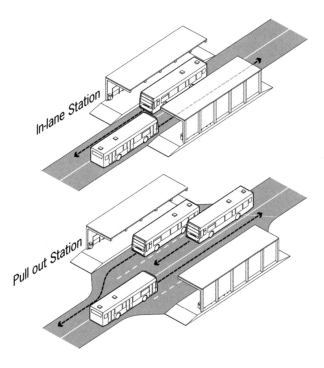

Often, capacity is set by people, not technology. From 1939 to 1958, the San Francisco Bay Bridge carried two rail tracks. Trains (above left) were manual. In 1974, Transbay rail service returned with two tracks in a tunnel, fully automated (above right). But even today, BART is limited to 24 trains an hour through the tube, while the old line handled 57. Why? The bridge railroad had multiple tracks and platforms in San Francisco (right top). Now, every BART train that crosses the bay stops at the same platform (right bottom). Thus, capacity is limited by the time it takes passengers to get on and off the train.

Vehicle design affects capacity. Toronto's 2010 "Rocket" railcars (below) were the first in North America with open gangways between cars, turning the entire train into one compartment and increasing capacity by about 10%.

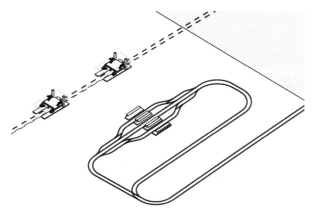

LEGIBILITY

A transit trip is a series of decisions: whether to take transit or not, which station to walk to, which platform to go to, which stop to get off at, where to go from there. Every one of those decisions requires information, and a good transit system provides that information when it is needed, in an easy to understand form. ■

Brand the network. A good transit system has a clear identity. In the US, every transit agency has a brand. Some are clever ("Sound Transit"), some are odd ("SORTA"), some are merely boring (the many variants of "Metro," or the two systems called "The Bus"). In addition to agency brands, individual modes often have their own brands. In Portland, TriMet's light-rail system is called "MAX," and in Norfolk, Hampton Roads Transit's trains are "The Tide." Denver's light rail used to be "The Ride," but RTD has dropped that. Wonderfully, Roaring Fork Transit Authority's rapid bus route (opposite, top right) is the VelociRFTA." Many agencies extend their main brand for modes: DC has "Metrorail," "Metrobus," "Metroway," and "MetroAccess." These brands become a big part of local culture; everyone in Boston knows "the T," and everyone in San Francisco knows BART. But they can be confusing, too. Multiple brands within a single agency or region also obscure the network: bus and rail should work together, but it is hard to figure that out when they go by two completely different names.

Identify lines. Within a network, distinguishing lines is critical. Almost every US bus network uses numbered routes, though Baltimore uses colors and Boulder has Hop, Skip, Jump, Bound, Dash, Stampede, and Bolt. One number can actually cover multiple branches. Some agencies use letters to distinguish them, and others simply hope riders figure out that the 5:13 bus goes somewhere different than the 5:21. Most rail lines use colors, but New York has so many lines that it has to use letters and numbers, and Philadelphia has always used names. Many BRT lines are colored, too, to send the message that they are like rail. Commuter-rail lines are usually named, sometimes by destination, sometimes for historical reasons. Within a metropolitan area, agencies rarely coordinate. Two different agencies may both have a #10 bus in the same city, going to different places.

Identify frequency. It is not enough for riders to know where lines go; they need to know how often they run. If there are multiple routes to a destination, some on frequent routes, some on hourly routes, and some on express routes that only run at certain items of day, it is important for a rider to be able to tell the difference quickly so that they can find the best route for their trip.

A good map can guide riders to the best service. Most transit maps distinguish by mode. Rail lines, even commuter-rail lines with only a few trips a day, get prominent thick lines, while bus routes, even the ones that run frequently all day, get thin lines. But some systems have started explicitly showing frequency. Los Angeles published a "12-Minute Map" of frequent bus service; Portland and Minneapolis have designated "frequent networks" that include bus and rail. Minneapolis and Portland both have special signs at bus stops to identify frequent routes.

Identify stops. Stop names help riders figure out where to get off. A good stop name also helps riders build a strong mental geography of the city. In the United States, station names are standard for rail lines and BRT. Bus stops, however, rarely get names.

Clarify transfers. Where riders change from one route to another, signage is critical for making the transfer easy. Rail-to-rail transfers within the same network generally get handled pretty well, though some systems are better than others. Rail-to-bus signs are more erratic. Transfers between agencies are sometimes ignored altogether.

Simplify networks. The easiest network to figure out is one that is simple to start with. Modern smartphone apps can make navigating easier, but they are no match for a network that is easy to decipher and easy to remember. Many US transit networks are needlessly complex. That includes bus networks, but also some rail lines; several heavy-rail lines and light-rail networks have some peak-only routes, and different weekday and weekend service, and commuter-rail lines often have some trains that skip certain stops, which works well for people who travel at the exact same time every day, can learn their schedule, and optimize their commute, but can be very confusing for first-time riders or those whose travel schedules are irregular, leaving them on a train that bypasses their destination. Several US cities have undertaken redesigns of their entire route networks with simplicity as a major goal.

Create a legible experience. When a transit agency considers everything, it can create a wonderfully intuitive, legible experience. The A-Line in the Twin Cities (opposite bottom) is a great example. The route has a clear name, and a simple, easy to understand "L"-shaped route following two streets and making connections to two rail lines. The buses are distinctively branded, and that branding is carried through to the stops, which are easily visible from a distance with tall beacon signs. Every stop has a name. The signage at the stop clearly shows which direction the bus is going, and an information pal includes a route map, schedules, fares, and simple "how to ride" information. A digital display announces the next bus. There are maps on board too, and onboard announcements match the route names at the stations. At every step, a rider knows what they need to know, and there is continuous reassurance that they are headed in the right direction. All transit should aspire to an experience this legible.

Germany (left) has national transit branding; all subways are marked with a blue "U" and frequent commuter-rail networks with a green "S." In the United States, signage varies greatly from city to city and mode to mode. In Seattle, light-rail signs (below left) are easier to read and have more information than bus signs (below right.)

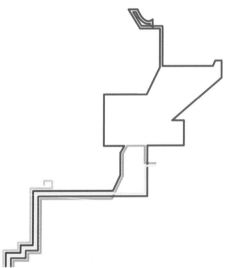

Route 54 in St. Paul, with five different service patterns (above) is typical of US bus networks. Houston's 2015 redesign simplified such routes, and the new map (right) differentiates among bus routes that run every 15 minutes or more frequently (red), bus routes that run every 30 minutes (blue), and bus routes than run hourly (green).

INCLUSIVITY

It seems obvious to say that transit systems should be designed to welcome everyone, but transit often has been designed in ways that exclude major segments of the population. Fundamentally, most US and Canadian transit has been designed by non-disabled white men in a way that best serves non-disabled white men.

Often this is intentional. Transit systems have racism built into their schedules, their fleets, their route structures and their infrastructure. Much of this is in pursuit of what Dr. Destiny Thomas calls "White Comfort." Agencies seek to attract white suburban "choice riders," and many of those riders are uncomfortable around people who don't look like them. So agencies have used alignments, schedules, fares, and policing to create what are often effectively separate systems.

Exclusivity can also be less intentional. Women, for example, have different travel patterns than men: they travel more outside peak hours, are more likely to "chain" trips together, and are more likely to be traveling with groceries or strollers. Agencies often ignore those needs. It seems likely that the people who write the policies at many agencies that require strollers to be folded when boarding never navigated transit with a toddler. ∎

Don't overspend to chase "choice riders" and don't take "dependent riders" for granted. These terms sound neutral (even thoughtful) but lead to inequitable policy. These terms reflect a pejorative, dated and inaccurate way of thinking about transit ridership that has profoundly shaped our transit networks by encouraging agencies to spend lots of money to lure new transit riders while not focusing on making trips better for existing riders (like in New Orleans, below, which built low-ridership tourist-oriented streetcars, but not bus shelters at its most important transfer hub). Reliability, frequency, and faster trips benefit everyone, and deploying them where they will help the most people will build more equitable networks.

Acknowledge racism. Federal Title VI regulations require that any changes to a transit system—schedule changes, fare changes, or new routes—be analyzed to make sure that they do not have a disparate impact on any racial or ethnic groups. But if the system was discriminatory to start with, that isn't enough. Transit will never be just unless we acknowledge and try to remedy past injustice.

Make networks accessible. Making networks easy to use for people who have impaired mobility, who are blind, or who are deaf offers freedom and economic opportunity and benefits other riders too, by making systems easier to navigate with baggage or simply easier to understand.

Consider families. Raising children is a central part of human life—but transit agencies make life difficult for families in many ways. An inclusive network has fares that are affordable for families, vehicles, stations, and faregates that are easy to use in groups, and family-friendly policies like allowing strollers on board.

Focus on safety, not policing. Transit needs to be safe for its riders, and that means addressing crime as well as societal issues like mental health and homelessness. There is little evidence, though, that putting lots of police officers on transit makes transit safer, and lots of evidence that it results in police targeting riders of color. Many agencies use unarmed fare-enforcement officers, and some have started deploying social workers to assist riders who are in distress and causing disruptions.

Make fares fair. Fares should not be an economic burden to people who need transit, and should not force those who have less money to use lower-quality services. Low-income fares, applied equally across all modes, make transit more equitable.

Select diverse leadership. Transit networks will always reflect the perspectives of the people who create them: board members, agency staff, and consultants. Having people in those positions with backgrounds that reflect riders and the public as a whole will lead to more inclusive networks. (And, of course, having people who actually ride transit in these positions will help too.)

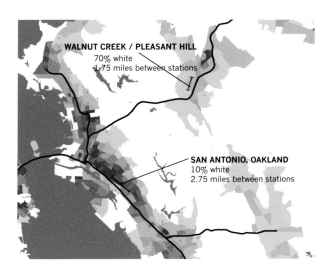

WALNUT CREEK / PLEASANT HILL
70% white
1.75 miles between stations

SAN ANTONIO, OAKLAND
10% white
2.75 miles between stations

Racism is evident both in infrastructure and in operations. When BART (left) was planned in the 1960s, it was literally designed to speed white suburban commuters past Black inner-city residents. In Oakland's San Antonio—the most racially diverse neighborhood in the city, and one of the densest parts of the Bay Area—BART trains run nearly three miles without stopping. In suburban Walnut Creek and Pleasant Hill, less than half as dense, BART stations are only 1¾ miles apart. Fifty years later, that racism is still built into the system, and it's amplified by how the system is operated. BART police are disproportionately deployed in stations that serve Black neighborhoods, and while only 10 percent of BART riders are Black, 50 percent of "code of conduct" citations issued by BART police in 2019 were to Black riders.

The Americans with Disabilities Act, signed into law in 1990, requires that all new transit stations be fully accessible to people in wheelchairs (and have other accessibility features, like tactile warning strips at platform edges and announcements both audibly and visually). It also requires that existing transit systems identify "key stations" and retrofit them to be accessible. Some older systems have done that aggressively; all but one of the stations on Boston's heavy-rail system are accessible, and Chicago (below left) has been retrofitting elevators so that 70 percent of its "L" stations are accessible. In New York (bottom right), on the other hand, only 110 of 472 stations are accessible, and those are concentrated in Manhattan. The stations that are accessible are often plagued by months-long elevator shutdowns. A person in a wheelchair is excluded from the majority of North America's busiest transit system.

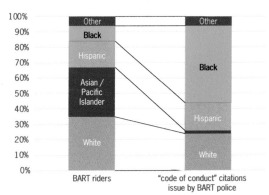

BART riders

"code of conduct" citations issue by BART police

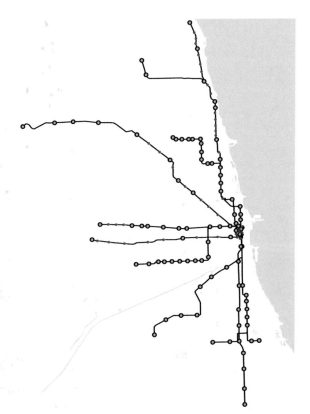

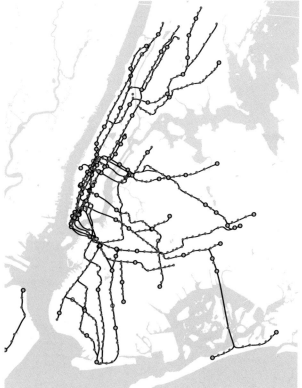

GOOD IDEAS FROM ABROAD

US transit has taken many ideas from overseas, but it still suffers from a "not-invented-here" mindset. Pushed on New York's high construction costs in 2017, the MTA chair explained that New York has "unique challenges" like high ridership, old infrastructure, historic buildings, and density. Transit agencies in London, Paris, and Tokyo, which have built far more new transit in recent decades than New York, probably find those challenges familiar. The world has some great transit systems and there are many good ideas that US systems could implement.

The United States was a pioneer in **transit automation**. In 1962, New York City operated one of the first automated heavy-rail trains in the world. But today, even computerized systems like San Francisco's BART have operators in the cab. Across the world, most new heavy-rail lines, like Singapore's Circle Line, are fully automated. This brings several key advantages. With no driver error, automated rail lines are safer, and since the trains stop precisely in the same place every time, stations can have platform edge doors that prevent passengers for falling onto the tracks. For peak periods, automated rail lines are higher capacity since trains can run closer together. Off-peak, they allow higher-frequency service since there's no need to pay an operator for each train, so running a two-car train every 5 minutes costs the same as running a four-car train every 10.

In the United States, light rail is largely used on long routes to the suburbs alongside old rail lines and freeways. Europe, where the idea of light rail originated, builds **urban light rail** in dense, walkable places inside the core. These lines aren't like American streetcars, which have small vehicles that share lanes with cars. European urban light rail has dedicated lanes and large vehicles, providing high reliability and high capacity, so these lines are a significant upgrade to urban buses. They're being deployed in the corridors that have the highest transit demand, and they're carrying lots of people. Even though it overlaps an extensive subway system, the Viennese tram network (below) carries 500,000 trips a day, more than twice as many as the busiest US light-rail network. The 10 tram lines in Paris carry nearly a million trips a day.

The United States has commuter rail while the rest of the world has **regional rail**. US networks are focused on getting suburban 9-to-5 commuters to downtown in the morning and home in the evening. Service is good at peak hours in the peak direction, but many lines have no midday or weekday service at all, and the ones that do are infrequent. That means people who are headed to suburban job centers, who work service jobs, who are going to school, or who want to use transit for all their daily needs don't benefit from commuter rail. Elsewhere, commuter rail is run as all-day, all-purpose transit. In Germany, S-Bahn networks, which cover entire metropolitan areas, typically run on 20- or 30-minute frequencies all day. The majority of the London Overground network (left), which shares track with freight, runs every 15 minutes all day, and every 4 minutes on some lines.

Bus lanes can be very cheap, very quick to implement, and very effective at making transit faster, more reliable, and more useful. From 2004 to 2006, Seoul implemented 60 miles of two-way bus lanes on major arterials (opposite top left) in the most congested parts of the city simply by restriping, adding signs, and building simple boarding islands. These are used by the city's ordinary bus routes. Across the world, bus lanes aren't seen as a special feature for BRT, but rather as an upgrade for any urban service.

further differentiate between heavy-rail fares and bus fares, and even between local and limited stop buses. Getting from point "A" to point "B" will cost differently depending on what type a vehicle a transit rider uses to get there. This makes the system harder to understand, drives lower-income riders onto slower modes, and forces transit agencies to maintain duplicate networks. Some other countries don't make these distinctions; Zurich, for example, has buses, light rail, and commuter rail, but the fares for all of these are identical, based only on the distance traveled.

US transit agencies don't believe in **modal equality**: they usually treat each mode as a different system. There is a bus network and a rail network. With that come different standards: typically, all light-rail stations have, at a minimum, a name, a shelter, ticket-vending machines, digital displays, and detailed passenger information, while even brand-new bus stops are guaranteed only a sign and a concrete pad. At transfer stations these differences are particularly evident. But none of these features have anything to do with the technological differences between bus and rail; they simply reflect a stated or unstated hierarchy which places rail (and rail riders) above bus (and bus riders). In Germany, transit agencies are much more likely to treat bus and rail as peers. At Münchner Freiheit (above), Munich buses and light-rail trains share a single station canopy, treated identically except for the steel rails and the overhead wire.

Unified fares transform a transit network. In the United States, commuter-rail fares are almost always different (and higher) then other transit fares, and many cities

In the United States and Canada, there is a firm division, enforced by regulatory agencies, between light rail / streetcar / heavy rail on one hand and commuter rail / Amtrak on the other. In Europe and Japan, that divide doesn't exist, and **hybrid rail systems** are common. In Kassel, Germany, for example, the "RegioTram" light-rail vehicles run on mainline railroad lines (shared with commuter trains, freight rains, and even high-speed rail) for part of their trip (above top), then take a track connection on the rails of the local streetcar network and run right into downtown on city streets (above bottom). Some lines use electrified rail routes; on others, onboard diesel generators allow the trains to run onto non-electrified routes. This combines the low capital cost of commuter rail with the one seat downtown service of light rail. There's nothing technological preventing this from being implemented in the US.

PART 3
METRO AREAS

Fifty-seven metropolitan areas in the United States and Canada have rail transit or BRT. This section of the book includes every one of them, orderd by population, largest (New York City) to smallest (Fort Collins). The numbering reflects each area's rank by population among all metropolitan areas (not just those with rail or BRT). The metropolitan areas are the largest units that the Census Bureau or Statistics Canada defines (either Core-Based Statistical Areas, Combined Statistical Areas, or census metropolitan area). This definition combines some cities together—Washington and Baltimore, San Francisco and San Jose, Boston and Providence—into multi-centric regions. In general, rail-transit systems are confined to only one of these areas. (Some systems, like Philadelphia's SEPTA, do touch an adjacent metropolitan area at their outer ends; the Hartford Line commuter rail crosses three metropolitan areas). The official name of the area is shown on the first page, along with the population. These metro areas can be quite large, often extending across multiple states, but often the outermost portions have no rail or frequent bus and may not be mentioned in the text.

For this book, transit is a regularly scheduled service that is open to the public (though it could be privately operated), operates for most of the day for at least five days a week (so the Kenosha streetcar, which operates   weekends only during the winter, doesn't count), serves trips within a metropolitan area (so Amtrak doesn't count), is not contained within a single in-stitution (so no airport peoplemovers, univer-sity campus shuttles, or amusement park monorails), and is not solely operated as a museum.

Frequent transit (whether it is bus or rail) is defined as routes that that run at least every 15 minutes on weekdays from 7:00 a.m. to 6:00 p.m. This is not average frequency, but maximum headway—two buses every 10 minutes followed by two every 20 does not count. Multiple overlapping routes count as "frequent" only if they are specifically marketed as a combined service.

At the beginning of each metro area section, logos (right, top) show all transit agencies that operate rail, BRT, or frequent bus in the metro area. The agency names used reflect their public branding.

Each agency may operate multiple sys-tems. Each system has an information box (right, 2nd from top) with key data. A system is generally defined as one or more lines, of the same mode, operated by the same agency, that connect to each other and share one brand.

In the pages that follow, tags at the top of the page call out large and small systems, high-performing or low-performing systems, "legacy" systems that predate World War II, and systems that are under construction or currently suspended. The mileage is two-way miles; a mile or route that is traveled in one direction only counts as half a mile. Likewise, stations served in one direction only count as half a station.

Every metropolitan area has two maps, at the same scale across the entire book. The first map (right, 3rd from top) shows the physical form of the transit system. Modes—heavy rail, light rail, BRT, streetcar, commuter rail—are color coded. The line types show whether the line is at ground level, in a street, elevated, in a freeway, or in a subway. Lines under construction as of 2020 are shown. Lines that are planned but not yet under construction are not. These maps also show frequent-bus routes as well as major airports and Amtrak, VIA or other intercity-rail (like Florida's privately owned Brightline) stations on corridors that have more than one train a day. These maps show how the transit system is built and connected.

The second map (right, 4th from top) shows the frequent-transit network. Areas outlined in thick black lines are within one half mile of a frequent-rail station. Areas in thin black are within one half mile of a frequent-bus route. The shaded areas are more than one half mile from any frequent transit. Not all rail lines are frequent, so some don't show up. The background shows census data: yellow-orange-red shading shows population density, and purple outlines show employment density. Green dots show large college campuses. Callouts indicate large job centers. Use these maps to understand what a transit system serves.

Some cities also have detailed maps (right bottom) of major transit hubs. These are at a much larger scale than the big maps that show the entire metropolitan areas, but these detail maps are at a consistent scale with each other.

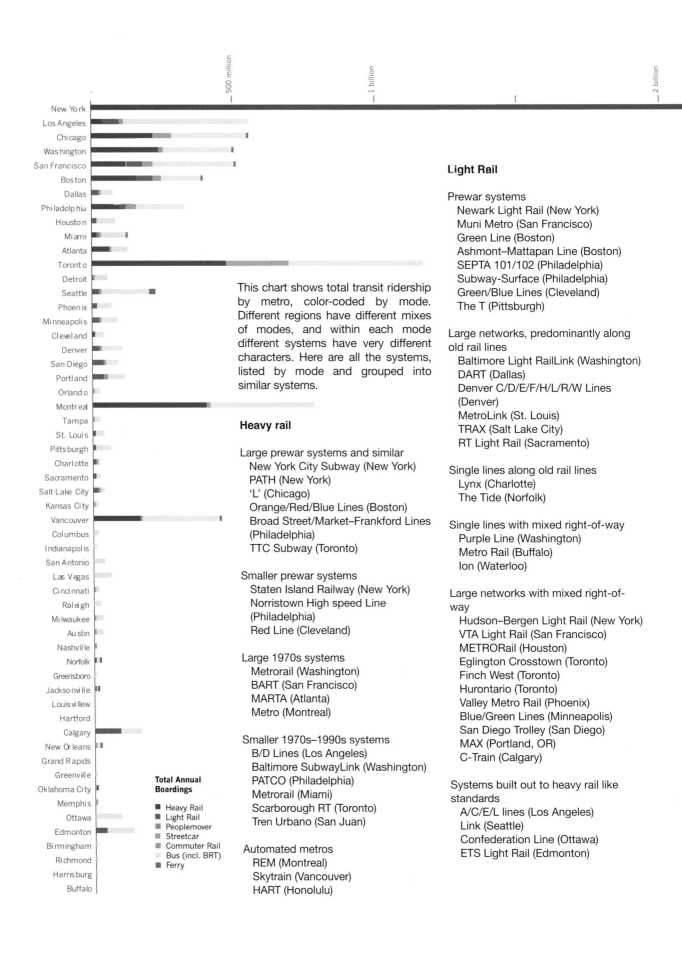

500 million · 1 billion · 2 billion

New York · Los Angeles · Chicago · Washington · San Francisco · Boston · Dallas · Philadelphia · Houston · Miami · Atlanta · Toronto · Detroit · Seattle · Phoenix · Minneapolis · Cleveland · Denver · San Diego · Portland · Orlando · Montreal · Tampa · St. Louis · Pittsburgh · Charlotte · Sacramento · Salt Lake City · Kansas City · Vancouver · Columbus · Indianapolis · San Antonio · Las Vegas · Cincinnati · Raleigh · Milwaukee · Austin · Nashville · Norfolk · Greensboro · Jacksonville · Louisville · Hartford · Calgary · New Orleans · Grand Rapids · Greenville · Oklahoma City · Memphis · Ottawa · Edmonton · Birmingham · Richmond · Harrisburg · Buffalo

This chart shows total transit ridership by metro, color-coded by mode. Different regions have different mixes of modes, and within each mode different systems have very different characters. Here are all the systems, listed by mode and grouped into similar systems.

Heavy rail

Large prewar systems and similar
 New York City Subway (New York)
 PATH (New York)
 'L' (Chicago)
 Orange/Red/Blue Lines (Boston)
 Broad Street/Market–Frankford Lines (Philadelphia)
 TTC Subway (Toronto)

Smaller prewar systems
 Staten Island Railway (New York)
 Norristown High speed Line (Philadelphia)
 Red Line (Cleveland)

Large 1970s systems
 Metrorail (Washington)
 BART (San Francisco)
 MARTA (Atlanta)
 Metro (Montreal)

Smaller 1970s–1990s systems
 B/D Lines (Los Angeles)
 Baltimore SubwayLink (Washington)
 PATCO (Philadelphia)
 Metrorail (Miami)
 Scarborough RT (Toronto)
 Tren Urbano (San Juan)

Automated metros
 REM (Montreal)
 Skytrain (Vancouver)
 HART (Honolulu)

Total Annual Boardings

■ Heavy Rail
■ Light Rail
■ Peoplemover
■ Streetcar
■ Commuter Rail
  Bus (incl. BRT)
■ Ferry

Light Rail

Prewar systems
 Newark Light Rail (New York)
 Muni Metro (San Francisco)
 Green Line (Boston)
 Ashmont–Mattapan Line (Boston)
 SEPTA 101/102 (Philadelphia)
 Subway-Surface (Philadelphia)
 Green/Blue Lines (Cleveland)
 The T (Pittsburgh)

Large networks, predominantly along old rail lines
 Baltimore Light RailLink (Washington)
 DART (Dallas)
 Denver C/D/E/F/H/L/R/W Lines (Denver)
 MetroLink (St. Louis)
 TRAX (Salt Lake City)
 RT Light Rail (Sacramento)

Single lines along old rail lines
 Lynx (Charlotte)
 The Tide (Norfolk)

Single lines with mixed right-of-way
 Purple Line (Washington)
 Metro Rail (Buffalo)
 Ion (Waterloo)

Large networks with mixed right-of-way
 Hudson–Bergen Light Rail (New York)
 VTA Light Rail (San Francisco)
 METRORail (Houston)
 Eglington Crosstown (Toronto)
 Finch West (Toronto)
 Hurontario (Toronto)
 Valley Metro Rail (Phoenix)
 Blue/Green Lines (Minneapolis)
 San Diego Trolley (San Diego)
 MAX (Portland, OR)
 C-Train (Calgary)

Systems built out to heavy rail like standards
 A/C/E/L lines (Los Angeles)
 Link (Seattle)
 Confederation Line (Ottawa)
 ETS Light Rail (Edmonton)

Streetcar

Prewar systems
   Cable Cars (San Francisco)
   15 Girard (Philadelphia)
   TTC Streetcars (Toronto)
   RTA Streetcars (New Orleans)

1980s-2000s "heritage" systems
   F Market (San Francisco)
   McKinney Avenue Trolley (Dallas)
   Galveston Trolley (Houston)
   TECO Line (Tampa)
   MATA Trolley (Memphis)
   El Paso Streetcar (El Paso)
   METRO Streetcar (Little Rock)

2000s stand-alone "modern" systems
   Q-Line (Detroit)
   KC Streetcar (Kansas City)
   Cincinnati Bell Connector (Cincinnati)
   The Hop (Milwaukee)
   OKC Streetcar (Oklahoma City)
   Sun Link (Tucson)

2000s "modern" systems connected to larger rail networks
   OC Streetcar (Los Angeles)
   DC Streetcar (Washington)
   Dallas Streetcar (Dallas)
   Atlanta Streetcar (Atlanta)
   Tempe Streetcar (Phoenix)
   Seattle Streetcar (Seattle)
   Tacoma Link (Seattle)
   Portland Streetcar (Portland, OR)
   CityLYNX (Charlotte)
   S-Line (Salt Lake City)

Peoplemover / Aerial Tram

   Roosevelt Island Tram (New York)
   Las Colinas APT (Dallas)
   Metromover (Miami)
   Detroit People Mover (Detroit)
   Monorail (Seattle)
   Portland Aerial Tram (Portland, OR)
   Las Vegas Monorail (Las Vegas)
   Skyway (Jacksonville)

BRT

Urban and suburban street-running
   sbX (Los Angeles)
   Metroway (Washington)
   Tempo (San Francisco)
   Van Ness (San Francisco)
   Rapid 522 (San Francisco)
   Silver Line (Houston)
   Viva (Toronto)
   HealthLine (Cleveland)
   South Bay BRT (San Diego)
   UVX (Salt Lake City)
   Red Line (Indianapolis)
   Deuce (Las Vegas)
   Pulse (Richmond)
   ART (Albuquerque)
   EmX (Eugene)
   MAX (Fort Collins)
   Pie-X (Montreal)

Circulators
   Loop Link (Chicago)
   Lymo (Orlando)
   MallRide (Denver)

Regional busways, rail conversions, and subways
   J Line (Los Angeles)
   G Line (Los Angeles)
   Silver Line SL1/L2/SL3 (Boston)
   Mississauga Transitway (Toronto)
   Busways (Pittsburgh)
   Transitway (Ottawa)
   Rapibus (Ottawa)
   CTfastrak (Hartford)
   RT (Winnipeg)
   Orange Line (Minneapolis)

Commuter Rail

Prewar systems
   NJ Transit Rail (New York)
   MTA Long Island Rail Road (New York)
   MTA Metro-North Railroad (New York)
   Metra (Chicago)
   South Shore Line (Chicago)
   MARC Train (Washington)
   Caltrain (San Francisco)
   MBTA Commuter Rail (Boston)
   SEPTA Regional Rail (Philadelphia)
   Exo (Montreal)

DMU startups (2000s onward)
   SMART (San Francisco)
   eBART (San Francisco)
   A-Train (Dallas)
   Silver Line (Dallas)
   TexRail (Dallas)
   River LINE (Philadelphia)
   UP Express (Toronto)
   Sprinter (San Diego)
   WES (Portland, OR)
   Capital MetroRail (Austin)
   Trillium Line (Ottawa)

Diesel locomotive startups (1960s onward)
   Shore Line East (New York)
   Metrolink (Los Angeles)
   Arrow (Los Angeles)
   VRE (Washington)
   ACE (San Francisco)
   Trinity Railway Express (Dallas)
   Tri-Rail (Miami)
   GO Transit (Toronto)
   Sounder (Seattle)
   SunRail (Orlando)
   Northstar (Minneapolis)
   Coaster (San Diego)
   FrontRunner (Salt Lake City)
   West Coast Express (Vancouver)
   Music City Star (Nashville)
   Hartford Line (Hartford)
   RailRunner (Albuquerque)

Electric Startups (2010s)
   A/B/G/N Lines (Denver)

BEST AND WORST

Different metro areas have taken very different approaches to transit. As the chart on the previous page shows, some cities outperform their peers and some cities underperform. Here are some decisions that turned out well—and some that didn't. ■

Best Transit Cities

No place in the Western Hemisphere has as busy— and useful —a transit network as New York City.

Toronto is Canada's version of New York—a big city that has long been built around effective transit.

Boston's crowded streets would not function without the trains running underneath and the buses that feed them.

San Francisco doesn't have nearly as much rail and BRT as it needs, but its walkability makes up for the lack of transit infrastructure.

Before it had rail, Seattle already had a strong bus-riding culture. Now it is building a rail system that is connecting key activity centers and making transit trips much faster.

Vancouver has been completely transformed around Skytrain.

It is hard to imagine Washington, DC without its subway. Transit has reshaped the city and its suburbs.

Best Light-Rail Networks

The Green Line serves the heart of Boston: downtown, Back Bay, Fenway, cultural institutions, and universities. It has a subway and dedicated lanes elsewhere, and runs more frequently than any other light rail.

Minneapolis–St. Paul's two-line network connects the region's most important centers and serves a series of walkable neighborhoods. The Green Line carries 39,000 people a day without a single park-and-ride lot.

Houston's network is small. But few lines can match the original 7.5-mile Red Line for its usefulness.

Los Angeles's rapidly expanding network runs from the Pacific to the San Gabriel Valley, and the trains are packed.

Calgary carries more ridership than any other North American system on less than 40 miles.

Toronto's Eglinton Crosstown replaces a busy bus route with a well-connected line through dense areas that benefits existing riders and will draw new ones.

Best Heavy-Rail Networks

The New York City subway carries a quarter of all US transit trips, and seventy-five percent of the city's residents are within walking distance. No other rail network is as comprehensive.

Like the New York City subway, Chicago's 'L' runs into the heart of dozens of dense, walkable neighborhoods. Unlike New York, though, it has been extended and modernized.

BART carries two-thirds of the people crossing the bay into San Francisco from the east at rush hour. The Bay Area would not function without it.

Washington's MetroRail still feels modern after 40 years. The stations where two lines cross make connections simpler and more legible than any other network.

Vancouver's automated Skytrain runs the most frequent all-day rail service in North America.

The Montreal METRO is second only to New York in boardings per mile on a compact modern system.

Best BRT Lines

Hartford's CTFastTrak has a BRT route every 7–12 minutes on weekdays from New Britain to downtown Hartford. The same busway also carries express commuter buses and local routes that branch out across the region.

Cleveland's Healthline follows the city's strongest corridor, connecting downtown with universities, hospitals, and cultural institutions with dedicated lanes most of the way. It carries more people than the city's light-rail lines.

The Indianapolis Red Line shows what a smaller city can do with a good corridor, good service, and extensive dedicated lanes created by reallocating street space.

Best Commuter Rail

Chicago's Metra links a busy downtown to dozens of walkable suburbs. Despite sharing its tracks with some of the country's busiest freight-rail routes, it has on-time performance of 96 percent—better than Long Island or Boston, which control most of their own tracks.

Denver's A Line, connecting downtown to the airport, is the only commuter-rail line in the US that runs every 15 minutes all day, every day.

Caltrain was built to bring commuters from sleepy suburban towns into San Francisco. Now that the orchards at its south end have become Silicon Valley, though, it is busy both ways, carrying more riders on 77 miles than Los Angeles has on 412. And now it's electrifying to offer even more service.

Ottawa's Trillium Line was operating the most frequent commuter-rail service in North America on a single track.

Best Frequent Bus Networks

Minneapolis has a large, branded, frequent-bus network. Its A-Line is the first of a series of "Arterial BRT" projects that will upgrade the busiest routes with faster, more frequent service and better stops.

Portland, Houston, Baltimore, and Jacksonville redesigned their networks to create more frequent routes.

El Paso's new rapid-bus lines are creating a comprehensive frequent network in a relatively small city.

Best Streetcars

Toronto's streetcar network (below) not only survived, as central to the neighborhoods it runs through as it was a century ago; it's been linked closely to the subway and some lines have been upgraded with dedicated lanes.

San Francisco's F Market runs beautiful vintage cars, but what makes it special is its long and useful route, its frequent service, and its high ridership.

The Kansas City Streetcar stands out from its peers with a simple route that connects multiple activity centers.

Best Bus-Rail Integration

Unlike its peers in San Francisco or DC, Atlanta's MARTA heavy-rail system uses the same fare structure as local bus, and bus-rail transfers are free. Some of the stations were built with bus-transit centers inside faregates to make those transfers easy. The three other bus systems in the region also have free transfers to and from MARTA.

Houston redesigned its new bus network around rail lines, feeding bus riders into rail for quick trips downtown while creating new crosstown connections.

Portland (Oregon) redesigned its network in the 1980s, and today rail and bus work together in a frequent grid and share the downtown transit mall.

Calgary and Edmonton both have extensive suburban bus networks feeding into light rail.

Most Useless Rail-Transit Lines

Nashville's Music City Star cost only $41 million, but it carries only 1,200 people, which is less than a typical bus route.

The Cincinnati Bell Connector should have connected four major activity centers, but got cut back to only one.

Civic leaders love the ideas of circulators within major activity centers, but riders don't. Jacksonville spent two decades building its elevated Skyway, which carries only 5,000 people day.

The St. Clair County MetroLink line running east from St. Louis literally serves corn fields.

In the 1990s, Cleveland concluded the key to revitalization was stadiums, the Rock and Roll Hall of Fame, and the Waterfront Line. Only 400 people a day ride the light-rail extension.

eBart was designed as a lower cost version of a 10-mile BART extension to Antioch, but still cost $525 million for two suburban park-and-ride stations, and every one of the 5,600 riders has to transfer. An express bus could have done the same thing for less.

Missed Opportunities

SEPTA regional rail has the infrastructure of a heavy-rail system: a downtown tunnel, largely double track lines, and 100% electrification. But it is operated as commuter rail, with infrequent trains and premium fares. Just by reforming fares and adding service, Philadelphia could have a heavy-rail system with no construction at all.

DART, serving Dallas, has built the biggest light-rail network in the United States. But despite being expansive, it reaches remarkably few places. It skips a dense concentration of jobs in Uptown, barely serves the city's biggest medical district, stops outside of walking distance of several universities, and misses Love Field's airport terminal by half a mile. As a result, it carries half as many people per mile as San Diego, Phoenix, or Houston.

In the past decade, the MTA has spent $18.9 billion on New York City subway and commuter–rail expansion. That pays for only three new subway stations and one commuter-rail station. New York is paying over $2 billion a mile for new subway lines. As Alon Levy pointed out on his "Pedestrian Observations" blog, London, Amsterdam, Tokyo, Paris, and Barcelona are building new lines in dense urban areas for 1/3 to 1/8 as much. New York could have had 10 or 20 new stations for what they paid for three.

Toronto could have built a simple and effective light-rail line to Scarborough; instead it was forced into proprietary new technology that didn't do anything more for riders. Now, as that is wearing out, elected officials have committed to a $5.5 billion CDN subway with fewer stops that won't be ready in time for the shutdown of the old line.

INTERCITY RAIL

Amtrak
federal
intercity rail

VIA Rail Canada
federal
intercity rail

Nominally, the United States and Canada have national rail passenger networks. Both Amtrak and Via Rail were created in the 1970s to "save" dying privately operated intercity trains with a political mandate to cover the country. But both are underfunded, and much of that service is minimal: Amtrak's intercity trains, like the California Zephyr (above, in central Colorado), typically run once a day, and the only train across Western Canada—the Toronto-Vancouver Canadian— only runs two days a week. These trains function as vacation experiences, as transportation for people unwilling or unable to fly (Amish and Mennonites are common on trains), and, in a few places, rural transportation lifelines (in Canada, where trains serve areas with no roads).

But where cities are a few hours apart, and service is frequent, trains can compete with planes and cars. Amtrak and VIA both inherited high-density corridors: Washington–Boston and Windsor–Quebec. The Amtrak corridor has better service (with trains every half hour all day on the busiest segment) and better infrastructure (electrification from DC to Boston, built in stages from 1905 to 2000, and 150 mph top speeds). Amtrak carries more people between Washington and Boston than the airlines do.

Even outside of the Northeast, with diesel trains on tracks shared with freight, Amtrak corridors can draw thousands of riders a day. Amtrak's governing legislation allows states to fund service and infrastructure upgrades. In the Northeast, Maine, New York, Pennsylvania, and Virginia have used this to extend Northeast Corridor service. In the Midwest, Northwest, and California, states have created successful corridors with up to 15 trains a day.

High-speed rail on new tracks has been discussed for decades. Only recently has there been some progress. California committed in 2008 to building high-speed rail (at 220 mph), and one segment is under construction. In Florida, Brightline is building the first privately operated intercity passenger train in 40 years, including 40 miles of brand new 125-mph track. ■

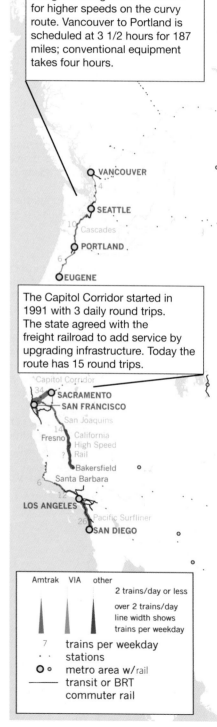

The Vancouver-Seattle-Portland-Eugene Cascades use Spanish-designed tilting trains that allow for higher speeds on the curvy route. Vancouver to Portland is scheduled at 3 1/2 hours for 187 miles; conventional equipment takes four hours.

The Capitol Corridor started in 1991 with 3 daily round trips. The state agreed with the freight railroad to add service by upgrading infrastructure. Today the route has 15 round trips.

Amtrak	VIA	other	
			2 trains/day or less
			over 2 trains/day line width shows trains per weekday
7			trains per weekday
∙ ∙			stations
O ● ∘			metro area w/ rail
—			transit or BRT commuter rail

brightline

Brightline
private
intercity rail

> There are no roads to Churchill, Manitoba -- it is reachable only by plane or 2-day-a-week VIA Rail train.

Intercity Rail (Amtrak)

PREWAR SYSTEM

Opened: 1831, nationalized 1971
Last Expanded: 2012
Length: 21,400 miles
Stations: 528
Frequency: 100 trains/day - 3 trains/week
Avg dail ridership:
34,250 on Northeast Corridor
42,190 on state supported corridors
12,600 on long distance routes

Intercity Rail (Via Rail)

PREWAR SYSTEM

Opened: 1853, nationalized 1977
Last Expanded: 1978
Length: 7,800 miles
Stations: 121
Frequency: 16 trains/day - 2 trains/week
Avg daily ridership:
13,000 on Quebec-Windsor Corridor
617 on other routes

> Three remote passenger-rail services in northern Canada exist to serve native settlements; two are owned and operated by First Nations.

> New York–Albany is Amtrak's fourth highest ridership corridor, but also a missed opportunity. It is a double-track line that could easily support twice as many trains, with 40-year-old cars and bare-bones snack service.

Quebec
11
OTTAWA 12 MONTREAL
20 13
Corridor
35
TORONTO 8
KITCHENER 6 Portland
41 10 Downeaster
BUFFALO Albany BOSTON
Empire 6 HARTFORD
Corridor 26 40
MILWAUKEE Hiawatha
16 DETROIT NEW YORK
CHICAGO 8 Wolverine 105
Illinois Zephyr / Harrisburg 28 Northeast Corridor
Carl Sandburg 8 PHILADELPHIA
Quincy 4
KANSAS Lin- Illini / WASHINGTON
CITY coln Saluki 18
4 6 RICHMOND 83
ST. LOUIS Carbondale 4
Missouri NORFOLK
River 4
Runner 8
Piedmont
CHARLOTTE Raleigh

Heartland Flyer
2

Intercity Rail (Brightline)

SMALL SYSTEM

ORLANDO Brightline
17

Opened: 2018
Last Expanded: N/A
Length: 70 miles (170 miles U/C)
Stations: 3 (4 under construction)
Frequency: 17 trips/day
Avg daily ridership: 2,400

MIAMI

> Amtrak's statutory requirements limit short-distance service to where states pay for it. That is why there is no corridor service in a huge chunk of the US south of Charlotte and east of San Diego.

1. NEW YORK

New York-Newark, NY-NJ-CT-PA

population 22,589,036 (1st)   **served by frequent transit** 43%   **daily trips per 1000** 522

No other North American city is as dependent on rail transit as New York City. It accounts for two thirds of US rail-transit ridership and one third of all transit ridership. New York City has only one car for every four people. Most of the population uses public transit not just to get to work but for errands and entertainment. Even in the suburbs, where car ownership is typical and freeways cross the landscape, commuter rail carries almost a million people to work daily.

The first rail transit line in the United States—horse-drawn streetcars—started regular service in lower Manhattan in 1832. From then on, New York grew around rail lines. Streetcars allowed the city to grow beyond walking distance. But those got stuck in traffic, and the solution was grade separation. By 1880, Manhattan had 81 miles of elevated railroad carrying 61 million passengers a year. In 1904, the government of the newly unified city opened a 23.9-mile subway system in Manhattan, Brooklyn, and the Bronx. It immediately increased possible commuting distances. The first major round of subway expansion started in 1913 and added 110 miles to the system, linking it to existing elevated lines in Brooklyn and bringing rapid transit to Queens for the first time. The result was the rapid growth of the city into the outer boroughs. In 1910, half of New York's population was in Manhattan; in 1940 it was only a quarter. Meanwhile, suburbs developed around the city on steam railroad lines. By the 1860s, railroads were selling commutation tickets. From the 1900s through the 1930s, railroads invested huge sums of money on widening lines, elevating them above streets, and electrification. A dedicated subway system got passengers from New Jersey terminals into Manhattan, and the Pennsylvania Railroad built tunnels to get direct access to the island.

Today, the area's rail-transit system is in the hands of government agencies representing three different states. All inherited well-engineered, lavishly built infrastructure. But that is a curse as well as a blessing: all that infrastructure requires a lot of maintenance. The Metropolitan Transit Authority spent $2.2 billion on subway cars, stations, and track in 2003—enough to build 50 miles of light rail—without adding a single mile of track or new station. Here in the capitol of rail transit, there hasn't been a major new subway line built in 50 years, only short extensions or connections, and the commuter-rail system has expanded only slightly since its low point of the 1970s. The story here is one of undoing years of deferred maintenance and improving existing infrastructure to carry ever-increasing passenger loads. ∎

MTA
independent agency
Heavy Rail
Frequent Bus
Commuter Rail

PATH
independent agency
Heavy Rail

New Jersey Transit
independent agency
Heavy Rail
Frequent Bus

CT Transit
state agency
Commuter Rail
Frequent Bus

nice

NICE
county
Frequent Bus

Bee-Line
county
Frequent Bus

RIOC
independent agency
Aerial Tram

+ **Biggest and busiest subway system in North America**
+ **Most extensive US commuter-rail system in the United States, with seven-day all-day service on many lines**
+ **Dense core city with 3/4 of residents within walk of frequent rail and 60% car-free households**
− **Poor transit service in very dense areas outside of New York City**
− **Antiquated and unreliable subway infrastructure**

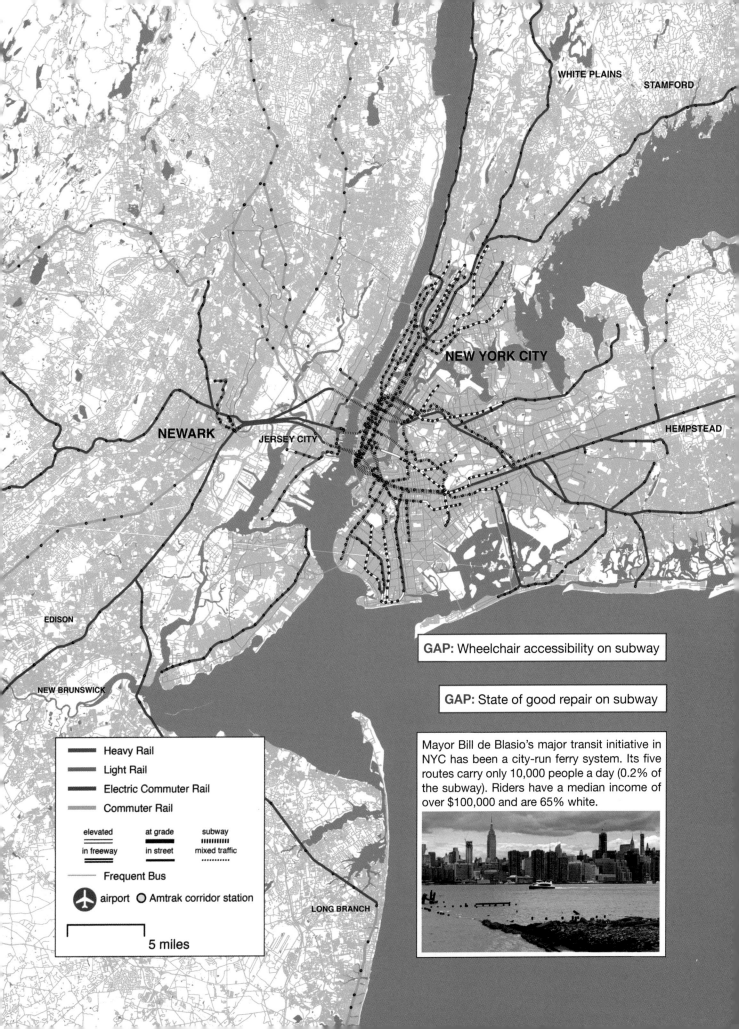

WHITE PLAINS

STAMFORD

NEW YORK CITY

NEWARK

JERSEY CITY

HEMPSTEAD

EDISON

NEW BRUNSWICK

LONG BRANCH

GAP: Wheelchair accessibility on subway

GAP: State of good repair on subway

Mayor Bill de Blasio's major transit initiative in NYC has been a city-run ferry system. Its five routes carry only 10,000 people a day (0.2% of the subway). Riders have a median income of over $100,000 and are 65% white.

Heavy Rail
Light Rail
Electric Commuter Rail
Commuter Rail

| elevated | at grade | subway |
| in freeway | in street | mixed traffic |

Frequent Bus

✈ airport ◎ Amtrak corridor station

5 miles

Heavy Rail (New York Subway)

EXTREMELY HIGH PERFORMER
LARGE SYSTEM
PREWAR SYSTEM

Opened: 1904
Last Expanded: 2017
Length: 233 miles
Stations: 424
Frequency: 2-10 min peak, 4-10 midday, 8-15 evenings/weekends, 20 overnight (24 hr service)
Avg weekday ridership: 9,117,400
Ridership per mile: 39,130

Heavy Rail (Staten Island Railway)

LOW PERFORMER
SMALL SYSTEM
PREWAR SYSTEM

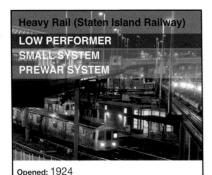

Opened: 1924
Last Expanded: N/A
Length: 14 miles
Stations: 22
Frequency: 15 min; 30 overnight/ weekend (24 hr service)
Avg weekday ridership: 28,500
Ridership per mile: 2,036

Aerial Tram (Roosevelt Island Tram)

Opened: 1976
Last Expanded: N/A
Length: 0.6 miles
Stations: 2
Frequency: 7 min peak, 15 min midday/ evening/weekend
Avg weekday ridership: 6,179
Ridership per mile: 10,298

With 2.3 million riders on an average weekday, the bus system in New York City is the second busiest transit network in the country, behind only the New York City subway. They provide frequent all-day service across nearly the entire city, and they are an essential lifeline for the city's low-income residents (above), especially in parts of Queens, Brooklyn, and the Bronx beyond the reach of subway. Buses offer a key connection for crosstown trips and the only wheelchair-accessible citywide network.

But the bus system has been neglected. The average bus speed in Manhattan is 6 mph. It's common on 42nd Street to watch pedestrians outpace the bus. The outer boroughs don't do much better; buses in Brooklyn and Queens average just over 7 mph. Reliability is similarly bad, and stops often have minimal amenities and get blocked by illegally parked cars, piles of trash, and snow. In 2008, the city started working with MTA to implement "Select Bus Service," with limited stops, bus lanes, and signal priority. In 2019, cameras on board buses started enforcing those lanes. FourteenthStreet in Manhattan (below) is now a busway, with only limited local-access car traffic allowed. These measures, though, only helped a small part of the network, and the rollout of bus priority has consistently been slower than initially announced, due in part to NIMBY opposition.

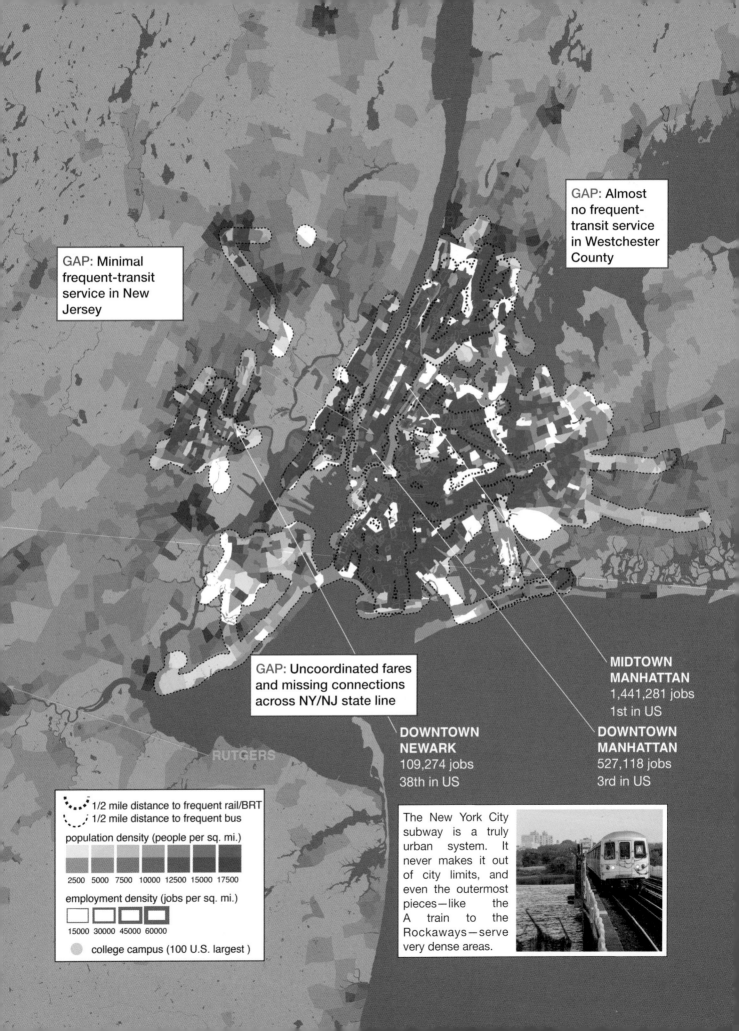

GAP: Minimal frequent-transit service in New Jersey

GAP: Almost no frequent-transit service in Westchester County

GAP: Uncoordinated fares and missing connections across NY/NJ state line

RUTGERS

MIDTOWN MANHATTAN
1,441,281 jobs
1st in US

DOWNTOWN NEWARK
109,274 jobs
38th in US

DOWNTOWN MANHATTAN
527,118 jobs
3rd in US

1/2 mile distance to frequent rail/BRT
1/2 mile distance to frequent bus

population density (people per sq. mi.)

2500 5000 7500 10000 12500 15000 17500

employment density (jobs per sq. mi.)

15000 30000 45000 60000

college campus (100 U.S. largest)

The New York City subway is a truly urban system. It never makes it out of city limits, and even the outermost pieces—like the A train to the Rockaways—serve very dense areas.

The 232-mile New York City subway was largely built from 1900 to 1940. The burst of construction enabled the city's population to double (right). But since 1940, the city's transit system has actually shrunk.

When the city built the first subway line, it chose a private company, Interborough Rapid Transit Company, to operate it. The company also owned all of the elevated lines and half the streetcar lines in Manhattan. To prevent a monopoly, the 1913 subway expansion included a second private company, Brooklyn-Manhattan Transit. It linked its existing elevated lines in Brooklyn into newly built subway lines in Manhattan and new lines in Queens. The IRT, meanwhile, expanded into the Bronx and Queens and added another Manhattan line. The two systems operated as separate, money-making enterprises. In the 1920s the city began construction of another round of subway lines, the Independent system, operated by the city to counteract the power of the private companies. Some IND lines were purposefully located to provide competition to the private lines, especially in the Bronx and upper Manhattan.

The subway officially became one system with the "unification" of 1940, when the city bought out the BMT and IRT. In 1968, the subways were taken over by the MTA, an independent state-level agency. The system it operates is still largely the system it inherited. On today's subway map, old IRT lines are still designated with numbers while BMT and IND lines carry letters. Different design standards, require the MTA to maintain two separate fleets of subway cars with different sizes. Adjacent stations that belonged to different systems were built without connections, resulting in several "out-of-system transfers" where passengers exit fare gates, walk on the street, and enter another set of fare gates to change lines. There is also significant duplication. There are five north-south lines in the two-mile width of

New York City Population

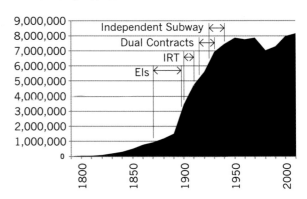

midtown Manhattan, but they are all concentrated at the center of the island since each system needed to serve the business districts. As a result, on an island with three subway stations per square mile, the United Nations headquarters is half a mile from the nearest subway.

There has been little subway construction since the 1930s, and, with the closure of the last Els, New York actually has fewer rapid-transit stations today than it did in the 1960s. Postwar projects include the conversion of a commuter-rail line into the Rockaway line, and a number of minor additions: a half-mile subway in 1967 to link BMT lines in Brooklyn with IND lines in Manhattan; a three-station subway in 1988 to replace an elevated line in Jamaica, Queens; a new East River crossing to the system in 1989; a single-station extension to the Hudson Yards redevelopment in 2015; and a two-mile, three-station segment of the Second Avenue Subway in 2016.

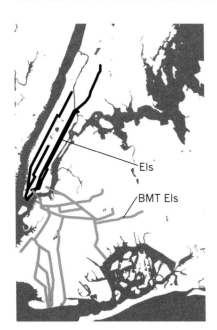

New York City rapid transit before 1908

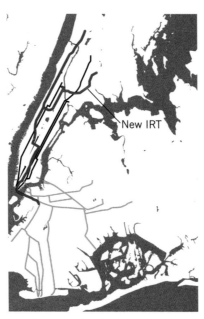

IRT contracts 1 and 2, built 1900–1908

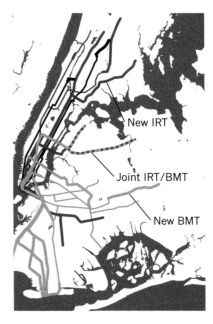

Dual Contracts, built 1913–1931

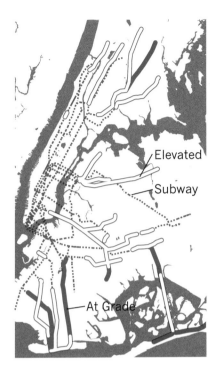

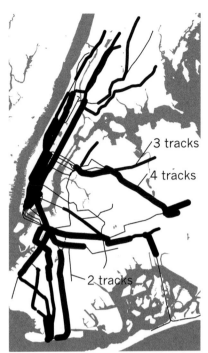

"Subway" is a misnomer; some 70 miles of the system are elevated, and another 23 are on the surface (top left). New York has more miles of elevated track than the Chicago 'L', and unlike in Chicago, almost all of those are above city streets. The cost of putting lines underground will keep trains running above NYC streets for a long time. Most of the surface tracks are old railroad lines, built when those parts of the city were still rural.

Much of the subway's capacity and convenience is due to express tracks (shown as thick lines on the map top right). The Manhattan main lines, and several lines in Queens and Brooklyn, have four tracks with all-day express service. On these lines, express stations, served by all trains, typically have center platforms designed for easy transfers, while the intermediate stations are served only by local trains.

Several more lines have three tracks with part-time service in the rush-hour direction, and there are unused express tracks on several lines, like the N/W in Astoria, Queens (left). These tracks also allow 24-hour service to continue while one or two tracks are under construction. No other subway has this much express service. Due to the high cost of building a four-track subway, it is likely that none ever will.

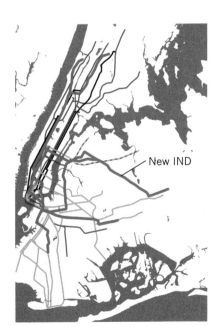

Independent Subway, built 1925–1940

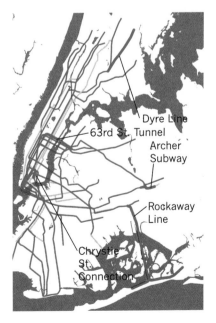

Unified System, 1940– (abandoned lines shown in light grey)

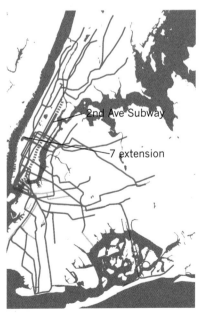

Current expansion (dashed lines are unfunded)

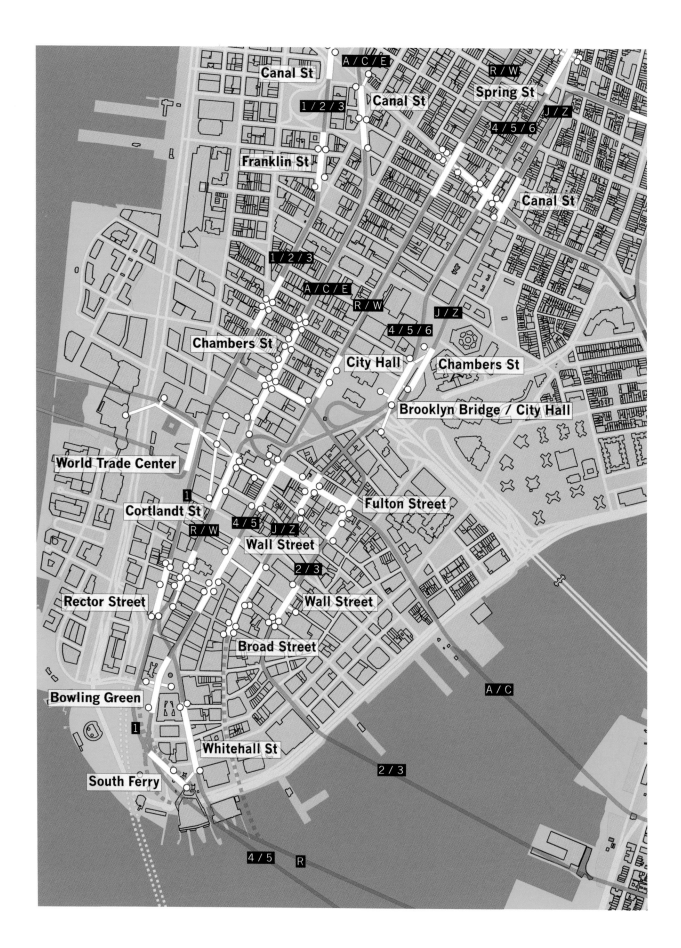

Lower Manhattan (opposite) has the densest network of subway lines in North America. It was built as four different systems: IRT (1, 2, 3, 4, 5), BMT (J, R, W, Z), IND, and the Hudson & Manhattan Railroad (PATH). Each was trying to serve a relatively small but very dense business district. This results in incredible capacity: nearly 150 trains an hour pass through this area during rush hour. Alex Marshall of the Regional Plan Association noted that providing sufficient surface parking for the workers at the World Trade Center if they did not take transit would require paving over most of this map. Fifty freeway lanes would need to be added to bring them into Manhattan. Public transit is the lifeblood of New York City.

The tangle of routes is a relic of history, created by irregular streets laid out by Dutch settlers and the competition of privately operated transit. Because the transit systems were competing, they had little reason to interconnect their routes. Nobody would design a transit system like this today.

Over time, the different systems have been linked. When the system was unified, the Transit Authority removed fare gates to create free transfer where passages existed. The construction of the World Trade Center created links between IRT, BMT, IND, and PATH via an underground shopping concourse. Following the WTC's destruction by terrorists in September 2001, the Port Authority built a new station, and the MTA built a new transit center at Fulton Street (below), combining four stations. A concourse connects these facilities, bringing PATH and 11 subway lines together. But not all of these connections happen within the same set of fare gates, and PATH and the subway still use separate fare systems.

Another relic of subway competition will be harder to fix: duplicated routes leave sections of Manhattan a long walk from the nearest station—particularly the Lower East Side and the Battery Park City development along the Hudson River. The Second Avenue Subway would help, adding three stations closer to the East River. But it is not funded, and there are no plans for rail, or even dedicated lanes for buses, to Battery Park City.

The Staten Island Railway (above) is a story of what might have been. In 1925, work began on a subway tunnel to connect Brooklyn with Staten Island, and the commuter-rail line on the island was electrified and upgraded with equipment that matched the subway. But the tunnel was never completed, and the Verrazano Narrows Bridge was built in 1965 with no provision for rail.

Thus, every morning, commuters on Staten Island enact an old ritual: they get off a train and onto a boat. This is the last of many rail-transit operations across the United States that depend on ferry connections to downtown employment centers. The Staten Island Ferry (bottom) remains an important connection between Staten Island and Manhattan. But the railway is not nearly as significant. Three-quarters of ferry riders arrive by car and bus. Less than a quarter of the island is within walking distance of a rail station. Unlike elsewhere in New York, rail is not the fastest mode of transportation here. An all-stops trip the length of the line takes 40 minutes, the ferry trip to lower Manhattan takes 25 minutes, and continuing on to Midtown takes another 15-minute subway ride. Express bus service via the Verrazano Bridge takes 45 minutes for the whole trip, though it costs more. Staten Island residents have the longest commutes in New York City.

Like the rest of New York City, Staten Island is a case study in the effects of transit on the development of cities. It shows what happens without good transit links. If either the BMT or the Hudson & Manhattan had linked to the island, it would be as dense as Brooklyn or Queens. Instead, it is the forgotten borough, with a little-known rail-transit line.

Commuter Rail (Long Island Rail Road)

HIGH PERFORMER

LARGE SYSTEM

PREWAR SYSTEM

Opened: 1834
Last Expanded: ongoing
Length: 319 miles (4 in construction)
Stations: 124 (1 in construction)
Frequency: 30-min all-days service on some lines; rush hour only on others
Avg weekday ridership: 385,400
Ridership per mile: 1,208

Commuter Rail (Metro-North Railroad)

HIGH PERFORMER

LARGE SYSTEM

PREWAR SYSTEM

Opened: 1849
Last Expanded: 2000
Length: 272 miles
Stations: 113
Frequency: 30 min–3 hour off-peak; more frequent peak
Avg weekday ridership: 311,800
Ridership per mile: 1,146

Commuter Rail (Shore Line East)

LOW PERFORMER

Opened: 1990
Last Expanded: 2001
Length: 90 miles
Stations: 15
Frequency: 20–45 min peak, 1–3 hr midday/evening/weekend
Avg weekday ridership: 2,200
Ridership per mile: 24

New York City has the Western Hemisphere's most extensive and intensive commuter-rail system. Three major commuter-rail operations enter the city from the north, the east, and the west, combining for 1.7 million weekday trips. That is more than all other US commuter-rail systems combined.

That high ridership results from a concentration of jobs, a lack of competition, transit-friendly development patterns, and all-day service. Highway options are limited: only a few tunnels and bridges lead to Manhattan and its 2.4 million jobs. Because the New York City subway does not extend beyond city limits, commuter rail serves trips that would use heavy rail elsewhere. Across all three states, small towns are centered on rail stations. On the Long Island Rail Road in 2012–2014, nearly a quarter of riders walked from their homes to the station, and less than 40% drove alone and parked. Because many lines have all-day service, locals use commuter rail for all sorts of trips. New Jersey Transit's Northeast Corridor has trains in both directions every 30 minutes or more from 4:00 a.m. to well past midnight. Only 60% of Long Island Rail Road riders headed toward New York are going to work. Employment centers have also developed around suburban stations in places like Stamford, Connecticut (below), and Metropark, New Jersey.

All of this is made possible by the best commuter-rail infrastructure in the country. In the early twentieth century, New York's railroads made massive investments that continue to serve commuters well today. These include extensive double track, electrification on four separate railroads, and numerous grade-separation projects.

Arguably, this infrastructure is actually underused. In other cities, the kinds of job and population densities served by commuter rail in New York support light-rail or heavy-rail service every 10–15 minutes. That would be much more useful for shorter trips. Trips not bound for Manhattan would also benefit from running trains through New York City, rather than having every train terminate there.

The commuter-rail network shares tracks and stations with busy intercity rail corridors. Amtrak runs 150-mph Acela service and 100-mph regional service under electric wires to Boston, Philadelphia, and Washington out of Penn Station, as well as diesel service to Springfield, Massachusetts, and Albany, New York.

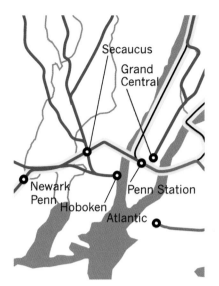

There are two commuter-rail stations in Manhattan. Grand Central Terminal serves Metro-North trains from the north and the northeast. It is reached by a four-track line (opposite top) that is elevated through Harlem and then tunnels under Park Avenue. Penn Station serves Long Island Railroad trains from the east and New Jersey Transit and Amtrak trains. Its approach tracks tunnel under both the Hudson and East Rivers. A new tunnel now under construction will bring some LIRR trains into Grand Central.

Commuter Rail (NJ Transit Rail)

HIGH PERFORMER
LARGE SYSTEM
PREWAR SYSTEM

Opened: 1839
Last Expanded: 2009
Length: 419 miles
Stations: 157
Frequency: varies from 30 min all day to a few trains a day
Avg weekday ridership: 303,949
Ridership per mile: 725

Small towns in New York, New Jersey, and Connecticut developed around the railroad, so the densest, most walkable areas tend to cluster at stations.

Shore Line East service, launched in 1990, connects to Metro-North in New Haven and extends eastward along the Connecticut coast.

New Haven and Stamford are destinations in their own right, creating two-way travel demand on Metro-North.

Dense development extends outside New York City into Long Island and New Jersey around closely spaced commuter-rail stations with all-day service.

At its eastern end, 116 miles and 3 hours from New York City, the LIRR serves upscale beach towns and small fishing ports.

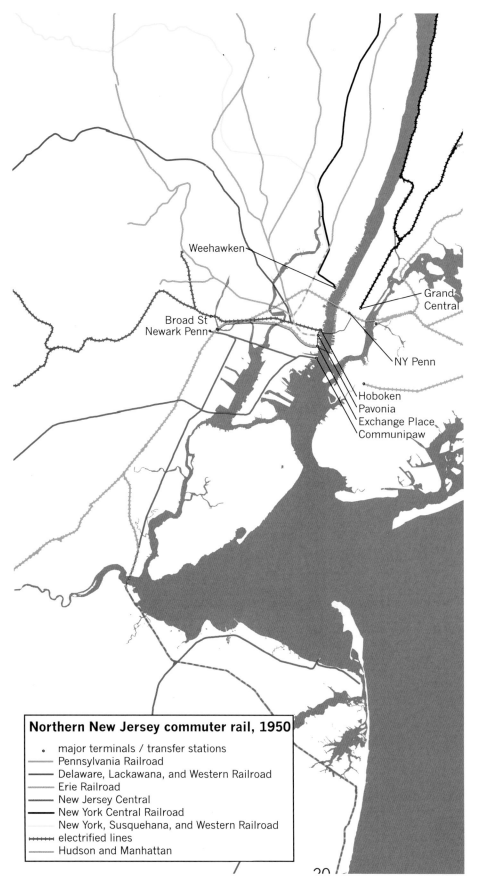

Weehawken

Grand Central

Broad St
Newark Penn

NY Penn

Hoboken
Pavonia
Exchange Place
Communipaw

Northern New Jersey commuter rail, 1950

∘   major terminals / transfer stations
——   Pennsylvania Railroad
——   Delaware, Lackawana, and Western Railroad
——   Erie Railroad
——   New Jersey Central
——   New York Central Railroad
——   New York, Susquehana, and Western Railroad
++++   electrified lines
——   Hudson and Manhattan

From the 1850s to the 1950s, New York was the largest population center and largest port in the United States as well as a major manufacturing center. It is no wonder that every major eastern railroad tried to make it to the city. As the city grew, most ended up operating commuter service.

But the Hudson River stood as a moat between Manhattan and the west. Only one railroad—the Pennsylvania—had the resources to cross it, and it took until 1910 to do that. All the others ended on the New Jersey waterfront, within sight of Manhattan. Jersey City and Hoboken became a tangle of rail lines, with five major passenger terminals within five miles, as well as countless freight facilities.

Passengers had two ways to make it to their jobs across the river. Every terminal had its own ferry slips (below) where the railroads operated their own boats to another set of terminals across the river. Three of the terminals were also served by the Manhattan Tubes (today's PATH) whose trains were faster and immune to storms or ice on the river.

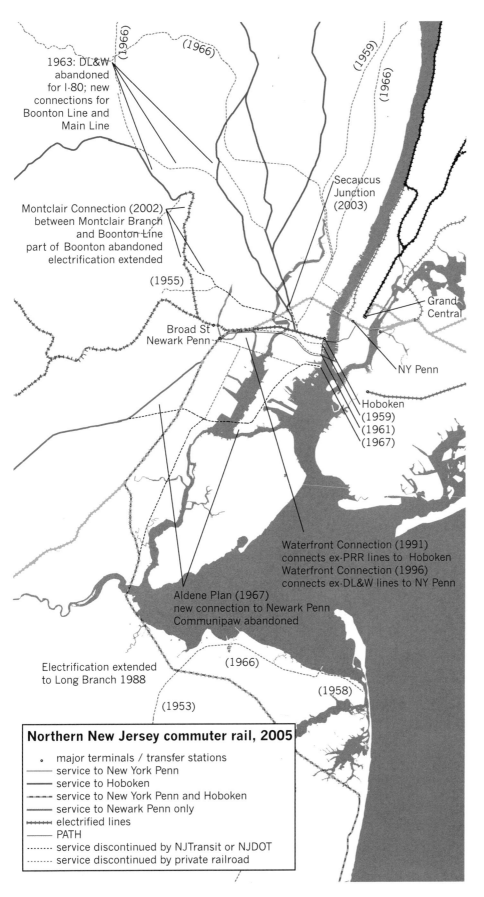

1963: DL&W abandoned for I-80; new connections for Boonton Line and Main Line

Montclair Connection (2002) between Montclair Branch and Boonton Line part of Boonton abandoned electrification extended

(1955)

(1966)

(1966)

(1959)

(1966)

Secaucus Junction (2003)

Grand Central

Broad St
Newark Penn

NY Penn

Hoboken
(1959)
(1961)
(1967)

Waterfront Connection (1991) connects ex-PRR lines to Hoboken
Waterfront Connection (1996) connects ex-DL&W lines to NY Penn

Aldene Plan (1967) new connection to Newark Penn Communipaw abandoned

Electrification extended to Long Branch 1988

(1966)

(1958)

(1953)

Northern New Jersey commuter rail, 2005

- major terminals / transfer stations
— service to New York Penn
— service to Hoboken
–·–· service to New York Penn and Hoboken
— service to Newark Penn only
+++ electrified lines
— PATH
······ service discontinued by NJTransit or NJDOT
······ service discontinued by private railroad

In the freeway era of the 1950s and 1960s, New Jersey's commuter rail service began to disappear. The real prospect of losing the remaining service prompted public takeover.

The state of New Jersey has spent the last 30 years consolidating New Jersey's commuter rail lines into one interconnected system. The first step used new track connections to reroute New Jersey Central's commuter service into Newark Penn Station. This left two groups of lines: former Pennsylvania Railroad lines that ran via Newark Penn Station into New York Penn Station, and a set of former Erie-Lackawanna lines that ran into Hoboken. New Jersey Transit then built a pair of connection tracks, allowing some trains that formerly ran to Penn to run to Hoboken, and some that formerly ran to Hoboken to run to Penn. A little farther east, other Hoboken lines crossed the Penn Station lines. Here, in 2003, NJT opened Secaucus Junction, a two-level transfer station. Thus all of northern New Jersey's commuter rail lines are now one system.

The Port Authority of New York and New Jersey never intended to operate a transit system; it was a dock, bridge, and tunnel operator that wanted to get into commercial real estate. But to build the World Trade Center, the PA needed the land occupied by the headquarters and downtown terminal of the Hudson & Manhattan Railroad. Thus, in the interest of real estate—and to pacify New Jersey politicians—the PA acquired the third-oldest subway in the United States. PATH is an oddity. It does not connect residential areas with business districts, or carry people from one part of a city to another. It was opened in 1908 with a single purpose: getting passengers from New Jersey commuter trains into Manhattan. That remains its primary mission. The opening of Newark Penn Station (below) in 1937 completed the system and created easy transfers between commuter rail, the Tubes, and local transit. The Newark Station was intermodal before the word intermodal. PATH trains from Downtown Manhattan enter the station at roof level (below) to discharge passengers onto a mezzanine with stair access to outbound commuter-train platforms, then reverse and collect passengers at a track just across the platform from inbound commuter trains. Two levels below are subway platforms for the Newark City Subway, built in the 1930s to take Newark streetcars off city streets and converted into light rail in 2002-2006, with a one-mile branch to Newark Broad Street, the second commuter-rail station in downtown Newark.

The consolidation of the New Jersey commuter-rail system connected PATH to commuter-rail lines in two locations: Newark Penn Station and Hoboken Terminal. For passengers arriving at Hoboken, PATH is the way to get to either Downtown or Midtown Manhattan. Most trains through Newark go directly to Penn Station in Midtown, but PATH offers a shortcut to lower Manhattan.

With the closure of the remaining rail terminals, two PATH stations were left marooned in weedy fields. But empty tracts of land across the river from Manhattan with excellent rapid-transit access would not stay empty for long. Starting in the 1980s, the New Jersey waterfront was redeveloped with high-rise offices and apartments, with PATH linking them to the city. The Hudson-Bergen Light Rail System, which connects with PATH at both those stations, now acts as a feeder system.

In the morning (above), most of the PATH boardings are at Newark Penn Station and Hoboken Terminal, where riders transfer from commuter trains to get to New York City. In the afternoon (below), the pattern reverses, with the largest number of boardings at the World Trade Center and 33rd Street in Manhattan. Likewise, Journal Square—with 15 connecting bus routes—is also largely an A.M. origin and P.M. destination. But the Exchange Street and Newport stations, which are surrounded by office and residential towers, see two-way traffic.

With the completion of One World Trade Center, the PATH station was integrated into the basement concourse of that complex, and rebuilt (above) following the 2001 terrorist attacks. It is well located at the edge of the downtown financial district, a five-minute walk from Wall Street.

New Jersey has the largest privately operated for-profit transit system in the United States. Many different private companies, coordinating to various degrees, operate multiple jitney corridors, connecting to two Manhattan bus terminals and the Journal Square PATH station. While the system evolved from very informal operations, it now offers regularly scheduled service: buses run on predefined routes, many of which (right) have relatively predictable all-day frequent service. Regular passengers find it convenient, but the system is arcane and hard to discover and understand for first-time users.

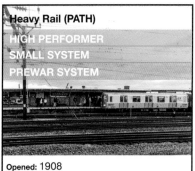

Heavy Rail (PATH)

HIGH PERFORMER
SMALL SYSTEM
PREWAR SYSTEM

Opened: 1908
Last Expanded: 1937
Length: 13.8 miles
Stations: 13
Frequency: 4–7 min peak, 10 min midday, 15 min weekends/overnight (24–hr service)
Avg weekday ridership: 306,700
Ridership per mile: 22,225

Light Rail (Hudson-Bergen Light Rail)

HIGH PERFORMER

Opened: 2000
Last Expanded: ongoing
Length: 16.6 miles (0.7 in construction)
Stations: 24 (1 in construction)
Frequency: 5–10 min peak, 8–20 min midday, 10–30 min evening/weekends
Avg weekday ridership: 52,957
Ridership per mile: 3,190

Hoboken and Jersey City (above) have always been the poor relations of New York City, which lies just across the Hudson River. This is also true for rail transit. While this part of New Jersey had lots of transit facilities—six commuter railroad terminals and the Hudson & Manhattan Railroad—all of these were designed for suburban commuters passing through on their way to Manhattan. In fact, the sprawling rail yards acted as an impediment to local travel.

In the 1990s, the waterfront, now dubbed the "Gold Coast," was redeveloped with office towers, malls, and condos. Some of these were built directly around PATH stations. Between the late 1980s and 2000, ridership increased by 11,800 at Pavonia-Newport and 8,600 at Exchange Place; that new traffic represents 10% of system ridership. For the rest of the new development, and for connections north and south, New Jersey built the Hudson-Bergen Light Rail. It serves several distinct purposes. It directly serves one business district (the New Jersey waterfront) and connects to two more (Downtown and Midtown Manhattan) via subway and ferry connections. Some commuters use HBLR to get to the Gold Coast from New Jersey, some commuters use HBLR to get to Manhattan from New Jersey, and some use it to get from New York to the Gold Coast. The system also provides local service for neighborhoods in Bayonne, Jersey City, Hoboken, and North Bergen.

The basic concept of the system is a central segment that serves the office centers with a mix of private right-of-way and street-running lines, which connects to the outer segments along abandoned railroad lines. The system design is typical for a 1990s light-rail system: a mix of rights of way, moderate use of overpasses and elevated segments, low-floor vehicles, and proof-of-purchase ticketing. The original design included street running in Hoboken, but due to local opposition that was changed to an old railroad line farther inland. This delayed construction. The first segment opened in 2000, but trains did not make it to Hoboken Terminal until 2002, and to the northern end of the line in 2006.

Light Rail (Newark Light Rail)

HIGH PERFORMER
SMALL SYSTEM
PREWAR SYSTEM

Opened: 1935
Last Expanded: 2006
Length: 6.3 miles
Stations: 17
Frequency: 3–10 min peak, 10 min midday, 10–30 min evening, 20–25 min weekends
Avg weekday ridership: 20,880
Ridership per mile: 3,314

2. LOS ANGELES

Los Angeles–Long Beach, CA

population 18,711,436 (2nd)   **served by frequent transit** 22%   **daily trips per 1000** 83

Los Angeles is known as the archetypical automobile city. But Los Angeles is a generation older than other Sun Belt cities like Houston, Dallas, or Phoenix. It was one of the ten largest cities in the United States by 1910, and it more than doubled in size in the next decade. This growth was supported by what was then the world's largest electric railway system, the Pacific Electric, with over 1,000 miles of track (including a short downtown subway) that connected the city to its suburbs. Before LA was a freeway city, it was a transit city; the first segment of the Hollywood Freeway even included Pacific Electric tracks in the median.

Though Los Angeles's first rail system was gone by 1963, it left a city that is still friendly to transit. An average of 8,000 people per square mile live within the city limits of Los Angeles, about the same as Seattle and Baltimore and more than twice as many as Houston, Dallas, Phoenix, or Denver. Much of the city has a regular street grid, and the climate is conducive to walking. Transit never went away. The streetcar lines evolved into the nation's second-largest bus system, carrying 1.1 million boardings on an average weekday.

Planning for a new rail-transit system began even before the old system was torn up. The Los Angeles Metropolitan Transit Authority, the ancestor of today's MTA, was created in 1951 to study monorail between Los Angeles and Long Beach. In 1968, 1974, and 1976, voters turned down rail proposals. In 1980, a rail plan finally passed. Work began on three different lines: a subway west from downtown under Wilshire (the same route where ground had been broken on in 1962), a light-rail line to Long Beach (on the same corridor as the Pacific Electric rail line that MTA itself abandoned in 1961), and another light-rail line in the Century Freeway, on right-of-way preserved as a result of local opposition to the freeway project.

The early years of the rail construction were difficult. The Red Line (now called the B and D lines) ran into concerns about gas pockets, leading to a 1985 federal law prohibiting construction of a subway under Wilshire. The route, already under construction, was frantically redesigned to turn north instead, leaving an odd one-mile spur on the original alignment. The Green Line (C) was designed to connect population areas to defense plants near LAX. By the time the line opened in 1995, the Cold War was over and the original ridership projections have still not been met. But the Blue Line (A), opened in 1990, has been widely successful. With 90,000 weekday boardings, it is now the busiest single light-rail line in the country. The opening of rail built momentum for more. Meanwhile, the Southern California Regional Rail Authority, spanning five counties, spent $450 million to buy 175 miles of freight rail lines in 1990 and began operating commuter rail the following year. That system is

+ **Successful (and expanding) light-rail system serving dense urban places**
+ **Extensive frequent bus network**
+ **High-quality BRT line**
− **Inadequate connections outside LA County**

Metro

Metro
independent agency
Heavy Rail
Light Rail
BRT
Frequent Bus

METROLINK
Southern California Regional Rail Authority
independent agency
Commuter Rail

Omnitrans
independent agency
Frequent Bus
BRT

Foothill Transit
independent agency
Frequent Bus

LADot
municipal
Frequent Bus

Big Blue Bus
municipal
Frequent Bus

Long Beach Transit
independent agency
Frequent Bus

GTrans
municipal
Frequent Bus

Montebello
BUS LINES
Montebello Bus Lines
municipal
Frequent Bus

OCTA
OCTA
independent agency
Frequent Bus

now the second-longest commuter-rail system in the United States at 412 miles.

There has been rail construction in LA in every year since 1986, and a steady stream of openings: subway to North Hollywood in 2000, light rail to Pasadena in 2003, East LA in 2009, Culver City in 2012, Santa Monica in 2016. Today, two major projects are under construction and three more are in planning.

LA has also made dramatic improvements to its bus system. A grid of "Rapid" buses, in mixed traffic on major streets, provides high-frequency, limited-stop service across the urban area. In the San Fernando Valley, G Line (formerly Orange Line) BRT vehicles run in a dedicated busway, serving LRT-like stations and connecting to the subway. Busways along the San Bernardino Freeway and the Harbor Freeway carry numerous local and express bus lines as well as J Line (formerly Silver Line) BRT vehicles.

But the experience of taking transit in LA can still be frustrating. Despite the success of the Rapid system, attempts to dedicate street lanes for transit have failed. LA bus riders spend their time stuck in the same traffic as automobile drivers. Despite exclusive right-of-way, the rail system can be frustratingly indirect. The L Line heads straight towards downtown but stops short, forcing passengers to transfer to the subway. The C Line gets within half a mile of LAX runways but doesn't serve the terminal. The densest employment corridor in the region—Wilshire Boulevard from downtown through Wilshire Center, the Miracle Mile, Beverly Hills, Century City, and Westwood to Santa Monica does not have a rail line, leaving many of the city's jobs outside convenient transit access.

LA could be one of the great transit success stories of the next few decades. In 2016, voters approved new taxes that will yield $120 billion over 40 years for new transit projects. These projects promise to fix many of the system's gaps with new rail corridors and better connections. The density is there to support high ridership, and the relentlessly congested freeways make transit attractive. Well-designed rail lines in the right places—coupled with reliable bus service—could make transit the preferred way to move around LA. ∎

Heavy Rail (B/D Lines)

Opened: 1993
Last Expanded: ongoing
Length: 17.8 miles (9.1 under construction)
Stations: 16 (7 under construction)
Frequency: 5–10 min peak, 6–15 min midday, 10–20 min evening, 6–15 min weekends
Avg weekday ridership: 130,900
Ridership per mile: 7,354

Light Rail (A/C/E/L Lines)
LARGE SYSTEM

Opened: 1990
Last Expanded: ongoing
Length: 88.2 miles (19.5 under construction)
Stations: 80 (15 under construction)
Frequency: 6–12 min peak, 12–15 min midday, 10–20 min evening, 7–20 min weekend
Avg weekday ridership: 161,300
Ridership per mile: 1,829

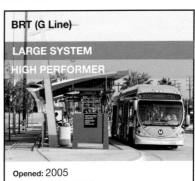

BRT (G Line)
LARGE SYSTEM
HIGH PERFORMER

Opened: 2005
Last Expanded: 2012
Length: 18 miles (18 guideway miles)
Stations: 17 (guideway only)
Frequency: 4–10 min day, 20 min evening
Avg weekday ridership: 21,663
Ridership per mile: 1,202

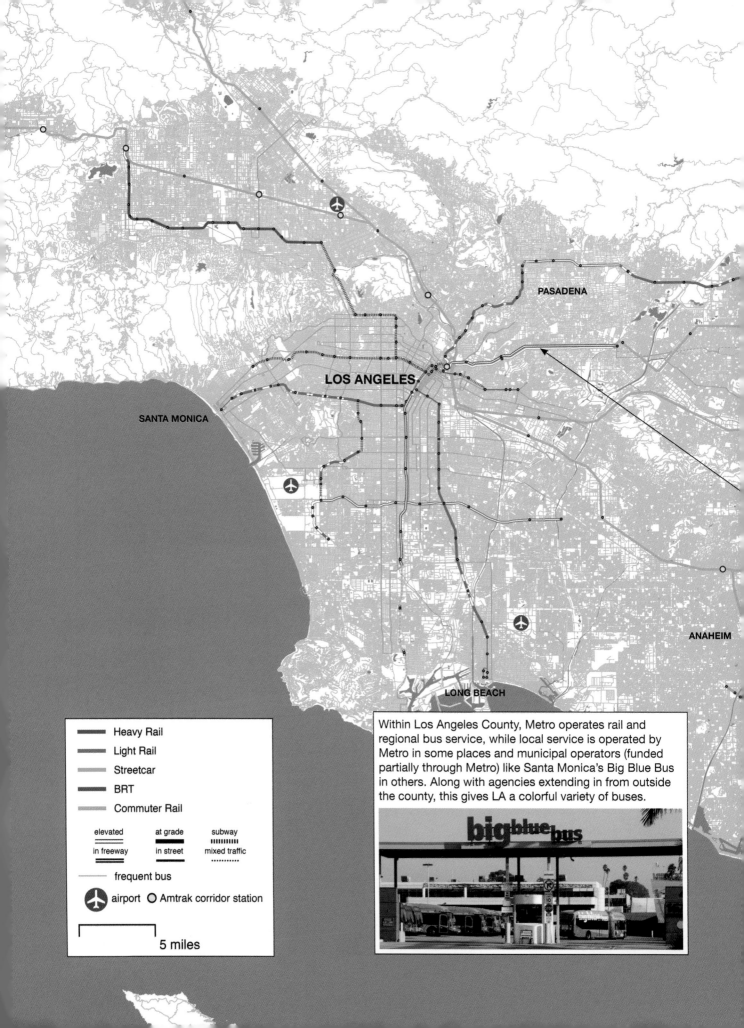

Legend

▬▬▬	Heavy Rail
▬▬▬	Light Rail
▬▬▬	Streetcar
▬▬▬	BRT
▬▬▬	Commuter Rail

elevated	at grade	subway
in freeway	in street	mixed traffic

frequent bus

✈ airport   ○ Amtrak corridor station

5 miles

SANTA MONICA

LOS ANGELES

PASADENA

ANAHEIM

LONG BEACH

Within Los Angeles County, Metro operates rail and regional bus service, while local service is operated by Metro in some places and municipal operators (funded partially through Metro) like Santa Monica's Big Blue Bus in others. Along with agencies extending in from outside the county, this gives LA a colorful variety of buses.

big blue bus

San Bernardino's Arrow commuter-rail line will share stations with Metrolink, but it will be operated using DMUs, with transfers in San Bernardino, where it will also connect to SBX BRT and local buses. Some Metrolink express service may use the same tracks.

LA's El Monte busway (now a HOT lane) opened alongside I-10 in 1973, before anyone knew to call the buses that run on it BRT. It carries around 16,000 bus passengers a day on the Metro J Line, the Foothill Transit Silver Streak, and multiple express routes. The Metrolink San Bernardino Line runs alongside the busway (here at the LA County USC Medical Center busway station); it carries half as many passengers even though it is five times as long. Metrolink trains run every hour or less off-peak; the buses run every 15 min or better. The end of the busway is at El Monte Station, a two-level, 29-bay bus transit center (said to be the largest in the US west of Chicago) that serves 22,000 passengers a day as the terminus of the J Line and a major hub for Foothill Transit.

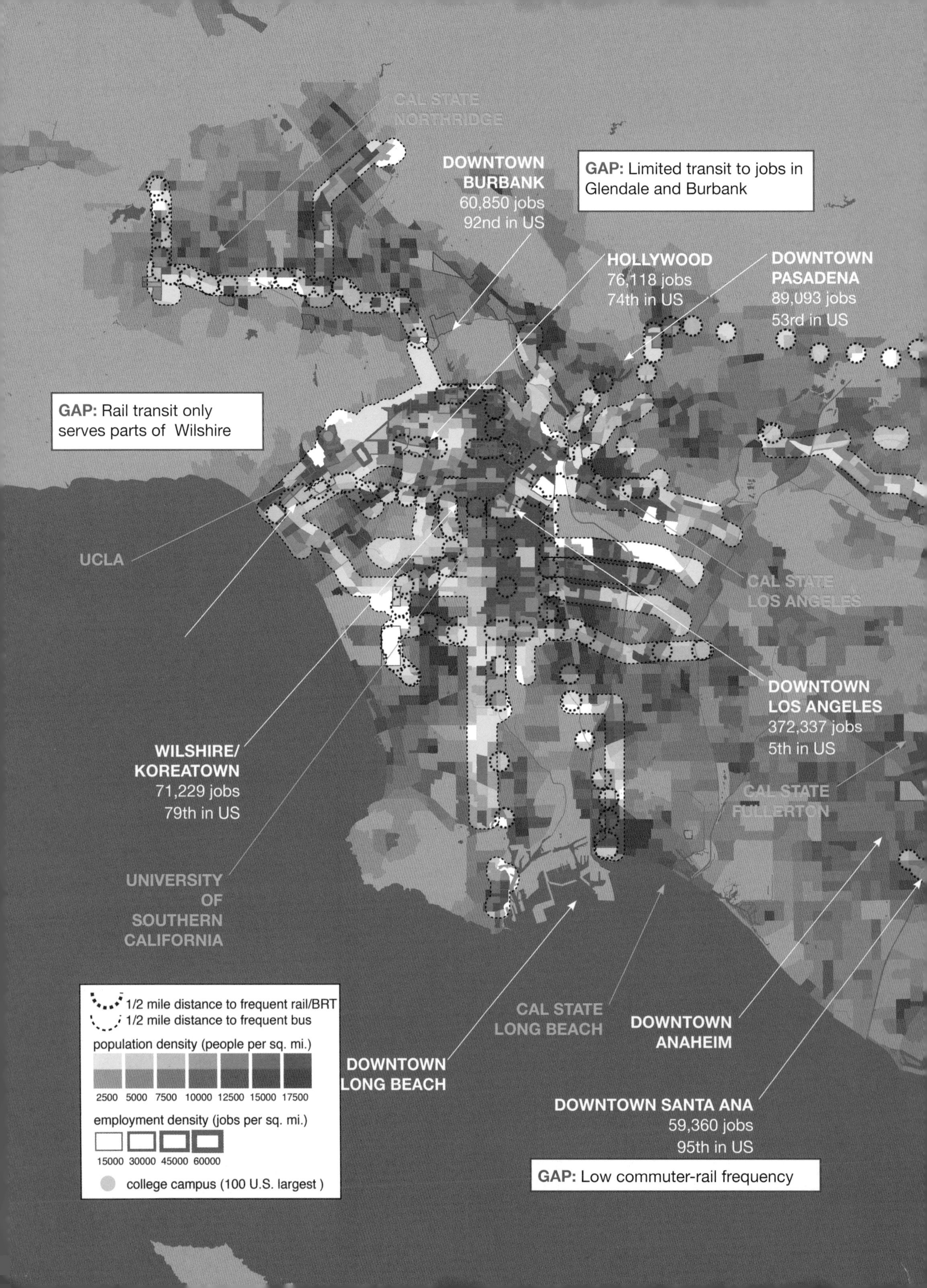

DOWNTOWN BURBANK
60,850 jobs
92nd in US

GAP: Limited transit to jobs in Glendale and Burbank

HOLLYWOOD
76,118 jobs
74th in US

DOWNTOWN PASADENA
89,093 jobs
53rd in US

CAL STATE NORTHRIDGE

GAP: Rail transit only serves parts of Wilshire

UCLA

CAL STATE LOS ANGELES

DOWNTOWN LOS ANGELES
372,337 jobs
5th in US

WILSHIRE/ KOREATOWN
71,229 jobs
79th in US

CAL STATE FULLERTON

UNIVERSITY OF SOUTHERN CALIFORNIA

CAL STATE LONG BEACH

DOWNTOWN ANAHEIM

DOWNTOWN LONG BEACH

DOWNTOWN SANTA ANA
59,360 jobs
95th in US

GAP: Low commuter-rail frequency

1/2 mile distance to frequent rail/BRT
1/2 mile distance to frequent bus

population density (people per sq. mi.)

2500 5000 7500 10000 12500 15000 17500

employment density (jobs per sq. mi.)

15000 30000 45000 60000

college campus (100 U.S. largest)

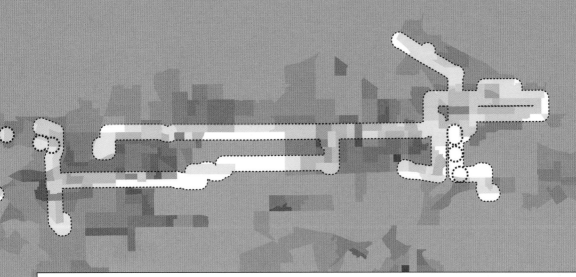

Los Angeles has long-standing dense concentrations of low-income residents south and southeast of Downtown; these areas account for much of the ridership on the LA Metro bus and light-rail network. But Southern California's poverty also sprawls outward, with dense pockets far away from the central city, in places that transit doesn't serve well.

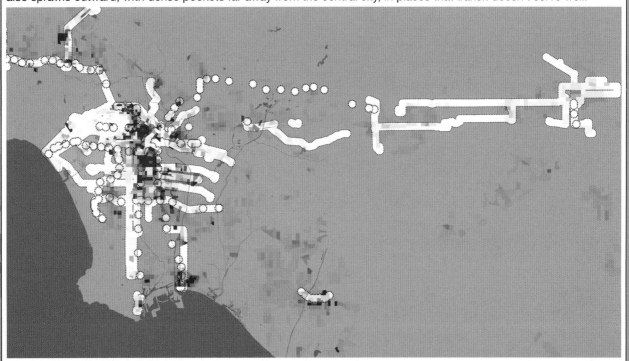

GAP: Frequent-transit service in Orange County

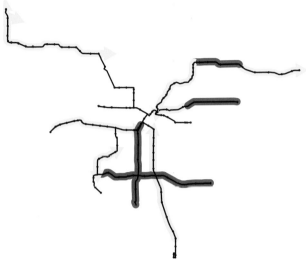

The majority of LA's rail-transit system, and all of its busways, are built in freeways (red above) or abandoned rail lines (yellow). These available rights-of-way simplified construction, lowered costs, and reduced political objections, but they also came at a cost.

On LA's first two light-rail lines, many stations ended up in industrial or low-density suburban surroundings, a long walk away from any destinations. At a station like Hawthorne on the C Line (left top), the freeway and its ramps occupy much of the land around the station that would otherwise be within walking distance. Unfortunately, transit engineers have made the problem worse. At Rosa Parks station, for example, the transit lines (left, 2nd from top) often look industrial and dangerous, and bus ramps around that station (left, 3rd from top) leave pedestrians to fend for themselves in an over-scaled sea of concrete.

Newer lines integrate into the city much better. The East Side Gold Line, now the L Line (left, 4th from top) uses street running and tunnels to get into the heart of the neighborhood where no freeway or railroad existed, and the new K Line, now under construction, combines a section of rail line with subway under Crenshaw and street running to create a crosstown connection. While the L Line to Pasadena and the E Line (formerly Expo Line) to Santa Monica also follow old rail lines, those lines extend right where people want to go, like Mission Street in South Pasadena (left, bottom) and downtown Santa Monica (opposite, bottom). In some ways this is historical good fortune; the E Line carried electric rail transit from 1911 to 1953, and neighborhoods developed around it. But it also reflects good decisions about which corridors to use, and a willingness to move forward despite political opposition. On newer projects, Metro has also paid more attention to urban design, resulting in stations that blend into the city better.

1980: Proposition A sales tax passes to fund first rail projects
1973: El Monte Busway
1990: Blue Line
1993–2000: Red/Purple Line
1995: Green Line

1990: Proposition C sales tax passes
1996: Harbor Transitway
2003: Gold Line to Pasadena
2005: Orange Line
2009: Gold Line to East LA

2008: Measure R sales tax passes
2012–2016: Expo Line
2012: Orange Line to Chatsworth
2016: Gold Line to APU
2019: Creshaw Line
2021: Regional Connector
2023–2024: Purple Line extension

2016: Measure M sales tax passes with $120 billion in transit projects

The Orange Line, now known as the G Line, (above right), the highest ridership BRT line in the country, wasn't intended to be BRT. It follows an old rail corridor through the San Fernando Valley, connecting to the Red Line North Hollywood station westward. Logically, it should be an extension of the heavy-rail Red Line, but local residents opposed elevated rail and even persuaded the state legislature to pass legislation that prohibited any rail in the corridor except a deep subway. Metro did not have the funding to build a subway, so the only alternative left was a busway.

BRT is often described as "light rail, but with buses" and the G Line fits that well. The rail line, which often paralleled local streets, and even ran in a street median for a stretch, was converted to a two-lane, bus-only roadway, with signal priority at intersections and light-rail-like stations every mile or so. Buses run every four to eight minutes from 5:00 a.m. to 7:00 p.m., with less frequent evening and overnight service. The G Line was conceptually designed like light rail. Every bus stops at every station, no routes other than the G Line use the busway, and, except for a short loop through Warner Center, Orange Line buses don't leave the busway.

G Line ridership has been strong since it opened in 2005. Planners projected 5,000–7,500 trips a day; instead the line got 22,700 daily in its first year, and now carries more than 28,000. That exceeds most modern light-rail systems, and the line is straining under the load. The 60-foot buses, the longest allowed under state law, are packed at peak hours, and more-frequent service would disrupt cross traffic at intersections that already handle a bus (in one direction or the other) every two minutes. Metro is now studying a series of improvements, including grade separations at the busiest cross streets and railroad-style crossing gates to enable the buses to run faster. Long-term plans call for conversion to light rail, which is now possible since the legislation prohibiting rail in the corridor was repealed in 2014. The G Line is a BRT success story, but it likely should have been light rail from the beginning.

BRT (J Line)

LARGE SYSTEM

Opened: 2009

Last Expanded: N/A

Length: 38 miles (22 guideway miles)

Stations: 12 (guideway only)

Frequency: 5–10 min peak, 10–15 min midday, 20–40min evening, 15–40 min weekend

Avg weekday ridership: 17,588

Ridership per mile: 463

BRT (sbX)

LOW PERFORMER

Opened: 2014

Last Expanded: N/A

Length: 15.7 miles (5.4 guideway miles)

Stations: 6 (guideway only)

Frequency: 10 min peak, 15 min midday/evening (Mon–Fri only)

Avg weekday ridership: 2,908

Ridership per mile: 185

Streetcar (OC Streetcar)

Open: 2022

Last Expanded: N/A

Length: 0 (4.15 miles in construction)

Stations: 0 (10 in construction)

Frequency: 10 -15 min

Avg weekday ridership: N/A

Ridership per mile: N/A

The Los Angeles subway (below), built starting in 1986, is one of the last of its kind. It resembles the systems in San Francisco, Washington, Atlanta, Baltimore, and Miami, all of which date from the 1960s and 1970s. Its $4.5-billion cost for 17.4 miles, hints at why heavy rail has fallen out of favor. The expense is driven by stations designed for six-car trains and an alignment that is entirely in subway (except for the maintenance facility). But with the intense ridership in LA is getting on its small heavy rail system—142,300 boardings on an average weekday—the cost is justified. At 8,000 boardings a mile, the D and B lines (formerly the Red and Purple Lines) are among the most intensely used rail lines in the country, ranking behind only large Northeastern cities like New York, Philadelphia, and Boston. These lines are the spine of the transit system, and with the planned "subway to the sea" along LA's densest employment corridor, they will become even more important.

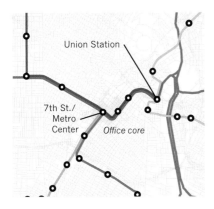

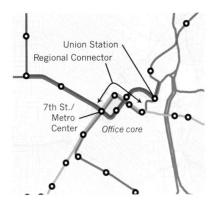

From the east side of LA, the L Line (opposite, top right) heads straight toward the skyscrapers of downtown (below), and then turns away half a mile short. Instead, it goes to Union Station, the downtown transit hub for Los Angeles. The 1939 station now offers nearly 150 commuter trains a day on five lines including light-rail trains to Pasadena and East Los Angeles, bus rapid transit to the San Gabriel Valley, and express buses to Los Angeles International Airport (LAX). But Union Station was built where the rail lines were, not where people are trying to go. It is half a mile from City Hall and one and a half miles from Pershing Square in the heart of downtown. Thus nearly all commuter-rail and light-rail passengers are forced to transfer. Most take the B/D subway to get to the employment core. Light rail serves downtown better from the south, where the A Line and E Line pass the convention center and entertainment district and terminate underground at Metro Center. But even from here, much of downtown is more than a 15-minute walk, and anyone headed from the A or E Lines to the L Line has to transfer to the B/D Line at Metro Center, then transfer again at Union Station.

Remarkably, this awkward arrangement (left, top) in LA's biggest employment center is not the result of historical accretion. All of these lines were planned together and built over only 25 years by the same agency.

In 2022, nearly 20 years after the L Line opened, a new subway will bring its trains into downtown for the first time. The "Regional Connector" (left, center) will turn three light-rail lines—the A Line and E Line dead-ending into downtown from the south, and the L Line skirting it on the north—into two, both running through the center of downtown. This will give downtown-bound passengers a one-seat ride (without the B/D transfer), allow passengers bound elsewhere to ride right through downtown or make a single transfer, and give Metrolink passengers at Union Station a connection to parts of downtown not served by the subway.

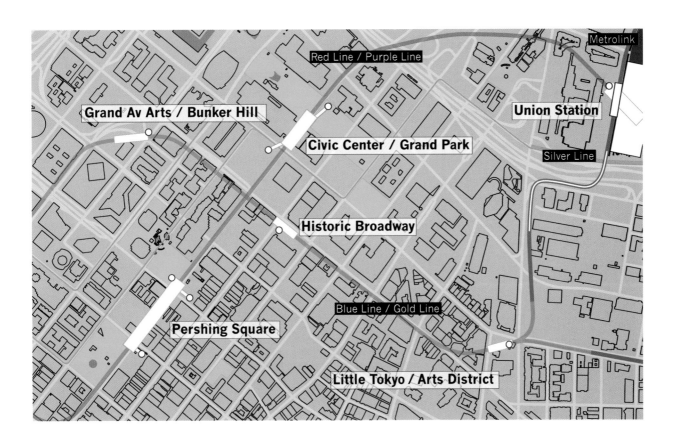

Los Angeles is a multi-centric region. It contains 10 of America's 100 largest employment hubs. But the transit system has been slow to address that. The initial rail-transit system focused on downtown (seen in the distance above). In 2000 (below), with two heavy-rail, two light-rail, five light-rail, and one bus-rapid-transit lines in operation, the large concentration of jobs on the west side in Century City, Westwood, and Santa Monica still wasn't served.

Newer rail and BRT lines have added major employment hubs like Santa Monica and Pasadena to the network, and when lines under construction open (below), the subway will have made it to the edge of Century City. But the commuter-rail system will still be focused on downtown, and the Glendale area will be served only by infrequent trains. It will take the next round of transit expansion to serve more centers and create crosstown connections.

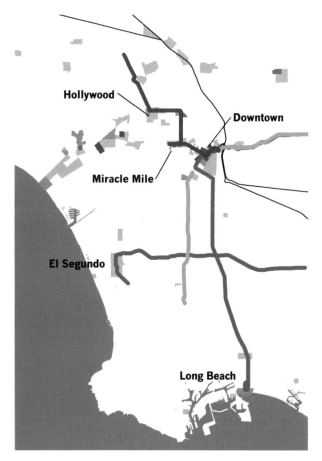

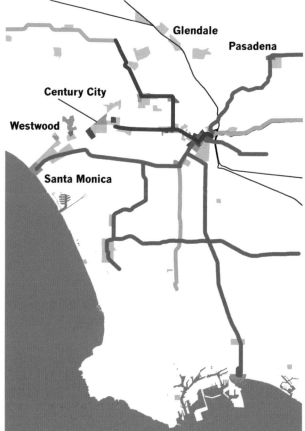

Commuter Rail (Metrolink)

LARGE SYSTEM

Opened: 1992
Last Expanded: 2016
Length: 407 miles
Stations: 62
Frequency: 20–40 min rush hour; limited off-peak
Avg weekday ridership: 38,500
Ridership per mile: 95

Commuter Rail (Arrow)

SMALL SYSTEM

Open: 2022
Last Expanded: N/A
Length: 0 (9 miles in construction)
Stations: 0 (5 in construction)
Frequency: 20–40 min rush hour; limited off-peak
Avg weekday ridership: N/A
Ridership per mile: N/A

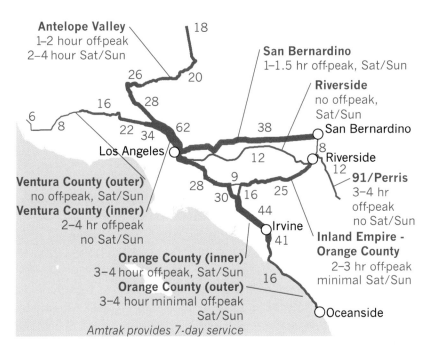

Antelope Valley
1–2 hour off-peak
2–4 hour Sat/Sun

San Bernardino
1–1.5 hr off-peak, Sat/Sun

Riverside
no off-peak, Sat/Sun

18 26 20 16 28 6 8 22 34 62 38 San Bernardino 8 Los Angeles 12 Riverside 12

91/Perris
3–4 hr off-peak
no Sat/Sun

Ventura County (outer)
no off-peak, Sat/Sun
Ventura County (inner)
2–4 hr off-peak
no Sat/Sun

28 9 30 16 25 44 Irvine 41

Inland Empire - Orange County
2–3 hr off-peak
minimal Sat/Sun

Orange County (inner)
3–4 hour off-peak, Sat/Sun
Orange County (outer)
3–4 hour minimal off-peak
Sat/Sun
Amtrak provides 7-day service

16 Oceanside

Los Angeles Union Station is the hub of Metrolink, the largest commuter-rail startup in US history, growing to 512 miles in its first decade of service. That is similar to Chicago and more than Philadelphia or Boston. Trains run 71 miles from Union Station (right) to Ventura, 77 miles to Lancaster, 57 miles to San Bernardino (above), and 87 miles to Oceanside, where they meet San Diego's Coaster service.

But while Metrolink is expansive, it is not intensive. All lines (left) have service every 20–40 minutes during rush hour, but the off-peak service is no better than hourly on any line, and some lines have no off-peak or weekend service at all, though all have transit connections and destinations like universities, beaches, and entertainment districts. Forty-four thousand passengers a day ride Metrolink, but many more could use it if there were more service.

3. CHICAGO

Chicago–Naperville, IL-IN-WI

population 9,825,325 (3rd)   **served by frequent transit** 29%   **daily trips per 1000** 154

CTA
independent agency
Heavy Rail
BRT
Frequent Bus

The way to really fly.

Metra
independent agency
Commuter Rail

South Shore Line
independent agency
Commuter Rail

Pace
independent agency
Frequent Bus

Chicago has always been a transit city. In the late 1800s and early 1900s, it built more rapid transit, more quickly, than any city other than New York. It had commuter trains operated by a dozen railroads. Unlike most other cities, Chicago kept investing in that network after World War II, opening new rapid-transit lines in every decade from the 1950s through the 1990s. The commuter railroads kept investing too, pioneering new technologies like bi-level cars and push-pull trains. In recent decades the CTA has extensively rehabilitated and reconstructed its rail network, largely avoiding the infrastructure issues that have plagued New York and Washington, DC. The city's urban fabric reflects this extensive and useful network. Downtown Chicago, fed by heavy-rail and commuter-rail lines, is the second-biggest employment hub in the country. Walkable, mixed-use neighborhoods stretch more than five miles from downtown in every direction.

The core of the Chicago network is the 'L' (the local nickname for elevated trains, now adopted as an official brand), which accounts for one third of all the transit trips in the metropolitan area. It was built, starting in the 1890s, by four private companies. They were among the earliest elevated rail-transit lines in the country—only New York preceded them—and the tight clearances, tight curves, and short stations they built have shaped the system ever since. At under 50 feet, Chicago's railcars are the shortest of any North American heavy-rail system, and at six or eight cars, the trains are among the shortest. The elevated lines were connected in 1897 by the most famous part of Chicago's transit infrastructure, the elevated "Loop" around downtown Chicago, where all the lines met. The government got involved with the network in the 1930s with the construction of a federally funded downtown subway. When the state created the Chicago Transit Authority in 1947, it acquired the network. The CTA closed some low-ridership branches, but also began to upgrade and expand the system, adding a second downtown subway, replacing some elevated sections, and building lines to both airports. The 'L' covers much of the city; 48 percent of Chicago's residents are within a half mile of a station. Those who aren't are connected to it by an extensive bus network. Chicago's highly regular street grid is reflected in the network design. Most bus routes are crosstowns, connecting to the radial 'L.' The 9 and 9X Ashland, for example, connects to four CTA rail stations along its 17-mile north–south route and makes 27,000 trips a day. But, while the 'L' has been steadily gaining ridership since the 1990s, the bus system has not. This is likely due to speed and reliability; the Ashland bus averages only 8.7 miles per hour. An ambitious CTA plan announced in 2012 would upgrade several key routes, including Ashland, to BRT. However, public opposition has stalled the plan, and Chicago's only BRT to date is Loop Link, a short but useful set of bus lanes and stations in downtown used by seven routes. Chicago also has one of the country's most extensive commuter-rail systems, second only to New York's in ridership and length. The network—operated today by Metra in Illinois and Wisconsin and South Shore Line in Indiana—was inherited from seven private railroads. Six had their corporate headquarters in Chicago, and the volume and quality of the service reflected that. Today, eight of 11 routes have seven-day-a-week service, and between 5:00 and 5:59 p.m. 72 trains leave downtown's four commuter-rail terminals. Unlike the networks in New York and Philadelphia, these lines are largely shared with intense freight-rail operations. Despite this complex choreography, on-time performance is 96 percent. All along these lines, suburbs grew up around train stations, and commuter rail is part of the fabric of life in Chicago's suburbs. ∎

+ **'L' network serving walkable neighborhoods**
+ **Frequent bus grid**
+ **Busy commuter rail**
− **No integration between local transit and commuter rail**

Indiana's South Shore Line was opened as an interurban electric railway in 1908 and upgraded in pieces over time. In 2020 trains still run down the middle of a residential street, but reconstruction will start soon to separate the trains and the automobiles.

EVANSTON

SCHAUMBURG

CHICAGO

NAPERVILLE

GARY

JOLIET

Legend

— Heavy Rail
— BRT
— Electric Commuter Rail
— Commuter Rail

| elevated | at grade | subway |
| in freeway | in street | mixed traffic |

— frequent bus

✈ airport   ○ Amtrak corridor station

5 miles

Chicago's original lines like the Blue Line at Western, opened in 1895, (right) were largely elevated. Unlike in other cities, though, they are not above streets but above alleys, allowing them to blend into the city in a way that elevated lines in Philadelphia and New York do not.

1963

1970

In the 1950s, Chicago pioneered the construction of rapid transit in freeway medians. Three of Chicago's major freeways—the Dan Ryan, Kennedy, and Eisenhower (right) incorporated transit lines into their design. These lines replaced some existing elevated lines but also extended the system outward.

1980

1990

Chicago's newest line, the Orange to Midway Airport (right), opened in 1993, serving neighborhoods that had never had 'L' service. It largely follows freight-rail lines.

2000

One third of the metro area's low-income residents live in the city, which is served by extensive bus and rail.

DOWNTOWN CHICAGO
609,902 jobs
2nd in US

UNIVERSITY OF ILLINOIS
116,261 jobs
47th in US

GAP: Southwest Chicago served only by local bus and infrequent commuter rail despite high density

••••• 1/2 mile distance to frequent rail/BRT
- - - 1/2 mile distance to frequent bus

population density (people per sq. mi.)

2500 5000 7500 10000 12500 15000 17500

employment density (jobs per sq. mi.)

15000 30000 45000 60000

● college campus (100 U.S. largest)

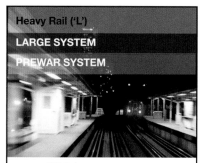

Heavy Rail ('L')

LARGE SYSTEM

PREWAR SYSTEM

Opened: 1892

Last Expanded: 2006

Length: 102.8 miles

Stations: 145

Frequency: up to 3 min peak; 8–12 min midday; 6–30 min weekends, 20 min overnight (24-hr service on some lines)

Avg weekday ridership: 695,300

Ridership per mile: 6,794

BRT (Loop Link)

SMALL SYSTEM

Opened: 2015

Last Expanded: N/A

Length: Open BRT (0.8 guideway miles)

Stations: 4 (guideway only)

Frequency: 1 min peak, 4 min off-peak

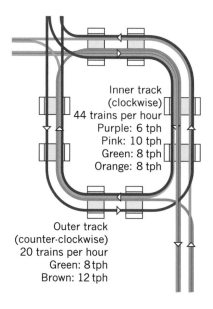

Inner track
(clockwise)
44 trains per hour
Purple: 6 tph
Pink: 10 tph
Green: 8 tph
Orange: 8 tph

Outer track
(counter-clockwise)
20 trains per hour
Green: 8 tph
Brown: 12 tph

Metra and South Shore commuter trains run into five different downtown stations. Inconveniently, none are directly connected to the 'L.' The Ogilvie (above) and LaSalle stations are less than a block from the 'L,' but Union Station is three blocks away. One solution is the Loop Link BRT (below) running east–west through the Loop. The stations are branded, but there is no specific Loop Link service. Instead, the bus lanes and stations are the downtown segment of seven routes that then extend in multiple directions. This improves reliability on each of these routes, and also creates a downtown circulator.

Downtown Chicago is defined by the elevated Loop (left). It is a one-of-a-kind transit facility. The Green Line is the only line that actually runs through the Loop to create a crosstown route. The other lines (Brown, Purple, Pink, and Orange) enter the Loop, circle, and come back the way they came. This unusual arrangement means that each of these four lines serves all eight of the downtown stations, maximizing the number of commuters who can get close to their job without changing trains. The tradeoff is a complex operation; more than a train a minute passes through the complex intersection at the northwest corner, and any disruption rapidly impacts all of the lines.

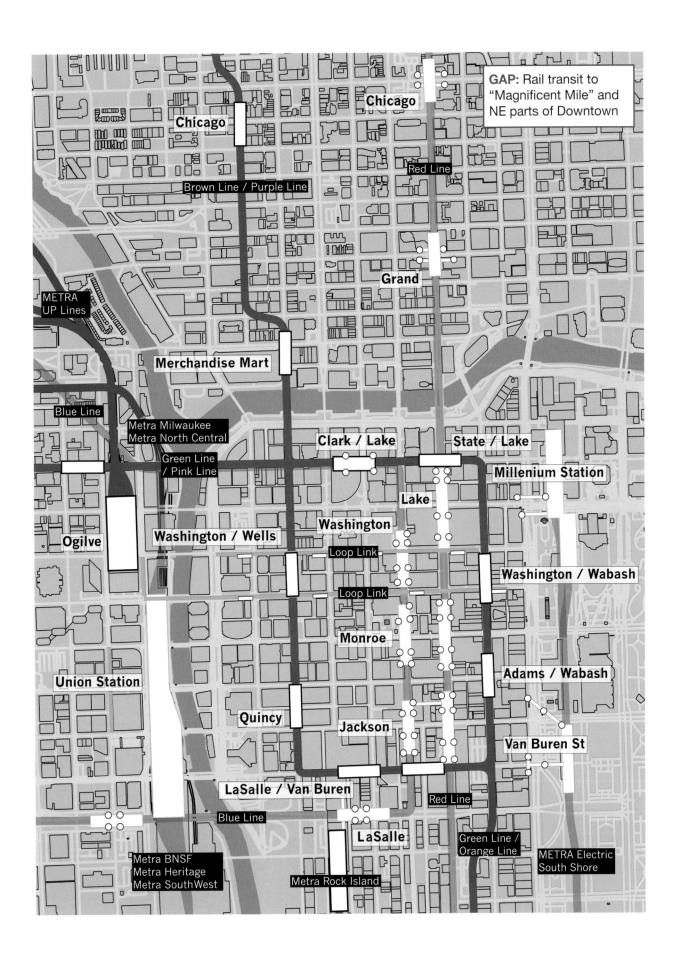

GAP: Rail transit to "Magnificent Mile" and NE parts of Downtown

Chicago

Chicago

Red Line

Brown Line / Purple Line

Grand

METRA
UP Lines

Merchandise Mart

Blue Line

Metra Milwaukee
Metra North Central

Clark / Lake

State / Lake

Green Line
/ Pink Line

Millenium Station

Lake

Washington

Ogilve

Washington / Wells

Loop Link

Washington / Wabash

Loop Link

Union Station

Monroe

Adams / Wabash

Quincy

Jackson

Van Buren St

LaSalle / Van Buren

Red Line

Blue Line

LaSalle

Green Line /
Orange Line

METRA Electric
South Shore

Metra BNSF
Metra Heritage
Metra SouthWest

Metra Rock Island

Diesel/Electric commuter rail (Metra)

HIGH PERFORMER
LARGE SYSTEM
PREWAR SYSTEM

Opened: 1850
Last Expanded: 2006
Length: 487.7 miles
Stations: 241
Frequency: 10–50 min peak, 1–4 hours off-peak; weekend service on most lines
Avg weekday ridership: 274,000
Ridership per mile: 562

Electric commuter rail (South Shore Line)

PREWAR SYSTEM

Opened: 1909
Last Expanded: 1992
Length: 90.9 miles
Stations: 20
Frequency: 7–29 trains each way a day weekday; 7–9 trains each way a day weekend
Avg weekday ridership: 10,900
Ridership per mile: 120

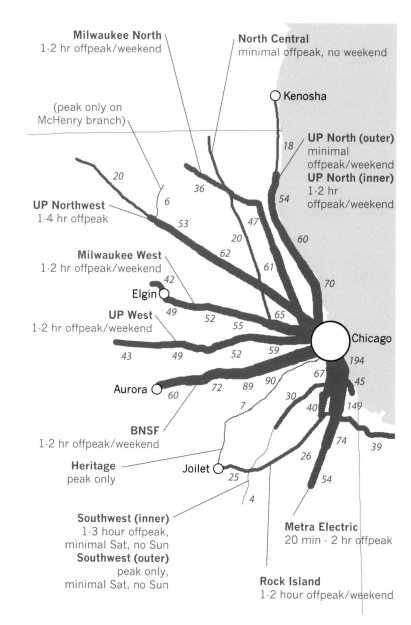

Milwaukee North
1·2 hr offpeak/weekend

North Central
minimal offpeak, no weekend

Kenosha

(peak only on McHenry branch)

UP North (outer)
minimal offpeak/weekend
UP North (inner)
1·2 hr offpeak/weekend

UP Northwest
1·4 hr offpeak

18

20

36

6

53

54

47

20

60

62

61

70

Milwaukee West
1·2 hr offpeak/weekend

42

Elgin

UP West
1·2 hr offpeak/weekend

49

52

55

65

Chicago

43

49

52

59

194

Aurora

60

72

89

90

67

45

7

30

40

149

BNSF
1·2 hr offpeak/weekend

74

39

Heritage
peak only

Joilet

26

25

54

4

Southwest (inner)
1·3 hour offpeak,
minimal Sat, no Sun
Southwest (outer)
peak only,
minimal Sat, no Sun

Metra Electric
20 min · 2 hr offpeak

Rock Island
1·2 hour offpeak/weekend

As in the Northeast, commuter trains have been part of the fabric of Chicago suburbia for over a century. Towns like Oak Park (right) grew up around the stations, so riders getting off the train find themselves in walkable main streets. Most Metra lines (above) run midday service—roughly a train an hour—and weekend service, so they are useful for many trips, not just 9-to-5 commutes. Twenty-five percent of weekend trips are not peak-direction rush-hour trips. While weekend ridership is much lower than weekdays, Metra still carries 75,000 trips on an average Saturday, and 48,000 on an average Sunday.

The image above shows the everyday railroad in Chicago: a Metra UP-West Line train passes two Union Pacific trains waiting for clearance to move. The Green Line 'L' train on the right has its own track, but Metra doesn't. All three tracks are used by passenger and freight trains. A UP dispatcher in Omaha, Nebraska, is guiding the passenger train through the freight traffic. No freight railroad would ever accept the complexity and liability of such an operation were it proposed today, but it works in Chicago. That is due to heavy-duty infrastructure, long-established history (freight and passenger trains have been sharing this particular line since 1848), institutional ties (this Metra train is actually operated by Union Pacific employees under contract), and a culture of cooperation.

The Metra Electric lines (center right) are unique in Chicago. In the 1920s, the Illinois Central electrified its commuter rail and completely separated it from freight rail. The surrounding neighborhoods are much denser than other Chicago commuter-rail corridors. The University of Chicago, Soldier Field, and McCormick Place convention center are along the way, and there is no 'L' line nearby. Thus, in terms of infrastructure and travel demand, Metra Electric resembles heavy rail or light rail more than it does commuter rail; a branch even runs right through the middle of the street in South Chicago (bottom right). But because it is operated by Metra, it is operated like commuter rail, with rush-hour–focused service, conductors on board each train, and higher fares than local transit. Were it operated like an 'L,' with more frequency and lower fares, it would undoubtedly serve many more people.

4. WASHINGTON

Washington–Baltimore–Arlington, DC-MD-VA-WV-PA

population 9,814,928 (4th)   **served by frequent transit** 17%   **daily trips per 1000** 140

No other city has undergone as complete a transit transformation since World War II as Washington, DC. As of 1960, the city had buses and a few infrequent commuter-rail routes to the suburbs. Since then, the growth of the federal government has transformed DC to one of the largest   and richest   metropolitan areas in the country. Transit has been an integral part of the city's transformation. Today, DC has the second busiest rail system in the country. Transit has completely transformed not just how people move around in the city (40 percent of DC residents use public transit, a higher share than any other city except New York), but the shape of the city itself.

First opened for the Bicentennial in 1976, Metrorail comes from the same era as BART in San Francisco. Like BART, Metrorail connects downtown employment to suburban park-and-ride lots. There are a total of 61,721 spaces at 44 suburban stations. But unlike BART, Metrorail was designed to serve the city as well. Rather than one line through the city, Metrorail has half a dozen. Some of DC's densest residential areas have subway stations in their heart. And, more than any other modern rail system in the country, Metrorail serves dense, walkable places outside the city center. A series of activity centers have grown up around Metrorail stations. This is the result of deliberate planning. In Arlington, Virginia, local planners pushed for Metrorail to be built in a subway alignment under Clarendon Boulevard rather than in the median of Interstate 66 half a mile away, and then rezoned the single-story commercial strip along the boulevard to high-rise mixed use. That corridor now has 60,000 jobs. Metrorail's most recent expansion brought rail transit into the heart of Tysons Corner, the 36th-largest employment center in the United States, 15 miles from central DC. Those employment centers are being further served by new transit lines that link to Metrorail. Along the Potomac River in Alexandria, the Metroway BRT line links new development to Metrorail and to Crystal City. In Maryland, the 16-mile Purple Line will connect two major employment centers, the University of Maryland, and four Metrorail lines. The commuter-rail system, four lines in Maryland and two in Virginia, also services these suburban centers, and has multiple suburban Metrorail transfer stops. DC has spent four decades building a world-class transit system, and it has transformed the region.

+ **Modern heavy-rail network has transformed DC around it**
+ **Great transit service to walkable suburban activity centers**
- **Significant maintenance and capacity issues**
- **Inadequate and poorly located rail network in Baltimore**

WMATA
independent agency
Heavy Rail
BRT
Frequent Bus

Maryland DOT
state department
Heavy Rail
Light Rail
Commuter Rail
Frequent Bus

VRE
independent agency
Commuter Rail

Ride On
municipal
Frequent Bus

The Bus
municipal
Frequent Bus

DASH
municipal
Frequent Bus

d.

DC DOT
state department
frequent bus
streetcar

Fairfax Connector
municipal
frequent bus

**Charm City
Circulator**
municipal
Frequent Bus

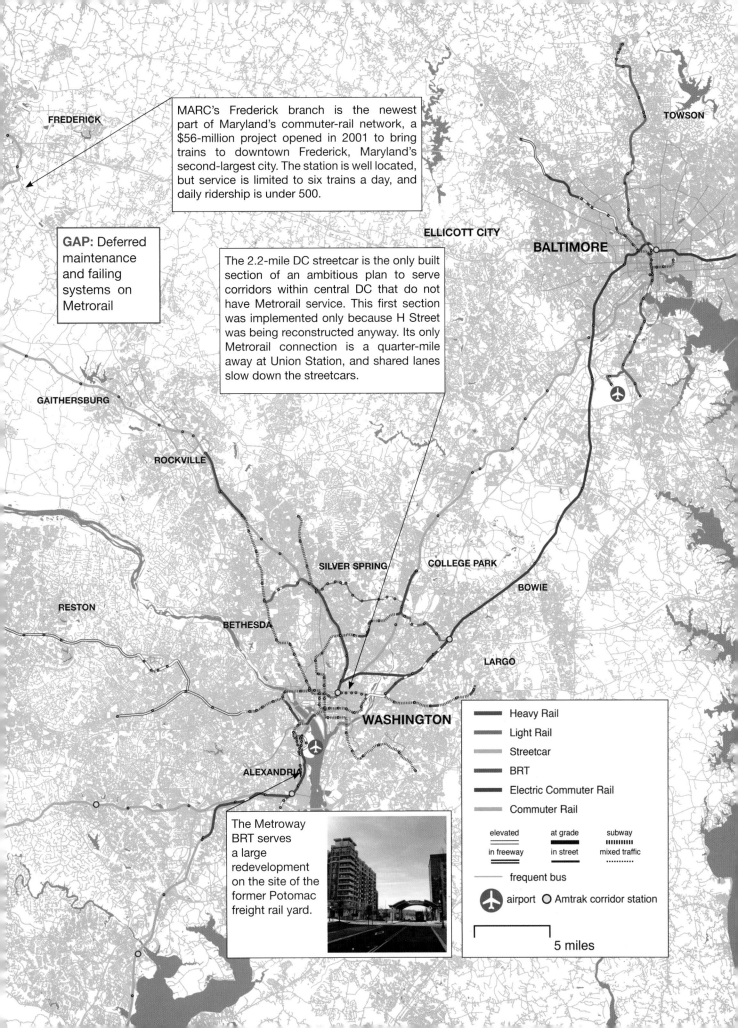

FREDERICK

MARC's Frederick branch is the newest part of Maryland's commuter-rail network, a $56-million project opened in 2001 to bring trains to downtown Frederick, Maryland's second-largest city. The station is well located, but service is limited to six trains a day, and daily ridership is under 500.

ELLICOTT CITY

TOWSON

BALTIMORE

GAP: Deferred maintenance and failing systems on Metrorail

The 2.2-mile DC streetcar is the only built section of an ambitious plan to serve corridors within central DC that do not have Metrorail service. This first section was implemented only because H Street was being reconstructed anyway. Its only Metrorail connection is a quarter-mile away at Union Station, and shared lanes slow down the streetcars.

GAITHERSBURG

ROCKVILLE

SILVER SPRING

COLLEGE PARK

BOWIE

RESTON

BETHESDA

LARGO

WASHINGTON

ALEXANDRIA

The Metroway BRT serves a large redevelopment on the site of the former Potomac freight rail yard.

Heavy Rail	
Light Rail	
Streetcar	
BRT	
Electric Commuter Rail	
Commuter Rail	

elevated	at grade	subway
in freeway	in street	mixed traffic

frequent bus

✈ airport   ○ Amtrak corridor station

5 miles

Heavy Rail (Metrorail)

LARGE SYSTEM

Opened: 1976

Last Expanded: ongoing

Length: 118 miles (11.5 in construction)

Stations: 91 (6 in construction)

Frequency: 4–8 min peak, 6–12 min midday, 6–20 min evening/weekends

Avg weekday ridership: 816,700

Ridership per mile: 6,921

BRT (Metroway)

SMALL SYSTEM

LOW PERFORMER

Opened: 2014

Last Expanded: N/A

Length: 6.8 miles (2.2 guideway miles)

Stations: 8.5 (guideway only)

Frequency: 6–12 min peak/midday, 15 min evenings, 20 min weekends

Avg weekday ridership: 2,431

Ridership per mile: 358

Light Rail (Purple Line)

UNDER CONSTRUCTION

SMALL SYSTEM

Open: TBD

Last Expanded: ongoing

Length: 0 miles (16.2 under construction)

Stations: 0 (21 under construction)

Frequency: 7.5 min (proposed)

Avg weekday ridership: N/A

Ridership per mile: N/A

Baltimore, 42 miles up Amtrak's Northeast Corridor, is DC's stepchild. A poor, economically declining city in a state that's increasingly focused on DC (notably, the hub of Maryland's commuter rail system is not Baltimore but DC's Union Station), it's seen sporadic and ineffectual transit investment. Planning in the 1970s resulted in a single line, following a freeway and serving no hubs other than downtown. It is among the lowest-performing heavy-rail systems nationally. A late 1980s push for light rail yielded a new north–south line following an old railroad right of way, which puts it in a fairly inaccessible valley through the densest parts of Baltimore, and in old industrial areas to the north and south. Poor location could not be fixed by further extensions and infrastructure improvements through the 1990s and 2000s, and that line, too, is a notably low performer. This isn't helped by exceptionally low frequencies. The airport branch only gets one train every 30 minutes at mid-day on a weekday. Unlike DC, three decades of rail investment have done little for Baltimore. ■

In Silver Spring, Maryland (above), the new light-rail Purple Line will meet heavy-rail Metrorail trains, MARC commuter trains, and RideOn and WMATA buses amid office buildings, retail, and high-rise residential. Tysons Corner, Virginia (right), grew up around highways and now has rail extended through it.

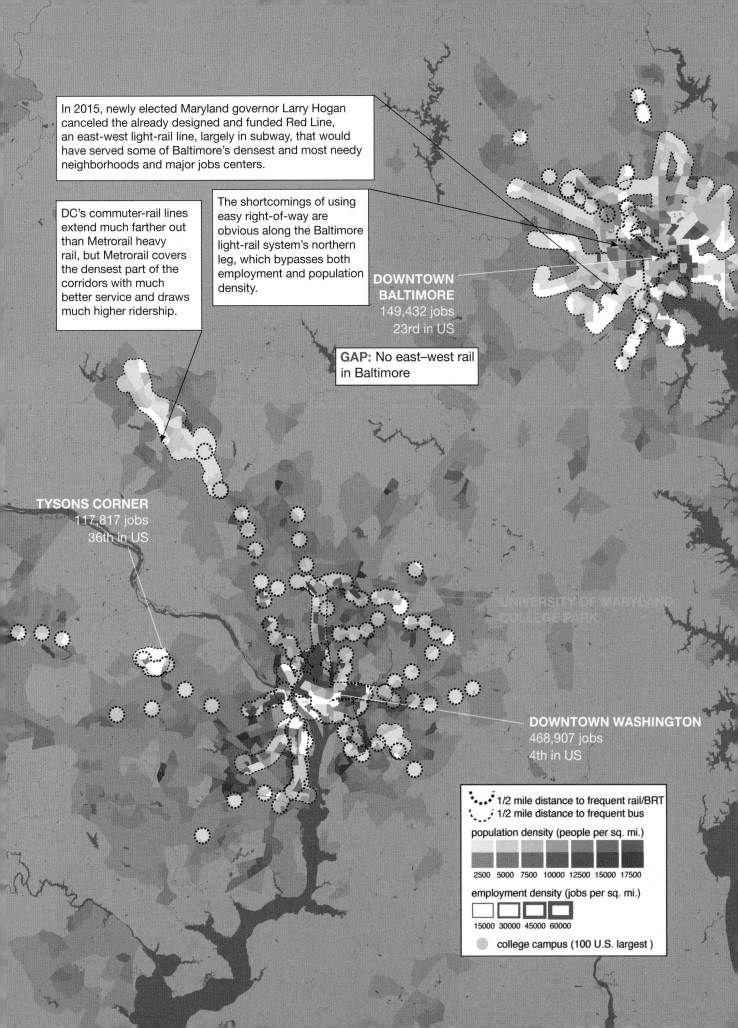

In 2015, newly elected Maryland governor Larry Hogan canceled the already designed and funded Red Line, an east-west light-rail line, largely in subway, that would have served some of Baltimore's densest and most needy neighborhoods and major jobs centers.

DC's commuter-rail lines extend much farther out than Metrorail heavy rail, but Metrorail covers the densest part of the corridors with much better service and draws much higher ridership.

The shortcomings of using easy right-of-way are obvious along the Baltimore light-rail system's northern leg, which bypasses both employment and population density.

DOWNTOWN BALTIMORE
149,432 jobs
23rd in US

GAP: No east–west rail in Baltimore

TYSONS CORNER
117,817 jobs
36th in US

UNIVERSITY OF MARYLAND COLLEGE PARK

DOWNTOWN WASHINGTON
468,907 jobs
4th in US

1/2 mile distance to frequent rail/BRT
1/2 mile distance to frequent bus

population density (people per sq. mi.)
2500 5000 7500 10000 12500 15000 17500

employment density (jobs per sq. mi.)
15000 30000 45000 60000

college campus (100 U.S. largest)

Streetcar (DC streetcar)

Opened: 2016
Last Expanded: N/A
Length: 2.5 miles
Stations: 8
Frequency: 10–15 min
Avg weekday ridership: 2,400
Ridership per mile: 960

No other postwar US rail-transit system serves its downtown (opposite) as well as DC's does. The three central Metrorail routes serve all of the concentrations of federal office buildings (Federal Triangle, Federal Center Southwest, and Capitol Hill) as well as the private office areas around K Street and DC's traditional downtown (bottom left). The great expenditures on multiple core lines, and the grand transfer stations like Metro Center (above), are a large part of what has made Metrorail so useful. Metrorail also links well to commuter rail, which tunnels under Capitol Hill (center left).

Outside the core, Metrorail also went to considerable effort to serve many destinations. While all lines follow railroad and freeway corridors (yellow and red in the map below) in places, they frequently deviate from those relatively easy alignments. Fully 40% of the system is in tunnels.

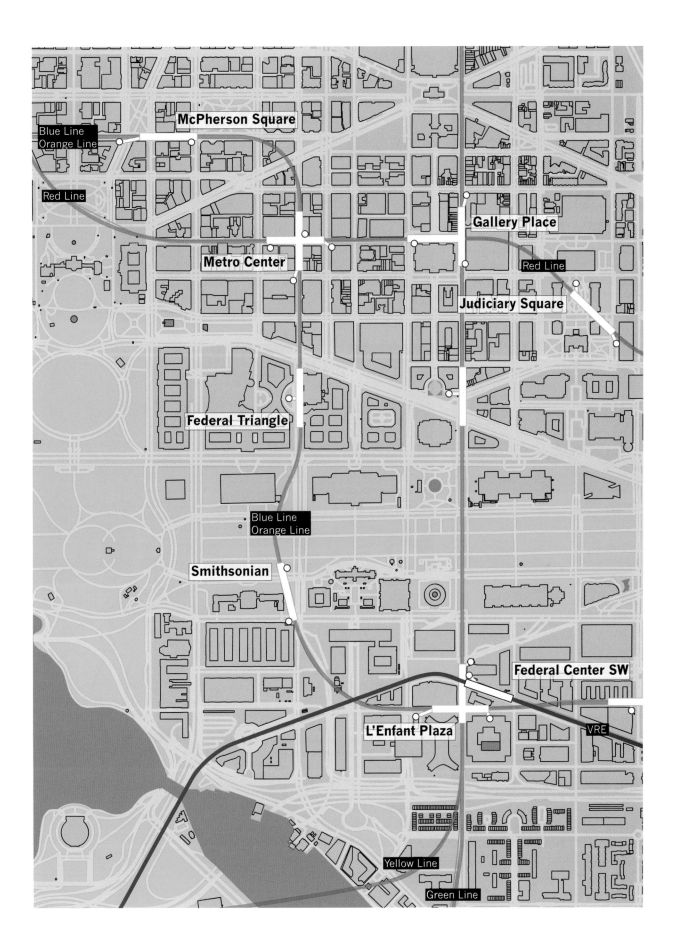

McPherson Square

Blue Line
Orange Line

Red Line

Gallery Place

Metro Center

Red Line

Judiciary Square

Federal Triangle

Blue Line
Orange Line

Smithsonian

Federal Center SW

L'Enfant Plaza

VRE

Yellow Line

Green Line

Heavy Rail (Metro SubwayLink)

LOW PERFORMER
SMALL SYSTEM

Opened: 1983
Last Expanded: 1995
Length: 15.5 miles
Stations: 14
Frequency: 8 min peak, 10 min midday/evening, 15 min weekend
Avg weekday ridership: 36,600
Ridership per mile: 2,361

Light Rail (Light RailLink)

LOW PERFORMER

Opened: 1992
Last Expanded: 1997
Length: 30 miles
Stations: 33
Frequency: 10–20 min peak, 15–30 min midday/evening/weekends
Avg weekday ridership: 25,300
Ridership per mile: 843

Unlike DC, Baltimore built its rail-transit systems around available right of way (shown in below yellow for railroad lines and red for freeway). Both lines go into the center of downtown, where the light rail makes a slow trip down Howard Street (top), while the subway tunnels underneath. Past there, the Metro follows a rail line and then a freeway (left), while the light rail follows a rail line up a valley (above), offering riders fine views of lakes and forests, but few actual destinations.

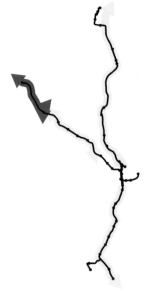

Diesel/Electric Commuter Rail (MARC)

PREWAR SYSTEM

Opened: 1835
Last Expanded: 2001
Length: 187 miles
Stations: 43
Frequency: Penn Line: 30–60 min weekdays, 6–9 trains a day weekend. Others: 3–10 trains a day each way, weekday peak only.
Avg weekday ridership: 30,000
Ridership per mile: 160

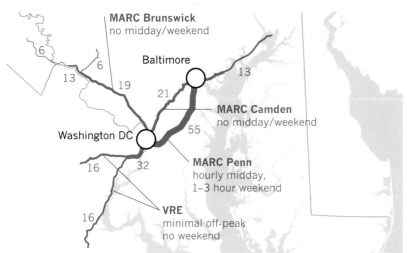

MARC Brunswick
no midday/weekend

6

Baltimore

6

13

19

21

13

MARC Camden
no midday/weekend

55

Washington DC

16   32

MARC Penn
hourly midday,
1–3 hour weekend

16

VRE
minimal off-peak
no weekend

Diesel Commuter Rail (VRE)

Opened: 1992
Last Expanded: 2015
Length: 90 miles
Stations: 19 (1 under construction)
Frequency: 8 trains each way a day weekday (no weekend service)
Avg weekday ridership: 17,200
Ridership per mile: 191

DC's commuter-rail system (above) is among the oldest in the US. Passenger trains have been running continuously here since the 1830s. Compared to Boston, New York, and Philadelphia, though, the network is small and service is sparse. Only MARC's Penn Line has all-day, seven-day-a-week service. The other two MARC lines and the two VRE lines (below) run at weekday rush hour only. Harpers Ferry, West Virginia (top), sees only three trains inbound in the morning and three trains outbound in the afternoon.

5. SAN FRANCISCO

San Jose–San Francisco–Oakland, CA

population 9,665,887 (5th)   **served by frequent transit** 17%   **daily trips per 1000** 145

The San Francisco Bay Area, divided by water and hills and centered on three major cities (San Francisco, Oakland, and San Jose), is a place of contrasts. San Francisco itself, seven miles square, is the oldest city on the West Coast. Surrounded by water on three sides, it is dense, mixed-use, and walkable. At the south end of the bay, San Jose, which was still surrounded by orchards in the 1960s, is now a sprawl of low-rise, car-oriented office parks known as Silicon Valley. The more the Bay Area population grows, the more the prewar core cities densify, and the rest of the area grows outwards, pushing waves of stucco houses into the farmlands of the Central Valley.

The Bay Area's transit, split into many systems by geography and history, reflects these contrasts in land use. San Francisco has one of the most comprehensive transit networks in the country. Nearly all residents are within walking distance of all-day frequent service. As a result, 25 percent of trips in San Francisco are made on transit. The Geary local bus route alone serves 55,000 riders a day, more than half of the rail-transit systems in the United States. MUNI Metro ranks among the three top systems in the country by total ridership and ridership per mile. In San Jose, however, transit struggles. Its light-rail system is one the worst performers in the country. With 42 miles, its light-rail system is longer than San Francisco's, but it carries only a quarter as many riders. San Jose has spent a lot of money on transit, but it has also spent a lot of money on roads and enforced land-use restrictions that limit density. Its tallest building is only 22 stories.

The transit network is tied together by BART, which, like the Bay Area, has a split personality. It was the first modern heavy-rail system in the United States, opened in 1972 as public opinion turned against new freeways. Its single line in San Francisco crosses the bay and then splits into four lines in the East Bay. In its core, it is a busy urban-rail system, tunneling under walkable places, fed by bus routes, and useful for short trips. At its extremities, it acts more like commuter rail, picking up suburbanites from vast parking lots. Pittsburg—the far eastern end of the system—is 40 miles, 55 minutes, and two mountain ranges away from Downtown San Francisco. BART has become essential: it carries 60 percent of peak-hour trips crossing the bay into San Francisco.

The Bay Area is politically disjointed, and the transit system reflects this. There are more than 30 separate transit operators. The region's complex politics also make it hard to make good decisions on capital projects. Ironically, the region's transit-friendly politics can make things worse by ensuring that any project, whether it makes sense or not, can be funded. The region's track record on investments is not good. BART's extensions since 1995 have increased system mileage by 45 percent, but only 20 percent

+ Dense and transit-intense core city with extensive frequent bus and successful light-rail and streetcar systems
+ Heavy-rail system acting as a regional spine and cross-bay conduit
+ Busy commuter rail with all-day service and employment at both ends
– Major investments in low-ridership suburban rail while neglecting urban areas
– Complex and often uncoordinated mix of agencies

BART
independent agency
Heavy Rail

MUNI
municipal
Frequent Bus
Light Rail
BRT
Streetcar
Cable Car

VTA
independent agency
Light Rail
BRT
Frequent Bus

AC Transit
independent agency
Frequent Bus
BRT

SamTrans
independent agency
Frequent Bus

Wheels
independent agency
Frequent Bus

County Connection
independent agency
Frequent Bus

Caltrain
independent agency
Commuter Rail

Altamont Corridor Express
independent agency
Commuter Rail

SMART
independent agency
Commuter Rail

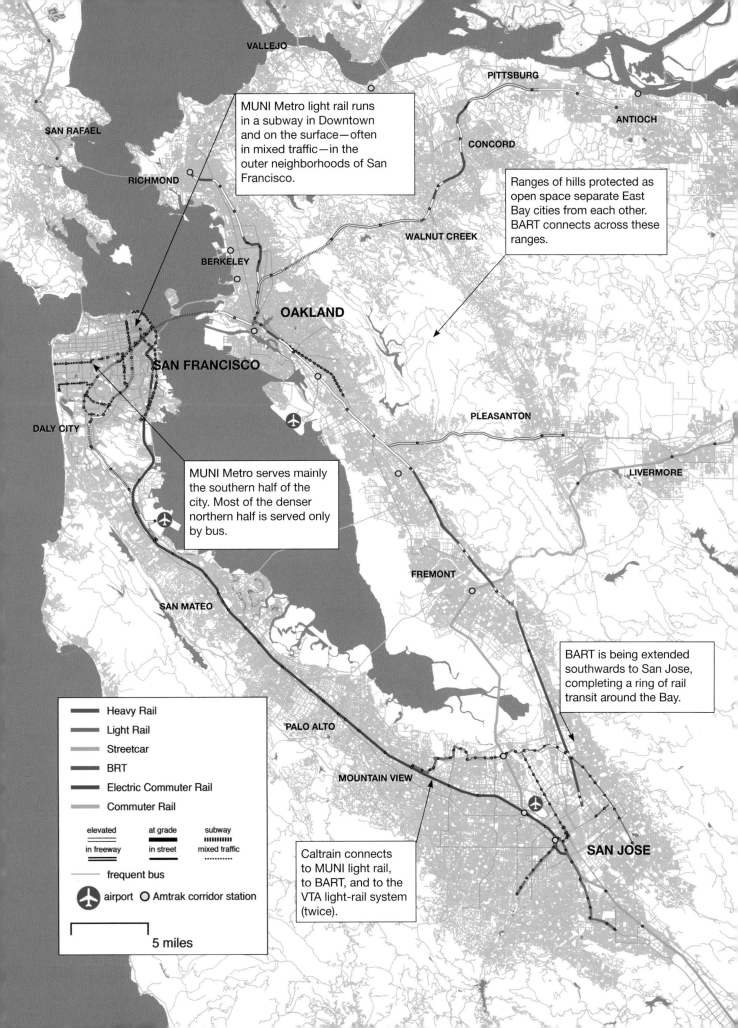

MUNI Metro light rail runs in a subway in Downtown and on the surface—often in mixed traffic—in the outer neighborhoods of San Francisco.

Ranges of hills protected as open space separate East Bay cities from each other. BART connects across these ranges.

MUNI Metro serves mainly the southern half of the city. Most of the denser northern half is served only by bus.

BART is being extended southwards to San Jose, completing a ring of rail transit around the Bay.

Caltrain connects to MUNI light rail, to BART, and to the VTA light-rail system (twice).

VALLEJO

PITTSBURG

ANTIOCH

SAN RAFAEL

RICHMOND

CONCORD

BERKELEY

WALNUT CREEK

OAKLAND

SAN FRANCISCO

PLEASANTON

DALY CITY

LIVERMORE

SAN MATEO

FREMONT

PALO ALTO

MOUNTAIN VIEW

SAN JOSE

Heavy Rail
Light Rail
Streetcar
BRT
Electric Commuter Rail
Commuter Rail

elevated   at grade   subway
in freeway   in street   mixed traffic

frequent bus

airport ◯ Amtrak corridor station

5 miles

Light Rail (Muni Metro)

HIGH PERFORMER
PREWAR SYSTEM

Opened: 1917
Last Expanded: ongoing
Length: 35.7 miles (1.7 under construction)
Stations: 119 (4 under construction)
Frequency: 2-10 peak, 2-10 midday, 3-20 evening/weekend
Avg weekday ridership: 143,863
Ridership per mile: 4,030

Streetcar (F Market)

HIGH PERFORMER
LARGE SYSTEM

Opened: 1995
Last Expanded: 2000
Length: 5.9 miles
Stations: 30
Frequency: 6–7 min peak/midday, 10–15 min evening/weekends
Avg weekday ridership: 14,367
Ridership per mile: 2,435

Streetcar (Cable Cars)

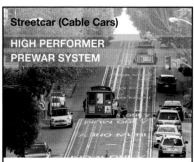

HIGH PERFORMER
PREWAR SYSTEM

Opened: 1878
Last Expanded: 1890
Length: 4.3 miles
Stations: numerous
Frequency: 4–10 min peak midday, 4–12 min evening/weekends
Avg weekday ridership: 13,837
Ridership per mile: 3,218

of trips involve one of those stations. Two new commuter-rail projects—eBART in Pittsburg and SMART in Marin—carry only 8,000 and 3,000 people a day. Meanwhile, some of the densest parts of the region—where tens of thousands of existing transit riders are stuck in traffic on buses every day—are not even being considered for anything beyond basic BRT. For decades, transit investments here have favored middle-class suburbanites, not city residents, and surely not low-income minority residents.

The Bay Area can be one of the best places in the United States to be a transit rider. In San Francisco transit can get you everywhere, and a third of households don't even own cars. Around the Bay Area, there are great walkable places connected to each other by fast, reliable transit. But those rail stations are far apart, and the network of high-frequency bus routes is limited. Most of the Bay Area, like most of the United States, is fundamentally car-oriented, and, as housing gets more and more expensive in the core, people have no choice but to live in the outskirts. ■

For San Francisco transit, topography is destiny. The city's hills (below, circa 1956) led to the invention of the cable car in 1873 and caused San Francisco to hang onto the technology long enough that the preservationists were able to save it. Likewise, the only reason any of the streetcar lines stayed in service to be converted to light rail was infrastructure like the Sunset Tunnel (bottom), which is too narrow to carry buses. The commuter train, now Caltrain, originally took a roundabout hilly route into the city. A 1907 direct route that tunneled through a series of ridges improved travel times and ensured it remained a good commute option even in the freeway age.

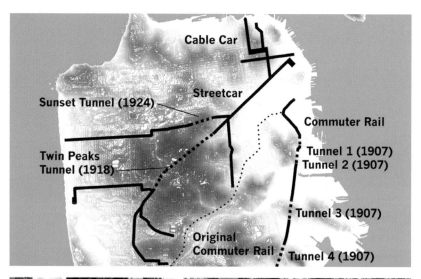

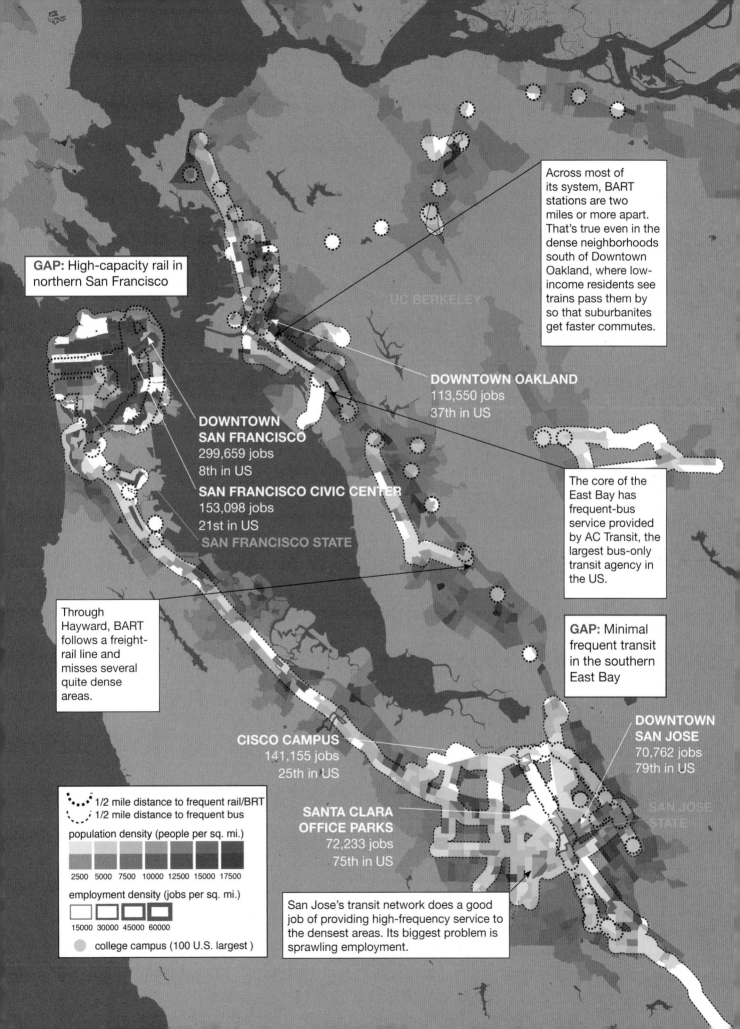

GAP: High-capacity rail in northern San Francisco

Across most of its system, BART stations are two miles or more apart. That's true even in the dense neighborhoods south of Downtown Oakland, where low-income residents see trains pass them by so that suburbanites get faster commutes.

UC BERKELEY

DOWNTOWN OAKLAND
113,550 jobs
37th in US

DOWNTOWN SAN FRANCISCO
299,659 jobs
8th in US

SAN FRANCISCO CIVIC CENTER
153,098 jobs
21st in US

SAN FRANCISCO STATE

The core of the East Bay has frequent-bus service provided by AC Transit, the largest bus-only transit agency in the US.

Through Hayward, BART follows a freight-rail line and misses several quite dense areas.

GAP: Minimal frequent transit in the southern East Bay

DOWNTOWN SAN JOSE
70,762 jobs
79th in US

SAN JOSE STATE

CISCO CAMPUS
141,155 jobs
25th in US

- - - ◡ 1/2 mile distance to frequent rail/BRT
····◡ 1/2 mile distance to frequent bus

population density (people per sq. mi.)

2500 5000 7500 10000 12500 15000 17500

employment density (jobs per sq. mi.)

15000 30000 45000 60000

● college campus (100 U.S. largest)

SANTA CLARA OFFICE PARKS
72,233 jobs
75th in US

San Jose's transit network does a good job of providing high-frequency service to the densest areas. Its biggest problem is sprawling employment.

Light Rail (VTA Light Rail)

LOW PERFORMER

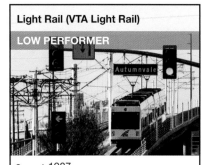

Opened: 1987
Last Expanded: ongoing
Length: 40.4 miles (2.4 U/C)
Stations: 59 (2 U/C)
Frequency: 7.5–15 min weekdays,
9–20 min weekends
Avg weekday ridership: 26,700
Ridership per mile: 661

BRT (Van Ness)

UNDER CONSTRUCTION

SMALL SYSTEM

Opened: 2021
Last Expanded: N/A
Length: Open BRT (0 guideway miles,
2 under construction)
Stations: 0 (8.5 in construction, guideway
only)
Frequency: 6 min

BRT (Rapid 522)

SMALL SYSTEM

LOW PERFORMER

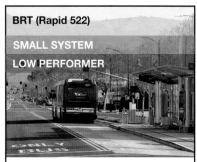

Opened: 2017
Last Expanded: N/A
Length: 25 miles (1 guideway miles)
Stations: 2 (guideway only)
Frequency: 10 min peak, 12 min off-peak,
15 min weekend
Avg weekday ridership: 5,228
Ridership per mile: 209

The San Jose light-rail system is centered on downtown San Jose (above). With only 70,000 jobs, it is one of the smallest downtowns that any US light-rail line serves, smaller than Buffalo, and with only 3,000 more jobs than Norfolk. The light-rail system does try to serve more jobs outside downtown with a winding route through corporate campuses in Sunnyvale (below). However, the overall job density is low, walking distances are long, and the environment isn't friendly to pedestrians.

Santa Rosa

34

SMART
2–3 hr midday
2–4 hr weekend

San Rafael

San Francisco

Stockton

8

ACE
no off-peak, Sat/Sun

92

CALTRAIN
1 hr off-peak,
weekend

San Jose

6

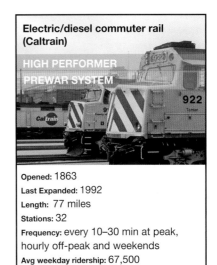

**Electric/diesel commuter rail
(Caltrain)**

HIGH PERFORMER
PREWAR SYSTEM

922

Opened: 1863
Last Expanded: 1992
Length: 77 miles
Stations: 32
Frequency: every 10–30 min at peak,
hourly off-peak and weekends
Avg weekday ridership: 67,500
Ridership per mile: 877

The level of service among the Bay Area's commuter-rail lines varies dramatically (above). Caltrain, which has considerably upgraded the corridor it owns from San Francisco to San Jose, offers service in both directions at least once an hour, seven days a week. During rush hour, there are as many as five trains an hour. Some of those are "Baby Bullet" express trains, which use segments of quadruple track (below) to pass the local trains, connecting San Francisco to San Jose in 65 minutes rather than 95. Caltrain's electrification, now under construction, will allow even higher service levels; current plans are for all-day service every 15 minutes or better, making it one of only two frequent commuter-rail lines in the United States. By contrast, the Altamont Commuter Express (ACE) is limited by agreement with Union Pacific, which own the tracks, to only four   trains a day each way, all at rush hours.

Like Caltrain, Marin's new SMART train owns its own tracks. But service will be much more limited, with rush-hour service plus a single midday train. On the other hand, eBART, a diesel train built as an extension of BART's heavy-rail service, will run every 20 minutes all day. SMART and ACE are tailored to the 9-to-5 commute, whereas Caltrain and eBART can serve all sorts of work schedules and types of trips.

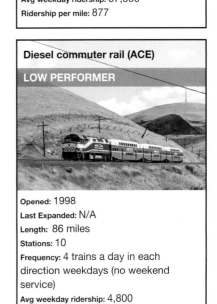

Diesel commuter rail (ACE)

LOW PERFORMER

Opened: 1998
Last Expanded: N/A
Length: 86 miles
Stations: 10
Frequency: 4 trains a day in each direction weekdays (no weekend service)
Avg weekday ridership: 4,800
Ridership per mile: 56

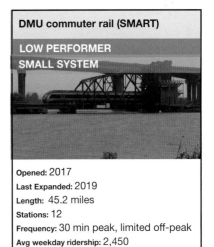

DMU commuter rail (SMART)

LOW PERFORMER
SMALL SYSTEM

Opened: 2017
Last Expanded: 2019
Length: 45.2 miles
Stations: 12
Frequency: 30 min peak, limited off-peak
Avg weekday ridership: 2,450
Ridership per mile: 54

Heavy Rail (BART)
LARGE SYSTEM

Opened: 1972
Last Expanded: 2020
Length: 119.2 miles
Stations: 47
Frequency: 3–15 min peak, 15 min weekday, 20 min night/weekend
Avg weekday ridership: 421,100
Ridership per mile: 3,533

DMU Commuter rail (eBART)
HIGH PERFORMER
SMALL SYSTEM

Opened: 2018
Last Expanded: N/A
Length: 10 miles
Stations: 3
Frequency: 15 min weekday, 20 min weekend
Avg weekday ridership: 8,200
Ridership per mile: 820

BRT (Tempo)

Opened: 2020
Last Expanded: N/A
Length: 9.5 miles (7.6 guideway miles)
Stations: 21 (guideway only)
Frequency: 7 min peak
Avg weekday ridership: N/A
Ridership per mile: N/A

GAP: BART capacity across San Francisco Bay

All of BART's lines meet in Oakland. From there, a train crosses the San Francisco Bay every 2.5 minutes during rush hour. The above map shows how BART ridership (shown by the thickness of the lines) is concentrated in the region's core where density is greatest and multiple lines come together (below) to cross San Francisco Bay. The outer ends of the system have a fraction of the ridership that the core does. The entire system, however, is built to the same standard—two full grade-separated tracks—so the core is overloaded while the outer ends have expensive infrastructure not justified by the ridership. BART's expansions (highlighted in yellow) since the original 1970s system have been on comparatively low-ridership segments.

BART was designed as a park-and-ride system, and just over half of passengers arrive by car. But transit connections have been a key part of the system from the beginning. Nearly every station (like Union City, below) has a bus-transit center, and 21 percent of riders arrive at the BART station by transit. AC Transit's new BRT line, which replaced a busy local bus route, connects to BART at both ends. BART has also been working with cities and developers to build more housing and jobs next to stations (like Contra Costa Center, above) allowing more people to walk to BART. BART now offers discounted fares for low-income residents, many of whom live near the lines in the East Bay (right). But BART fares are still higher than local bus, and transfers aren't free. It doesn't quite serve as the spine of regional transit that it could be.

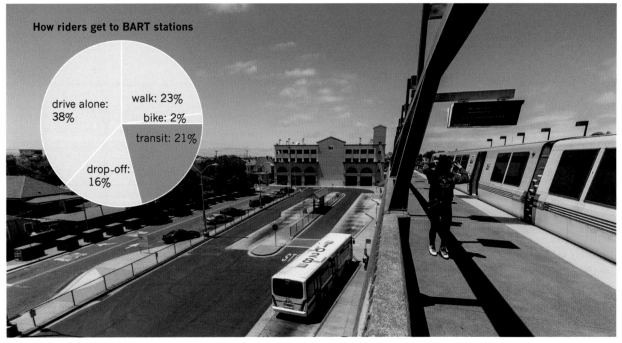

How riders get to BART stations

drive alone: 38%

walk: 23%

bike: 2%

transit: 21%

drop-off: 16%

6. BOSTON

Boston–Worcester–Providence, MA-RI-NH-CT

population 8,287,710 (6th)   **served by frequent transit** 14%   **daily trips per 1000** 134

MBTA
independent agency
Heavy Rail
Light Rail
Frequent Bus
Commuter Rail

RIPTA
independent agency
Frequent Bus

Boston has a long transit history. A local railroad offered America's first commuter tickets in 1843. The Orange Line is one of the oldest heavy-rail lines in the country. The light-rail Tremont Street subway, still in operation as part of the MBTA's Green Line, was the first subway line in the United States, and the third in the world. That history is still obvious. Park Street station, with ridiculously tight curves and low-level platforms, feels like a relic. Some Red Line subway cars are nearly 50 years old and the Ashmont-Mattapan shuttle that links to one of the south ends of the Red Line operates with cars built in 1945–46.

But Boston's transit system is also quite modern. No other prewar rail-transit network in the United States has transformed like Boston's, with old elevated lines rebuilt in new corridors, and lines extended further into the suburbs to new park-and-ride stations. Boston was the first US city to convert a railroad line to light rail. The commuter-rail system has been expanded from a low of 240 miles in 1980 to 400 miles in 2018.

Despite all of Boston's investment, though, there are notable gaps. Some lines are missing. Traveling a mile and a half from Hynes Convention Center station in Back Bay to Central Station in Cambridge requires either a roundabout 21-minute subway trip with a transfer downtown, or a 15-minute bus ride in congested traffic. Some connections are poorly designed, like the open-air walk between subway and commuter rail at North Station, or the silly loop of the Silver Line on the South Waterfront. Some lines don't have enough service, like commuter-rail lines that run only hourly at midday where density would support more trips. Much of the system is unreliable, like Green Line stations where hundreds of daily riders board from traffic lanes and intersections where packed trains wait for traffic signals. Overall, many of Boston's transit dollars have gone where they were least needed: $600 million for a bus tunnel under a brand new district with plenty of space for reserved lanes on the surface, and $534 million for a commuter-rail line that carries 5,500 trips a day from a suburb that already had express ferry service to Boston. Boston is a transit city. Thirty-seven percent of households do not have a car. Rail covers the city's major employment centers and dense urban neighborhoods and a dense network of frequent-bus routes fill in the gaps. The city is—and always has been—walkable and mixed-use. Even the suburban commuter-rail system gets a quarter of its ridership from people walking to the stations. It is a great place to ride transit, but it could be much better. ■

+ **Effective, modernized, heavy-rail network**
+ **Busy urban light rail with dedicated lanes and downtown subway**
− **Major investments in commuter rail focus on 9-to-5 trips**
− **Lack of BRT/Rail connections for trips not going through downtown**

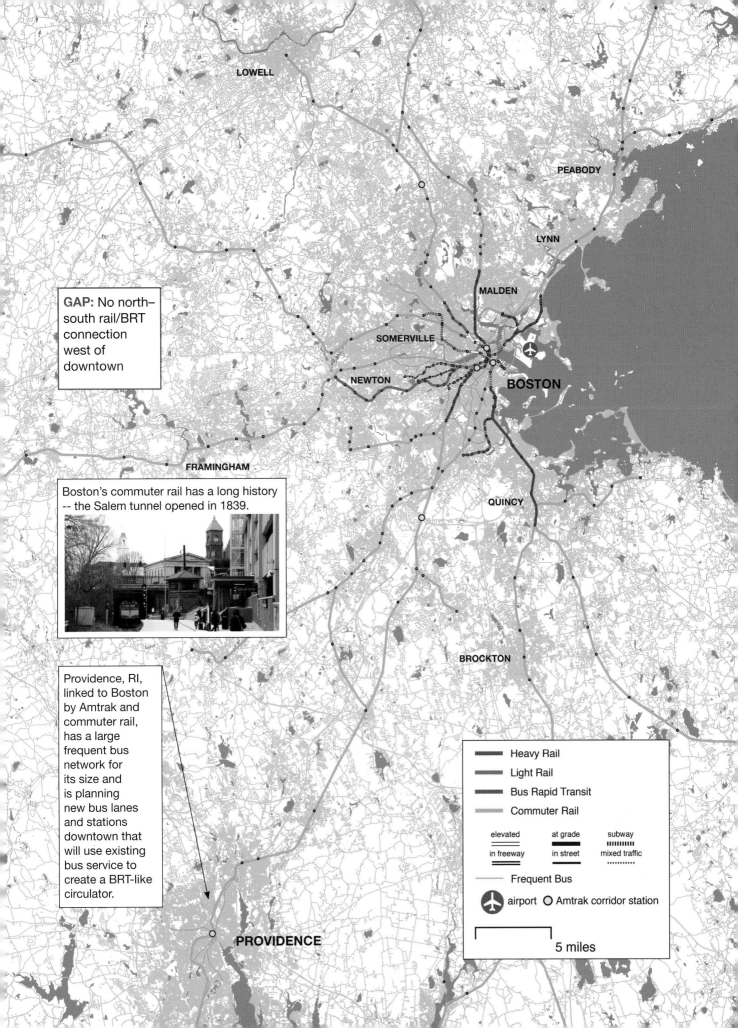

LOWELL

PEABODY

LYNN

MALDEN

SOMERVILLE

NEWTON

BOSTON

GAP: No north–south rail/BRT connection west of downtown

FRAMINGHAM

Boston's commuter rail has a long history -- the Salem tunnel opened in 1839.

QUINCY

BROCKTON

Providence, RI, linked to Boston by Amtrak and commuter rail, has a large frequent bus network for its size and is planning new bus lanes and stations downtown that will use existing bus service to create a BRT-like circulator.

PROVIDENCE

| Heavy Rail |
| Light Rail |
| Bus Rapid Transit |
| Commuter Rail |

| elevated | at grade | subway |
| in freeway | in street | mixed traffic |

Frequent Bus

✈ airport ○ Amtrak corridor station

5 miles

Heavy Rail (Orange/Red/Blue Lines)

LARGE SYSTEM
PREWAR SYSTEM

Opened: 1901
Last Expanded: 1987
Length: 38 miles
Stations: 53
Frequency: 5–9 min peak, 9–14 min midday, 10–12 min evening, 9–15 min weekends
Avg weekday ridership: 475,300
Ridership per mile: 12,508

Commuter Rail (MBTA Commuter Rail)

LARGE SYSTEM
PREWAR SYSTEM

Opened: 1834
Last Expanded: ongoing
Length: 402 miles (36 in construction)
Stations: 138 (6 in construction)
Frequency: 30–60 min peak, 60 min off-peak on some lines, weekday service on some lines
Avg weekday ridership: 121,700
Ridership per mile: 303

Light Rail (Ashmont-Mattapan Line)

SMALL SYSTEM
PREWAR SYSTEM

Opened: 1929
Last Expanded: N/A
Length: 2.5 miles
Stations: 8
Frequency: 5 min peak, 8 min midday, 12 min evening, 12–26 min weekend
Avg weekday ridership: 4,637
Ridership per mile: 1,855

Boston's heavy-rail system dates back to 1901, but 70% of today's network was built since World War II. In 1950, the Red, Orange, and Blue lines made up a 19.1-mile system. Since, 7.7 miles have been closed, and 26.8 miles of new line have opened. The new lines are not a strict replacement. The new south end of the Orange Line (above), built in a joint corridor with Amtrak and commuter rail, is parallel to the old elevated line on Washington Street, but half a mile away. Many of the new corridors parallel rail lines, like the southern Red Line at Savin Hill (below). The two leftmost tracks are the Red Line to Braintree, built in 1971, the center track is the South Shore commuter rail, and the right two tracks are the original Red Line from 1927.

1952, 1954

The Blue Line is extended to Wonderland.

1971, 1980

A new Red Line branch opens to Braintree.

1960

1975, 1977

The Orange Line to Charlestown is replaced with a new line to Oak Grove.

1984, 1985

The Red Line is extended to Alewife in two stages.

1980

1987

As part of the Southwest Corridor Project, the Orange Line along Washington Avenue is replaced with a new line to Forest Hills.

1990

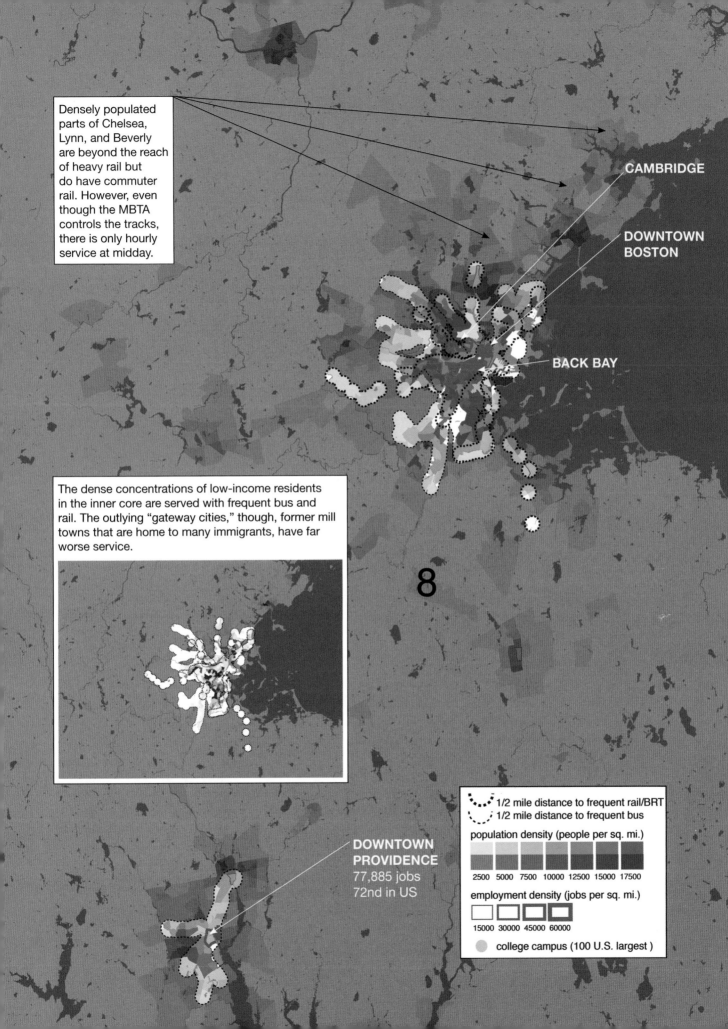

Densely populated parts of Chelsea, Lynn, and Beverly are beyond the reach of heavy rail but do have commuter rail. However, even though the MBTA controls the tracks, there is only hourly service at midday.

CAMBRIDGE

DOWNTOWN BOSTON

BACK BAY

The dense concentrations of low-income residents in the inner core are served with frequent bus and rail. The outlying "gateway cities," though, former mill towns that are home to many immigrants, have far worse service.

8

DOWNTOWN PROVIDENCE
77,885 jobs
72nd in US

1/2 mile distance to frequent rail/BRT
1/2 mile distance to frequent bus

population density (people per sq. mi.)

2500 5000 7500 10000 12500 15000 17500

employment density (jobs per sq. mi.)

15000 30000 45000 60000

college campus (100 U.S. largest)

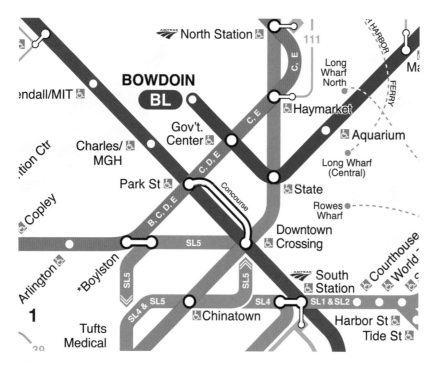

All of MBTA's heavy-rail, light-rail, BRT, and commuter-rail lines (above) come together amid the tight colonial streets of downtown Boston (right). Because of the city's complicated transit history, these connections don't always come together. South Station, for example, has only one connection into downtown, and getting from South Station to North Station requires a transfer. The Silver Line from the south waterfront connects only to the Red Line, and the Blue and Red lines come within a quarter mile of each other but don't connect. However, the MBTA has rebuilt the North Station and Government Center light-rail and heavy-rail stations to improve transfers. Nearby Back Bay (below), Boston's second downtown, was part of a 1960s vision for a "high spine" of high rises stretching west from downtown. It is connected to downtown by the heavy-rail Orange Line and the light-rail Green Line and has a commuter-rail and Amtrak Station.

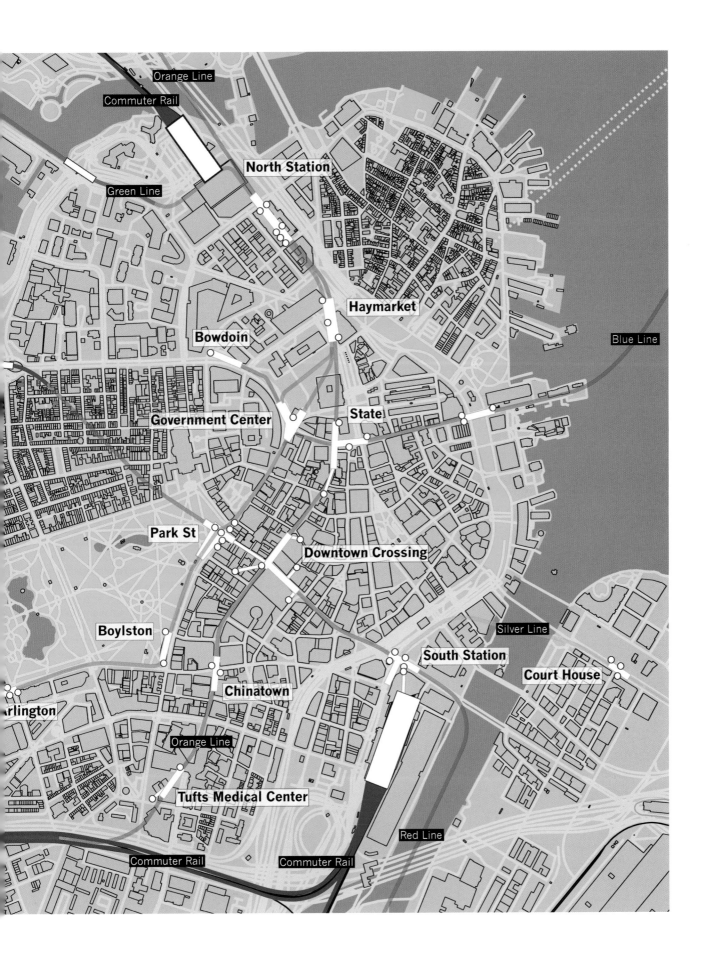

North Station

Orange Line

Commuter Rail

Green Line

Haymarket

Bowdoin

Blue Line

Government Center

State

Park St

Downtown Crossing

Boylston

Silver Line

South Station

Court House

rlington

Chinatown

Orange Line

Tufts Medical Center

Red Line

Commuter Rail

Commuter Rail

Light Rail (Green Line)

HIGH PERFORMER
PREWAR SYSTEM

Opened: 1889
Last Expanded: ongoing
Length: 23 miles (4.7 in construction)
Stations: 66 (6 in construction)
Frequency: 2–6 min peak, 3–9 min midday/evening, 3–12 min weekend
Avg weekday ridership: 133,063
Ridership per mile: 5,785

BRT (Silver Line SL1/SL2/SL3)

HIGH PERFORMER

Opened: 2004
Last Expanded: 2018
Length: 8.8 miles (2.4 guideway miles)
Stations: 12 (guideway only)
Frequency: 3–10 min peak, 8–15 min off-peak
Avg weekday ridership: 23,819
Ridership per mile: 2,702

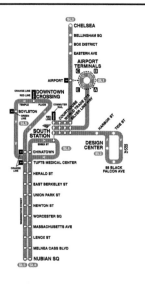

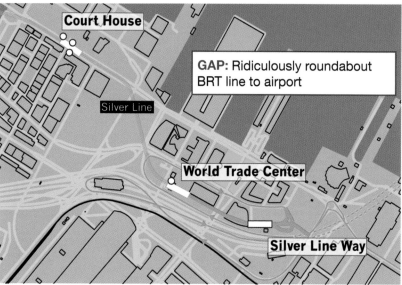

Court House

GAP: Ridiculously roundabout BRT line to airport

Silver Line

World Trade Center

Silver Line Way

The Silver Line (left) is an ungainly creation, a mix of major infrastructure and odd compromises. The south waterfront section (above) was built as part of a major redevelopment of old port facilities into a new civic and commercial district. Buses travel in a 1.5-mile subway with three stations from South Station to a portal (top), then branch. One line runs on surface streets farther along the waterfront. The other enters the highway tunnel under Boston Harbor and runs to Logan Airport. Amazingly, even though the subway and the tunnel were built at the same time, less than 100 feet apart, there is no connection, and buses must make a ¾-mile loop out of their way. Westbound buses actually stop at the street entrance of the World Trade Center station, then stop again inside the station four minutes later. This route was extended in 2018 to Chelsea (below right), partially along a commuter-rail line. The Dudley Square section of the Silver Line is a surface bus in poorly enforced bus lanes (below left). No buses run through the two sections, though a transfer is possible at South Station.

The Green Line (below) is America's busiest light-rail system, with 222,000 boardings on an average weekday. A short elevated section on the north end leads into the downtown subway (above), which runs through down- town and splits into two branches in the Back Bay. From there, the trains emerge onto the surface. Three of the four branches are street-running. Unlike similar systems in San Francisco and Philadelphia, almost all the street trackage is in reserved lanes (right, top). The Watertown and Arborway branches, which shared lanes with cars, were abandoned in 1969 and 1985. The fourth branch, Riverside, opened in 1959 as the first of the now numerous light-rail lines in the United States built by taking over a former rail line (right, middle photo). While this is the longest branch, it is not the busiest, and all three surface branches draw more riders per mile. Street stops like Coolidge Corner (right, bottom photo), which sees 3,500 boardings on an average weekday, are in the heart of Brookline and West Boston neighborhoods. Green Line tracks also run through the campuses of Northeastern University, Boston University, and Boston College.

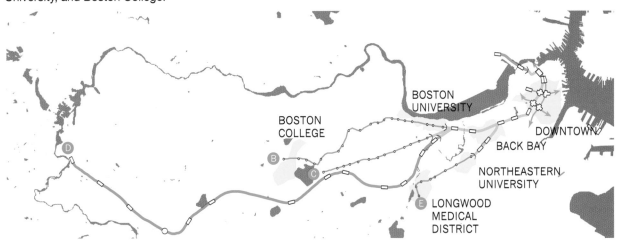

7. DALLAS

Dallas–Fort Worth, TX-OK

population 8,057,796 (7th)   **served by frequent transit** 3%   **daily trips per 1000** 26

The Dallas Metroplex has opened more than 150 miles of all-day rail service since 1995, more than any other US metropolitan area. Downtown Dallas has seven light-rail lines, two streetcar lines, and a commuter-rail line radiating out in every direction. It is an impressive accomplishment, and it has taken great political will. Dallas Area Rapid Transit has no fewer than 13 member cities, so spending $5.4 billion on light rail required a consensus between urban and suburban areas. In 2000, a measure to speed up construction by issuing bonds passed with 77 percent of the vote. That pro-transit attitude extends beyond DART's borders too. The Fort Worth "T" partnered with DART to extend commuter rail into Tarrant County and is now building its own commuter-rail line. Denton County has its own commuter-rail line to serve a population of only 780,000.

This transit investment has also led to major private investment. DART's member cities compete aggressively for new development, and many have focused on creating mixed-use areas around stations. Along the DART Red Line, for example, there is infill retail and residential development at Mockingbird Station in Dallas, a mixed-use town center with performing arts center at Galatyn Park, a major new office complex for State Farm at City Line, and 1,000 new residential units in historic downtown Plano. Private developers have invested as much in development around the stations as DART spent on the system.

But the same ambition that created this massive system, and promoted development around it, has also limited its ridership. From the beginning, DART's goal was scale. The 1988 master plan called for a 93-mile system. When success is measured in miles of track, the logical approach is to find easy rights-of-way. DART purchased a total of 125 miles of freight railroad right-of-way in the 1980s and 1990s, and built its lines straight down those pre-cleared paths. DART light-rail lines skirt the medical center rather than running through it, pass within 600 feet of the Love Field runway but don't serve the terminal, stop on the opposite side of freeways from both Southern Methodist University and the University of Dallas, and miss the densest neighborhoods in Dallas. Thus it is not surprising that while DART's 93-mile light-rail system is the longest in the country, it doesn't make the top five in ridership. It is behind not only legacy systems in San Francisco and Boston, but also San Diego, Portland, and Los Angeles.

+ **Major investment in transit**
- **Low-frequency, low-ridership light-rail network bypassing key destinations**
- **Lack of frequent service**

DART
independent agency
Light Rail
Streetcar
Commuter Rail
Frequent Bus

Trinity Metro
independent agency
Commuter Rail
Frequent Bus

McKinney Avenue Transit Authority
non-profit
Streetcar

Trinity Railway Express
independent agency
Commuter Rail

DCTA
independent agency
Commuter Rail

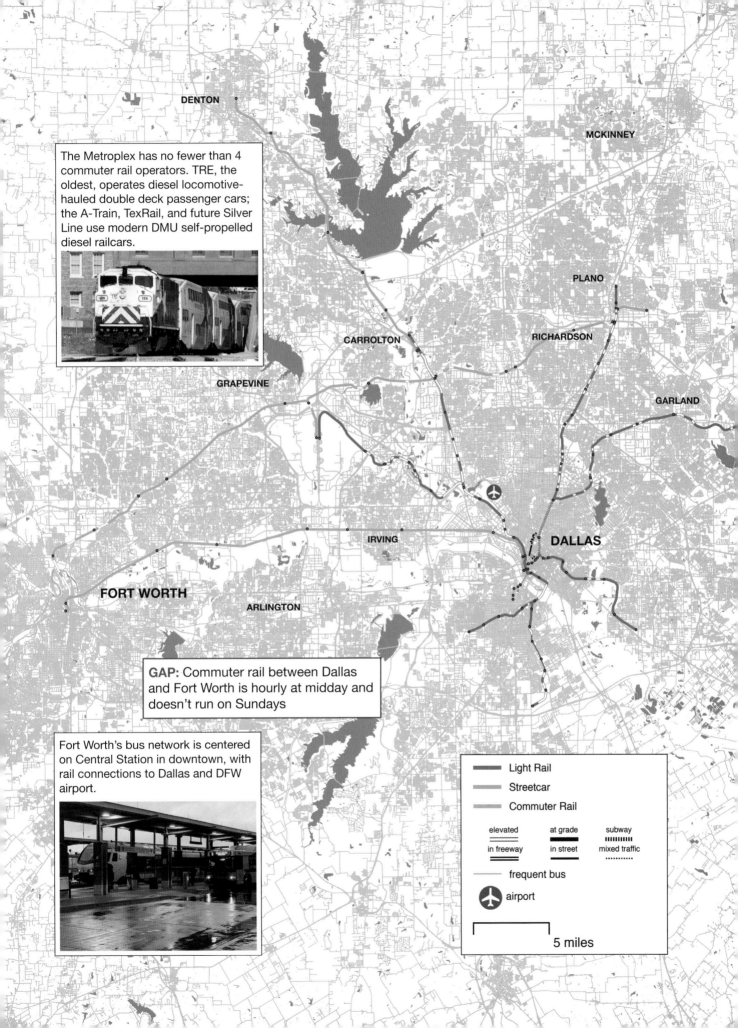

DENTON

MCKINNEY

The Metroplex has no fewer than 4 commuter rail operators. TRE, the oldest, operates diesel locomotive-hauled double deck passenger cars; the A-Train, TexRail, and future Silver Line use modern DMU self-propelled diesel railcars.

PLANO

CARROLLTON

RICHARDSON

GRAPEVINE

GARLAND

IRVING

DALLAS

FORT WORTH

ARLINGTON

GAP: Commuter rail between Dallas and Fort Worth is hourly at midday and doesn't run on Sundays

Fort Worth's bus network is centered on Central Station in downtown, with rail connections to Dallas and DFW airport.

▬▬	Light Rail
▬▬	Streetcar
▬▬	Commuter Rail

elevated	at grade	subway
in freeway	in street	mixed traffic

— frequent bus

✈ airport

5 miles

Light Rail (DART)

LARGE SYSTEM

LOW PERFORMER

Opened: 1996
Last Expanded: 2016
Length: 92.6 miles
Stations: 64
Frequency: 8–15 min peak, 10–20 min midday/evening/weekend
Avg weekday ridership: 92,000
Ridership per mile: 994

Streetcar (McKinney Avenue Trolley)

LOW PERFORMER

Opened: 1989
Last Expanded: 2015
Length: 4.1 miles
Stations: 25
Frequency: 17 min weekday, 22 min weekend
Avg weekday ridership: 1,644
Ridership per mile: 401

Streetcar (Dallas Streetcar)

SMALL SYSTEM

LOW PERFORMER

Opened: 2015
Last Expanded: 2016
Length: 2.4 miles
Stations: 6
Frequency: 20 min
Avg weekday ridership: 475
Ridership per mile: 198

LA carries more than twice as many riders as Dallas on less track. The member cities supported this approach so that they would get their stations. Plano, Rowlett, and Carrolton are all 20 miles from downtown Dallas in different directions, but all now have rail service. Ten of the 13 member cities have rail stations within walking distance, and the DART board voted in 2018 to proceed with the $1.1 billion Cotton Belt commuter-rail line, projected to carry only 16,000 riders, in part so that Addison would be the 11th city with service. Arguably, DART has achieved its primary design goals; high ridership was just not one of them.

Today, Dallas has the most impressive rail system in Texas, but Houston, San Antonio, Austin, and El Paso all have higher per-capita transit ridership. Dallas has only one frequent bus route, and only 16 of the 64 light-rail stations get more than one train every 20 minutes mid-day on a weekday. If Dallas had focused as much on service as it has on infrastructure, a lot more people might be on the trains. ■

The McKinney Avenue Trolley started as a passion project but has transformed into genuinely useful transit. A street reconstruction revealed long-abandoned street car tracks on McKinney Avenue, and a local restauranteur and rail fan with a collection of vintage trolley cars founded a nonprofit to build and operate the line. The first cars ran in 1989, funded by local businesses to draw patrons. DART started contributing operating funding in 2002, when a northward extension to the West Village development (above) and the DART Cityplace station opened, and the line was extended into downtown in 2015. Today, the streetcar serves a dense corridor (right) that is bypassed by the light-rail subway, connecting apartments, hotels, office buildings, and the arts district to the center of downtown with daily service every 17 minutes. It now carries 1,700 trips a day.

Dallas's second streetcar line also started as a grassroots effort, first rolled out as a website for the fictional "Oak Cliff Transit Authority" but quickly adopted by the City of Dallas, which received a federal grant and opened the line in 2015. Unlike McKinney, however, the line doesn't go into downtown, and the trains don't run more than every 20 minutes, even at rush hour. Ridership is a paltry 300 trips a day.

Many of DFW's low-income residents are in dense clusters of suburban apartments far from ether light-rail or frequent-bus service.

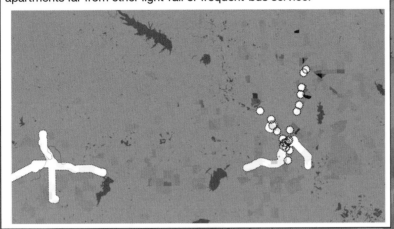

GAP: No frequent transit to densest parts of Dallas

DOWNTOWN FORT WORTH
80,068 jobs
66th in US

OFFICE PARK IRVING
93,250 jobs
48th in US

UT MEDICAL CENTER
190,285 jobs
15th in US

DOWNTOWN DALLAS
167,514 jobs
19th in US

GAP: McKinney Avenue Trolley—which serves denser corridor than light rail—is infrequent and slow.

1/2 mile distance to frequent rail/BRT
1/2 mile distance to frequent bus

population density (people per sq. mi.)

2500 5000 7500 10000 12500 15000 17500

employment density (jobs per sq. mi.)

15000 30000 45000 60000

college campus (100 U.S. largest)

Light Rail (METRORail)

HIGH PERFORMER

Opened: 2004
Last Expanded: 2016
Length: 22.3 miles
Stations: 39
Frequency: 6–12 min peak/midday, 6–18 evenings/weekends
Avg weekday ridership: 60,300
Ridership per mile: 2,704

BRT (Silver Line)

Opened: 2020
Last Expanded: N/A
Length: 4.7 miles (4.7 guideway miles)
Stations: 10
Frequency: 6 min
Avg weekday ridership: N/A
Ridership per mile: N/A

Streetcar (Galveston Trolley)

OPERATIONS SUSPENDED

Opened: 1988
Last Expanded: 2005
Length: 0 miles (3.1 under construction)
Stations: 0 (22 under construction)
Frequency: not operating
Avg weekday ridership: N/A

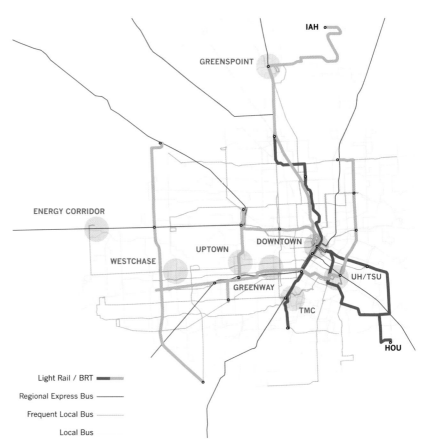

Light Rail / BRT
Regional Express Bus
Frequent Local Bus
Local Bus

The METRONext plan (above) creates four networks: rail and BRT that link major activity centers, regional express bus to the suburbs, a grid of frequent local bus routes, and the local bus network, all interconnected. In many ways, the plan builds on the redesigned bus network, upgrading some of the highest ridership bus corridors (below) to rail or BRT.

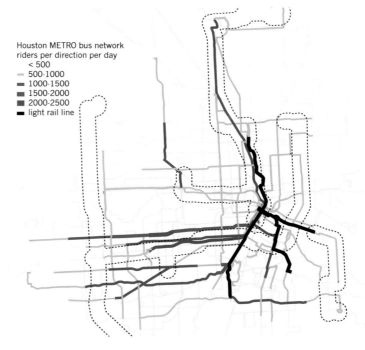

Houston METRO bus network
riders per direction per day
< 500
500-1000
1000-1500
1500-2000
2000-2500
light rail line

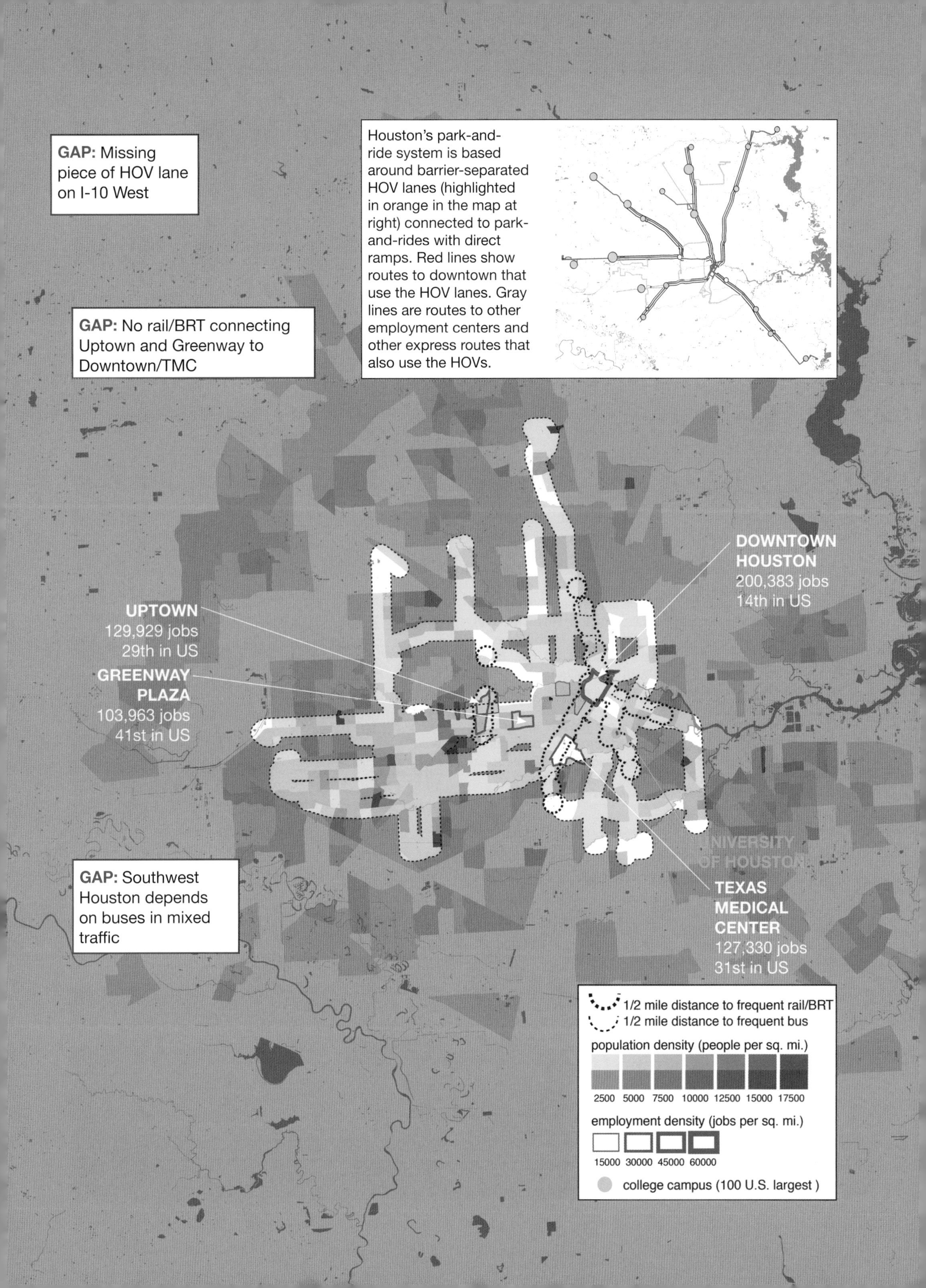

GAP: Missing piece of HOV lane on I-10 West
GAP: No rail/BRT connecting Uptown and Greenway to Downtown/TMC
Houston's park-and-ride system is based around barrier-separated HOV lanes (highlighted in orange in the map at right) connected to park-and-rides with direct ramps. Red lines show routes to downtown that use the HOV lanes. Gray lines are routes to other employment centers and other express routes that also use the HOVs.
DOWNTOWN HOUSTON
200,383 jobs
14th in US
UPTOWN
129,929 jobs
29th in US
GREENWAY PLAZA
103,963 jobs
41st in US
UNIVERSITY OF HOUSTON
GAP: Southwest Houston depends on buses in mixed traffic
TEXAS MEDICAL CENTER
127,330 jobs
31st in US
1/2 mile distance to frequent rail/BRT
1/2 mile distance to frequent bus
population density (people per sq. mi.)
2500 5000 7500 10000 12500 15000 17500
employment density (jobs per sq. mi.)
15000 30000 45000 60000
college campus (100 U.S. largest)

All three of Houston's light-rail lines cross in the center of Downtown (opposite) at Capitol and Rusk (above), surrounded by office buildings and lofts. Main Street (in Midtown, below) was extensively rebuilt for rail, going from six traffic lanes to two, with exclusive lanes for rail, a planted median between stations, and wider sidewalks.

Houston's bus and rail networks are closely integrated. Sixteen of the 25 stations on the Red Line offer connections to local bus routes, either at transit centers like Downtown Transit Center (right) or at ordinary street intersections.

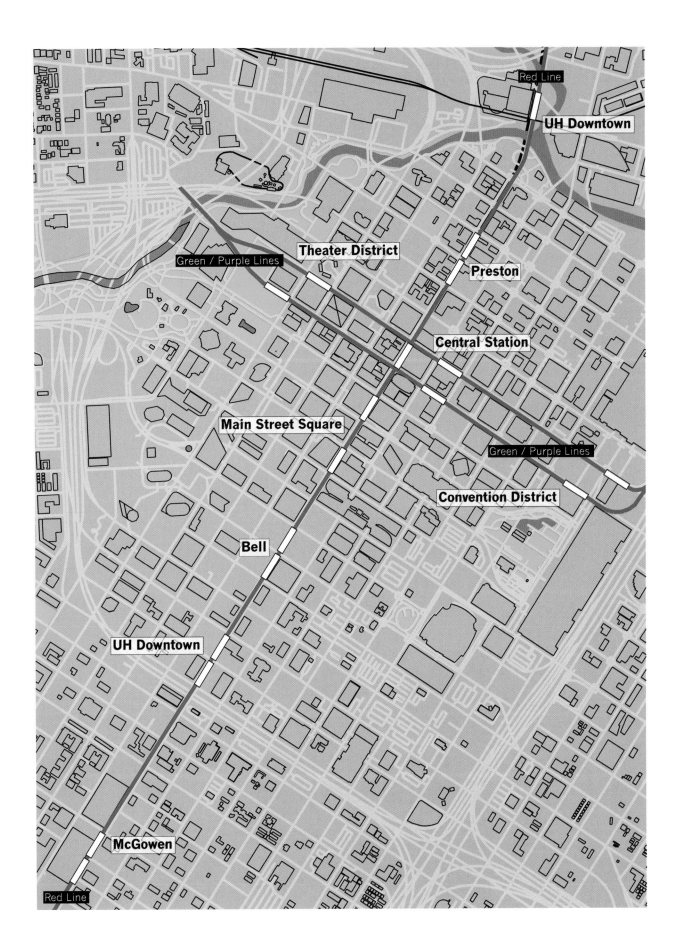

9. PHILADELPHIA

Philadelphia–Reading–Camden, PA-NJ-DE-MD

population 7,209,620 (9th)   **served by frequent transit** 22%   **daily trips per 1000** 124

SEPTA
independent agency
Heavy Rail
Light Rail
Streetcar
Frequent Bus
Commuter Rail

New Jersey Transit
independent agency
Commuter Rail
Frequent Bus

Delaware River Port Authority
independent agency
Heavy Rail

Post-WWII Philadelphia inherited a spectacular transit infrastructure. The city had two heavy-duty electrified commuter-rail networks, the only four-track subway outside New York City, a comprehensive streetcar network including a downtown subway, interurban lines reaching into the suburbs, and well-designed intermodal stations linking them.

But the story since then has been one of decline. Pennsylvania's transit dollars—granted at the whim of a legislature that is balanced between urban and rural interests—have gone toward maintaining what exists already. Most of the streetcar network is gone. A new commuter-rail tunnel through downtown created a single regional system, but the service it provides is still traditional commuter rail, and large sections of commuter rail that served significant destinations like Reading (a metro area of 415,000) are gone. Only across the river in New Jersey, where state government has been more generous, has there been meaningful rail-system expansion. While most of New Jersey Transit's rail system is focused on New York City (and covered in that section of the book), two lines, both built in the last 30 years, serve the Philadelphia suburbs of southern New Jersey.

Nevertheless, thanks to those long-ago investments, Philadelphia has one of the best transit systems in the country. Frequent buses and streetcars blanket the city, feeding into two busy subway lines. Half the city's 1.5 million residents can get to Center City in 30 minutes or less by transit. PATCO trains cross the river into New Jersey 24 hours a day. Commuter-rail and light-rail trains link walkable suburbs and nearby cities like Trenton, New Jersey, and Wilmington, Delaware, into the city. Thirty-three percent of Philadelphia households do not have a car, and a quarter of the city's residents commute by transit. The numbers are impressive, but it is sobering to think about what the city might look like if it had been growing its transit system for the past 50 years rather than shrinking it. ■

+ **Useful urban heavy-rail and light-rail network**
+ **Extensive commuter-rail network with downtown tunnel**
− **Low off-peak commuter-rail frequency and uncoordinated fares**

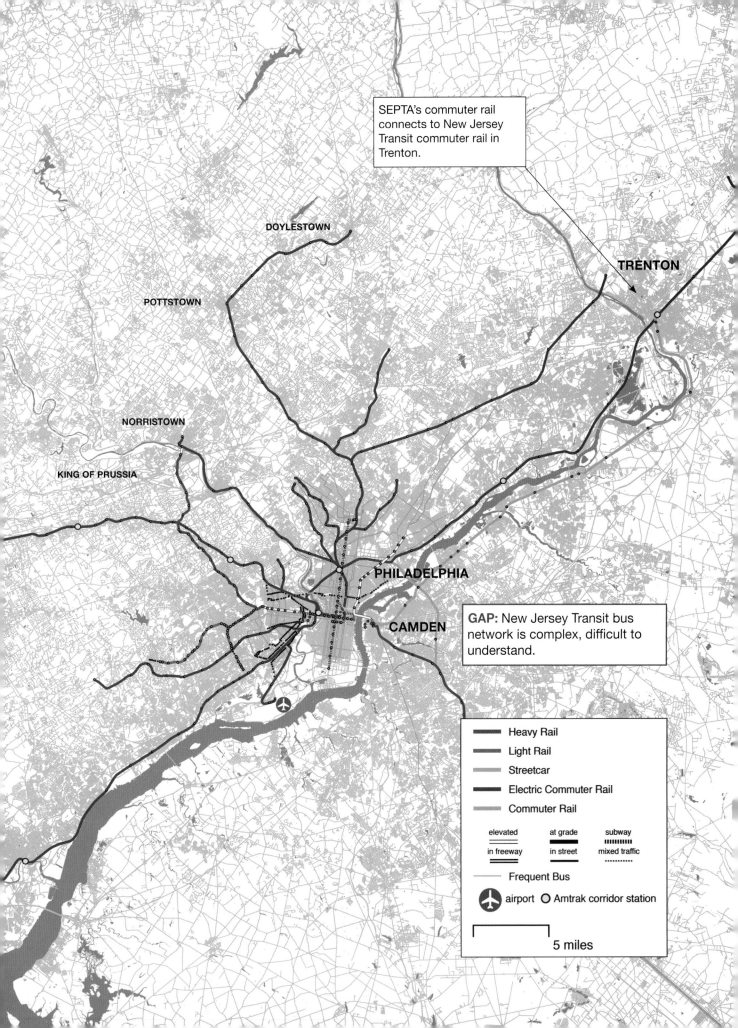

SEPTA's commuter rail connects to New Jersey Transit commuter rail in Trenton.

DOYLESTOWN

POTTSTOWN

TRENTON

NORRISTOWN

KING OF PRUSSIA

PHILADELPHIA

CAMDEN

GAP: New Jersey Transit bus network is complex, difficult to understand.

Heavy Rail
Light Rail
Streetcar
Electric Commuter Rail
Commuter Rail

| elevated | at grade | subway |
| in freeway | in street | mixed traffic |

Frequent Bus

✈ airport   ◯ Amtrak corridor station

5 miles

**Heavy Rail
(Broad St./Market-Frankford)**

HIGH PERFORMER

PREWAR SYSTEM

Opened: 1907
Last Expanded: 1973
Length: 24.9 miles
Stations: 52
Frequency: 4–7 min peak/midday, 10–12 min evening, 10–20 min weekend
Avg weekday ridership: 329,200
Ridership per mile: 13,221

Light Rail (SEPTA 101/102)

LOW PERFORMER

SMALL SYSTEM

PREWAR SYSTEM

Opened: 1906
Last Expanded: 1913
Length: 11.9 miles
Stations: 52
Frequency: 20 min weekday, 30 min weekend
Avg weekday ridership: 7,732
Ridership per mile: 650

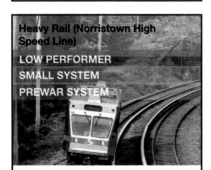

Heavy Rail (Norristown High Speed Line)

LOW PERFORMER

SMALL SYSTEM

PREWAR SYSTEM

Opened: 1907
Last Expanded: 1912
Length: 13.5 miles
Stations: 22
Frequency: 5–15 min peak, 15–30 min midday, 2–30 min evening, 20–30 min weekend
Avg weekday ridership: 10,543
Ridership per mile: 781

Philadelphia has two heavy-rail lines within city limits. The Broad Street Line (below), entirely in subway, runs north and south from Center City, and the Market Frankford Line, in a tunnel in the center and elevated (left) beyond, runs west and northeast. They cross under City Hall. Trains come as often as every four minutes during rush hour, and the Broad Street line has express trains as well, a feature found only here, New York, and Chicago. Together they carry more that 300,000 people on an average weekday. Of all the rail systems in the United States, only New York and Boston have more boardings per mile.

SEPTA's rail system has a sharp break at the city line. The two subway lines, the streetcars, and the subway-surface light-rail trains, originally built by the city and by private companies awarded franchises by the city, stay within the city. In the suburbs, other companies built streetcars and electric interurban lines. Three of these lines survive, all feeding into the Market-Frankford subway at 69th street. Two (the 101 and 102, below) are light rail, operating in a mix of private right-of-way and streets, and the third, the Norristown High Speed Line, is heavy rail, albeit with light-rail-sized vehicles.

These areas, developed with single-family homes in the early 1900s, are walkable but significantly less dense than the city. It is no surprise that ridership is thus much lower than the urban lines. But the low level of service may make a difference, too. The 20- or 30-minute midday frequencies are low compared to systems serving less dense areas in places like Denver and Salt Lake City, and so is ridership.

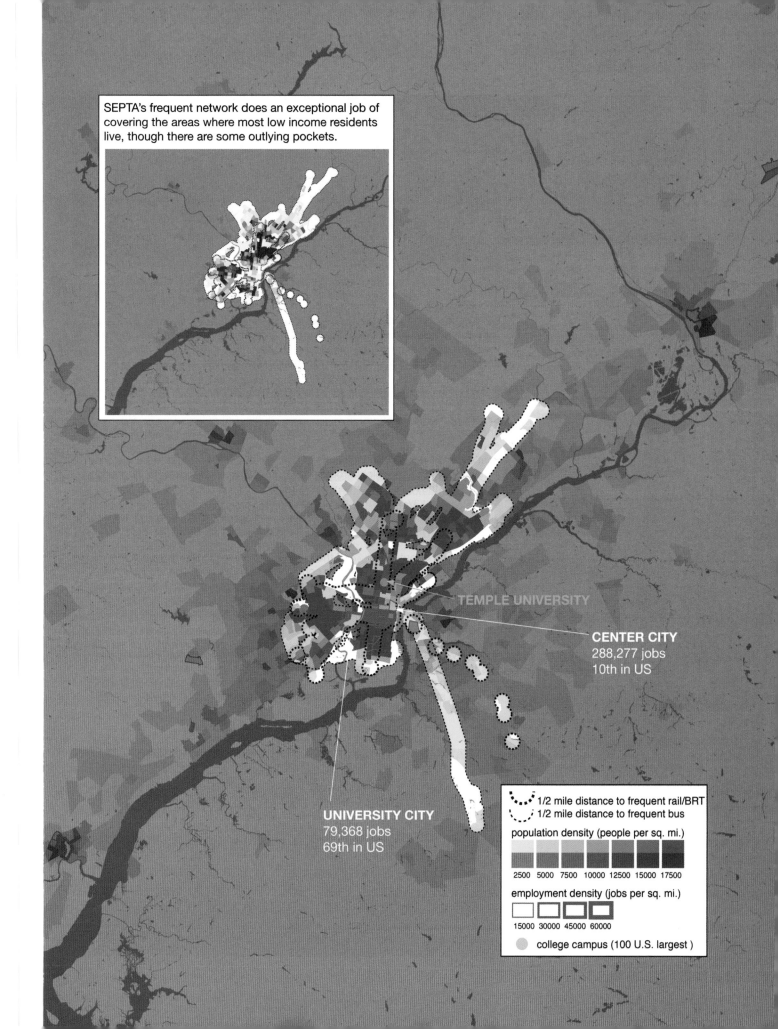

SEPTA's frequent network does an exceptional job of covering the areas where most low income residents live, though there are some outlying pockets.

TEMPLE UNIVERSITY

CENTER CITY
288,277 jobs
10th in US

UNIVERSITY CITY
79,368 jobs
69th in US

1/2 mile distance to frequent rail/BRT
1/2 mile distance to frequent bus

population density (people per sq. mi.)
2500 5000 7500 10000 12500 15000 17500

employment density (jobs per sq. mi.)
15000 30000 45000 60000

college campus (100 U.S. largest)

Commuter Rail (SEPTA Regional Rail)

HIGH PERFORMER

LARGE SYSTEM

PREWAR SYSTEM

Opened: 1832

Last Expanded: ongoing

Length: 280 miles (3 in construction)

Stations: 153 (1 in construction)

Frequency: 18–49 peak, 30–60 midday/evening, 30–90 weekend (peak only on one line)

Avg weekday ridership: 134,600

Ridership per mile: 481

No US downtown is as conveniently served by the city's entire rail network as Center City Philadelphia (right). The Broad Street subway, running north–south, and the Market-Frankford Line, running east–west, cross under City Hall. The subway-surface streetcars loop around the building. The regional rail lines stop just a block away, and PATCO is four blocks south. All these stations are connected with the extensive underground Center City Concourse (below), which also links to numerous downtown office buildings.

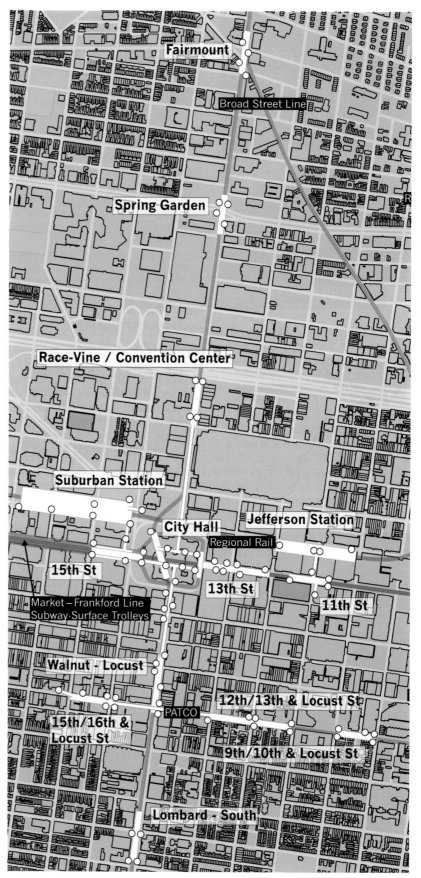

PENNSYLVANIA   RAILROAD

SUBURBAN   STATION

In 1984, SEPTA completed a tunnel under Center City Philadelphia, linking two previously unconnected commuter rail systems—six former Reading Railroad lines and six former Pennsylvania Railroad lines plus a new airport line—into a single system. Instead of terminating at stub end stations, trains now run through, stopping at 30th Street, Suburban Station (above), Jefferson Station (right), and Temple University (bottom right). The resulting system is one of the most comprehensive, and highest ridership, commuter-rail systems in the United States. But, despite its depiction alongside subway and light rail on SEPTA's rail map (below), it's still a very traditional commuter-rail system, with infrequent midday, night, and weekend service, conductors collecting tickets, and separate fares from local transit.

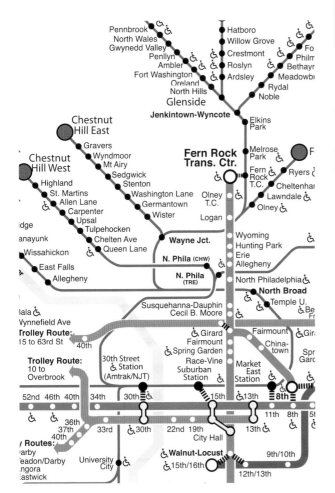

10. MIAMI

Miami–Fort Lauderdale–Port St. Lucie, FL

population 6,889,936 (10th)   **served by frequent transit** 12%   **daily trips per 1000** 49

The Miami metropolitan area needs a good transit system. It is big, with 6.5 million people. It is far-flung, stretching north–south over 100 miles. It is poor, with a per-capita income of only $20,454, by far the lowest of any of the 20 largest US metropolitan areas, and full of recent immigrants, with 37 percent of the population born outside the United States. It is also a major tourist attraction.

In the 1970s, Miami set out to build a world-class rail system. The plan called for 50 miles of elevated computer-controlled heavy rail. Construction started in 1980 on the first 21-mile line, which opened in segments from 1983 to 1985. By the time that those segments opened, though, momentum had faded. The logical southward extension was built as a busway. It took until 2003 for the next rail segment to open, and that only added a little more than a mile of track. But MetroRail has proven to be useful, connecting to buses from the north and south, attracting new development, and growing ridership from 20,000 a day after opening to 60,000 by the mid-2000s. That built public support, and in 2002 voters overwhelmingly passed a sales tax to fund 89 miles of additional rail, serving current high-ridership, frequent-bus corridors. But, due to over-optimistic assumptions and epic mismanagement, only 2.4 miles, and one station, have been built. Clearly, Miami could have done better. It is not dissimilar in scale and density to Atlanta, where 48 miles of rail carry 213,000 people a day.

Meanwhile, Miami got a commuter-rail line. Tri-Rail opened in 1989 as a temporary measure while parallel highways were under construction. Ridership was just high enough—7,000 on an average weekday by the mid-1990s—that it was made permanent. Over time, service has been increased and stations improved. But Tri-Rail serves the wrong corridor and goes to the wrong place. Its inland route is away from major destinations and notably less dense than the Florida East Coast Railroad corridor. It terminates, illogically, at the airport. Downtown Miami is another 20-minute Metrorail ride away. There is a need for a north–south corridor through the metro area, but Tri-Rail isn't it.

Oddly, Miami's one transit success story looks like a toy. The Metromover, little cars running on elevated tracks around downtown, came from the same generation of downtown peoplemovers as Jacksonville and Detroit, both widely considered failures. But Metromover has actually worked. It serves as a downtown distributor for Metrorail and connects high-rise residential to the north and south, carrying 33,000 trips a day. It is an accomplishment, but Miami deserves more. ■

Miami-Dade
Transit
municipal
Heavy Rail
Peoplemover
Frequent Bus

Tri-Rail
independent agency
Commuter Rail

BROWARD COUNTY
Transit
Broward County Transit
county
Frequent Bus

CORAL GABLES
THE CITY BEAUTIFUL
Coral Gables
municipal
Frequent Bus

MIAMIBEACH **TROLLEY**
Miami Beach Trolley
municipal
Frequent Bus

+ Effective downtown peoplemover
– Incomplete rail network and inadequate frequent transit network

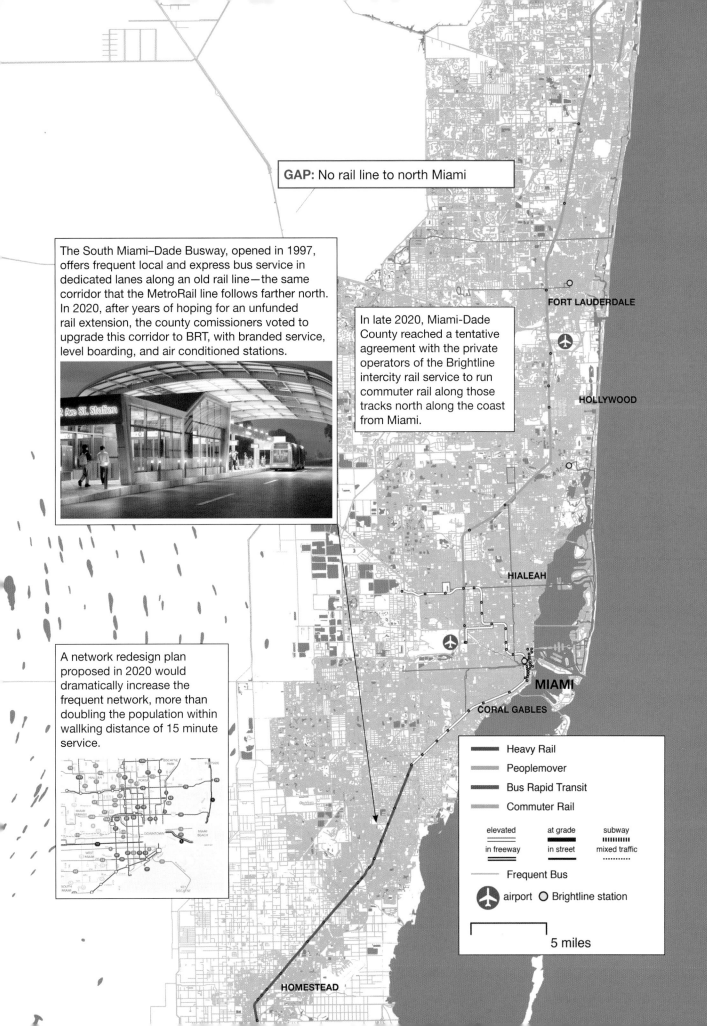

GAP: No rail line to north Miami

FORT LAUDERDALE

The South Miami–Dade Busway, opened in 1997, offers frequent local and express bus service in dedicated lanes along an old rail line—the same corridor that the MetroRail line follows farther north. In 2020, after years of hoping for an unfunded rail extension, the county commissioners voted to upgrade this corridor to BRT, with branded service, level boarding, and air conditioned stations.

In late 2020, Miami-Dade County reached a tentative agreement with the private operators of the Brightline intercity rail service to run commuter rail along those tracks north along the coast from Miami.

HOLLYWOOD

HIALEAH

A network redesign plan proposed in 2020 would dramatically increase the frequent network, more than doubling the population within wallking distance of 15 minute service.

MIAMI

CORAL GABLES

	Heavy Rail
	Peoplemover
	Bus Rapid Transit
	Commuter Rail

elevated	at grade	subway
in freeway	in street	mixed traffic

Frequent Bus

✈ airport ◯ Brightline station

5 miles

HOMESTEAD

Heavy Rail (Metrorail)
LOW PERFORMER

Opened: 1984

Last Expanded: 2012

Length: 24.3 miles

Stations: 23

Frequency: 7.5–15 min peak/midday, 15–30 min evening/weekends

Avg weekday ridership: 62,600

Ridership per mile: 2,576

BRT (Metromover)
HIGH PERFORMER

Opened: 1986

Last Expanded: 1996

Length: 3.5 miles

Stations: 20

Frequency: 1.5 min peak, 3 min off-peak

Avg weekday ridership: 31,800

Ridership per mile: 9,086

Diesel Commuter Rail (TriRail)

Opened: 1989

Last Expanded: 1998

Length: 70.9 miles

Stations: 18

Frequency: 20–30 min peak; 1 hr midday/evening/weekend

Avg weekday ridership: 14,800

Ridership per mile: 209

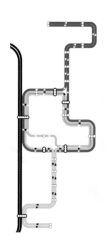

Metrorail stops at the edge of downtown Miami (below), and the MetroMover (above right) goes right into the heart of it. It is the only place in the United States where a major urban rail system relies on a downtown circulator to distribute riders. The central loop serves most downtown office buildings, the government complex, and Miami College (above left). The northern and southern extensions connect to areas of hotels and high-rise condos. Another connection was created in 2018: the nine-acre MiamiCentral development (in yellow), alongside MetroRail and Metromover, includes three-million square feet of residential, office, commercial, and retail development as well as the Miami terminus of Brightline, a privately funded intercity passenger rail line to Palm Beach and eventually Orlando, and possible future commuter rail.

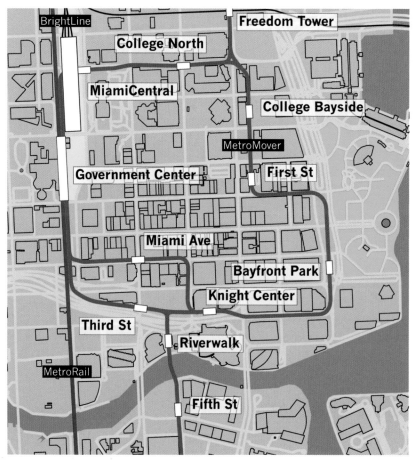

Miami activists worry about "climate gentrification": many of the low-income neighborhoods near downtown, relatively well-served by transit, are on (comparatively) high ground and could become more attractive for development as coastal parcels are threatened by sea-level rise.

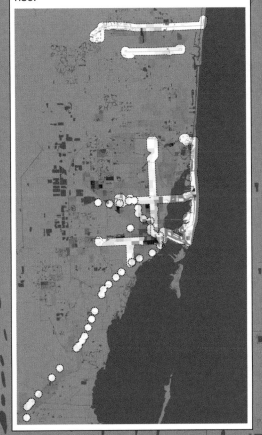

GAP: Commuter rail misses downtowns

DOWNTOWN FORT LAUDERDALE
58,216 jobs
99th in US

DOWNTOWN MIAMI
188,003 jobs
16th in US

GAP: Frequent network misses many dense neighborhoods

1/2 mile distance to frequent rail/BRT
1/2 mile distance to frequent bus

population density (people per sq. mi.)

2500 5000 7500 10000 12500 15000 17500

employment density (jobs per sq. mi.)

15000 30000 45000 60000

college campus (100 U.S. largest)

11. ATLANTA

Atlanta–Athens-Clarke County–Sandy Springs, GA

population 6,853,392 (11th)   **served by frequent transit** 5%   **daily trips per 1000** 52

MARTA
independent agency
Heavy Rail
Frequent Bus

Atlanta Streetcar
municipal
Streetcar

In the 1970s, Atlanta was deliberately reinventing itself into a national and global hub that now has the country's third-largest concentration of Fortune 500 companies, the broadcast headquarters of one of the world's largest news organizations, and a major international airline hub. Major public works were integral to that transformation, supporting the city's growth and serving as visible symbols of its new status. In 1974, work began on a world-class convention venue. In 1977–80, the airport was completely rebuilt with innovative midfield terminals connected by a peoplemover. A new rail-transit system was part of the same vision.

Ground was broken for MARTA in 1975. It was the first modern rail-transit system in the Southeast, built when rail was still a Northeast and West Coast phenomenon. It used essentially the same technology (including air-conditioned aluminum cars and an automatic train-control system) as San Francisco's BART, which had been operating for only three years, and Washington's Metrorail, which would open the following year. Like BART and Metrorail, MARTA was intended to move suburban commuters quickly and comfortably to downtown jobs. Twenty-four of 38 stations have a total of 25,000 parking spaces. With station spacing of over a mile, trip times beat congested highways. Crowds of commuters getting off at Peachtree Center each morning, and the office buildings that have sprung up around MARTA stations in Uptown, show the system's success. Unlike BART and METRO, MARTA was designed from the start as an integral part of the city's bus system, which is operated by the same agency. A single flat fare covers the entire bus–rail system. Nearly every local bus route connects to a rail station. As a result, the rail system carries 46 percent of the region's transit trips.

From the start, MARTA was limited by regional politics. Three suburban counties chose not to join. Even today, suburbs populated by "white flight" are resistant to transit. The transit network reflects the region's segregation. Cobb County, which is 62 percent white (compared to 38 percent within the city of Atlanta), has only limited bus service and no rail. In the 1990s, the political momentum behind MARTA's expansion ran out. The last new station was opened in 2000. That left key places unconnected. Emory University, for example, is not on the rail network, and neither are many of the denser neighborhoods in the core of the city. The frequent-bus network has only a handful of routes—fewer than most similar cities—and feeds into the radial rail system rather than creating crosstown connections. The only recent rail project is a short downtown streetcar that is generally slower than walking. Today, though, Atlanta seems poised for another expansion. In 2016, voters approved city and MARTA ballot measures that will add rail stations and frequent-bus routes, build BRT and light-rail lines, including the "belt line" past Emory, that will fill gaps in the rail network in the densest parts of the region. ∎

+ **Strong heavy-rail network integrated with buses**
- **No rail to some major universities and dense neighborhoods**
- **Anti-transit suburbs**

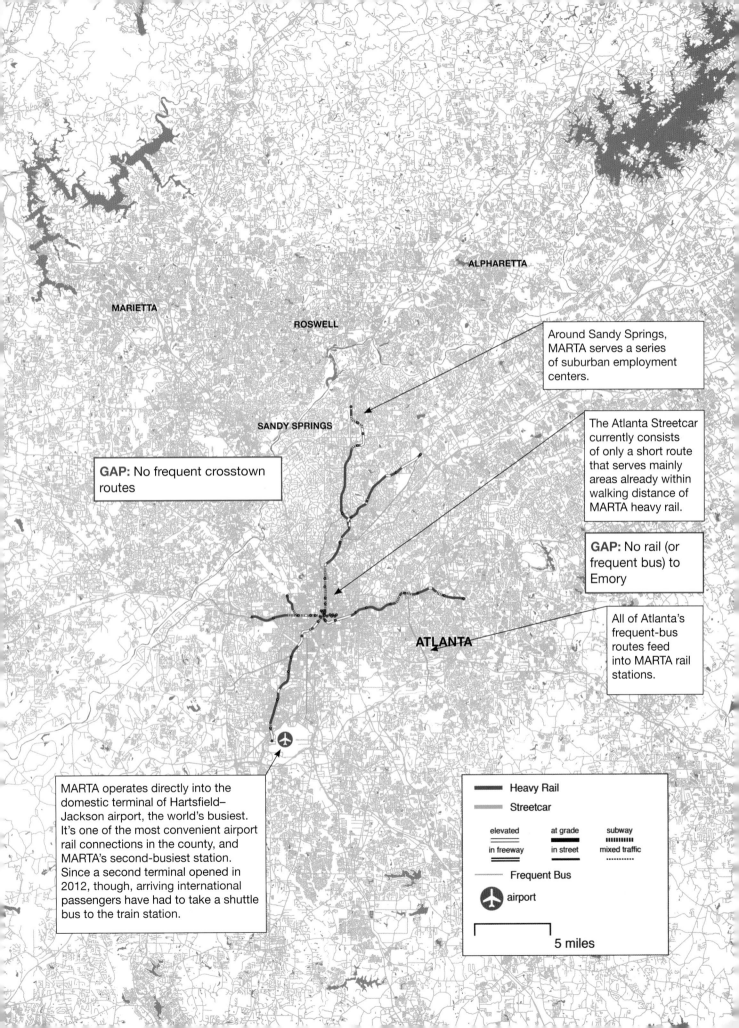

ALPHARETTA

MARIETTA

ROSWELL

Around Sandy Springs, MARTA serves a series of suburban employment centers.

SANDY SPRINGS

The Atlanta Streetcar currently consists of only a short route that serves mainly areas already within walking distance of MARTA heavy rail.

GAP: No frequent crosstown routes

GAP: No rail (or frequent bus) to Emory

All of Atlanta's frequent-bus routes feed into MARTA rail stations.

ATLANTA

MARTA operates directly into the domestic terminal of Hartsfield–Jackson airport, the world's busiest. It's one of the most convenient airport rail connections in the county, and MARTA's second-busiest station. Since a second terminal opened in 2012, though, arriving international passengers have had to take a shuttle bus to the train station.

▬▬▬	Heavy Rail
▬▬▬	Streetcar

| elevated | at grade | subway |
| in freeway | in street | mixed traffic |

▬▬▬ Frequent Bus

✈ airport

5 miles

Heavy Rail (MARTA)

Opened: 1979
Last Expanded: 2000
Length: 47.6 miles
Stations: 38
Frequency: 10 min peak, 15 min midday, 20 min nights/weekends
Avg weekday ridership: 207,700
Ridership per mile: 4,363

Streetcar (Atlanta Streetcar)

SMALL SYSTEM

LOW PERFORMER

Opened: 2014
Last Expanded: N/A
Length: 1.3 miles
Stations: 7
Frequency: 10–15 min weekdays and weekend
Avg weekday ridership: 700
Ridership per mile: 538

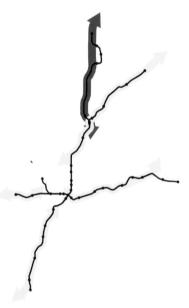

Like systems from the same era in San Francisco and Baltimore, MARTA is in a tunnel in Downtown (above) and makes extensive use of freight-rail (yellow, left) and highway (red) rights-of-way outside it. This simplifies construction and saves money, but often bypasses important destinations that don't happen to be on that highway or freight-rail line. Planners in San Francisco and Baltimore accepted that tradeoff, but planners in Atlanta made deliberate choices to leave easy paths to reach key destinations. In Decatur, the county seat of Dekalb County (below), the freight-rail line that MARTA follows is a quarter-mile away from the center of Downtown. Instead of putting the station there, MARTA built a short piece of tunnel that places the station in the center of Downtown.

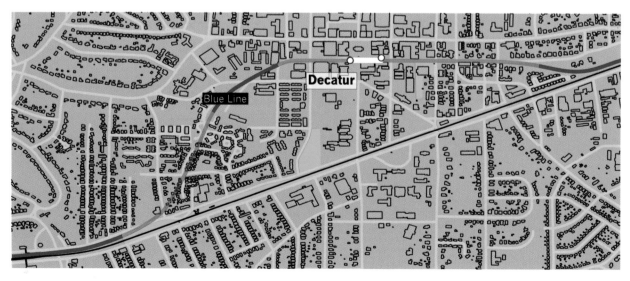

The northern end of MARTA runs through clusters of suburban job sites. These suburban areas became major employment centers partially because of the rail line, but the wide streets and empty space between buildings can be forbidding for transit riders.

MARTA CENTER - SANDY SPRINGS
89,968 jobs
51st in US

Some of the densest parts of the core—former streetcar neighborhoods—have neither rail nor frequent bus.

EMORY UNIVERSITY

MIDTOWN ATLANTA
103,767 jobs
42nd in US

GEORGIA STATE

DOWNTOWN ATLANTA
142,759 jobs

1/2 mile distance to frequent rail/BRT
1/2 mile distance to frequent bus

population density (people per sq. mi.)

2500 5000 7500 10000 12500 15000 17500

employment density (jobs per sq. mi.)

15000 30000 45000 60000

college campus (100 U.S. largest)

12. **TORONTO**

Toronto - Mississauga - Brampton - Markham - Vaughan, ON

population 5,928,040 (12th)   **served by frequent transit** 59%   **daily trips per 1000** 544

Toronto is, and always has been, a transit city. It's second only to New York among US and Canadian metro areas in transit ridership. It's the only true legacy rail system in Canada.

The Toronto Transit Commission, founded in 1921 as one of the first publicly owned transit agencies in North America, has been operating streetcars for its entire existence, and its busiest routes today were among its busiest 100 years ago.

Toronto is a peer to Chicago, Philadelphia, New York and Boston—a historic city full of dense, walkable neighborhoods surrounding a downtown that is still a center of retail and entertainment as well as employment. Like those cities, it has century-old rail lines still carrying hundreds of thousands of people every day. Unlike those cities, Toronto has been aggressively expanding transit. There has been rail expansion and upgrade work going on nearly continuously since the end of World War II. Every US city, and every other Canadian city, had a contraction of their transit systems in the 1950s and 1960s. This was followed (usually) by new starts and expansions in the 1970s and beyond. Toronto's transit system is not a surviving subset of a legacy system, or a blank sheet creation. It is the result of continuous evolution.

Toronto is also a modern city. It did not become Canada's largest city and eclipse Montreal as a financial center until well after World War II. A new postwar subway transformed Toronto's skyline. Its commuter-rail system was started more or less from scratch in the 1960s and expanded in the 70s, and 80s. It now carries more passengers than any other North American commuter-rail system except New York and Chicago. The region has the most robust suburban transit network in North America, with extensive suburban BRT, ambitious BRT and light-rail projects, plans for a transformation of

TTC
municipal
heavy rail
light rail
streetcar
frequent bus

Metrolinx
independent agency
light rail
commuter rail
frequent bus

Miway
municipal
BRT
Frequent Bus

YRT
municipal
BRT
Frequent Bus

Brampton Transit
municipal
Frequent Bus

Durham Region Transit
municipal
Frequent Bus

+ **High ridership subway, streetcar, and commuter rail networks**
+ **Highly interconnected multimodal regional system**
- **Erratic planning driven by municipal and provincial politics**

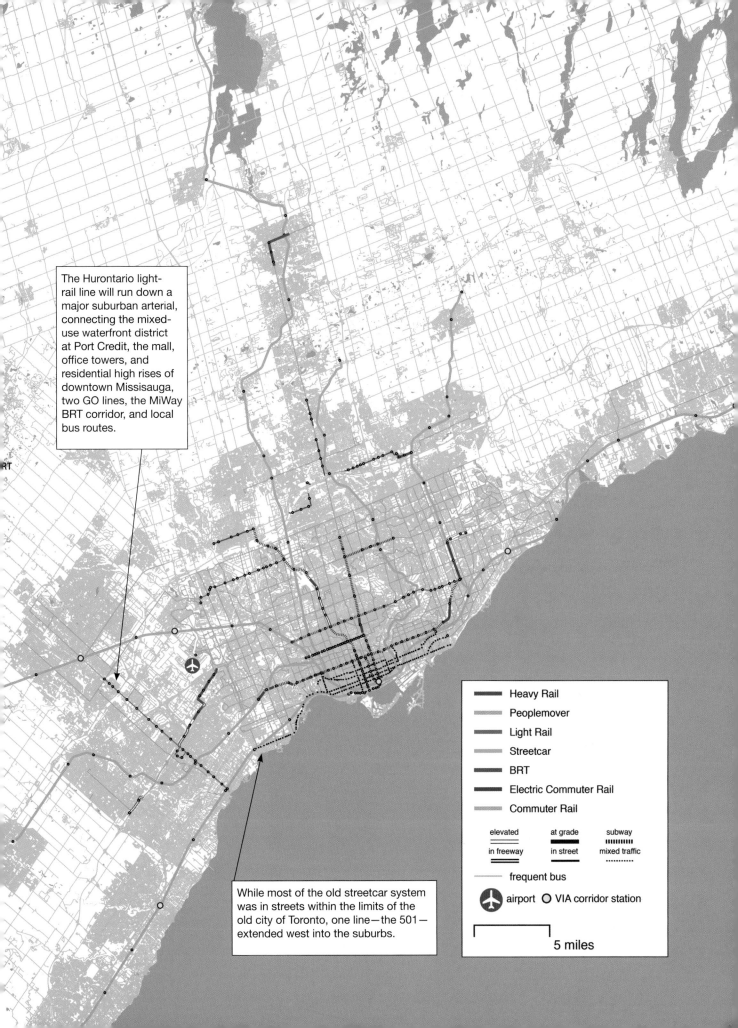

The Hurontario light-rail line will run down a major suburban arterial, connecting the mixed-use waterfront district at Port Credit, the mall, office towers, and residential high rises of downtown Missisauga, two GO lines, the MiWay BRT corridor, and local bus routes.

While most of the old streetcar system was in streets within the limits of the old city of Toronto, one line—the 501—extended west into the suburbs.

	Heavy Rail
	Peoplemover
	Light Rail
	Streetcar
	BRT
	Electric Commuter Rail
	Commuter Rail

| elevated | at grade | subway |
| in freeway | in street | mixed traffic |

frequent bus

✈ airport   ◯ VIA corridor station

5 miles

commuter rail with all-day frequent service, and a comprehensive network of frequent bus routes.

This continual investment, though, is not as orderly as it might appear. The streetcar network was nearly abandoned even as it was one of the busiest rail-transit networks in North America. Subway expansion has been approved and funded in fits and starts. Master plans have been unveiled, adopted, argued about, and cancelled. The subway is run by the city, but funded by the province, so succeeding mayors and premiers have tried to build their own vision of transit.

The political argument usually isn't about whether transit in and around Toronto should be expanded; it's about where and how. Liberal governments have often focused within the city, where ridership is highest and their political support is greatest, while conservative governments support extensions to their electoral base in the suburbs. Transit mode has also been very political. The 1972 Go-Urban plan and the 2007 Transit City plan both proposed to greatly expand the reach of the rail network by using new lower-cost technologies. But suburban conservative leaders (prominently Rob Ford, mayor of Toronto from 2010 to 2014) have argued that the suburbs also deserve real subways, even if ridership is lower, and that any technology that takes space away from cars—like street-running light rail—is unacceptable. The politics of job creation have also been prominent. The Go-Urban plan, and the Scarborough light-rail line that resulted from it, were an attempt to build a transit industry in Ontario, building jobs across the region. It's no accident that Toronto's newest subway cars, streetcars, and commuter trains were all built in Thunder Bay, Ontario.

This historic messiness is not apparent to riders. Toronto has one of the best connected transit systems on the continent. TTC bus lines and streetcars feed into the subway lines, often running directly into the stations so passengers can transfer inside the fare gates. Suburban buses connect to the subway, and the regional GO system integrates buses with commuter rail, offering all-day service across the region. A regional farecard covers trips on 11 different transit systems. Toronto has always been a transit city, and it continues to build some of the best transit in North America. ■

GO-Urban
1972

The plan: an automated "Intermediate Capacity Transit System." Only one line – (Scarborough RT) was built.

Network 2011
1985

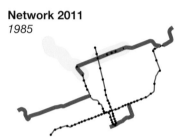

The plan: three new subway lines. Part of one line (Shepherd) was built. Instead of completing the plan, the province funded a line to the York Region.

Transit City
2007

The plan: seven new light rail lines. In 2010, new mayor Rob Ford tried to cancel all of them, but two survived with council support.

Active planning
2020

The oft-revised "Big Move" plan is for a light-rail extension (from TransitCity), subway extension, a new automated rail line (similar to Network 2011), and a subway replacing Scarborough RT.

The Toronto subway has left an indelible mark on the city. The Yonge street line created a continuous corridor of high rises through what were one- and two-story neighborhoods.

```
········· 1/2 mile distance to frequent rail/BRT
- - - - -  1/2 mile distance to frequent bus
```

population density (people per sq. mi.)

2500 5000 7500 10000 12500 15000 17500

no employment density data

The most unusual thing about Toronto transit is the streetcars. Toronto is the only city in North America that kept most of its historic streetcar network—52 miles—intact. Here it is still possible, in places like Parkdale, to see neighborhoods and commercial corridors that were built around streetcars a century ago and still have streetcars full of people gliding through them. It's a bit of a time capsule, full of archaic features like end-of-the-line loops and boarding from the street. It is an essential part of Toronto. The streetcars are the busiest surface routes in Toronto, with 468,800 boardings on an average weekday. That's more than any light-rail system in North America.

In downtown, there are four busy east-west streetcar lines in the space of one mile: King, Queen, Dundas, and College. Each connects to two subway stations.

On Queen Street (right), a streetcar is scheduled every four minutes at rush hour, running in traffic as it always has, with passengers boarding from the street.

The essence of Toronto streetcars is in the neighborhoods. At Broadview and Gerard (below), two double-track lines cross, with connecting tracks in three of the four quadrants. Streetcars squeal around the curves in front of a streetscape that exemplifies both the city's historic fabric and its diverse population. Nearby, streetcars photogenically run above the green slopes of Riverdale Park. West of Broadview, the streetcars run through typical streetcar suburbs—single-family residential neighborhoods, with scattered commercial enterprises, built around the lines (bottom). Streetcars have been making the same rounds since the 1910s.

Streetcar (TTC)

VERY LARGE SYSTEM

PREWAR SYSTEM

VERY HIGH PERFORMER

Opened: 1892
Last Expanded: 2016
Length: 52 miles
Stations: 685
Frequency: 4-10 min all day
Avg weekday ridership: 530,600
Ridership per mile: 10,204

The TTC streetcar system is the high-ridership core of Toronto's prewar network (right). While some lower ridership routes—particularly in northwest Toronto-were replaced by bus—TTC kept running the streetcars on the busiest lines, where they efficiently handle large crowds. Like many European cities, Toronto saw the subway as an upgrade of the streetcar, replacing streetcars on Yonge and Bloor and creating new connections for other routes. The plan was to ultimately replace streetcars entirely. But in 1972, after a successful campaign by local transit advocates, the TTC board voted to retain streetcars.

In the 1980s, the TTC began expanding the streetcars. The first new line, opened in 1990, was Harbourfront (below). In 1997, it was extended two miles up Spadina in dedicated lanes in the center of the street, replacing a bus line that had replaced a street line in 1948. The Spadina route crosses four other streetcar lines and, at its north end, it connects to both Toronto subway lines at Spadina Station. The Spadina Station streetcar terminal is underground, with a short tunnel leading into it. After Spadina, the TTC focused on the St. Clair line. This 4.3 mile line had been operating in mixed traffic since the 1930s Between 2005 and 2010 it was rebuilt with dedicated lanes in the street median (above). It connects twice to subway line 1.

TTC is also doing simpler upgrades to make streetcars more reliable. Some lines have new boarding platforms. A pilot project in 2017 severely restricted car traffic and created safe boarding areas for passengers on the busiest line, King Street. The changes have been made permanent.

1950

1978

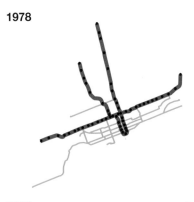

2020

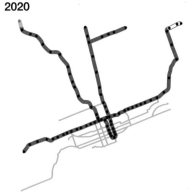

The subway has become an integral part of the life of Toronto, even creating a second downtown where the 1 and 2 lines cross at Bloor-Yonge. At 47 miles, the subway is not unusually long — less than half the size of San Francisco's BART or DC's Metrorail. But at 1.58 million boardings a day, the Toronto subway carries more people a day than any US rail system other than the New York City subway, or San Francisco's BART and Metrorail combined. Its newest trains are open gangway, like all modern subways should be. Nearly the entire subway is underground (right), but some of the older sections were built in open trenches — parallel to, not under, the street — and some remains visible above ground (above).

Most of the subway is in the old city of Toronto. At the outer ends, it connects to suburban transit. At Kennedy the subway meets the Scarborough RT, now called Line 3. Intended as a cheaper way to extend to the suburbs, it was designed as a grade-separated streetcar line. But it was built using ICTS automated technology developed by the Urban Transportation Development Corporation, which was owned by the province of Ontario (though it was later privatized) and provided politically valuable jobs. That same technology proved to be very successful in Vancouver, but it has not been used again in Toronto. Instead, politicians have pushed for full-sized subways because they're perceived as better, and the subway has been expended north into car-oriented suburbs. The current plan to replace the aging Line 3 is a full underground subway. This would end at Scarborough Centre, a shopping mall and civic complex that serves as the heart of Scarborough, a once independent city amalgamated into Toronto in 1998. These suburban downtowns, often very well served by transit, are a distinctive feature of the Toronto region.

Heavy Rail (Subway)

VERY HIGH PERFORMER

Opened: 1954
Last Expanded: 2017
Length: 43.8 miles
Stations: 70
Frequency: 2-5 min
Avg weekday ridership: 1,557,700
Ridership per mile: 35,564

The subway is fully integrated with the streetcars and buses. Toronto's transit system is a grid — buses and streetcars run east-west or north-south. Nearly every route intersects the subway (above). Stations are built to make transfers convenient and comfortable. Many stations feature aboveground bus loops like the one at Spadina (below), with the buses stopping directly at the station entry pavilions. Most of the streetcar lines terminate at similar loops. St. Clair West has an unusual below-ground loop (bottom). While it's underground, it's not a conventional subway station under the street, but a loop of track around an underground platform beside the street. Streetcars enter the subway, make a 90-degree turn to enter the loop, circle the loop, and then head back out into the street. Diesel buses use the same loop. Opened in 1978 with the subway station, it's a curious hybrid between a traditional streetcar loop and heavy infrastructure that offers passengers very fast and convenient connections. There is nothing else like this in North America.

Heavy Rail (Scarborough RT)

**HIGH PERFORMER
SMALL SYSTEM**

Opened: 1985
Last Expanded: N/A
Length: 4 miles
Stations: 6
Frequency: 4-6 min
Avg weekday ridership: 44,600
Ridership per mile: 11,150

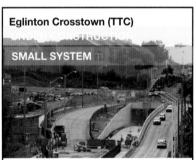

Eglinton Crosstown (TTC)

UNDER CONSTRUCTION

SMALL SYSTEM

Opened: 2022
Last Expanded: N/A
Length: 12 miles in construction
Stations: 25 in construction

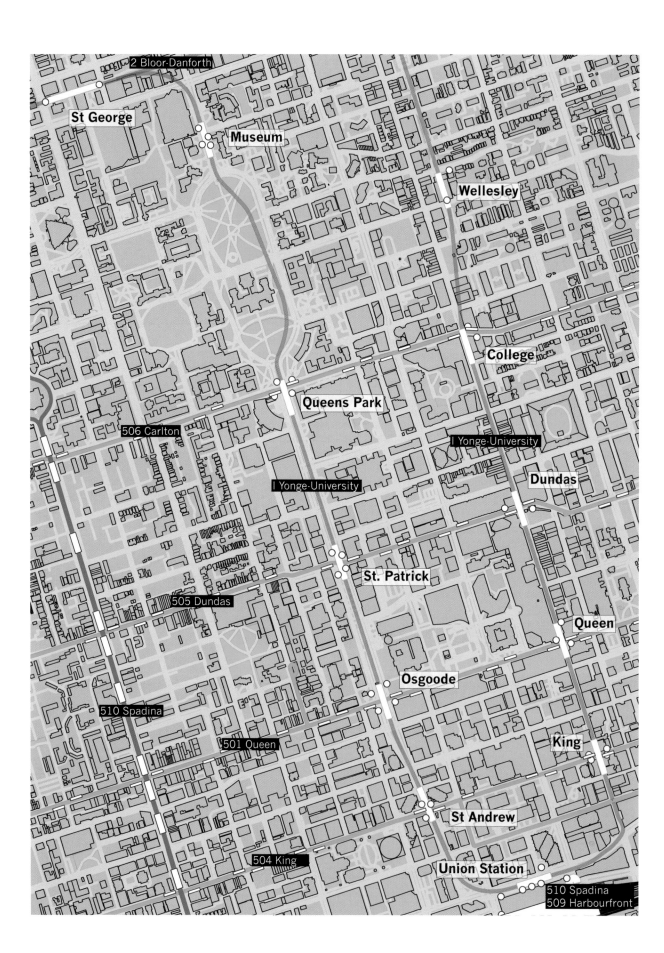

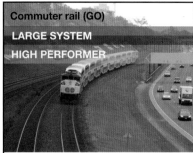

Commuter rail (GO)

LARGE SYSTEM

HIGH PERFORMER

Opened: 1967
Last Expanded: 2019
Length: 314.2 miles (2.2 in construction)
Stations: 68 (1 in construction)
Frequency: up to 30 min all-day; some lines are peak only
Avg weekday ridership: 230,500
Ridership per mile: 701

Union Station at the foot of downtown (left) near the shore of Lake Ontario, is the largest train station in Canada. With 16 tracks, it is the hub of both the regional GO Transit commuter-rail system and the national Via Rail system. West of the station, an underpass (below) simplifies the flow of trains into the station from the branching routes and from a Go Transit storage yard. Union Station has two underground stations: a subway station on the north side with a daily ridership of 143,640 people, and an underground streetcar station on the south side whose single platform is located on an alarmingly tight turning loop.

Union Station is also the downtown terminus for the Union Pearson Express. While it shares most of its tracks with GO Transit, it was conceived as a separate service, operated by a different division of the regional transit agency. The UP Express was targeted at a premium business travel market with only two stops (both with subway and GO transfers) between Union Station and the airport. Fares were $27 one way. This proved a failure, attracting only 2,000 riders a day (rather than the projected 5,000) at a subsidy of over $50 a ride. A fare reduction to $12 ($9 with a regional transit card) in 2016 increased ridership dramatically, to 10,000 passengers a day. The DMU trains reach the airport on a two-mile elevated spur (above) that branches from a GO line and connects directly to the terminal.

DMU Commuter rail (Union Pearson Express)

SMALL SYSTEM

HIGH PERFORMER

Opened: 2015
Last Expanded: N/A
Length: 14.5 miles
Stations: 4
Frequency: 15 min
Avg weekday ridership: 10,091
Ridership per mile: 696

Light Rail (Hurontario)
UNDER CONSTRUCTION
SMALL SYSTEM

Open: 2024
Last Expanded: N/A
Length: 11.2 miles under construction
Stations: 19 under construction

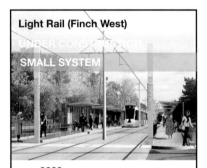

Light Rail (Finch West)
UNDER CONSTRUCTION
SMALL SYSTEM

Open: 2023
Last Expanded: N/A
Length: 6.8 miles under construction
Stations: 18 under construction

The Go Transit network, operated by Metrolinx, the regional transit agency, links the city to Greater Toronto. In many ways, it created the template for modern commuter rail in North America. It was the first new system after World War II, the first designed around park-and-ride lots, and the first to use the now ubiquitous Bombardier double deck cars. It's also typical in offering very limited off-peak commuter rail service, except for the Lakeshore line, which has trains every 15-30 minutes. But GO is reimagining commuter rail as regional rail. The regional plan calls for all day service at 15 minute frequencies on five lines using electric equipment.

GO Transit is more than a commuter-rail system – 61,000 of its 276,000 weekday boardings are on an extensive regional express-bus system. While many of these routes radiate out from Union Station downtown, GO also offers significant suburb-to-suburb service, connecting to other GO routes and local transit at hubs like Square One in the downtown of the suburb of Mississauga (below.)

Current service

Plans call for electric trains and all-day, seven-days-a-week frequent service on many GO lines. The agency now owns much of its own track, including almost 12 miles of dedi]cated track alongside freight track in the east. Most freight bypasses the core.

GO Expansion plan

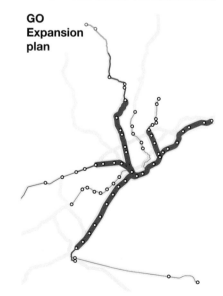

■ 15 min
■ 30 min
— 60 min
— some off-peak
----- peak only
▨ GO owned

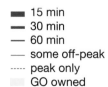

BRT (Mississauga Transitway)

Opened: 2014
Last Expanded: 2017
Length: Open BRT (7.4 guideway miles)
Stations: 9 (guideway only)
Frequency: at least every 15 min; more frequent peak

Toronto's suburban transit networks are extensive and busy. TTC ends at the Toronto city line; beyond that is the domain of Miway (serving Mississauga, pop. 721,599), YRT (Serving York Region, pop. 1,109,909), and Brampton Transit (pop. 593,638). All of these systems have over 100,000 boardings per day.

Two of these suburban networks have built high-quality BRT. Miway's Mississauga Transitway operates as a freeway express service west of the Square One transit hub, then uses an elevated busway. Central Parkway (above) is an elevated station, resembling heavy rail in everything but the rubber tires. From here, it takes its own grade-separated path through suburban office parks. The transitway hosts all-stops BRT service and express buses. Stations are designed with passing lanes so the express busses can pass through without stopping.

To the north of Toronto, York Region Transit is developing an extensive BRT network branded as Viva. Most of these lines are in the median of suburban arterials. The pink and purple lines, for example, have three miles of center-running bus-only lanes on Highway 7. At Enterprise Boulevard (below left), the lines follow a new transitway through the middle of a massive mixed-use development. Further to the west, where highway 7 turns into a grade-separated freeway, the buses run on the shoulders (below right). Viva connects to the Toronto subway at Vaughn Metropolitan Centre (which has a large BRT stop immediately outside the subway station) and at Finch, though the Finch line is still in mixed traffic. It also meets three GO lines. Toronto's suburban transit system continues to expand. One of three new light rail lines being built by Metrolinx is a north-south line on Hurontario in Mississauga and Brampton, connecting to Miway BRT and GO trains.

BRT (Viva)

LARGE SYSTEM

Opened: 2011
Last Expanded: 2020
Length: 52.2 miles (20.9 guideway miles)
Stations: 33 (guideway only)
Frequency: varies from every 15 minutes to peak only

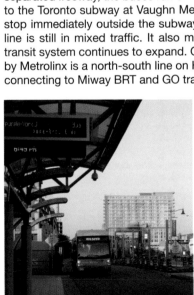

13. DETROIT

Detroit–Warren–Ann Arbor, MI

population 5,341,994 (13th)   **served by frequent transit** 8%   **daily trips per 1000** 27

Detroit's rail-transit history reads like a comedy. It has had four rail-transit systems in the modern era, only one of which was more than four miles long, and two of which are now gone. In 1974, the regional transit authority started funding commuter rail, but that was discontinued in 1983. In 1976, the city built a downtown streetcar line but that was abandoned by 2003. In 1987, the city opened a three-mile downtown peoplemover loop, but that was never expanded. A plan for a nine-mile light-rail line made it as far as environmental studies, but in 2011 the federal government pulled the funding in favor of a bus-rapid-transit plan that then fizzled, leaving a short streetcar line.

This series of stops and starts and token projects is part of a larger transit tragedy. The Detroit metropolitan area is actually relatively wealthy—its average household income of $49,000 exceeds that of Austin, Salt Lake City, or Dallas—but the city's median income is only $26,000, and a third of families are below the poverty line. The city's population has dropped for seven decades in a row and in 2021 was at only 36 percent of what it was in the 1950s. This dramatic decline is a testament to white flight, disinvestment, and economic segregation. Eighty-three percent of city residents are African American in a metropolitan area that is 70 percent white. The city of Detroit is poor not because of a lack of economic activity or money; it is poor because economic activity has been moved to suburbs and they do not want to share their wealth with the city.

This economic and racial segregation is directly reflected in the transit system. Detroit DOT buses serve city residents. The state-chartered regional transit authority, reorganized in 1989 to exclude the city and renamed SMART (Suburban Mobility Authority for Regional Transportation), runs bus service from the suburbs into the city, but within city limits SMART buses are drop-off-only in the morning and pick-up-only the afternoon, ensuring that city residents can't use them. Following decades of city financial trouble (and bankruptcy in 2013), DDOT only operates 40 percent as much service as it did in 1991. Detroit residents—in a city where 26 percent of households are carless—badly need access to jobs outside the city, but suburban interests have worked hard to prevent regional transit. The streetcar and the peoplemover are not useless, and the Detroit bus system isn't horrible either. But these are not nearly enough to help the city's residents get access to the opportunities they need. ■

- No regional express-transit network
- No regional integration
- Token downtown streetcar and peoplemover

M-1
private non-profit
Streetcar

DDOT
municipal
Frequent Bus

SMART
independent agency
Frequent Bus

Peoplemover (Detroit People Mover)

Opened: 1987
Last Expanded: N/A
Length: 1.5 miles
Stations: 6.5
Frequency: 3–5 min
Avg weekday ridership: 4,300
Ridership per mile: 2,867

Streetcar (Q-Line)

Opened: 2017
Last Expanded: N/A
Length: 3.3 miles
Stations: 12
Frequency: roughly 15 min
Avg weekday ridership: 2,490
Ridership per mile: 755

GAP: No rail/BRT on Woodward

GAP: Integration of urban and suburban transit networks

TROY

WARREN

LIVONIA

Peoplemover

Streetcar

elevated · at grade · subway

in freeway · in street · mixed traffic

frequent bus

airport ○ Amtrak corridor station

5 miles

DEARBORN

DETROIT

At 8 Mile Road, Detroit DOT buses reach city limits, and riders are forced to transfer to SMART buses.

Despite massive service cuts, Detroit DOT has maintained frequent service in key corridors.

WEST MALL AREA, TROY
63,884 jobs
88th in US

Woodward Avenue connects two job centers within Detroit—Downtown, and New Center—and extends out to suburban jobs.

MIDTOWN DETROIT
72,911 jobs
75th in US

1/2 mile distance to frequent rail/BRT
1/2 mile distance to frequent bus

population density (people per sq. mi.)

2500 5000 7500 10000 12500 15000 17500

employment density (jobs per sq. mi.)

15000 30000 45000 60000

college campus (100 U.S. largest)

The peoplemover system is limited to Downtown; the highest ridership days are special events like the Detroit Auto Show.

DOWNTOWN DETROIT
78,144 jobs
71st in US

14. PHOENIX

Phoenix–Mesa–Scottsdale, AZ

population 5,002,221 (14th)　　**served by frequent transit** 14%　　**daily trips per 1000** 39

Valley Metro
independent agency
Light Rail
Frequent Bus

Tempe Orbit
municipal
Frequent Bus

In the 2000s, Phoenix, a car-oriented city long hostile to transit, decided to build a light-rail line. The first line opened in 2008 to higher-than-expected ridership, and has been steadily expanding since. This is a familiar story, similar to Denver, Dallas, or Salt Lake City. On the ground, though, Phoenix's system is fundamentally different than the typical modern light-rail line. Nearly all of the first 20-mile line, as well as the extensions, run at grade down city streets. Phoenix is not building a light-rail express service to the suburbs, but rather a light-rail spine for its local transit network.

The light-rail line connects multiple activity centers. In downtown, it serves the cluster of office high-rises (relatively small for a city its size), the convention center, and the baseball stadium. From there it extends north to Uptown (another cluster of office buildings, below) past two major hospitals, through mixed single-family and multifamily neighborhoods, and past a major mall to the current terminus seven miles from downtown. In the other direction, the line extends east from downtown, passing the airport (with a convenient connection to the airport peoplemover system) on its way to Tempe, home of Arizona State University. It stops in downtown Tempe, then crosses through the campus and continues east (right) to the small-but-active mixed-use downtown of Tempe. There is parking at eight of the 35 stations, but every station is fundamentally walkable, integrated in the urban fabric. Seventy-five percent of rail riders walk to the train.

Phoenix is not fundamentally transit-friendly—it is a car-oriented city with a relatively small downtown. But its light-rail line (and the planned expansions) does an excellent job of putting transit where it can do the most good. ∎

+ **Light-rail line connecting major activity centers and dense neighborhoods**
– **Disconnected frequent-bus network**

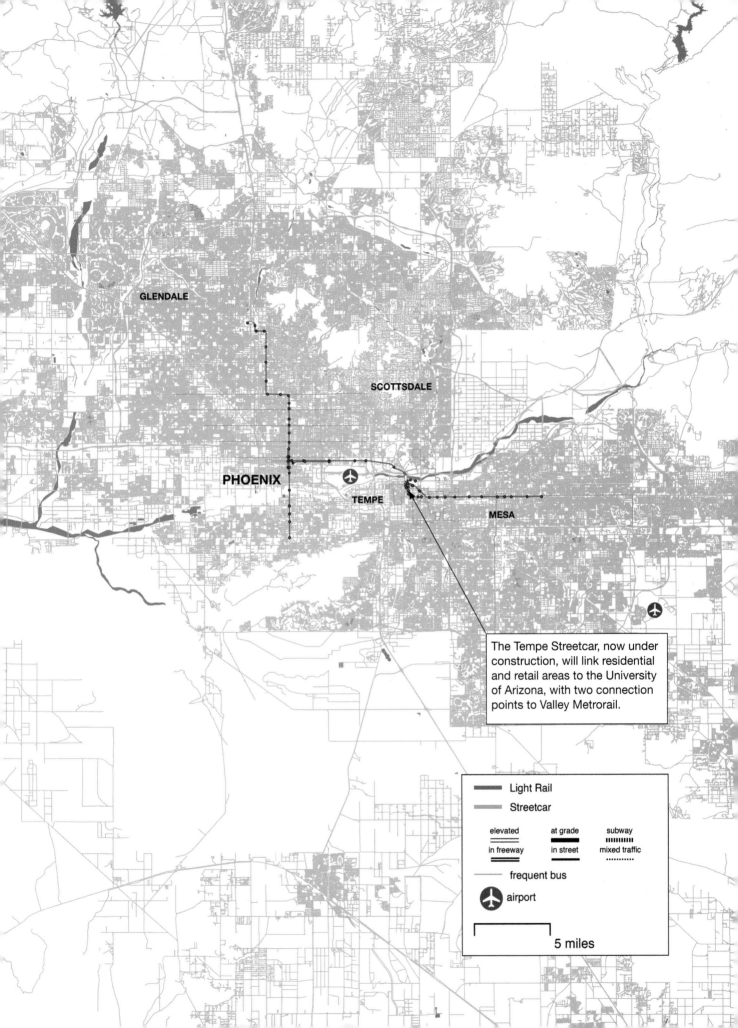

The Tempe Streetcar, now under construction, will link residential and retail areas to the University of Arizona, with two connection points to Valley Metrorail.

GLENDALE

SCOTTSDALE

PHOENIX

TEMPE

MESA

| | Light Rail |
| | Streetcar |

elevated	at grade	subway
in freeway	in street	mixed traffic
frequent bus		
airport		

5 miles

Light Rail (Valley Metro Rail)

Opened: 2008
Last Expanded: ongoing
Length: 28.5 miles (7.1 in construction)
Stations: 38 (10 in construction)
Frequency: 12 min peak/midday, 20 min evening, 15–20 min weekend
Avg weekday ridership: 47,000
Ridership per mile: 1,649

Streetcar (Tempe Streetcar)

UNDER CONSTRUCTION

Opened: 2021
Last Expanded: N/A
Length: 0 miles (3.4 under construction)
Stations: 0 (11 under construction)
Frequency: TBD
Avg weekday ridership: N/A
Ridership per mile: N/A

Arizona State University is a major destination for Valley Metrorail. Stu- dents are heavy light-rail users, with 17 percent of riders on the light rail going to the college. The light-rail line stops directly next to campus at the Tempe Transit Center (above), which also enables transfers to Tempe's Orbit bus systems (right). Next to the university, light rail stops directly on Mill Avenue, the center of downtown Mesa's office-and-retail district (below). The airport and downtown Phoenix are visible in the distance.

Planning is underway for a line heading west from Downtown, serving the state capitol and clusters of residential density along I-10. Although this will be the first freeway-light-rail alignment in Phoenix, it will still be pedestrian-focused; only 2 of 11 stations will have parking.

Scottsdale, an affluent city bordering Phoenix, operates its own transit system, linked to the rest of the region only by infrequent bus. Scottsdale City Council has repeatedly turned down light-rail plans, continuing that relative transit isolation.

GAP: Connections to Scottsdale

ARIZONA STATE

The residential density in Tempe and Mesa includes many apartments rented by students.

NORTH DOWNTOWN PHOENIX
79,551 jobs
68th in US

DOWNTOWN PHOENIX
107,859 jobs
39th in US

DOWNTOWN TEMPE
76,936 jobs
73rd in US

Phoenix has been expanding its frequent network, often by having higher-frequency service in the higher-ridership middle section of crosstown routes. But that service often falls just short of concentrations of low-income residents on the west side.

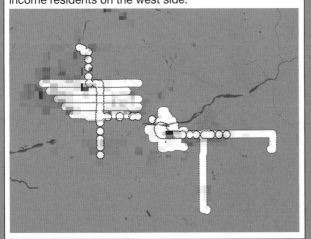

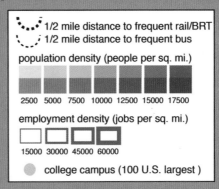

..... 1/2 mile distance to frequent rail/BRT
----- 1/2 mile distance to frequent bus

population density (people per sq. mi.)

2500 5000 7500 10000 12500 15000 17500

employment density (jobs per sq. mi.)

15000 30000 45000 60000

college campus (100 U.S. largest)

15. SEATTLE

Seattle–Tacoma, WA

population 4,903,675 (15th)   **served by frequent transit** 23%   **daily trips per 1000** 127

Sound Transit
independent agency
Light Rail
Streetcar
Commuter Rail
Frequent Bus

Seattle Streetcar
municipal
Streetcar

King County Metro
county
Frequent Bus

Community Transit
independent agency
Frequent Bus

In the twenty-first century, no other US city has committed to transit as dramatically as Seattle. In 2016, even as construction was still underway on projects approved by a 2008 ballot measure, voters approved a $53.8-billion transit expansion plan, backed by bonds and new taxes. That commitment is reflected on the ground, too, with new bus-priority lanes, redesigned bus networks tying into new light-rail stations, a regional fare card across seven transit operators, and new mixed-use centers built around transit. As transit agencies across the country lost ridership in 2017, Seattle increased both light-rail and bus ridership. By 2040, Seattle will have one of the largest—and likely most effective—regional rail networks in the country, with two light-rail subways crossing downtown and extending outwards to the dense core of Seattle, to older downtowns like Everett and Tacoma, and new employment centers in Bellevue and Redmond.

All of this is happening in a city that was already one of the most transit-friendly in the country. In 2015—before light rail opened to the university—the Seattle metro area already had per capita ridership on par with Boston and Philadelphia. In the neighborhoods of central Seattle, riding the bus is a normal part of life, and, thanks to decades of investment in HOV lanes, transit centers, and park-and-rides, suburban residents who work in Seattle are heavy transit users too. Only 30 percent of downtown Seattle employees drive to work alone; 47 percent use transit. From 2010 to 2016, downtown Seattle gained 45,000 jobs, and 95 percent of the added commute trips were handled by transit, biking, or walking.

Seattle's light-rail expansion builds on a transit network that had already been built up over decades. Light-rail trains and buses currently run through downtown in a tunnel opened in 1990 for commuter buses (though the buses will be evicted as rail expands). South of downtown (below), light-rail tracks parallel a busway. Across Lake Washington, freeway HOV lanes that have been carrying buses since 1989 are being converted to light rail, and trains will stop at the same transit centers that are already serving bus commuters. ■

+ **Regional light-rail network connecting major activity centers**
+ **Good frequent bus network**
− **Ineffective streetcars**

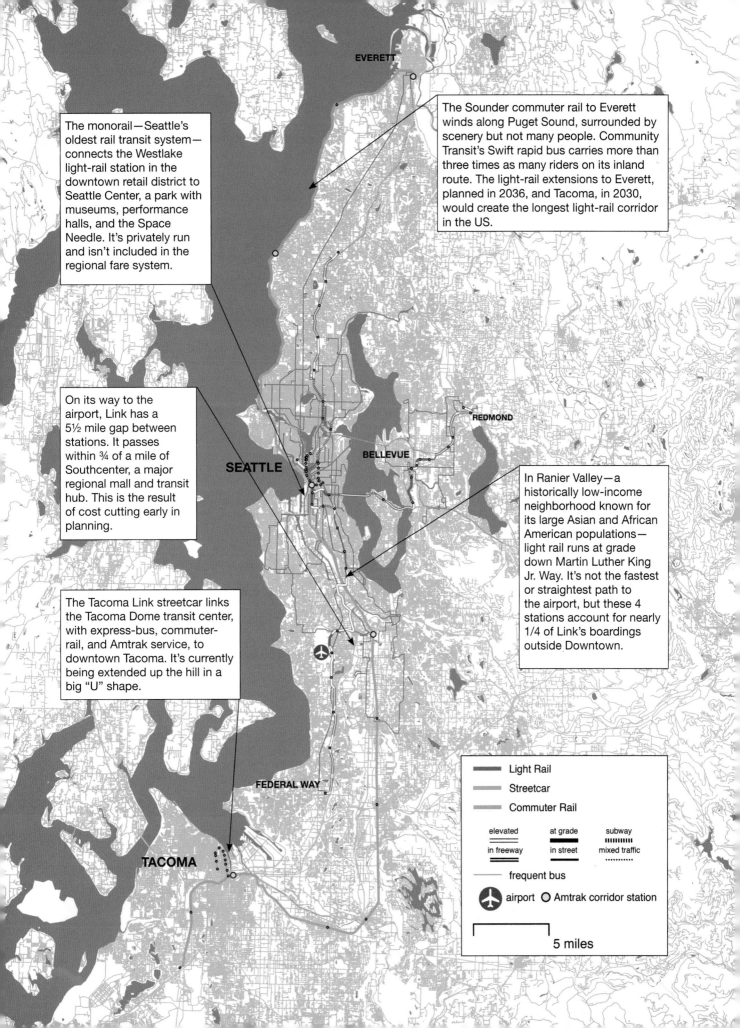

EVERETT

The Sounder commuter rail to Everett winds along Puget Sound, surrounded by scenery but not many people. Community Transit's Swift rapid bus carries more than three times as many riders on its inland route. The light-rail extensions to Everett, planned in 2036, and Tacoma, in 2030, would create the longest light-rail corridor in the US.

The monorail—Seattle's oldest rail transit system—connects the Westlake light-rail station in the downtown retail district to Seattle Center, a park with museums, performance halls, and the Space Needle. It's privately run and isn't included in the regional fare system.

On its way to the airport, Link has a 5½ mile gap between stations. It passes within ¾ of a mile of Southcenter, a major regional mall and transit hub. This is the result of cost cutting early in planning.

SEATTLE

REDMOND

BELLEVUE

In Ranier Valley—a historically low-income neighborhood known for its large Asian and African American populations—light rail runs at grade down Martin Luther King Jr. Way. It's not the fastest or straightest path to the airport, but these 4 stations account for nearly 1/4 of Link's boardings outside Downtown.

The Tacoma Link streetcar links the Tacoma Dome transit center, with express-bus, commuter-rail, and Amtrak service, to downtown Tacoma. It's currently being extended up the hill in a big "U" shape.

FEDERAL WAY

TACOMA

Light Rail
Streetcar
Commuter Rail

elevated   at grade   subway
in freeway   in street   mixed traffic

frequent bus

✈ airport   ◯ Amtrak corridor station

5 miles

Light Rail (Link)

LARGE SYSTEM

HIGH PERFORMER

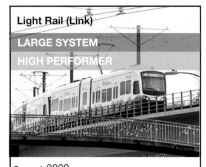

Opened: 2009
Last Expanded: ongoing
Length: 20.4 miles (38 in construction)
Stations: 16 (22 in construction)
Frequency: 6 min peak, 10 min midday, 15 min evening, 10–15 min weekend
Avg weekday ridership: 80,091
Ridership per mile: 3,926

Commuter Rail (Sounder)

Opened: 2000
Last Expanded: ongoing
Length: 83 miles
Stations: 12
Frequency: 4–13 trains each way a day (rush hour only, no weekend service)
Avg weekday ridership: 17,900
Ridership per mile: 216

Streetcar (Tacoma Link)

HIGH PERFORMER

Opened: 2003
Last Expanded: ongoing
Length: 1.6 miles (2.4 in construction)
Stations: 6 (6 in construction)
Frequency: 12 min peak/midday, 24 min evenings, 12–24 min weekends
Avg weekday ridership: 3,109
Ridership per mile: 1,943

The original Sound Transit plan in 1996 included Sounder, a north–south commuter-rail line. Because it shares track with BNSF freight trains, including a critical tunnel under downtown Seattle (above), its service is limited, with four daily round trips to the north and 13 to the south. Express bus (below left) is a more important part of the regional network, and light rail will eventually serve the same places as commuter rail with much more frequent service, using extensive grade separation (below right) for speed and capacity. That does not mean avoiding dense centers. In Bellevue (bottom), light rail will tunnel to serve the high-rises of downtown, then emerge to run through Bel-Red, a low-rise industrial area with dense residential, office, and retail.

BEL-RED

DOWNTOWN BELLEVUE

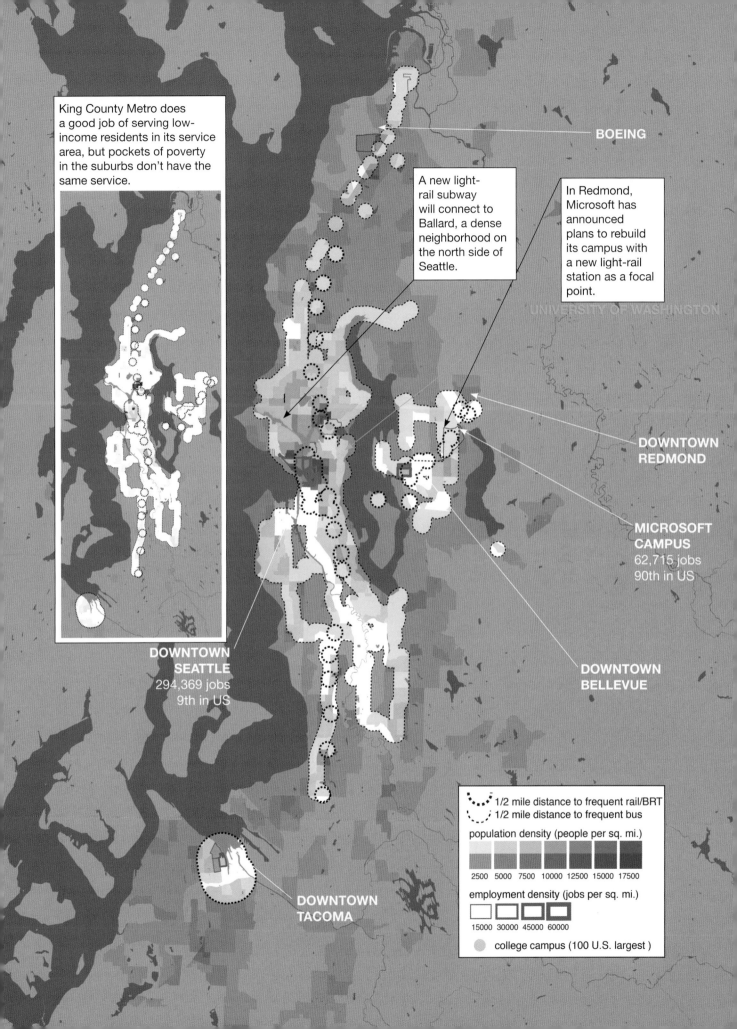

King County Metro does a good job of serving low-income residents in its service area, but pockets of poverty in the suburbs don't have the same service.

BOEING

A new light-rail subway will connect to Ballard, a dense neighborhood on the north side of Seattle.

In Redmond, Microsoft has announced plans to rebuild its campus with a new light-rail station as a focal point.

UNIVERSITY OF WASHINGTON

DOWNTOWN REDMOND

MICROSOFT CAMPUS
62,715 jobs
90th in US

DOWNTOWN BELLEVUE

DOWNTOWN SEATTLE
294,369 jobs
9th in US

DOWNTOWN TACOMA

1/2 mile distance to frequent rail/BRT
1/2 mile distance to frequent bus

population density (people per sq. mi.)

2500 5000 7500 10000 12500 15000 17500

employment density (jobs per sq. mi.)

15000 30000 45000 60000

college campus (100 U.S. largest)

The heart of Seattle transit network is in downtown (opposite). The Transit Tunnel (left) carries trains (and formerly buses as well) under the city's employment, retail, and cultural hubs. Above it, Third Avenue (above) is limited to transit only during rush hour, with local buses and RapidRide limited-stop routes. To the north of downtown, light rail tunnels into the heart of Capitol Hill (below on its way to the University of Washington). The trip from downtown to the university, once 25 minutes by bus, is now four minutes by train. Two streetcar lines connect to light rail. One serves First Hill and its hospitals and the other (bottom) serves the redeveloped South Lake Union area, headquarters of Amazon. Both run frequently, but unlike the light rail, they are slow, no faster than buses and sometimes slower than walking. Recent signal improvements and transit-only lanes, though, have helped the South Lake Union Line, and proposed new tracks through downtown connecting the two (and eliminating transfers for many downtown-bound riders) would have transit-only lanes.

Monorail (Seattle Monorail)

Opened: 1962
Last Expanded: N/A
Length: 1.2 miles
Stations: 2
Frequency: 10 min
Avg weekday ridership: 4,780
Ridership per mile: 3,983

Streetcar (Seattle Streetcar)

HIGH PERFORMER

Opened: 2007
Last Expanded: 2016
Length: 3.8 miles
Stations: 17
Frequency: 10 min peak/midday, 15 min nights/weekends
Avg weekday ridership: 6,000
Ridership per mile: 1,579

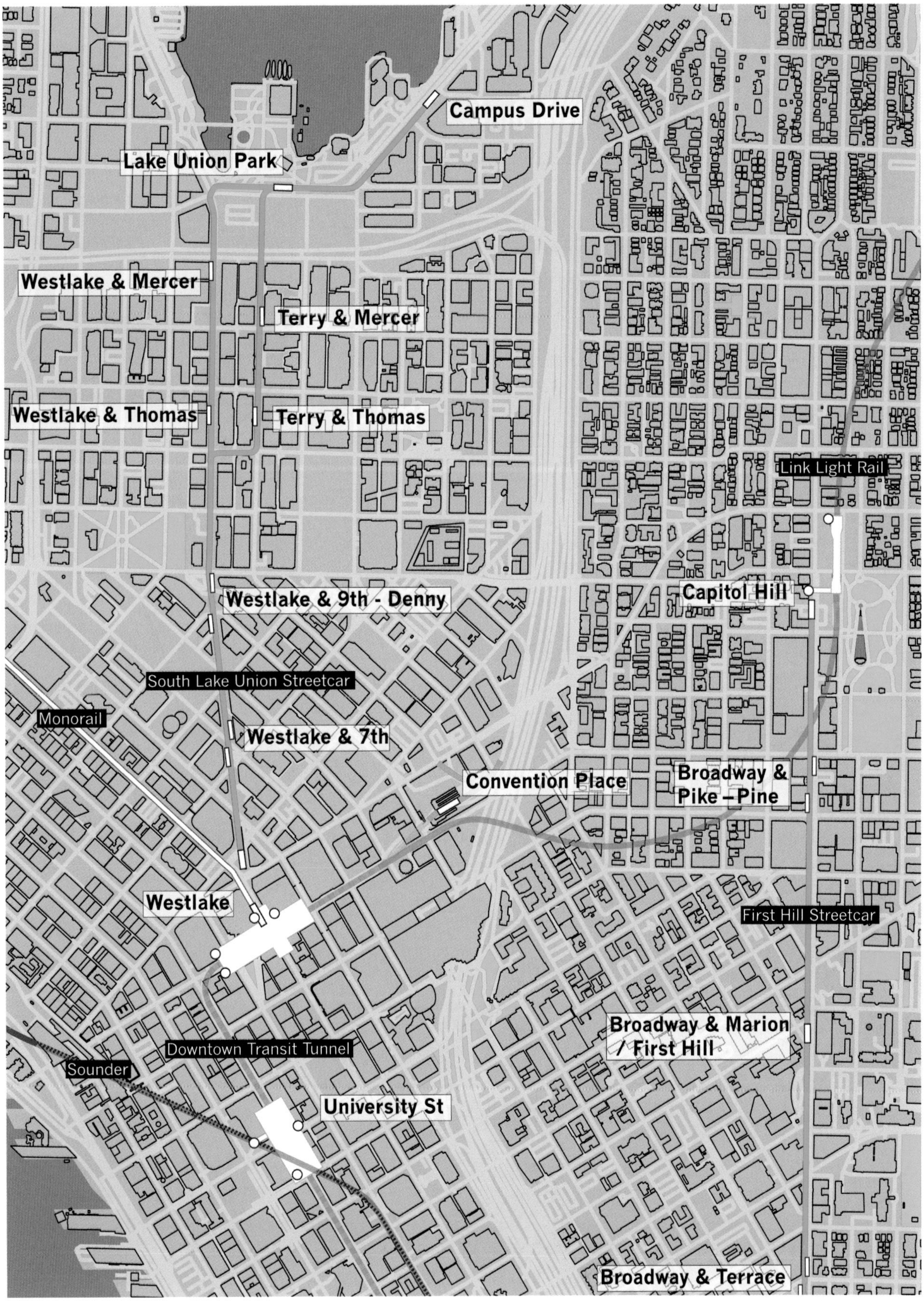

Campus Drive

Lake Union Park

Westlake & Mercer

Terry & Mercer

Westlake & Thomas

Terry & Thomas

Link Light Rail

Westlake & 9th - Denny

Capitol Hill

South Lake Union Streetcar

Monorail

Westlake & 7th

Convention Place

Broadway &
Pike – Pine

First Hill Streetcar

Westlake

Broadway & Marion
/ First Hill

Downtown Transit Tunnel

Sounder

University St

Broadway & Terrace

16. ORLANDO

Orlando–Deltona–Daytona Beach, FL

population 4,160,646 (16th)   **served by frequent transit** 2%   **daily trips per 1000** 19

LYNX
independent agency
BRT

SunRail
state department
Commuter Rail

There are two Orlandos.

One Orlando is the one everyone visits: theme parks, hotels, a huge convention center, and all the tourist-oriented sprawl that surrounds them. This is a surprisingly transit-oriented place (albeit private transit): the Disney Monorail carries more people every day than the Portland light-rail system, hotel shuttles run as frequently as major urban bus routes, and Disney's Magical Express is arguably the best airport transit connection in the country. The other Orlando, 10 miles northeast of the theme parks, is an ordinary city, with a downtown surrounded by bungalow neighborhoods, a major university, and the usual suburbs. Thus Orlando faces the transit challenges that all Sun Belt cities do: low-density, pedestrian-hostile development, and easy car access.

The first significant attempt to upgrade transit in Orlando was the Lymmo downtown circulator. It emerged from 1990s planning for a downtown streetcar. The city decided to build bus rapid transit instead. Lymmo's original three-mile loop has 100 percent dedicated lanes, traffic-signal priority, distinctive stations, and branded buses. It connects downtown employment and entertainment districts to the central bus-transit center with frequent service 17 hours a day. It was the first street-running BRT line in the United States, preceding the better known HealthLine in Cleveland by a decade.

Orlando's other significant transit investment is SunRail, a north–south commuter-rail line connecting suburban areas to downtown. It is unusually well connected for a commuter-rail startup, with stops within walking distance of downtown high-rises, at the downtown transit center (below right), and at a major hospital. It also offers relatively good service: every 30 minutes at peak and every hour off-peak, seven days a week. Florida owns the tracks and most freight trains have been rerouted onto other lines, so on-time performance is a stellar 96 percent. The stations are nice, the trains are comfortable, and the tickets are easy to use. But in a city with decentralized employment and relatively low traffic congestion, and on a corridor with low-density land uses, the market simply isn't that big. SunRail's ridership is about average for similar commuter-rail lines in postwar cities, but it carries about as many passengers on 30 miles of route as Lymmo carries on three. ∎

BRT (Lymmo Orange)
SMALL SYSTEM
HIGH PERFORMER
RIDE FREE

Opened: 1997
Last Expanded: 2004
Length: 1.3 miles (1.3 guideway miles)
Stations: 10.5 (guideway only)
Frequency: 5–7 min peak/midday, 15 min evening/weekend
Avg weekday ridership: 1,928
Ridership per mile: 1,483

Commuter Rail (SunRail)
SMALL SYSTEM

Opened: 2014
Last Expanded: ongoing
Length: 49 miles
Stations: 16
Frequency: 30 min peak, 1 hr off-peak, no weekend service
Avg weekday ridership: 6,300
Ridership per mile: 129

+ **Downtown BRT circulator in dedicated lanes playing a similar role as streetcars in other cities**
− **Well-executed commuter rail that doesn't serve enough jobs or homes**

SANFORD

ORLANDO

Bus Rapid Transit
Commuter Rail

elevated	at grade	subway
in freeway	in street	mixed traffic

Frequent Bus

✈ airport   ○ Brightline station

5 miles

Orlando's busiest bus route—with 7,000 trips on an average weekday—connects the central city to the resort district to the south.

KISSIMMEE

The suburbs served by Sunrail are very low density.

FULL SAIL UNIVERSITY

DOWNTOWN ORLANDO
104,290 jobs
40th in US

⋯⋮ 1/2 mile distance to frequent rail/BRT
⋯⋮ 1/2 mile distance to frequent bus

population density (people per sq. mi.)
2500 5000 7500 10000 12500 15000 17500

employment density (jobs per sq. mi.)
15000 30000 45000 60000

⬤ college campus (100 U.S. largest)

17. **MONTREAL**

Montreal - Laval - Longueuil, QC

population 4,098,927 (17th)   **served by frequent transit** 43%   **daily trips per 1000** 525

In the 1960s, the Quiet Revolution remade Quebec. Implemented by the government of Jean Lesage, elected in 1960, it was nationalistic, proudly modern, and proudly French. The government nationalized and massively expanded the hydroelectric system, creating a huge power-generating capacity that puts $2 billion in dividends directly into the provincial budget every year. It took over schools from the Catholic Church and created a strong social welfare system. It made French the primary language of government and commerce.

Montreal's Metro is an embodiment of that vision. Even though it's only a decade newer than the Toronto subway, its complex multi-level spaces, exposed concrete, and abstract art are unmistakably more modern. And the trains with their elegant rounded shape and their Michelin-designed rubber-tire system (its first use outside Paris) are distinctly French.

The Metro is the core of Montreal's transit system today. Its four lines carry 45% of Société de Transport de Montréal's passengers, and it serves as the spine of the city's grid-like bus network. Montreal is on an island, constrained by rivers to the north and the south and Mount Royal in the center, creating an area of high population density of a size found only in half a dozen North American cities. This is where the Metro is focused—only three of 68 stations are not on the island, and nearly the entire system is

STM
municipal
heavy rail
frequent bus
BRT

**Réseau express
métropolitain**
independent agency
heavy rail

Exo
independent agency
commuter rail

**Société de transport de
Laval**
independent agency
Frequent Bus

+ **Modern and busy subway**
+ **Excellent bus service in the city**
- **Weak suburban service**

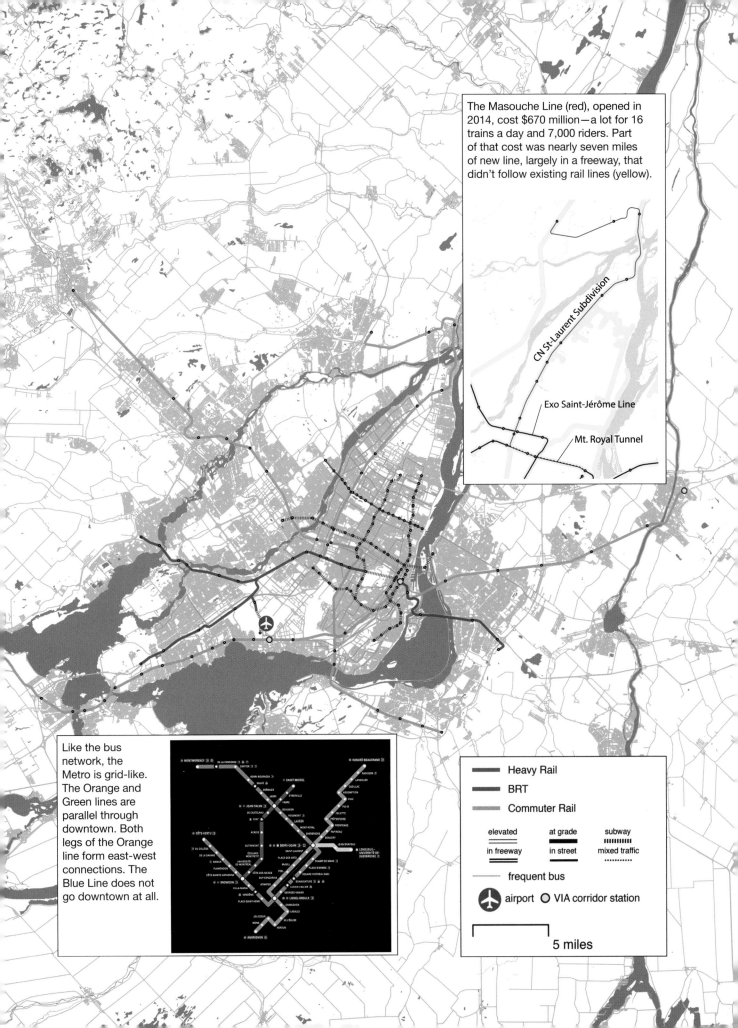

The Masouche Line (red), opened in 2014, cost $670 million—a lot for 16 trains a day and 7,000 riders. Part of that cost was nearly seven miles of new line, largely in a freeway, that didn't follow existing rail lines (yellow).

CN St-Laurent Subdivision

Exo Saint-Jérôme Line

Mt. Royal Tunnel

Like the bus network, the Metro is grid-like. The Orange and Green lines are parallel through downtown. Both legs of the Orange line form east-west connections. The Blue Line does not go downtown at all.

MONTMORENCY — DE LA CONCORDE — CARTIER — HONORÉ-BEAUGRAND
HENRI-BOURASSA — SAINT-MICHEL
SAUVÉ — LANGELIER
CHÉNIER — CADILLAC
JARRY — D'IBERVILLE — ASSOMPTION
JEAN-TALON — FABRE — VIAU
DE CASTELNAU — BEAUBIEN — PIE-IX
PARC — ROSEMONT — JOLIETTE
ACADIE — LAURIER — PRÉFONTAINE
CÔTE-VERTU — OUTREMONT — MONT-ROYAL — FRONTENAC
BERRI-UQAM — PAPINEAU
DU COLLÈGE — ÉDOUARD-MONTPETIT — SHERBROOKE — BEAUDRY
DE LA SAVANE — UNIVERSITÉ-DE-MONTRÉAL — SAINT-LAURENT — JEAN-GRAPEAU
NAMUR — CÔTE-DES-NEIGES — McGILL — LONGUEUIL-UNIVERSITÉ-DE-SHERBROOKE
PLAMONDON — GUY-CONCORDIA — PEEL — PLACE-DES-ARTS
CÔTE-SAINTE-CATHERINE — PLACE-D'ARMES
SNOWDON — ATWATER — CHAMP-DE-MARS
VILLA-MARIA — BONAVENTURE — SQUARE-VICTORIA-OACI
VENDÔME — LUCIEN-L'ALLIER
PLACE-SAINT-HENRI — GEORGES-VANIER
LIONEL-GROULX
CHARLEVOIX
JOLICOEUR — LASALLE
MONK — DE L'ÉGLISE
VERDUN
ANGRIGNON

Heavy Rail
BRT
Commuter Rail

elevated | at grade | subway

in freeway | in street | mixed traffic

frequent bus

✈ airport ○ VIA corridor station

5 miles

Heavy Rail (Metro)

VERY HIGH PERFORMER

Opened: 1966
Last Expanded: ongoing
Length: 43 miles; 3.5 miles under construction
Stations: 68; 5 under construction
Frequency: 2-5 min peak, 4-10 min midday, 6-12 min evening/weekend
Avg weekday ridership: 1,421,200
Ridership per mile: 33,051

Heavy Rail (REM)

Opened: 2021
Last Expanded: N/A
Length: 42 miles in construction
Stations: 26 in construction
Frequency: 2.5-10 min peak, 5-15 min offpeak

Commuter Rail (Exo)

HIGH PERFORMER

PREWAR SYSTEM

Opened: 1887
Last Expanded: 2014
Length: 132.5 miles
Stations: 51 (1 under construction)
Frequency: 2-5 min peak, 4-10 min midday, 6-12 min evening/weekend
Avg weekday ridership: 77,210
Ridership per mile: 583

in dense walkable neighborhoods. It is one of only two rail systems in North America that is entirely underground.

The Metro was completed in three spurts of construction. The first three lines were built between 1962 and 1967, opening in time for the 1967 World's Fair, Expo 67, which was held on an island in the river served by the Yellow Line. (The fair also had its own 3.5-mile rapid-transit line.) Extensions and the new Blue Line were built between 1971 and 1988. These were planned as part of the 1976 Olympics, but like the Olympics the expansion suffered from cost overruns and fighting between the city, the regional government, and the province. This resulted in the cancellation of some lines and delays in moving ahead with others. The final piece of today's system, a three-station, three-mile extension off the island into Laval funded by the province, was built between 2002 and 2007. A decade later, further expansion plans took shape. On the island the Blue Line will be extended northward by five stops, a "Pink Line" to north central Montreal was proposed by Valérie Plante, elected mayor of Montreal in 2017, and a new elevated rail line was proposed in 2020.

On the suburban south end of the island and off the island, the transit system drops off dramatically. Two major suburban bus operators—Laval in the north and Longueuil in the south—feed into Metro stations, carrying 85,360 and 133,537 boardings a day, respectively, adding up to less than 10% of the city's system. There are few frequent bus routes off the island. Unlike Toronto or Ottawa, major capital investments in transit outside the city have been minimal. Exo operates regional express bus and commuter rail. Only two commuter rail lines survived postwar cuts that extended into the 1980s by Canadian National and Canadian Pacific railroads. One is the Deux-Montagnes, an electrified line that starts in north-shore suburbs, extends through dense walkable neighborhoods built around the trains stations, and tunnels under Mount Royal into downtown. It has always had fairly good service—10 to 30 minutes at peak, hourly midday and on weekends—and carries 28,000 people a day. The other surviving line is the diesel-powered Vaudreuil–Hudson along the river through the south side of the island. It has always had much less-frequent midday service and only minimal weekend service, and carries about 16,000 people a day. In the late 1990s, the newly created regional agency, Agence Métropolitaine de Transport, began expanding commuter rail. A total of four lines were added in 1997 (initially as a temporary service during highway bridge construction), 2000, 2001, and 2014. All are peak focused, with minimal midday, and minimal or no weekend service. The original two lines carry nearly 60% of the commuter-rail ridership.

The next major expansion of regional transit comes as a long-delayed consequence of the Quiet Revolution. The Caisse de Dépôt et Placement du Québec, the investment arm of the province-wide pension plan created in 1995, is investing in a new automated heavy-rail system, opening in 2022. It will take over the Deux-Montagnes line, operating at much higher frequency, and add three routes, one to the airport, one to the south end of the island, and one to the south shore. ■

Only one Metro station is south (or, technically speaking, east) of the St. Lawrence River. Longueuil station is directly connected to a campus of the Université de Sherbrooke, but around that is a maze of freeway ramps and suburban sprawl. The station's major function is as a transfer. The bus terminal atop the station serves more than 60 suburban routes and five intercity bus lines. It's the fifth busiest station on the Metro.

Rail yards, industrial areas, and the airport separate the dense central part of the island from the more suburban (and largely English speaking) south end. The former Canadian Pacific Vaudreuil–Hudson line serves the southern edge of this area. The new REM line will follow the freeway through the center.

:•••:. 1/2 mile distance to frequent rail/BRT
:•••: 1/2 mile distance to frequent bus

population density (people per sq. mi.)

2500 5000 7500 10000 12500 15000 17500

no employment density data

BRT (Pie-X)

Open: 2023
Last Expanded: N/A
Length: 0 miles (8.1 in construction)
Stations: 0 (18 in construction)
Frequency: 10 min or better
Avg weekday ridership: N/A
Ridership per mile: N/A

The downtown Metro stations (Place-des-Arts station, top) and both commuter rail stations are integrated into the Underground City, 20 miles of tunnels and multi-level shopping centers linking the downtown high rises like Place Bonaventure (above the station tracks of Gare Central, left). In the winter, Montrealers can commute into downtown and never step outdoors once they get there.

Some commuters walk to Metro—one third of the island's population is within 1/2 mile of a station. Others take the bus—nearly the entire regional bus network feeds into Metro stations like Vendome (above.)

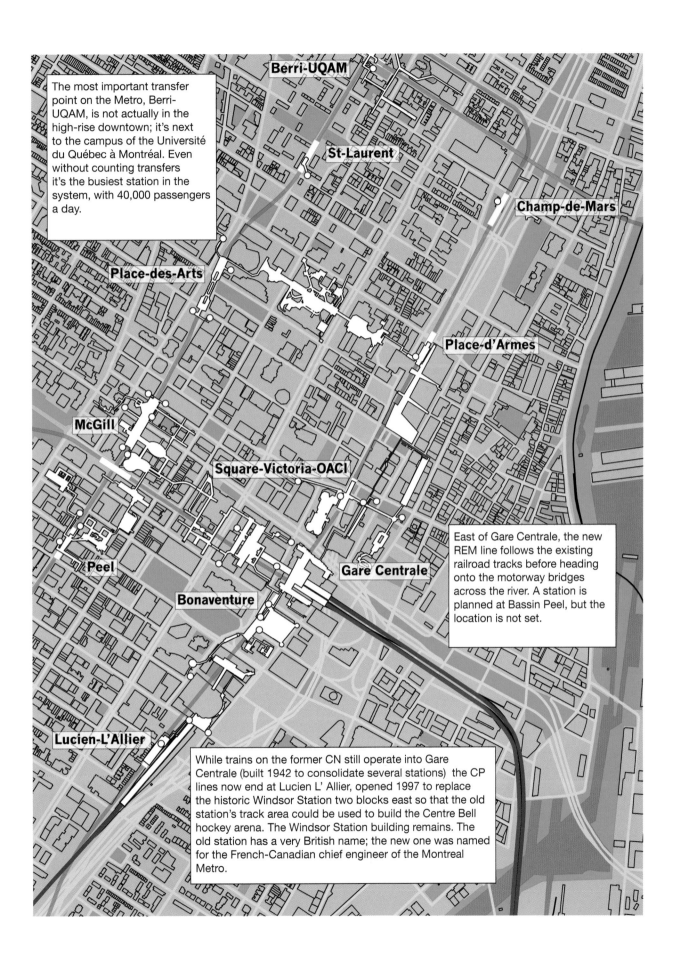

Berri-UQAM

The most important transfer point on the Metro, Berri-UQAM, is not actually in the high-rise downtown; it's next to the campus of the Université du Québec à Montréal. Even without counting transfers it's the busiest station in the system, with 40,000 passengers a day.

St-Laurent

Champ-de-Mars

Place-des-Arts

Place-d'Armes

McGill

Square-Victoria-OACI

Peel

Gare Centrale

East of Gare Centrale, the new REM line follows the existing railroad tracks before heading onto the motorway bridges across the river. A station is planned at Bassin Peel, but the location is not set.

Bonaventure

Lucien-L'Allier

While trains on the former CN still operate into Gare Centrale (built 1942 to consolidate several stations) the CP lines now end at Lucien L' Allier, opened 1997 to replace the historic Windsor Station two blocks east so that the old station's track area could be used to build the Centre Bell hockey arena. The Windsor Station building remains. The old station has a very British name; the new one was named for the French-Canadian chief engineer of the Montreal Metro.

Before the 1970s, Montreal was Canada's economic center, and from 1918 to 1996 it was headquarters for both of the national railroads. That left a legacy of infrastructure that Via Rail (above, crossing the Lachine Canal on a track that branches to Toronto and to the Victoria Bridge across to St. Lawrence) and Exo use today. Despite the fact that stations like Vendome (below) serve a wide variety of destinations, like the Royal Victoria hospital, the service is focused on 9-to-5 commutes into the downtown terminals, the historic Gare Central and the spartan Lucien L'Allier (left)

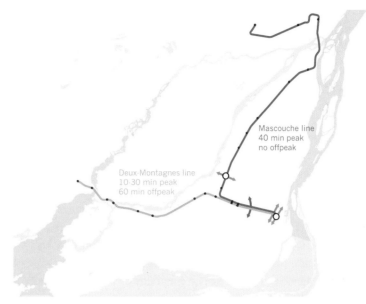

Canadian National, the last railroad to reach Montreal, decided that the only way it could reach downtown was to build a 3.2-mile tunnel (above left) right through Mount Royal. When it opened in 1918, it carried electric commuter-rail service. Modernized with new trains (center left) in 1995, the line continued to operate for a century. In 2014, it was joined through the tunnel by dual-mode diesel-electric locomotives on the new Masouche Line.

In 2020, that tunnel was closed for conversion to REM automated heavy rail. Three branches—the existing route and two new ones—will operate every 15 minutes or better all day, combining for trains every 2.5 to 5 minutes through the tunnel and then on a new route across the river. The project will also add two new stations in the tunnel, connecting to the Green and Blue Metro lines. The added routes, improved connections and dramatically better frequency will make the line useful to many more people. But, because it will replace the 10-car trains on the current line with four-car trains, peak capacity will actually be lower, and Mascouche Line passengers will need to transfer to REM or the Metro Orange Line (lower left.)

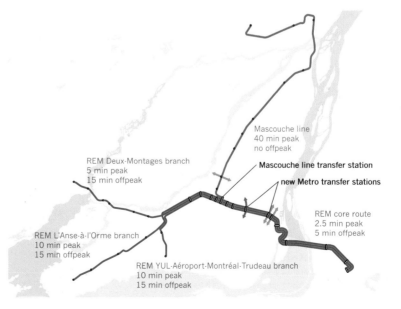

18. MINNEAPOLIS

Minneapolis–St. Paul, MN-WI

population 4,027,861 (18th)   **served by frequent transit** 12%   **daily trips per 1000** 61

Metro Transit
independent agency
Light Rail
Commuter Rail
Frequent Bus

The Twin Cities of Minneapolis and St. Paul do not seem to get the attention that Dallas, Denver, or Salt Lake City have for their major transit expansions. But, in its quiet Midwestern way, it has built one of the best transit systems in the country.

Minneapolis' transit focus long predates rail. Nicollet Mall, opened in 1967, was the first downtown transit mall in the United States. Minneapolis has also built up a significant commuter-bus network, bringing together five different transit agencies. But the 40 percent of downtown employees who use transit are not all coming from the suburbs. In the former streetcar neighborhoods of Minneapolis and St. Paul, bus riding is still a normal part of life. Twenty-five percent of bus riders in the Twin Cities have an annual household income over $50,000. This is due to a long focus on getting bus right. Metro Transit was one of the first US agencies to designate a frequent-transit network.

Thus, when the Twin Cities built light rail, they were building on an already successful network. The first two light-rail lines replaced busy bus corridors linking major activity centers. The Blue Line (right) connects downtown Minneapolis to the VA Medical Center, the airport, the suburban employment center of Bloomington, and the Mall of America. The Green Line connects Minneapolis, the University of Minnesota campus, and downtown St. Paul. The two rail lines serve all of the Twin Cities' major employment centers. The Blue Line, which is the busier of the two, runs down the center of University Avenue for six miles, through the center of a diverse series of neighborhoods, which include some of the highest concentrations of immigrants and low-income residents in the city. Every high-frequency bus route connects to at least one of the rail lines. Together, the Blue and Green lines make up one of the most successful light-rail net-

works in the United States, with more riders per mile than any other postwar light system (and most of the prewar systems as well).

But these high-ridership rail projects came with a tradeoff. The regional transit-financing authority, which imposes a half-cent sales tax for transit projects, is governed jointly by five counties, covering urban areas, suburbs, and small towns. The political compromise is that everyone gets something. That has already resulted in some remarkably low-ridership projects. The $317-million Northstar commuter rail, a 40-mile line through low-density suburbs, carries only 2,500 trips a day on six trains in each direction. The $127-million Red Line, a highway rapid-bus line with enclosed, heated stations, and pedestrian skywalks at key stops, carries fewer than 900 passengers a day. The next two light-rail lines, currently in planning, won't be quite that bad, but both avoid dense neighborhoods close to downtown to extend into low-density, car-oriented suburbs, and neither serves concentrated employment.

Nevertheless, the core of the Twin Cities transit network continues to get better. More routes are being added to the frequent network. The A Line, an improved local-bus service with limited stops, upgraded shelters and boarding areas, traffic signal priority, branding, and seven-day frequent service, increased ridership by 35 percent in its corridor. The Orange Line freeway BRT will provide express service to downtown Minneapolis linking to local bus routes. New developments are adding housing and retail around light-rail stations. The Twin Cities is continuing to transform into one of America's most transit-friendly metro areas. ■

+ **Light-rail lines connecting centers and focusing on strongest transit corridors**
+ **Frequent-bus network, integrated with rail, covering walkable urban neighborhoods**
– **Regional investment in low-ridership corridors**

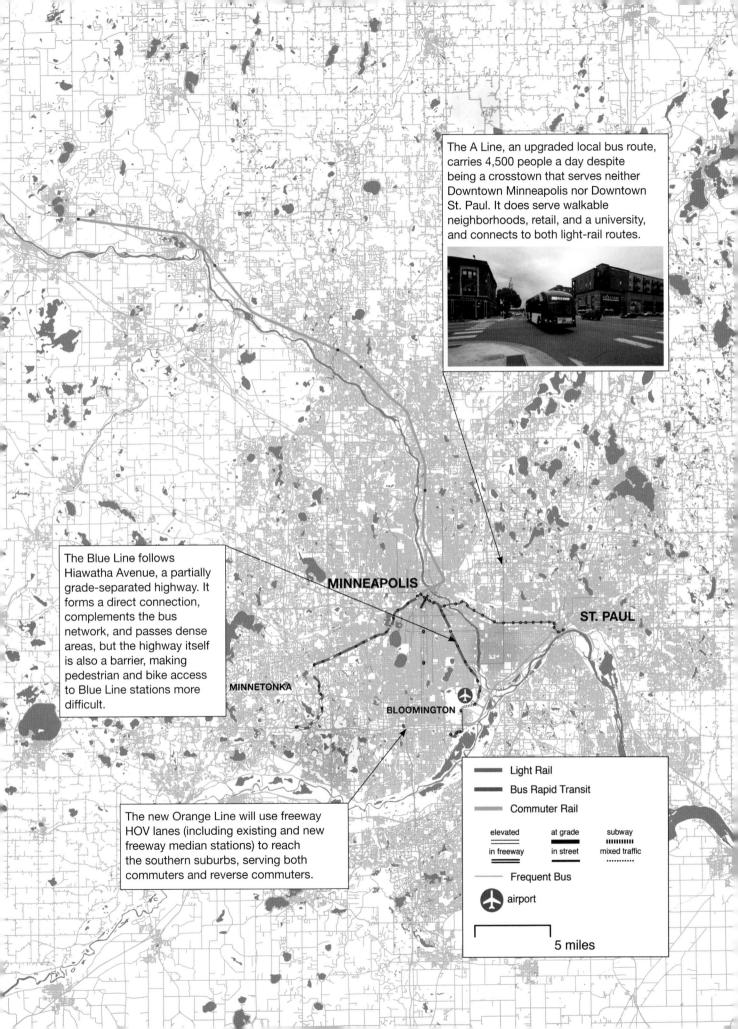

The A Line, an upgraded local bus route, carries 4,500 people a day despite being a crosstown that serves neither Downtown Minneapolis nor Downtown St. Paul. It does serve walkable neighborhoods, retail, and a university, and connects to both light-rail routes.

The Blue Line follows Hiawatha Avenue, a partially grade-separated highway. It forms a direct connection, complements the bus network, and passes dense areas, but the highway itself is also a barrier, making pedestrian and bike access to Blue Line stations more difficult.

The new Orange Line will use freeway HOV lanes (including existing and new freeway median stations) to reach the southern suburbs, serving both commuters and reverse commuters.

MINNEAPOLIS

ST. PAUL

MINNETONKA

BLOOMINGTON

Light Rail
Bus Rapid Transit
Commuter Rail

elevated   at grade   subway
in freeway   in street   mixed traffic

Frequent Bus

airport

5 miles

Light Rail (Blue/Green Lines)

HIGH PERFORMER

Opened: 2004

Last Expanded: ongoing

Length: 21.8 miles (14.5 in construction)

Stations: 37 (16 in construction)

Frequency: 10 min weekday/Saturday, 15 min Sunday

Avg weekday ridership: 75,300

Ridership per mile: 3,454

Commuter Rail (Northstar)

LOW PERFORMER
SMALL SYSTEM

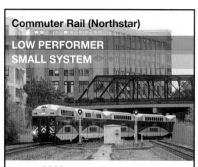

Opened: 2009

Last Expanded: N/A

Length: 40 miles

Stations: 7

Frequency: 6 trains each way a day weekdays, 3 trains a day each day weekends

Avg weekday ridership: 2,500

Ridership per mile: 63

BRT (Orange Line)

UNDER CONSTRUCTION

Opened: 2021

Last Expanded: N/A

Length: 17 miles (1 guideway miles)

Stations: 6 (guideway only)

Frequency: 15 min or better

Avg weekday ridership: N/A

Ridership per mile: N/A

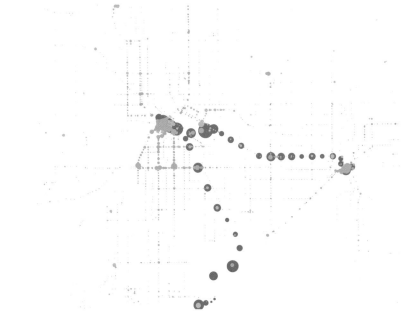

Nicollet Mall (top) carries five local bus routes, four of them frequent, through downtown Minneapolis. Buses ending their runs in downtown charge no fares on this segment, allowing the mall to act as a free circulator. A map of boardings by stop (above) shows how the frequent buses (orange) and the rail (blue) form the core of the transit system. There are high concentrations of ridership in the dense neighborhoods just south of downtown Minneapolis and along University Avenue (left) between Minneapolis and St. Paul.

The Twin Cities' next rail line, Southwest, follows existing rail corridors, bypassing urban neighborhoods with high potential ridership. A subway through Midtown Minneapolis (dashed) was considered but discarded for cost reasons. Since then, though, the supposedly lower-cost rail corridor has gotten more expensive due to local opposition. Ironically, the response to that opposition is to put part of the line underground, so there will be a tunnel after all, but through low-density, low-ridership areas. The Bottineau corridor to the northwest similarly would have followed rail lines, but the BNSF did not grant permission to follow its tracks, so that is being restudied.

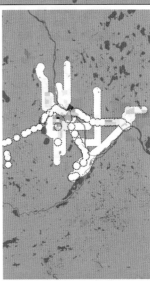

Despite their veneer of "Minnesota Nice," the Twin Cities, like all of the US, have a long history of racism. In the 1950s, I-94 was bulldozed through the middle of the Rondo, the center of the local Black community. In the 2000s, community activists rallied against early plans for the Green Line, which ran through the same neighborhoods. They convinced Metro Transit to engage communities—including long-time Black and Asian-American residents—in adding station locations and supporting equitable transit-oriented development. The transit police have also attempted more outreach to the homeless and recent immigrants. But, as the George Floyd murder showed, major problems with policing remain.

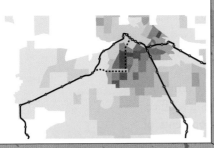

UNIVERSITY OF MINNESOTA

DOWNTOWN MINNEAPOLIS
232,458 jobs
12th in US

GAP: Rail or BRT to South Minneapolis

DOWNTOWN ST. PAUL
85,753 jobs
58th in US

- ⌐ 1/2 mile distance to frequent rail/BRT
- ⌐ 1/2 mile distance to frequent bus

population density (people per sq. mi.)

2500 5000 7500 10000 12500 15000 17500

employment density (jobs per sq. mi.)

15000 30000 45000 60000

● college campus (100 U.S. largest)

Light Rail (C/D/E/F/H/L/R/W Lines)

LARGE SYSTEM

Opened: 1994

Last Expanded: 2019

Length: 60.1 miles

Stations: 55

Frequency: 6–15 peak, 8–15 midday, 8–30 evening/weekend

Avg weekday ridership: 95,300

Ridership per mile: 1,586

Denver's rail system almost entirely follows rail lines (yellow below) and freeways (red). This has been effective for building a large system quickly. The alignment to the southeast, for example, was built by the Colorado Department of Transportation as part of freeway-widening project. But it means Denver has a lot of rail in sprawling, pedestrian-hostile places (along I-225, above) and even urban stations are often surrounded by infrastructure with no useful transit destinations (38th and Blake on the A Line, bottom.)

BRT (MallRide)

SMALL SYSTEM
HIGH PERFORMER

Opened: 1982

Last Expanded: 2014

Length: 1.4 miles (1.4 guideway miles)

Stations: 18 (guideway only)

Frequency: 2–15 min

Avg weekday ridership: 25,000

Ridership per mile: 17,857

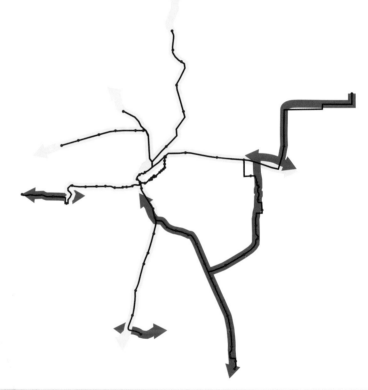

Commuter Rail (A/B/G/N lines)

HIGH PERFORMER
SMALL SYSTEM

Opened: 2016

Last Expanded: 2019

Length: 49.8 miles

Stations: 22

Frequency: Varies from 15 min to 1 hr, 7 days a week

Avg weekday ridership: 40,000

Ridership per mile: 803

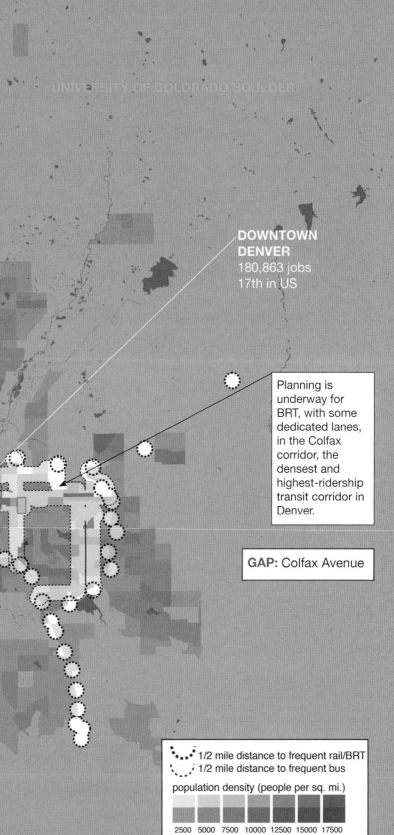

UNIVERSITY OF COLORADO BOULDER

**DOWNTOWN
DENVER**
180,863 jobs
17th in US

Planning is
underway for
BRT, with some
dedicated lanes,
in the Colfax
corridor, the
densest and
highest-ridership
transit corridor in
Denver.

GAP: Colfax Avenue

1/2 mile distance to frequent rail/BRT
1/2 mile distance to frequent bus

population density (people per sq. mi.)

2500 5000 7500 10000 12500 15000 17500

employment density (jobs per sq. mi.)

15000 30000 45000 60000

college campus (100 U.S. largest)

Downtown Denver has two light-rail alignments: the original 1994 line though the center of downtown (opposite) on Stout and California, and the 2002 line to Union Station. In 2007, when the major light-rail corridors offered a choice of both destinations, 80 percent of ridership was on the lines to Stout and California. But RTD decided to center its transit expansion on Union Station (left). The new West Line light rail, and all three commuter-rail lines, only operate there. Thus, the most important transit route in Denver is arguably the 16th Street Mall Ride (below), a free BRT line on a transit and pedestrian mall that runs every 2–15 minutes from 7:00 a.m. to midnight, seven days a week, from Union Station in the north to the Civic Center bus terminal in the south, connecting to all rail and commuter bus lines that run to downtown Denver.

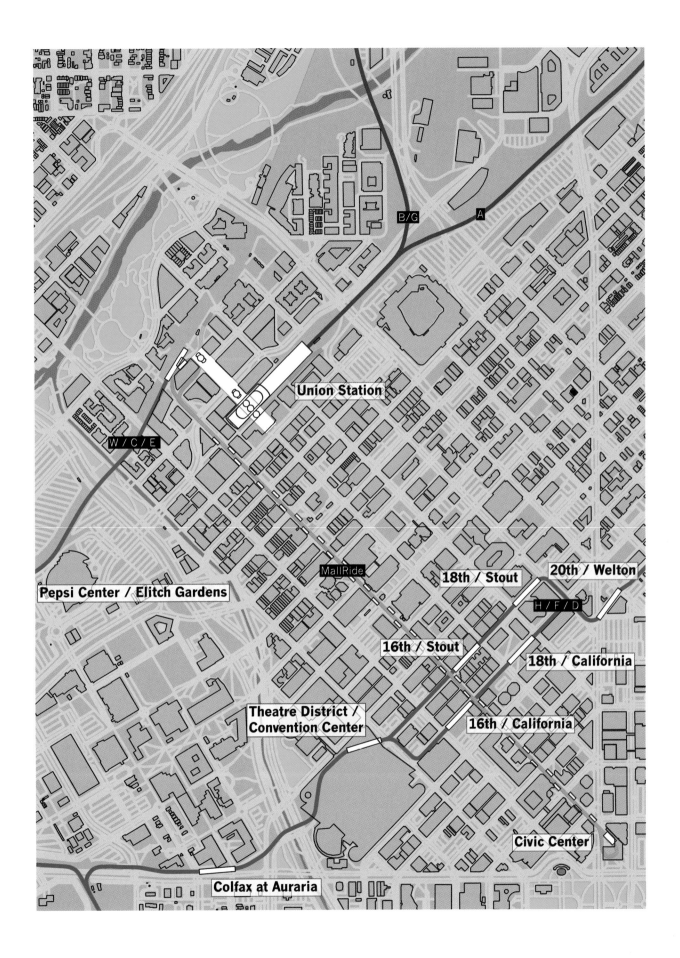

Union Station

B/G

A

W / C / E

Pepsi Center / Elitch Gardens

MallRide

18th / Stout

20th / Welton

H / F / D

16th / Stout

18th / California

Theatre District /
Convention Center

16th / California

Civic Center

Colfax at Auraria

20. CLEVELAND

Cleveland–Akron–Canton, OH

population 3,585,918 (20th)   **served by frequent transit** 5%   **daily trips per 1000** 31

RTA
independent agency
BRT
Heavy Rail
Light Rail
Frequent Bus

Fundamentally, the story of Cleveland in the last century is a story of decline. In the 1920s, it was America's fifth largest city, an economic powerhouse and a center of culture, and home to one of America's "big five" orchestras. In the 1940s the population peaked at over 900,000. Today it is less than half that. As they did elsewhere, residents left the city for the suburbs, but they weren't replaced. The overall metropolitan area shrank by 11 percent since 1970, even as US population grew by 51 percent.

Cleveland's rail-transit system is a reminder of that old, prosperous, ambitious Cleveland. The oldest segments date back to the 1920s. The Van Sweringen Brothers, who developed the suburb of Shaker Heights, built a streetcar line to serve it and wanted an express connection to Downtown. Therefore, they acquired the New York, Chicago, and St. Louis Railroad to use its right-of-way, and built Cleveland Union Terminal downtown, topping it with the tallest skyscraper west of New York City. That same right-of-way became the basis for the city's heavy-rail line, which actually shared tracks with the streetcars for three miles on its east-west path across the width of the city. The first heavy-rail segment opened in 1955; the last, a connection to the airport, in 1968. Chronologically, Cleveland is the first post-WWII rail-transit system in the United States, but, with its roots in planning in the 1920s, it is really the last of the prewar systems.

But the loss of city population and related suburban sprawl hasn't helped transit. The transit network faded in the car-oriented areas outside the city, and transit routes within the city lost ridership as population dropped. High-profile revitalization efforts have not made a meaningful difference. The light-rail system was extended in 1996 to the redeveloped waterfront, home of the Rock and Roll Hall of Fame, but the ridership has been so low at 400 trips a day that there has been serious consideration given to eliminating service on that segment.

In some ways, though, Cleveland is still a transit city. When the Cavaliers won the NBA championship in 2016, some 500,000 people took trains and buses downtown. The pre-WWII city is still there, with a walkable street grid and mixed-use neighborhoods. Fifty-eight percent of the city's residents live in housing units built before 1940, and those areas still have a good transit share. A strong frequent network covers the densest parts of the city. Its most important line is the Health Line BRT, opened in 2008, putting frequent transit, largely in dedicated lanes, down Euclid Avenue. It now carries 14,000 people a day, and Euclid has seen $6.3 billion in new development since construction started. The Health Line strings together some of Cleveland's greatest assets, all inheritances from that old, prosperous city: Case Western Reserve University, the art museum, the orchestra hall, the university hospitals, the Cleveland Clinic, Cleveland State University, the theaters at Playhouse Square, and Public Square in the heart of downtown. It is a national model for transit. ■

+ **Good BRT line**
− **Low-ridership heavy rail serving declining areas**
− **Infrequent light rail**

Cleveland is the only place in the United States where light rail and heavy rail run on the same tracks. In this section, stations have two sets of platforms: high for heavy rail, low for light rail. The RTA's next railcar order will likely be designed to be able to work both sets of lines.

EUCLID

CLEVELAND

LAKEWOOD

SHAKER HEIGHTS

The Cleveland light-rail lines were built as an integral part of the development of Shaker Heights, and that still shows today: the stores and apartments of Shaker Square (below) are built around the rail, and the two branches run in spacious medians through residential neighborhoods (bottom).

Heavy Rail

Light Rail

Bus Rapid Transit

| elevated | at grade | subway |
| in freeway | in street | mixed traffic |

frequent bus

 airport

5 miles

BRT (HealthLine)

HIGH PERFORMER

Opened: 2008
Last Expanded: N/A
Length: 6.8 miles (4 guideway miles)
Stations: 20 (guideway only)
Frequency: 10 min peak, 20 min off-peak
Avg weekday ridership: 8,678
Ridership per mile: 1,276

Heavy Rail (Red Line)

LOW PERFORMER
PREWAR SYSTEM

Opened: 1955
Last Expanded: 1968
Length: 18.9 miles
Stations: 18
Frequency: 10 min peak, 15 min midday/evening/weekend
Avg weekday ridership: 15,900
Ridership per mile: 841

The HealthLine (above) has dedicated lanes in the center of Euclid Avenue for four miles of its 6.8-mile length, with sheltered heated stops and level boarding. It is equipped with traffic signal priority to speed up trips, resulting in a 33-minute end-to-end trip, compared to 47 minutes for the local bus route. But that technology has been inactivated, apparently due to political pushback, resulting in 44-minute trips. The HealthLine meets the three rail lines at Tower City (right) in downtown Cleveland.

Light Rail (Green/Blue Lines)

LOW PERFORMER
SMALL SYSTEM
PREWAR SYSTEM

Opened: 1913
Last Expanded: 1996
Length: 15.3 miles
Stations: 35
Frequency: 7–15 min peak, 15–30 min midday/evening/weekend
Avg weekday ridership: 3,900
Ridership per mile: 255

The 1968 Red Line station (above) in the basement of Hopkins Airport was the first airport-terminal rail-transit connection in the United States.

The city of Cleveland itself is very poor—the white middle class left for the suburbs long ago. In this metropolitan area, the dense areas are almost all low income, which makes the lack of frequent transit in many of them all the more notable.

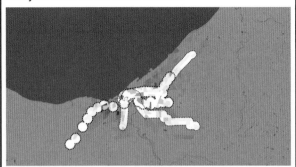

DOWNTOWN CLEVELAND
124,086 jobs
34th in US

UNIVERSITY CIRCLE
63,192 jobs
89th in US

1/2 mile distance to frequent rail/BRT
1/2 mile distance to frequent bus

population density (people per sq. mi.)

2500 5000 7500 10000 12500 15000 17500

employment density (jobs per sq. mi.)

15000 30000 45000 60000

college campus (100 U.S. largest)

21. SAN DIEGO

San Diego–Carlsbad, CA

population 3,338,330 (21st)   **served by frequent transit** 37%   **daily trips per 1000** 78

MTS
independent agency
Light Rail
Frequent Bus

North County Transportation District
independent agency
Commuter Rail
Frequent Bus

In 1978, San Diego started construction on the first modern light-rail system in the United States. It was a pragmatic choice. The region studied heavy rail, like the systems that San Francisco, Washington, and Atlanta had just built, but wasn't willing to bear the cost of such a system. Nevertheless, local leaders wanted rail in long corridors extending to the edges of the metro area, and they wanted it to run fast. The opportunity to do that presented itself when a tropical storm destroyed parts of the Southern Pacific's lines in the area, leaving the railroad happy to sell the lines to avoid the cost of rebuilding. One of these lines ran straight from downtown San Diego to the border with Tijuana, Mexico. Thus, San Diego's first light-rail line was 14.2 miles of converted freight rail linked to 1.7 miles of new downtown street-running track. Everything was done at minimal cost—the existing tracks were rehabilitated but not replaced, the stations were little more than concrete pads with bus shelters on them, and the downtown track was simply inserted into existing streets, with no further reconstruction. Unlike the heavy-rail systems that came before it, and also the light-rail systems that came after, the new San Diego Trolley involved no heavy infrastructure nor any attempt at urban design. But it worked very well; within five years the trolley was carrying 20,000 trips a day.

From that initial, simple project, San Diego has built one of the biggest rail networks in the country. Over time, the ambition and level of infrastructure has increased. The second trolley line, to El Cajon, followed another ex–Southern Pacific Line, but with more elaborate stations. The third, the Mission Valley Line, combined new right-of-way, elevated structures, and even a short subway to reach office parks, the football stadium, and San Diego State University. The next project, which started construction in 2016, will extend light rail northward onto the UC San Diego campus on its rugged plateau overlooking the Pacific. Meanwhile, new development has transformed the areas around light-rail stations. Opposite the old Santa Fe depot (below), where commuter and Amtrak trains head north along the coast to Oceanside and Los Angeles, a mixed-use high-rise wraps around the light-rail station. On the edges of downtown, new apartments and stores surround the tracks, and the streets have been rebuilt with wide sidewalks and street trees.

The Tijuana Line worked because it fit the city's geography. South of downtown, rail lines and people alike were squeezed into a narrow coastal plain, so the simple light-rail corridor matched population patterns. That remains the busiest line. The expansion of the trolley took great effort to make it to the two universities. But the densest parts of the city, and some of its key destinations like Balboa Park, remain beyond the reach of rail. ∎

+ **Regional light-rail network serving multiple centers and connecting to bus**
− **Densest neighborhoods dependent on buses in mixed traffic**

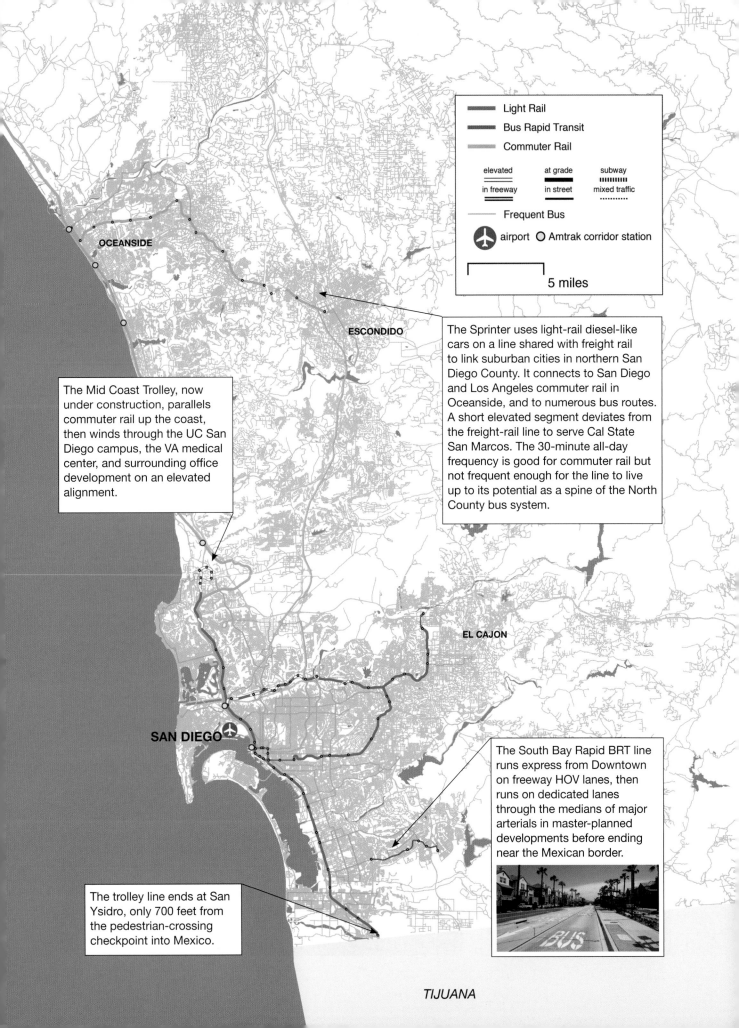

Light Rail

Bus Rapid Transit

Commuter Rail

elevated	at grade	subway
in freeway	in street	mixed traffic

Frequent Bus

✈ airport ◯ Amtrak corridor station

5 miles

OCEANSIDE

ESCONDIDO

The Sprinter uses light-rail diesel-like cars on a line shared with freight rail to link suburban cities in northern San Diego County. It connects to San Diego and Los Angeles commuter rail in Oceanside, and to numerous bus routes. A short elevated segment deviates from the freight-rail line to serve Cal State San Marcos. The 30-minute all-day frequency is good for commuter rail but not frequent enough for the line to live up to its potential as a spine of the North County bus system.

The Mid Coast Trolley, now under construction, parallels commuter rail up the coast, then winds through the UC San Diego campus, the VA medical center, and surrounding office development on an elevated alignment.

EL CAJON

SAN DIEGO

The South Bay Rapid BRT line runs express from Downtown on freeway HOV lanes, then runs on dedicated lanes through the medians of major arterials in master-planned developments before ending near the Mexican border.

The trolley line ends at San Ysidro, only 700 feet from the pedestrian-crossing checkpoint into Mexico.

TIJUANA

Light Rail (San Diego Trolley)

LARGE SYSTEM

Opened: 1981
Last Expanded: ongoing
Length: 51.8 miles (10.9 under construction)
Stations: 54 (9 under construction)
Frequency: 8–15 peak/midday, 30 evenings, 8–15 weekends
Avg weekday ridership: 117,700
Ridership per mile: 2,272

Commuter Rail (Coaster)

SMALL SYSTEM

Opened: 1995
Last Expanded: N/A
Length: 41 miles
Stations: 8
Frequency: 11 trains each way daily weekdays, 4 trains each way daily on weekends
Avg weekday ridership: 4,200
Ridership per mile: 102

DMU Commuter Rail (Sprinter)

HIGH PERFORMER
SMALL SYSTEM

Opened: 2008
Last Expanded: N/A
Length: 22 miles
Stations: 15
Frequency: 30 min peak/midday/evening, 30–60 min weekend
Avg weekday ridership: 7,800
Ridership per mile: 355

Barrio Logan (above) is typical of the older portions of the San Diego Trolley, built on existing freight-rail lines. Newer lines use heavier infrastructure, like a subway under the hilltop campus of San Diego State University that is reached through elevated viaducts above Interstate 8 (below left), to serve key destinations. New destinations have also developed around the rail lines, including residential (below right), the convention center, and the Petco Park baseball stadium (bottom).

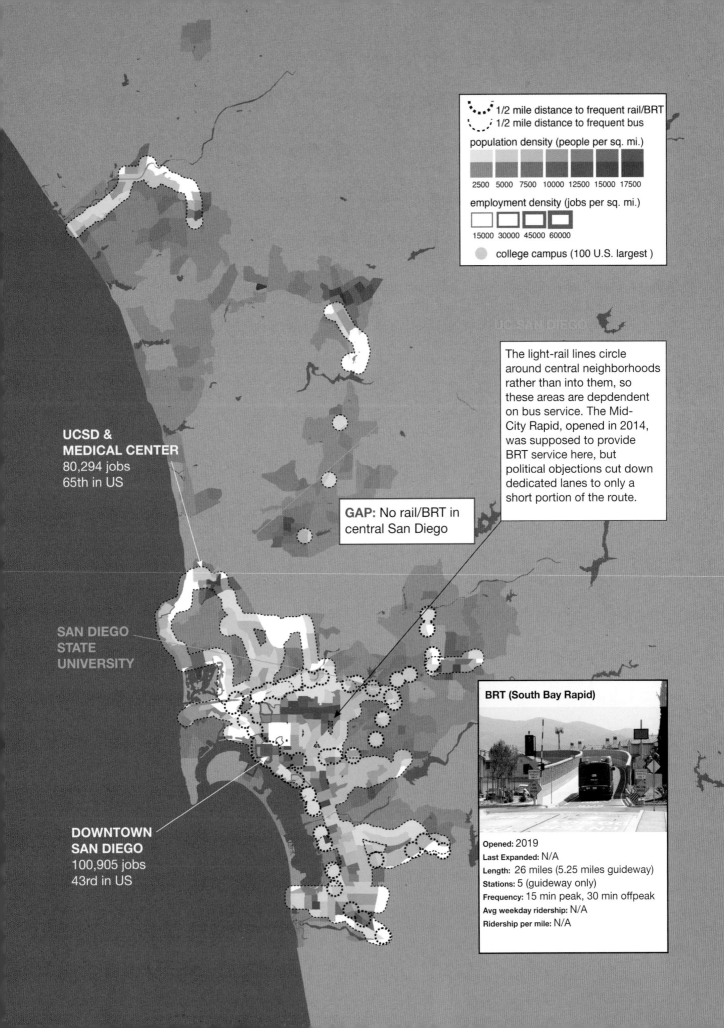

Legend

- ⌇ 1/2 mile distance to frequent rail/BRT
- ⌒ 1/2 mile distance to frequent bus

population density (people per sq. mi.)

2500 5000 7500 10000 12500 15000 17500

employment density (jobs per sq. mi.)

15000 30000 45000 60000

- ● college campus (100 U.S. largest)

UC SAN DIEGO

UCSD & MEDICAL CENTER
80,294 jobs
65th in US

The light-rail lines circle around central neighborhoods rather than into them, so these areas are depdendent on bus service. The Mid-City Rapid, opened in 2014, was supposed to provide BRT service here, but political objections cut down dedicated lanes to only a short portion of the route.

GAP: No rail/BRT in central San Diego

SAN DIEGO STATE UNIVERSITY

BRT (South Bay Rapid)

Opened: 2019
Last Expanded: N/A
Length: 26 miles (5.25 miles guideway)
Stations: 5 (guideway only)
Frequency: 15 min peak, 30 min offpeak
Avg weekday ridership: N/A
Ridership per mile: N/A

DOWNTOWN SAN DIEGO
100,905 jobs
43rd in US

22. PORTLAND

Portland-Vancouver-Salem, OR-WA

population 3,259,710 (22nd)   **served by frequent transit** 26%   **daily trips per 1000** 95

Tri-Met
independent agency
Light Rail
Commuter Rail
Frequent Bus

 PORTLAND STREETCAR

Portland Streetcar
municipal
Streetcar

Portland Aerial Tram
municipal
Aerial Tram

C-Tran
independent agency
Frequent Bus

Portland made three big decisions in the 1970s and 1980s that have created one of the best transit networks in the United States. The first was the state's adoption of an urban growth boundary in 1973, after a grassroots campaign by environmentalists and rural interests. Local governments—like Portland's Metro, created in 1979 to cover the three-county metro area—draw a line that encloses the metropolitan area, and no development can be built outside it. This line is expanded as the area grows, but it keeps metropolitan areas compact and contiguous. Portland has a relatively well-defined edge, with forests and farmlands beyond.

The second was the decision in 1974 to cancel the Mount Hood Freeway, proposed to run through residential neighborhoods (requiring the demolition of 1,750 homes) out to the suburb of Gresham. In 1978, the Tri-Met board decided to use the federal funds allocated for the freeway for a light-rail line. Unlike the San Diego or Los Angeles projects being developed at the same time, Portland put great emphasis on integrating the transit lines into the surrounding neighborhoods, with distinctive station architecture, redesigned streets, and integrated public spaces.

The third decision was the transformation of the local-bus network in 1982 from an infrequent radial network to a grid with strong frequent routes, two years before the new rail line opened.

Thus, Portland adopted some key ideas: transit as part of a livability strategy, rail as an alternative to highway expansion, an integrated bus-rail network, and urban design as a key part of transit. Those strategies have shaped transit across the United States, and in Portland they built one of the country's best transit networks.

The MAX light-rail network now includes six lines radiating out from downtown (below), reaching the edges of the metro area in most directions. These lines connect to the frequent bus grid, which covers the city's pre-World War II neighborhoods and extends out into some newer corridors. A streetcar network—started in 2001 as the first US streetcar to use modern vehicles—extends one to two miles beyond downtown, connecting neighborhood retail areas and waterfront redevelopment. An aerial tram connects the streetcar to the hilltop Oregon Health & Science University. It is a comprehensive, user-friendly and well-used network.

Of course, Portland is not a transit paradise. Jobs have sprawled and places including Intel's campus in Hillsboro and Nike's world headquarters in Beaverton are not served by rail. The growth boundary does not automatically lead to walkability, and much of the region beyond the prewar core is hostile to pedestrians and transit. Attempts have been made to insert transit in these areas, but ridership is poor. The 15-mile West Side Express commuter rail, connecting southwestern suburbia to light rail, carries only 1,700 trips a day.

+ **Successful light-rail network**
+ **Large frequent bus grid**
+ **Transit as part of a regional livability strategy**
− **Inadequate transit to suburban jobs**

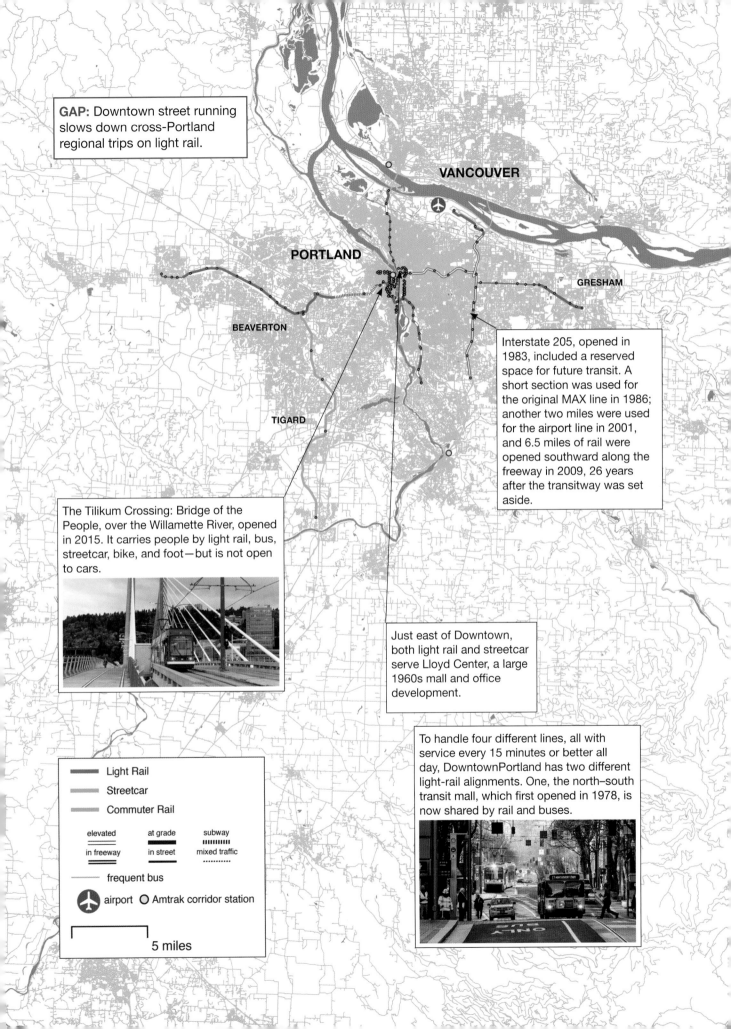

GAP: Downtown street running slows down cross-Portland regional trips on light rail.

VANCOUVER

PORTLAND

BEAVERTON

GRESHAM

TIGARD

Interstate 205, opened in 1983, included a reserved space for future transit. A short section was used for the original MAX line in 1986; another two miles were used for the airport line in 2001, and 6.5 miles of rail were opened southward along the freeway in 2009, 26 years after the transitway was set aside.

The Tilikum Crossing: Bridge of the People, over the Willamette River, opened in 2015. It carries people by light rail, bus, streetcar, bike, and foot—but is not open to cars.

Just east of Downtown, both light rail and streetcar serve Lloyd Center, a large 1960s mall and office development.

To handle four different lines, all with service every 15 minutes or better all day, DowntownPortland has two different light-rail alignments. One, the north–south transit mall, which first opened in 1978, is now shared by rail and buses.

▬▬▬	Light Rail
▬▬▬	Streetcar
▬▬▬	Commuter Rail

elevated	at grade	subway
in freeway	in street	mixed traffic

— frequent bus

✈ airport ◯ Amtrak corridor station

5 miles

Light Rail (MAX)

LARGE SYSTEM

Opened: 1986

Last Expanded: 2015

Length: 59.7 miles

Stations: 84

Frequency: 5–15 min weekdays, 15–30 min weekends

Avg weekday ridership: 119,600

Ridership per mile: 2,003

Streetcar (Portland Streetcar)

HIGH PERFORMER

LARGE SYSTEM

Opened: 2001

Last Expanded: 2015

Length: 9 miles

Stations: 36.5

Frequency: 7.5–15 min midday, 10–20 min morning/evening, 7.5–20 min weekends

Avg weekday ridership: 12,539

Ridership per mile: 1,567

Commuter Rail (WES)

SMALL SYSTEM

Opened: 2009

Last Expanded: N/A

Length: 14.7 miles

Stations: 5

Frequency: every 30 min peak only, 5 days a week (no weekend service)

Avg weekday ridership: 1,400

Ridership per mile: 95

Generally, the only transit-friendly places outside the core are transit-oriented developments at rail stations. As prime close-in neighborhoods have become more desirable, low-income residents have been priced out to these less accessible suburbs, and the parts of Portland with the best transit service have become increasingly affluent and white.

Still, there are few places in the United States where it is as easy to live a complete life on transit as in Portland. Since the 1970s, Portland has gone from a small fading industrial city to a national model for urbanism and a destination for hipsters from everywhere, and transit is an integral part of that story. ∎

Portland's light rail uses a variety of rights-of-way; a large section of the original line (above) and several later ones follow freeways, while the Yellow Line runs down Interstate Avenue (right) and the Red Line tunnels west of downtown. All are faster than the streetcar, which averages only 6.5 mph as it links the redeveloped Pearl District (below) to downtown.

Vancouver, Washington, just across the Columbia River, has its own separate transit system and turned down an opportunity for a light-rail extension to link to Portland.

GAP: Minimal transit connections across the Columbia River into Vancouver, Washington

DOWNTOWN PORTLAND
180.173 jobs
18th in US

The frequent network does a good job covering the neighborhoods where most of Portland's low-income residents live, but employment sprawl makes it harder to connect to jobs, and gentrification is displacing people from some of the most convenient neighborhoods.

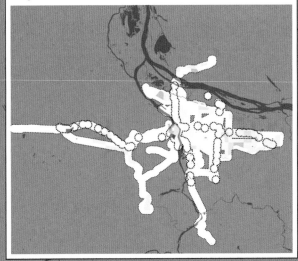

GAP: Car-oriented suburban campuses in Beaverton and Hillsboro with poor transit access

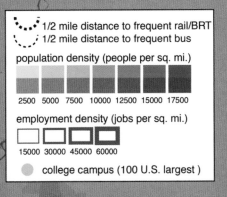

`···` 1/2 mile distance to frequent rail/BRT
`- -` 1/2 mile distance to frequent bus

population density (people per sq. mi.)

2500 5000 7500 10000 12500 15000 17500

employment density (jobs per sq. mi.)

15000 30000 45000 60000

⬤ college campus (100 U.S. largest)

Aerial Tram (Portland Aerial Tram)

HIGH PERFORMER

Opened: 2006
Last Expanded: N/A
Length: 0.6 miles
Stations: 2
Frequency: 6 min (no Sunday service except summer afternoons)
Avg weekday ridership: 10,000
Ridership per mile: 16,667

23. TAMPA

Tampa–St. Petersburg–Clearwater, FL

population 3,194,831 (21st) **served by frequent transit** 6% **daily trips per 1000** 23

In 2015, a *Tampa Bay Times* article examined how the TECO line streetcar, already in operation for over a decade, might increase ridership. The article pointed out that downtown employees who live along the line won't take it to work as long as it continues to run only after noon. That obvious conclusion is fitting for a metropolitan area that has never gotten its act together on transit. At first glance, the Tampa / St. Petersburg area ought to be a good place for transit. It has multiple downtowns separated by bodies of water that act as bottlenecks. But neither the service nor the infrastructure has lived up to that opportunity. The region has two major transit operators: HART in Hillsborough County (Tampa) and PSTA in Pinellas County (St. Petersburg and Clearwater). The two networks are connected only with infrequent cross-bay bus routes, and fare coordination is limited to a shared monthly pass.

The 25-mile corridor between St. Petersburg and Tampa could likely support a light-rail line or high-quality BRT. But, because of a lack of cross-county coordination, the corridor was never studied. HART did plan a north–south light-rail line following its busiest bus route, but county commissioners decided not to put that plan, which would need the support of a new sales tax, on the ballot in 2016. A light-rail line within St. Petersburg was rejected by voters in 2014.

Thus the only fixed-guideway transit in the region is the Tampa streetcar. It was built to connect the downtown waterfront to Ybor, an old cigar-manufacturing neighborhood that has been revitalized with lofts, restaurants, and bars. In 2010, the line was extended into the center of downtown. The historic replica cars, the span of service, and the frequency are designed to appeal to tourists, who aren't up early and aren't in a hurry. It does; when a cruise ship is in town ridership can spike to over 2,000 trips, compared to 400 on a typical weekday. Since that 2015 article, service hours and frequency have been increased, and in 2020 the state allocated funding to extend the line and reequip it with modern streetcars. Those are the kind of upgrades the streetcar needs to be truly useful. The entire regional network needs similar thinking. ■

HART
independent agency
Streetcar
Frequent Bus

PSTA
independent agency
Frequent Bus

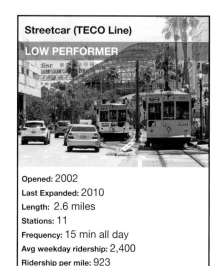

Streetcar (TECO Line)

LOW PERFORMER

Opened: 2002
Last Expanded: 2010
Length: 2.6 miles
Stations: 11
Frequency: 15 min all day
Avg weekday ridership: 2,400
Ridership per mile: 923

Ybor City (below) was redeveloped starting in the 1980s. Centro Ybor, at its center, has a movie theater, restaurants, and tourist-oriented stores. Like Little Rock, Tampa used brand-new vehicles built to resemble historic trolley cars, adding to the ambience.

- Useless tourist-oriented trolley
- Inadequate frequent network

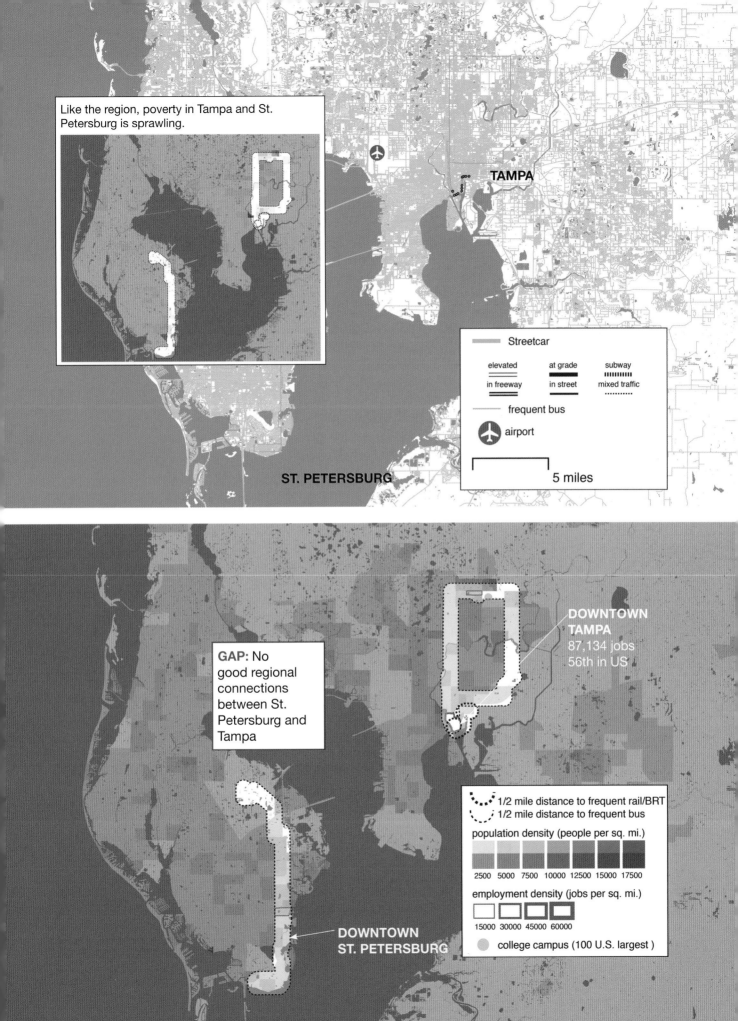

Like the region, poverty in Tampa and St. Petersburg is sprawling.

TAMPA

ST. PETERSBURG

Streetcar

| elevated | at grade | subway |
| in freeway | in street | mixed traffic |

frequent bus

✈ airport

5 miles

GAP: No good regional connections between St. Petersburg and Tampa

DOWNTOWN TAMPA
87,134 jobs
56th in US

DOWNTOWN ST. PETERSBURG

1/2 mile distance to frequent rail/BRT
1/2 mile distance to frequent bus

population density (people per sq. mi.)
2500 5000 7500 10000 12500 15000 17500

employment density (jobs per sq. mi.)
15000 30000 45000 60000

● college campus (100 U.S. largest)

24. ST. LOUIS

St. Louis–St. Charles–Farmington, MO-IL

population 2,907,648 (24th)   **served by frequent transit** 4%   **daily trips per 1000** 36

Metro
independent agency
Light Rail
Frequent Bus

No other city has been as fortunate in finding available right-of-way for a new rail-transit line as St. Louis. The Eads Bridge, built in 1874 as the first bridge crossing the Mississippi River, carried its last train in 1974, leaving two empty tracks across the region's biggest geographic barrier. At its west end, a pair of railroad tunnels, now unused, extended right under downtown, avoiding the need to lay any tracks in city streets. To the east and west, the railroad mergers that had reduced two dozen railroads serving St. Louis to only five left numerous lines abandoned. These lines connected the downtown employment core, two major universities, the medical center, the tourist area around the Gateway Arch, the newly redeveloped Union Station mall, the city's most important park, major museums, the zoo, and the airport. This available right-of-way enabled St. Louis to build 17 miles of light rail for only $465 million, $348 million of which came from federal funding.

The result, when the new light rail opened in 1993, was a dramatic transit success. Bus ridership in St. Louis had been steadily falling. But in the first five years that the new rail line was open, it increased ridership on the combined bus–rail system by 44 percent, including a five percent ridership increase on the buses. Further extensions have not been as fortunate. The 21-mile extension into Illinois, opened in 2001–3, used another abandoned rail line, but doesn't really connect to much. By the time it reaches the end of the line at Shiloh–Scott Air Force Base, it is literally running through cornfields. It has more than doubled the size of the system, but, remarkably, system-wide ridership went up by only one percent.

The Cross-County Extension, opened in 2006, added important destinations—it now stops right next to Washington University, formerly a 20-minute walk from rail, and serves the compact downtown of the county seat, Clayton. Ridership grew by 20 percent when the new line opened, but at a cost. This segment was much more expensive to build because it required a mix of tunnels and elevated structures. By the time it was done, the first contractor had been fired and the cost was $136 million over the original $550-million budget.

Metrolink's biggest challenge, though, is demographic. The combined population of the city and county of St. Louis has been declining for four decades. The 2020 population is 18 percent lower than it was in 1970. In that context, a light-rail system carrying 52,000 people, 80 percent of whom are new to transit, is impressive. ■

- **Light rail that misses urban density and serves cornfields**
- **Inadequate frequent network**

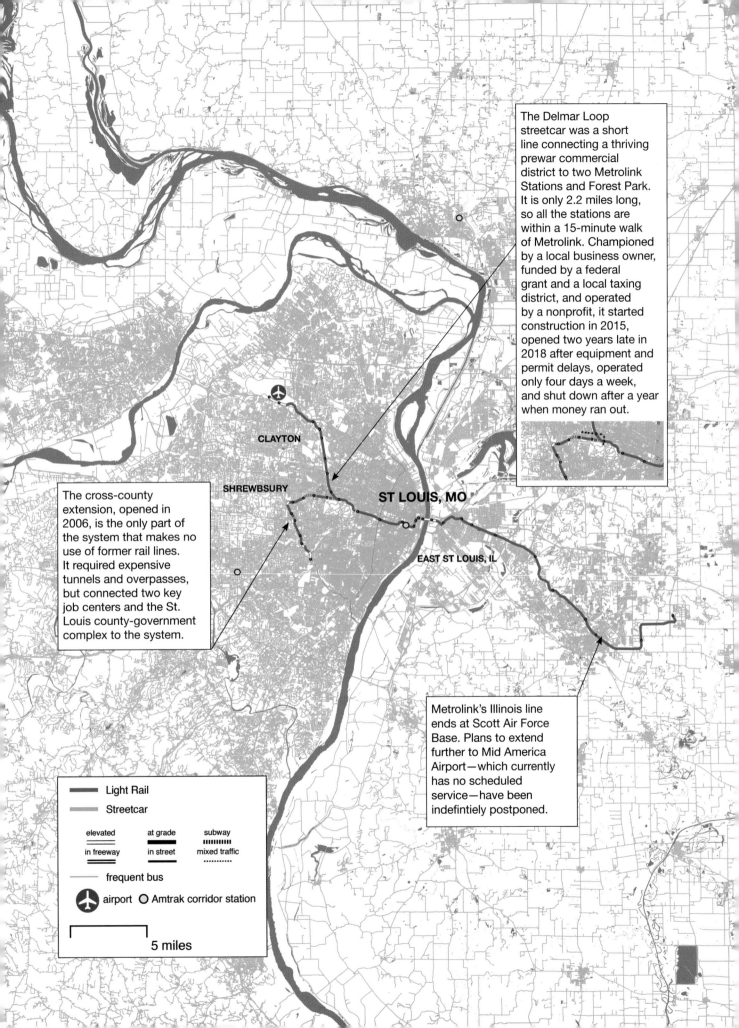

The Delmar Loop streetcar was a short line connecting a thriving prewar commercial district to two Metrolink Stations and Forest Park. It is only 2.2 miles long, so all the stations are within a 15-minute walk of Metrolink. Championed by a local business owner, funded by a federal grant and a local taxing district, and operated by a nonprofit, it started construction in 2015, opened two years late in 2018 after equipment and permit delays, operated only four days a week, and shut down after a year when money ran out.

The cross-county extension, opened in 2006, is the only part of the system that makes no use of former rail lines. It required expensive tunnels and overpasses, but connected two key job centers and the St. Louis county-government complex to the system.

Metrolink's Illinois line ends at Scott Air Force Base. Plans to extend further to Mid America Airport—which currently has no scheduled service—have been indefintiely postponed.

CLAYTON

SHREWBSURY

ST LOUIS, MO

EAST ST LOUIS, IL

Light Rail
Streetcar

elevated   at grade   subway
in freeway   in street   mixed traffic

frequent bus

airport   O Amtrak corridor station

5 miles

Light Rail (MetroLink)

LOW PERFORMER

Opened: 1993

Last Expanded: 2006

Length: 45.4 miles

Stations: 37

Frequency: 6–12 min peak, 10–20 min midday/evening/weekend

Avg weekday ridership: 38,900

Ridership per mile: 857

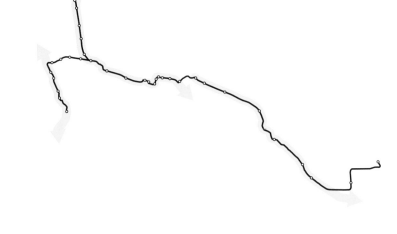

St. Louis was one of the great railroad centers of the United States, and the vast majority of Metrolink follows abandoned freight-rail lines (highlighted at top). Even the downtown subway uses a tunnel opened in 1875 for mainline railroad trains. Four stations—one at the tunnel entrance next to the ballpark (above), two in the tunnel itself, and one above the bank of the Mississippi River on the approach to the 1874 Eads Bridge (above left)—put all of Downtown within walking distance. Sometimes, the policy of following rail lines works well. Sometimes it leads to trains missing major activity centers or literally running through cornfields (left).

On the west side, Metrolink branches into the Red Line (to the airport) and the Blue Line (to Clayton). Each runs every 20 minutes off-peak, so only the area where the two lines overlap has all-day frequent service. That, combined with lack of frequent bus service (there are only two frequent routes) leaves some of the city's densest employment and population with low-quality service.

The region's only frequent bus route, the 70 Grand, serves dense, low-income, and largely Black neighborhoods on the north and south side of the city, but other similar neighborhoods have only infrequent service.

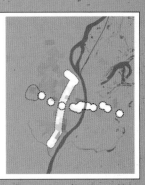

DOWNTOWN ST. LOUIS
97,167 jobs
44th in US

CLAYTON

GAP: Inadequate frequent network

GAP: No rail or frequent bus to the dense jobs and population of the West End

GAP: No north–south rail or BRT

A nighttime aerial view of St. Louis shows how much of the activity is on the Missouri side of the Mississippi River. But MetroLink is run by a bi-state authority. Thus, the agency's political structure trumped the geography of transit demand, and light rail was extended into rural Illinois.

⟍ 1/2 mile distance to frequent rail/BRT
⟍ 1/2 mile distance to frequent bus

population density (people per sq. mi.)

2500 5000 7500 10000 12500 15000 17500

employment density (jobs per sq. mi.)

15000 30000 45000 60000

◉ college campus (100 U.S. largest)

25. CHARLOTTE

Charlotte–Concord, NC-SC

population 2,797,636 (25th)   **served by frequent transit** 5%   **daily trips per 1000** 24

CATS
independent agency
Light Rail
Streetcar
Frequent Bus

Like Atlanta, Charlotte has transformed from a regional center to a global business city. As headquarters of Bank of America, and a major location of Wells Fargo, it is the second biggest banking center in the United States, after New York. Mecklenburg County has more than tripled in population since 1960 and is growing steadily by 30 percent a decade.

This growth has brought traffic congestion. It has also brought a more progressive attitude toward city planning. In 1998, the city, under Republican mayor Pat McCrory, adopted a new long-range plan integrating transportation and land-use policy. It identified five major corridors radiating out from downtown, proposed rail or BRT lines in those corridors, and called for focusing new office and multi-family development around those stations rather than dispersing it across the city. Voters approved a half-cent sales tax to pay for the plan.

The first major transit project to come out of the plan, also championed by McCrory, was the Lynx Blue Line, 9.6 miles of light rail south from downtown. The corridor was selected in 2000, construction started in 2005, and trains started running in 2007. The Blue Line follows a Norfolk Southern freight-rail corridor that had been partially abandoned. Its location, though, is prime: it runs through the center of downtown (and literally through the convention center, in a glass-enclosed tunnel) and then through the redeveloped South End. From there, it parallels a suburban commercial corridor, with park-and-ride lots serving the surrounding single-family neighborhoods. Ridership has been higher than expected—first-year ridership was 18,000 a day, rather than the projected 9,700. The line carries as many people per mile as Denver or Salt Lake City. Light rail has also been a stimulus for development; Uptown (right) in particular has boomed, with 12,000 apartments in place and another 2,600 under construction, and a Whole Foods directly on the light-rail station. The natural extension of the Blue Line, northeastward along the same north–south corridor, has similar promise: close-in neighborhoods ready for new development, and the University of North

Carolina campus anchoring the north end. It opened in 2018, and new development is on the way along it.

Other corridors in the 1998 plan haven't fared as well. The northward Red Line, was originally conceived as commuter rail and intended to open by 2012. But the transit authority, CATS, was unable to find funding, and Norfolk Southern did not agree to share its tracks, making the project much more expensive. It is now being rethought. CATS wasn't able to fund the east–west Gold Line either, so the city built an initial 1.5-mile segment as a streetcar in mixed traffic in conjunction with a street-reconstruction project and operated it using replica historic trolleys, originally used for a streetcar line that ran where the Blue Line is now. It's now being extended on both ends creating an east-west corridor across Downtown to complement the north-south light rail. Without dedicated lanes, though, it will not be as reliable. When east-west light rail is built (it's currently in planning stages) it may skip the center of Downtown entirely. Charlotte's Blue Line has been a success both in attracting ridership and in driving development. The nationwide attention that attracted got McCrory's successor, Democrat Anthony Foxx, appointed to be secretary of transportation under President Obama. But, so far at least, the region hasn't figured out a repeat. ■

+ **Light rail linking downtown, university, and new urban development**
- **Small frequent bus network**

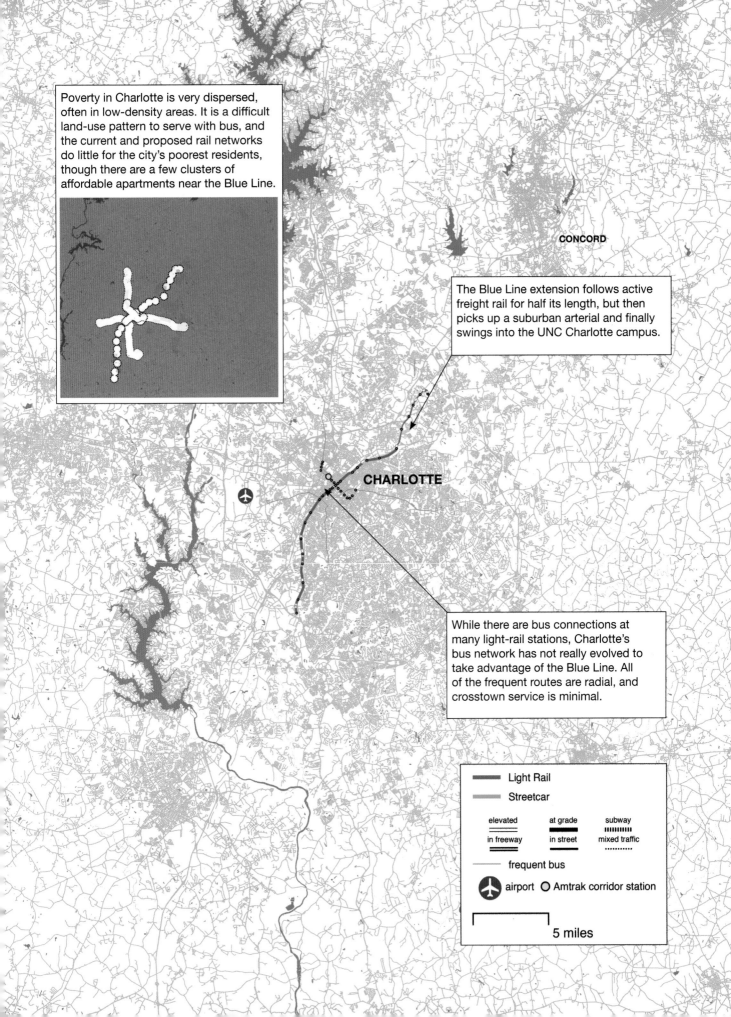

Poverty in Charlotte is very dispersed, often in low-density areas. It is a difficult land-use pattern to serve with bus, and the current and proposed rail networks do little for the city's poorest residents, though there are a few clusters of affordable apartments near the Blue Line.

CONCORD

The Blue Line extension follows active freight rail for half its length, but then picks up a suburban arterial and finally swings into the UNC Charlotte campus.

CHARLOTTE

While there are bus connections at many light-rail stations, Charlotte's bus network has not really evolved to take advantage of the Blue Line. All of the frequent routes are radial, and crosstown service is minimal.

Light Rail
Streetcar

| elevated | at grade | subway |
| in freeway | in street | mixed traffic |

frequent bus

✈ airport   ⊙ Amtrak corridor station

5 miles

Light Rail (Lynx)

SMALL SYSTEM

Opened: 2007
Last Expanded: 2018
Length: 19.3 miles
Stations: 26
Frequency: 10 min peak, 15 min midday, 20 min evening, 20–30 min weekends
Avg weekday ridership: 29,900
Ridership per mile: 1,549

Streetcar (CityLynx)

SMALL SYSTEM

Opened: 2015
Last Expanded: ongoing
Length: 1.5 miles (2.5 under construction)
Stations: 6 (11 under construction)
Frequency: 15 min peak, 20 min off-peak
Avg weekday ridership: N/A
Ridership per mile: N/A

In Downtown (top), the light-rail Blue Line (on the bridge in the background) connects to the downtown bus-transit center (left) and the Gold Line streetcar (foreground).

In the South End (center) new residential, office, and retail development surrounds stations.

The Blue Line ends at I-485 (bottom) with a 1,120-space parking garage. Initial plans extended the line another 1.5 miles to downtown Pineville, but, unlike in Charlotte, city officials de- cided not to zone for denser devel- opment around the station, and CATS planners concluded that current land uses didn't justify the cost.

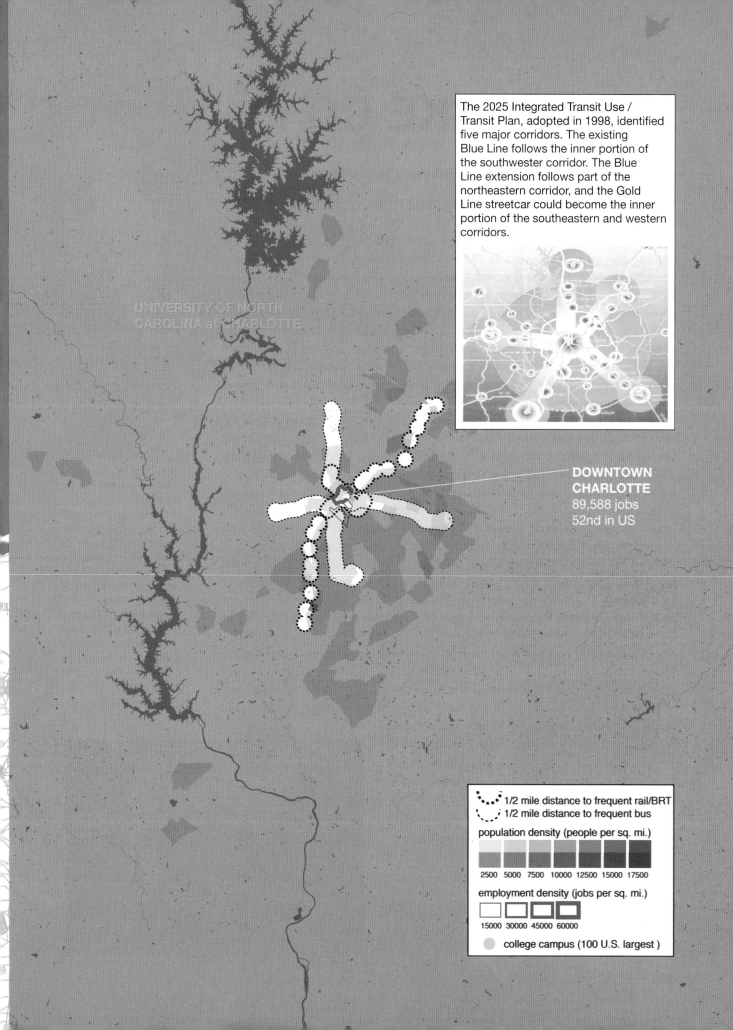

The 2025 Integrated Transit Use / Transit Plan, adopted in 1998, identified five major corridors. The existing Blue Line follows the inner portion of the southwester corridor. The Blue Line extension follows part of the northeastern corridor, and the Gold Line streetcar could become the inner portion of the southeastern and western corridors.

UNIVERSITY OF NORTH CAROLINA at CHARLOTTE

DOWNTOWN CHARLOTTE
89,588 jobs
52nd in US

⌒ 1/2 mile distance to frequent rail/BRT
⌒ 1/2 mile distance to frequent bus

population density (people per sq. mi.)
2500 5000 7500 10000 12500 15000 17500

employment density (jobs per sq. mi.)
15000 30000 45000 60000

● college campus (100 U.S. largest)

Light Rail (TRAX)

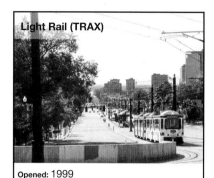

Opened: 1999

Last Expanded: 2013

Length: 44.7 miles

Stations: 50

Frequency: 7.5–15 min weekdays,
10–20 min weekends

Avg weekday ridership: 55,531

Ridership per mile: 1.242

Streetcar (S-Line)

**SMALL SYSTEM
LOW PERFORMER**

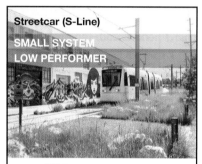

Opened: 2014

Last Expanded: N/A

Length: 2 miles

Stations: 7

Frequency: 20 min

Avg weekday ridership: 1,369

Ridership per mile: 685

Commuter Rail (FrontRunner)

Opened: 2008

Last Expanded: 2013

Length: 82 miles

Stations: 16

Frequency: 30 min weekday, 1 hr
weekend

Avg weekday ridership: 19,200

Ridership per mile: 234

Daybreak (above right), developed on 4,000 acres of former mining land, embodies Envision Utah ideals. It mixes single-family and multi-family residential, and each of the 20,000 units is within walking distance of a park. Seventy-three percent of children walk or bike to school. The major commercial centers, which will contain 9.1 million square feet of office and retail, are connected with bike trails and located around light-rail stations on the 2011 TRAX Mid-Jordan extension. But the commercial development was phased to follow single-family "rooftops," and the 2008 recession slowed development, leading to the odd sight of trains stopping in open fields (above left).

Unlike most modern commuter-rail lines, UTA's FrontRunner is largely separated from freight rail, running on its own tracks (above) alongside Union Pacific trains. This permits a relatively high level of service, with trains from 5:00 a.m. to past midnight, every 30 minutes during rush hour, and every hour for the rest of the day. Many of the stations, like Provo (below) are also bus transfer hubs.

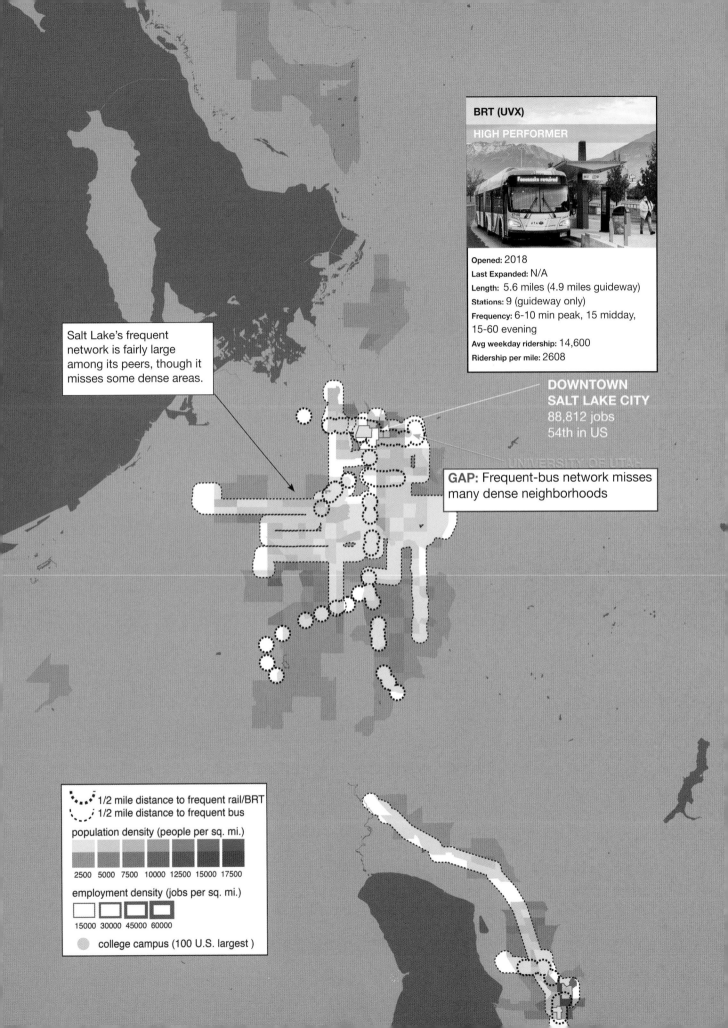

BRT (UVX)

HIGH PERFORMER

Opened: 2018
Last Expanded: N/A
Length: 5.6 miles (4.9 miles guideway)
Stations: 9 (guideway only)
Frequency: 6-10 min peak, 15 midday, 15-60 evening
Avg weekday ridership: 14,600
Ridership per mile: 2608

Salt Lake's frequent network is fairly large among its peers, though it misses some dense areas.

DOWNTOWN SALT LAKE CITY
88,812 jobs
54th in US

UNIVERSITY OF UTAH

GAP: Frequent-bus network misses many dense neighborhoods

1/2 mile distance to frequent rail/BRT
1/2 mile distance to frequent bus

population density (people per sq. mi.)

2500 5000 7500 10000 12500 15000 17500

employment density (jobs per sq. mi.)

15000 30000 45000 60000

college campus (100 U.S. largest)

27. SACRAMENTO

Sacramento–Roseville, CA

population 2,639,124 (27th)   **served by frequent transit** 10%   **daily trips per 1000** 29

SacRT
independent agency
Light Rail
Frequent Bus

Sacramento was a light-rail pioneer. Only Portland and San Diego had opened new light-rail systems when Sacramento opened its 18-mile line in 1987. It took significant local effort, and was a notable step for a metropolitan area that often seems to be an afterthought compared to Los Angeles, the San Francisco Bay Area, or San Diego.

Sacramento showed that smaller metropolitan areas could afford light rail. The initial line was funded with local funds, with no federal assistance. That limited budget is reflected throughout the project in simple stations, minimal urban design, and clever reuse of existing infrastructure. One segment—running west from downtown—followed a little-used freight-rail line. The other segments used city streets, a short section of old rail line, and right-of-way cleared for extending Interstate 80 through the city. The interstate extension project had been canceled in 1979 in favor of simply rerouting I-80 onto an already constructed freeway bypass to the north. The money already allocated for constructing this freeway section was used for light rail instead, an already-constructed freeway bridge was converted to rail, and existing pavement was repurposed as park-and-ride lots. The downtown segments that connect them were built at minimal cost, inserting tracks into existing streets without landscaping, or rebuilding sidewalks or any of the other parts of the street. A few key bridges were built single-track, reducing cost but restricting frequency. Stations were minimal, and when four-car trains stop at downtown stations they actually block cross streets. Later extensions, paid for with federal funds, have more elaborate infrastructure, but still follow a pattern of going along rail corridors with trains every 15 minutes (or every 30 on weekends), serving some inner neighborhoods, but primarily connecting park-and-ride lots to the state capitol and the surrounding office buildings. ∎

+ **Large regional light rail supporting downtown jobs**
- **Small frequent-bus network**

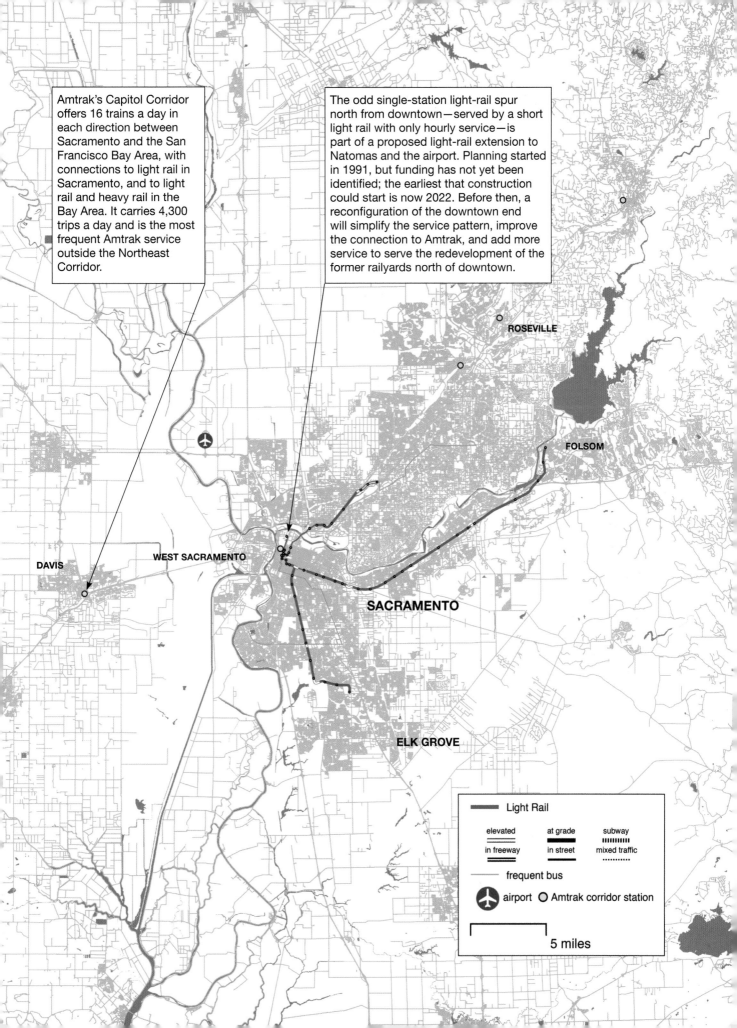

Amtrak's Capitol Corridor offers 16 trains a day in each direction between Sacramento and the San Francisco Bay Area, with connections to light rail in Sacramento, and to light rail and heavy rail in the Bay Area. It carries 4,300 trips a day and is the most frequent Amtrak service outside the Northeast Corridor.

The odd single-station light-rail spur north from downtown—served by a short light rail with only hourly service—is part of a proposed light-rail extension to Natomas and the airport. Planning started in 1991, but funding has not yet been identified; the earliest that construction could start is now 2022. Before then, a reconfiguration of the downtown end will simplify the service pattern, improve the connection to Amtrak, and add more service to serve the redevelopment of the former railyards north of downtown.

ROSEVILLE

FOLSOM

DAVIS

WEST SACRAMENTO

SACRAMENTO

ELK GROVE

Light Rail

elevated	at grade	subway
in freeway	in street	mixed traffic

frequent bus

✈ airport ◯ Amtrak corridor station

5 miles

Light Rail (RT Light Rail)

LOW PERFORMER

Opened: 1987

Last Expanded: 2015

Length: 42.8 miles

Stations: 50.5

Frequency: 15–30 weekdays, 30 weekends (no weekend service on one line)

Avg weekday ridership: 38,400

Ridership per mile: 897

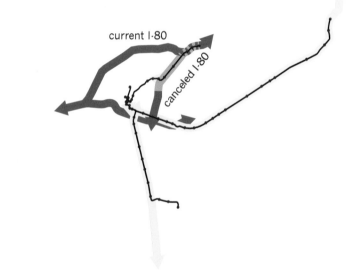

Sacramento's light-rail system (right) follows an abandoned freight-rail line, actually California's first railroad, incorporated in 1852 (yellow, top right), an active freight-rail line (also yellow, bottom right), right-of-way cleared for the alignment of a canceled freeway (red, and photo below) and city streets (above).

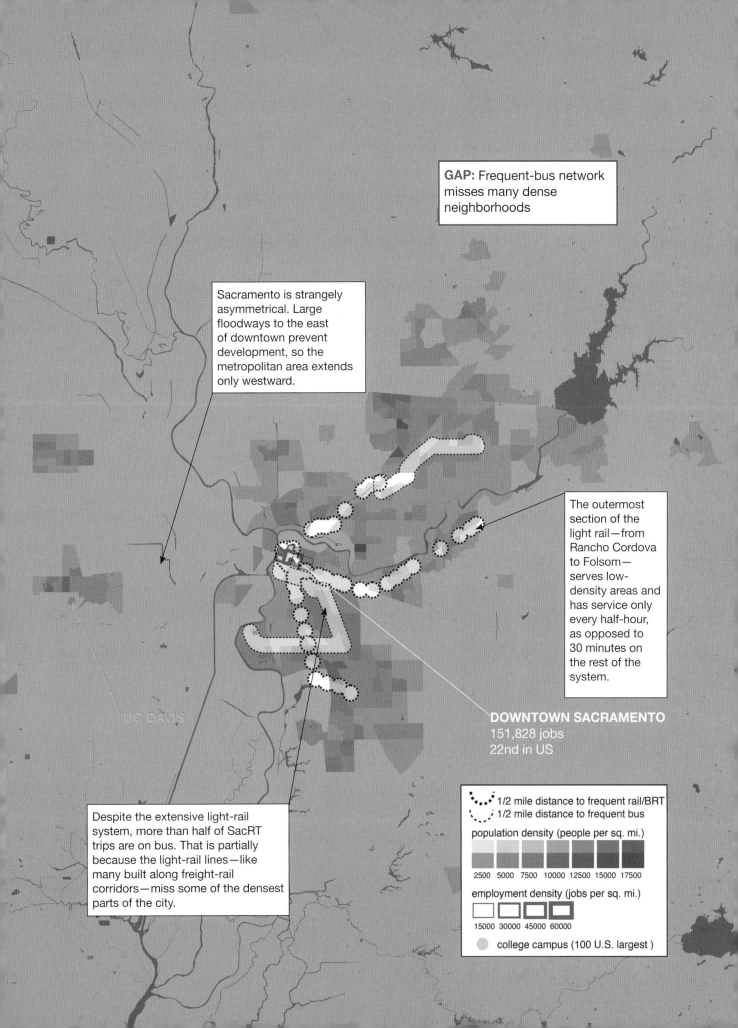

GAP: Frequent-bus network misses many dense neighborhoods

Sacramento is strangely asymmetrical. Large floodways to the east of downtown prevent development, so the metropolitan area extends only westward.

The outermost section of the light rail—from Rancho Cordova to Folsom—serves low-density areas and has service only every half-hour, as opposed to 30 minutes on the rest of the system.

UC DAVIS

DOWNTOWN SACRAMENTO
151,828 jobs
22nd in US

Despite the extensive light-rail system, more than half of SacRT trips are on bus. That is partially because the light-rail lines—like many built along freight-rail corridors—miss some of the densest parts of the city.

1/2 mile distance to frequent rail/BRT
1/2 mile distance to frequent bus

population density (people per sq. mi.)

2500 5000 7500 10000 12500 15000 17500

employment density (jobs per sq. mi.)

15000 30000 45000 60000

college campus (100 U.S. largest)

28. PITTSBURGH

Pittsburgh–New Castle–Weirton, PA-OH-WV

population 2,603,259 (28th)   **served by frequent transit** 8%   **daily trips per 1000** 68

Pittsburgh is a transit anomaly. As nearly every US city eliminated its streetcar system, Pittsburgh kept its intact. Then, as other cities began planning rail transit again, Pittsburgh tore up nearly all of its track. The remaining lines were modernized, but only partially. At the same time, the transit agency made massive investments in the country's most advanced busways. And now, in an era of cost-effective, street-running light-rail lines, Pittsburgh built a two-station line largely in subway. Pittsburgh's transit history is convoluted and sometimes confused, and that is reflected in the resulting system.

The most problematic aspect of Pittsburgh transit, though, is not infrastructure, but organization. In 1956, when the city of Pittsburgh proved unable to finance its own transit, the state legislature took the unusual step of creating the Port Authority of Allegheny County (which never actually built any port facilities) with transit as one of its missions, and in 1963 the authority bought the local private transit operators. That solved the immediate problem. But, unlike agencies in other states, the PAT does not have its own revenue source. Every year, the state legislature has to appropriate funding. In a state where the balance of power lies in rural areas and small towns, not cities, that funding is targeted every time state tax revenues are tight. So, even as the PAT has built new infrastructure with federal funds, it has frequently had to cut operations. Pittsburgh abandoned commuter rail in 1989, just as other cities were building new systems, and has the dubious distinction of being the first city to build a modern rail-transit line (the one-station Penn Park spur) and then take it out of service. ■

PortAuthority

Port Authority
independent agency
Light Rail
BRT
Frequent Bus

The historic roots of Pittsburgh's light rail are visible in suburban Bethel Park (below). The train is obviously modern, but the jointed track and the wooden poles are those of a 100-year-old rural streetcar line. In the background is Lytle, one of 25 modern high-platform stops on the system. They are outnumbered by 43 simple stops like the one at Center, in the foreground.

Another distinctive piece of legacy transit is the inclines (below left), which have been bringing people up the hills south of Downtown since the 1870s.

+ **High-ridership busways**
+ **Modernized, historic light rail serving walkable suburbs**
- **No BRT or light rail to major university / medical hub**

Three scenes from a light-rail trip: at top, a train leaves downtown Pittsburgh on a former Pennsylvania Railroad bridge; above, the street-running section in Beechview; below, the tunnel under the town center of Mt. Lebanon. The tunnel and the line over the bridge date from the 1987 modernization, and the street section was rebuilt at the same time.

Pittsburgh's topography has always made it a tough place to run transit. The 11 Fineview was once a streetcar; now it's a local bus, winding up steep hills and through narrow streets once an hour.

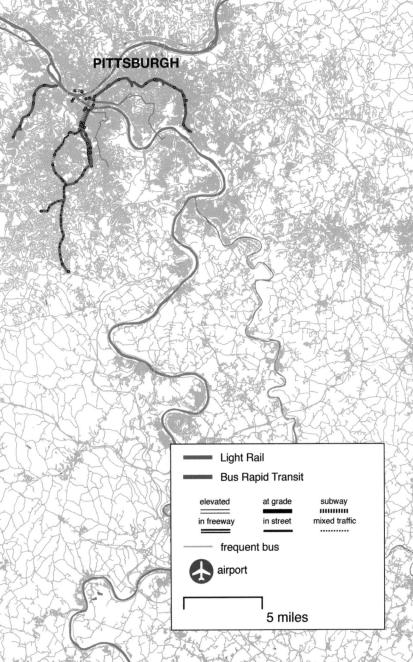

PITTSBURGH

	Light Rail
	Bus Rapid Transit

elevated	at grade	subway
in freeway	in street	mixed traffic

frequent bus

✈ airport

5 miles

Light Rail (The T)

LOW PERFORMER

PREWAR SYSTEM

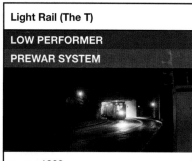

Opened: 1903
Last Expanded: 2012
Length: 22 miles
Stations: 53
Frequency: 4–15 peak, 8–30 midday,
30 evening, 15–30 weekend
Avg weekday ridership: 24,467
Ridership per mile: 1,203

BRT (Busways)

LARGE SYSTEM

Opened: 1977
Last Expanded: 2003
Length: open BRT (19 guideway miles)
Stations: 26 (guideway only)
Frequency: 6–8 min peak, 12–20 min
midday, 30–35 min weekend
Avg weekday ridership: N/A
Ridership per mile: N/A

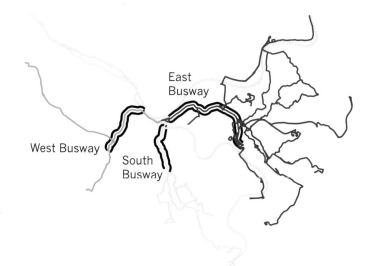

Pittsburgh's busway system is the largest of its kind in the United States. Three grade-separated, bus-only roadways with stations along them extend south, east, and west from Downtown.

The busways are operated as part of the overall bus network. Routes are named to show that they use the busways (any route whose number starts with a "G" runs on the West Busway, any route with a "Y" on the South Busway, and any route with a "P" on the East Busway) but the buses look no different than any other PAT bus. The East and West busways have "busway all stops" routes that run the length of the busway, stopping at all stations, and into downtown. But most of the 23 routes that use the busways extend beyond them (above), giving neighborhoods miles from the busways the benefit of faster and more-reliable service into downtown.

The busways were built where rights-of-way were available. The East Busway (below), extending along an active rail line into some of the densest and poorest parts of Pittsburgh, is the most successful, with 15 routes and an impressive 24,000 daily riders. The South Busway, which parallels light rail (and shares the Mt. Washington Tunnel with it), and the West Busway following an old railroad line through old industrial towns, each carry fewer routes and only 5,000 riders. Together, the three busways account for 17 percent of the Port Authority ridership, more than light rail. East Liberty Station (below left) was recently rebuilt.

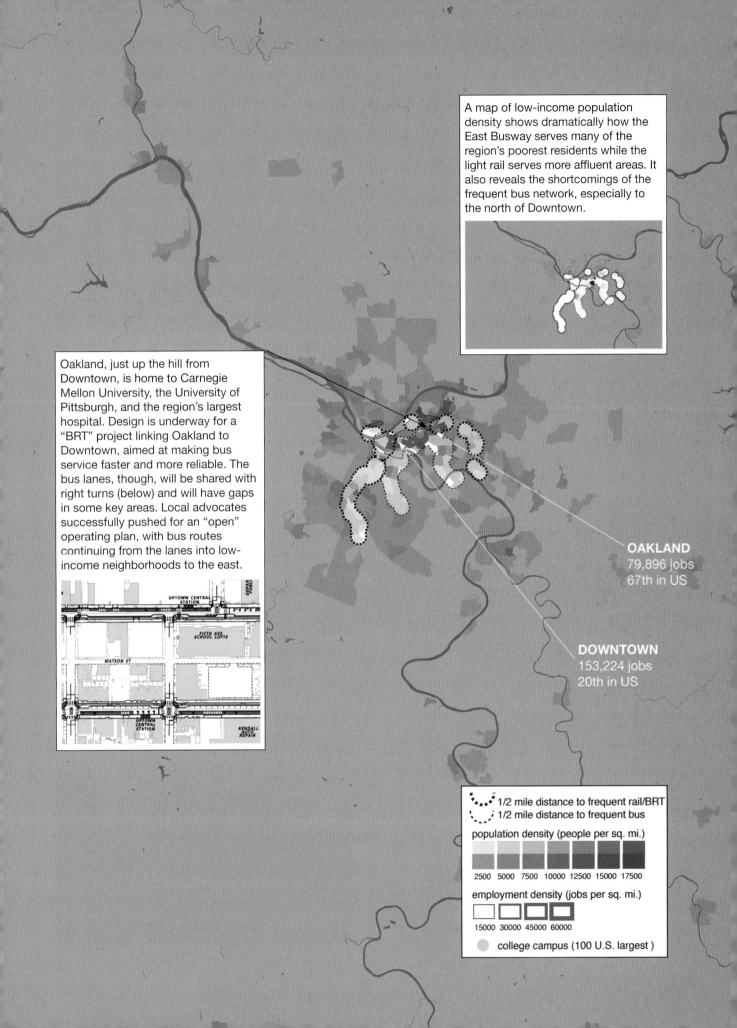

A map of low-income population density shows dramatically how the East Busway serves many of the region's poorest residents while the light rail serves more affluent areas. It also reveals the shortcomings of the frequent bus network, especially to the north of Downtown.

Oakland, just up the hill from Downtown, is home to Carnegie Mellon University, the University of Pittsburgh, and the region's largest hospital. Design is underway for a "BRT" project linking Oakland to Downtown, aimed at making bus service faster and more reliable. The bus lanes, though, will be shared with right turns (below) and will have gaps in some key areas. Local advocates successfully pushed for an "open" operating plan, with bus routes continuing from the lanes into low-income neighborhoods to the east.

OAKLAND
79,896 jobs
67th in US

DOWNTOWN
153,224 jobs
20th in US

'···' 1/2 mile distance to frequent rail/BRT
'··/ 1/2 mile distance to frequent bus

population density (people per sq. mi.)

2500 5000 7500 10000 12500 15000 17500

employment density (jobs per sq. mi.)

15000 30000 45000 60000

● college campus (100 U.S. largest)

As in San Francisco, Pittsburgh's light rail owes its survival to a tunnel. Pittsburgh's streetcars generally climbed the city's many hills rather than tunneling under them. That made them easy to replace with buses in the 1960s. But two old interurban lines, built to link Pittsburgh to the small towns of Washington and Charleroi, crossed under Mt. Washington just south of Downtown in a tunnel completed in 1904. Because the tunnel wasn't easy to convert to bus, they remained, cut short to the county line in 1953, betraying their original purpose with long segments of private right of way that now cut through well-to-do suburbs in the South Hills. The urge to replace 1940s streetcars with something modern and to nurture a local transit-manufacturing industry led to the 1964 "Skybus" plan, proposing new rubber-tired peoplemover technology to serve the South Hills. When that fizzled in 1972 due to cost and political disputes, a new task force was created and, four years later, chose light rail instead.

The modernization program proceeded in phases; arguably, it is still incomplete. The first step, built in 1981–87, had four parts. The most radical was a downtown subway, replacing street tracks on the Smithfield Street Bridge and in Downtown with a new river crossing on an abandoned railroad bridge and a three-station underground segment serving the central business district. Nearly as radical was the reconstruction of the route through suburban Beechview, with another new tunnel segment in Mount Lebanon replacing half a mile of street running. The plan also included a new suburban branch serving a park-and-ride garage at South Hills Village, also home to the system's new maintenance shop, which housed a fleet of new light-rail vehicles.

But the rebuilding was not total. The Overbrook Route, parallel to the Beechview line, was untouched, and its timber bridges continued to decay. The route to Drake was not upgraded for the new vehicles, so old street-cars continued running on it; in fact, the Downtown sub-way had to be designed to accommodate them. Most of the suburban stops were untouched, still consisting of no more than a patch of asphalt and perhaps a small shelter.

The second phase came after the Overbrook line finally decayed so much that all service had to be stopped. More funding was found, and the line was completely rebuilt, with new tracks, new bridges, and new handicapped-accessible stops. The project also included additional light-rail cars. In the interim, the route was closed for 11 years. At the same time, the last of the old streetcars were taken out of service, and the Drake line was abandoned. Meanwhile, planning was underway for a short northward expansion of the downtown subway under the Allegheny River to the sports stadiums and museums on the north side of the river. After 25 years of construction, the Pittsburgh light-rail system is an odd mix of old and new. Brand-new vehicles stop at 100-year-old stops that don't even have platforms. Nowhere, even in modern stations, are there ticket machines: fares are collected by station agents and train operators.

After nearly 40 years of construction, light-rail still serves only Downtown and one (affluent) slice of suburbs. It carries only 13 percent of Pittsburgh's transit riders, and misses the city's densest neighborhoods and significant activity centers like Oakland. Pittsburgh's light rail serves the area that it does not because that area had the highest transit demand, but because that area happened to be on the far side of a big mountain with a trolley tunnel running through it.

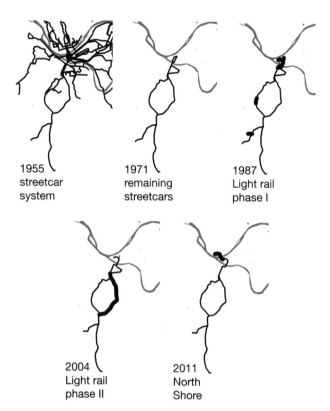

1955 streetcar system

1971 remaining streetcars

1987 Light rail phase I

2004 Light rail phase II

2011 North Shore

Pittsburgh's southern suburbs grew around the old streetcar lines that are now the "T." As a result, the tracks are embedded in the hearts of the small towns along the way. Below, an outbound train on the reconstructed Overbrook Line curves through Castle Shannon.

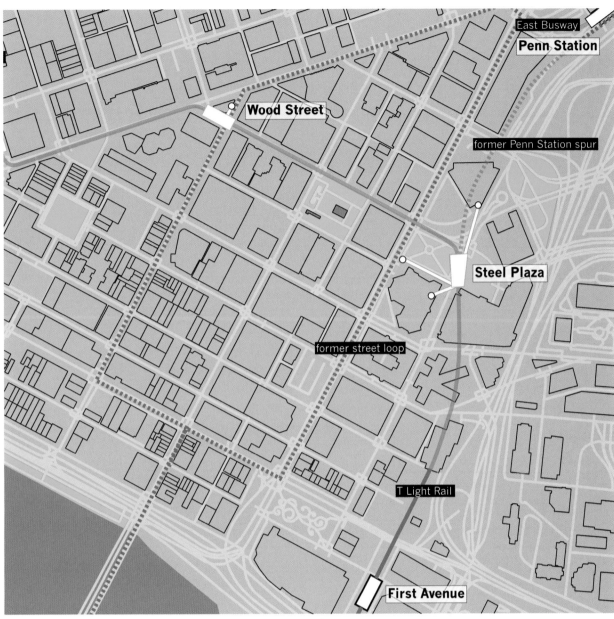

Wood Street

Penn Station

East Busway

former Penn Station spur

Steel Plaza

former street loop

T Light Rail

First Avenue

Downtown Pittsburgh is a small triangle, tightly confined by the Allegheny and Monongahela Rivers on two sides and steep slopes on the third. Until 1985, streetcars crossed the Monongahela on a road bridge and then looped through Downtown on city streets. The new downtown subway (right) replaced that with a new route along an abandoned rail line across the river to Steel Plaza and a new half subway from Steel Plaza to Gateway. Three stations (with a fourth, First Avenue, added later) put all of Downtown within walking distance of rail. A somewhat useless branch continued along the old rail line to Penn Station; service here was gradually reduced until it had the distinction of being the least-frequent light-rail line in the US (one passenger-carrying train a day, in one direction only) and then eliminated altogether, though it can still be used to store trains. In 2011, the subway was extended onward from Gateway, across the Allegheny.

29. KANSAS CITY

Kansas City–Overland Park–Kansas City, MO-KS

population 2,501,151 (31st)   **served by frequent transit** 6%   **daily trips per 1000** 20

RideKC Streetcar
independent agency
Streetcar

RideKC

**Kansas City Area
Transportation
Authority**
independent agency

Frequent Bus

For decades, Kansas City seemed like a transit backwater. As cross-state rival St. Louis built and expanded its light-rail system, Kansas City rejected a series of light-rail and streetcar ballot measures. The bus network was a confusing jumble of low-frequency routes. State and county boundaries divided the transit system into multiple operators with separate route-numbering systems and fare structures. Budget cuts reduced service. A series of major initiatives transformed that system. In 2005, a rapid-bus service, MAX, opened in the Main Street corridor. It has branded buses and distinctive stops with passenger information, service every 10-to-15 minutes all day on weekdays. Traffic signal priority, stops every 1/4 to 1/2 mile, and bus-only lanes in part of the corridor cut travel time by more than 20 percent, reducing a 24-minute trip to 18 minutes. Daily ridership in the corridor increased from 3,100 to 5,400. Main Street MAX was followed by a second corridor, Troost, in 2011, and a third is planned to open in 2020. In 2012, local routes were adjusted to simplify the network, make service more consistent, and increase frequencies. In 2015, four separate bus systems in Kansas City, Kansas; Kansas City, Missouri; Independence, Missouri; and Johnson County, Kansas, were coordinated into a single brand ("RideKC") and fare structure. This has created a coherent rider experience even as they continue to be governed and operated separately. Finally, and most visibly, a new streetcar line opened in 2016. Unlike many of its peers, it has been a clear success: with 6,800 daily riders on 1.9 miles, it is busier than most light-rail systems.

The streetcar, like MAX before it, is successful because it provides a direct route between major centers. It serves distinct major office areas —Downtown and Crown Center—which are too far apart to walk. It also serves retail and entertainment areas including River Market and the Power and Light District, numerous hotels, the central library, the redeveloping Crossroads area, and the museum complex at Union Station. MAX continues farther south to Country Club Plaza, a major retail area, and the University of Missouri–Kansas City. Work is now underway on extending the streetcar to the southern areas as well. Main Street is Kansas City's easy-to-understand, and frequent service along it while connecting to buses that serve the rest of the city. With the streetcar, as with MAX and the local-bus network, Kansas City has focused on the basics of good transit, and the public is noticing. The city has also now committed to making the entire system fare-free, hoping, the mayor said, to "build up a culture of bus riding." ∎

+ **High-ridership streetcar linking activity centers**
+ **Good bus–rail integration**
+ **Strong frequent-bus network**

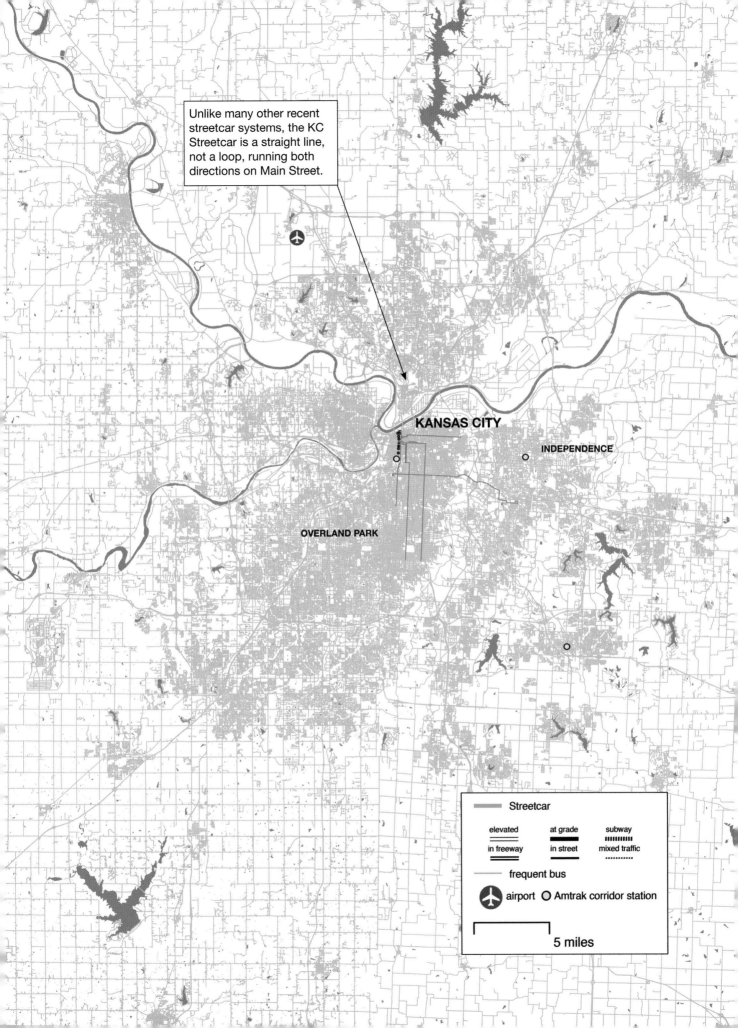

Unlike many other recent streetcar systems, the KC Streetcar is a straight line, not a loop, running both directions on Main Street.

KANSAS CITY

INDEPENDENCE

OVERLAND PARK

Streetcar

| elevated | at grade | subway |
| in freeway | in street | mixed traffic |

frequent bus

✈ airport   ◯ Amtrak corridor station

5 miles

Streetcar (KC Streetcar)

HIGH PERFORMER

SMALL SYSTEM

Opened: 2016

Last Expanded: N/A

Length: 1.9 miles

Stations: 10

Frequency: 10-15 min peak, 12-18 min off-peak

Avg weekday ridership: 6,107

Ridership per mile: 3,214

In mixed traffic, and without signal priority, the streetcar (right top) averages only about nine mph. It runs frequently enough, though, that it is significantly faster than walking (an average five-minute wait plus nine minutes in travel time from downtown to Union Station, compared to a 30-minute walk).

MAX (at Country Club Plaza, right) has distinctive red buses and named, branded stops with next-bus displays.

MAX, the local buses, and the streetcar systems are integrated into a single system. The streetcar connects to bus routes in all directions in Downtown, though the convenient 10th and Main transfer hub (below) has been replaced by on-street stops and the far-less convenient (albeit more spacious) East Village Transfer Center. Thus, the streetcar connects bus riders to the Crown Center area south of downtown. The streetcar also shares stops with MAX. Local bus and MAX use the same fares for easy transfers, and the streetcar is free. All three modes share coordinated branding.

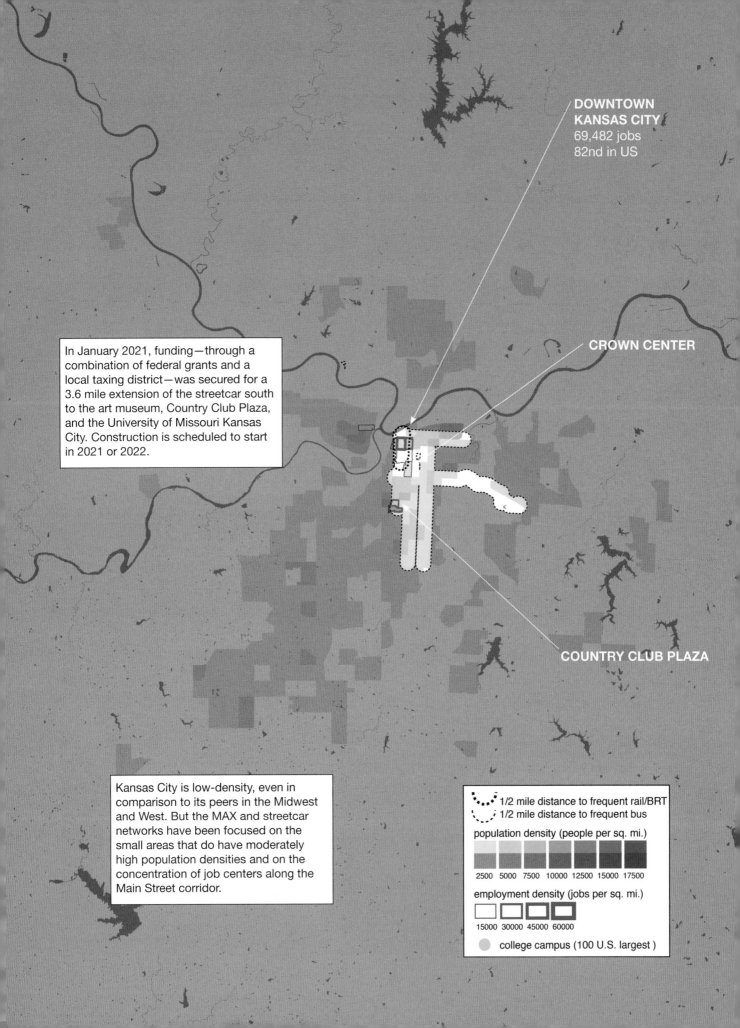

DOWNTOWN KANSAS CITY
69,482 jobs
82nd in US

CROWN CENTER

In January 2021, funding—through a combination of federal grants and a local taxing district—was secured for a 3.6 mile extension of the streetcar south to the art museum, Country Club Plaza, and the University of Missouri Kansas City. Construction is scheduled to start in 2021 or 2022.

COUNTRY CLUB PLAZA

Kansas City is low-density, even in comparison to its peers in the Midwest and West. But the MAX and streetcar networks have been focused on the small areas that do have moderately high population densities and on the concentration of job centers along the Main Street corridor.

1/2 mile distance to frequent rail/BRT
1/2 mile distance to frequent bus

population density (people per sq. mi.)
2500 5000 7500 10000 12500 15000 17500

employment density (jobs per sq. mi.)
15000 30000 45000 60000

college campus (100 U.S. largest)

30. VANCOUVER

Vancouver - Surrey - Barnaby, BC

population 2,463,431 (32nd)   **served by frequent transit** 66%   **daily trips per 1000** 502

Translink
independent authority
heavy rail
frequent bus
frequent ferry
commuter rail

Vancouver has been transformed around transit more than any other city in North America. The population of the metro area has doubled since 1981, and much of the growth has been in the form of high-rise residential towers clustered around Skytrain stops. This former industrial city has become a model for urban planning and one of the most diverse cities in North America. By some measures it is one of the most "livable" places on earth, and transit is at the center of that. Ninety percent of residents in the Vancouver city limits live within walking distance of frequent transit. Over half of all trips within the city are made by walking, biking, or transit, and car use is actually dropping. Ridership on Translink, the regional transit agency, has been rising steadily for decades, and increased 25% just between 2015 and 2019.

The Skytrain network is remarkable in two ways. The first is that it is the only completely automated large-scale rail network in North America. Some other cities like Miami and Detroit have short people-mover networks, but Vancouver is the only city operating full-sized trains on a large network with no drivers on board. This means that the cost of operating service does not go up dramatically with increased frequency, so Vancouver is able to provide better off-peak frequency than any other North American rail system. Expo Line trains come every 2-3 minutes at peak on most of the line, which matches the busiest rail lines in other cities. But, unlike those other cities, they come almost as frequently all day, every day. The least frequent service—late night until 1:00 am—is still every five minutes or better.

The second way in which the Skytrain network is remarkable is in its focus on transit-oriented development. The system has more transit-oriented development than any other North American rail system. Suburban stations that were surrounded by one-story commercial sprawl when they opened are now surrounded by clusters of residential high-rises. The core of Vancouver is dense and walkable, but what is most remarkable is just how urban the suburban parts of the network feel. ■

+ **Very high ridership automated heavy rail network**
+ **Transit-oriented development on a scale unmatched in North America**

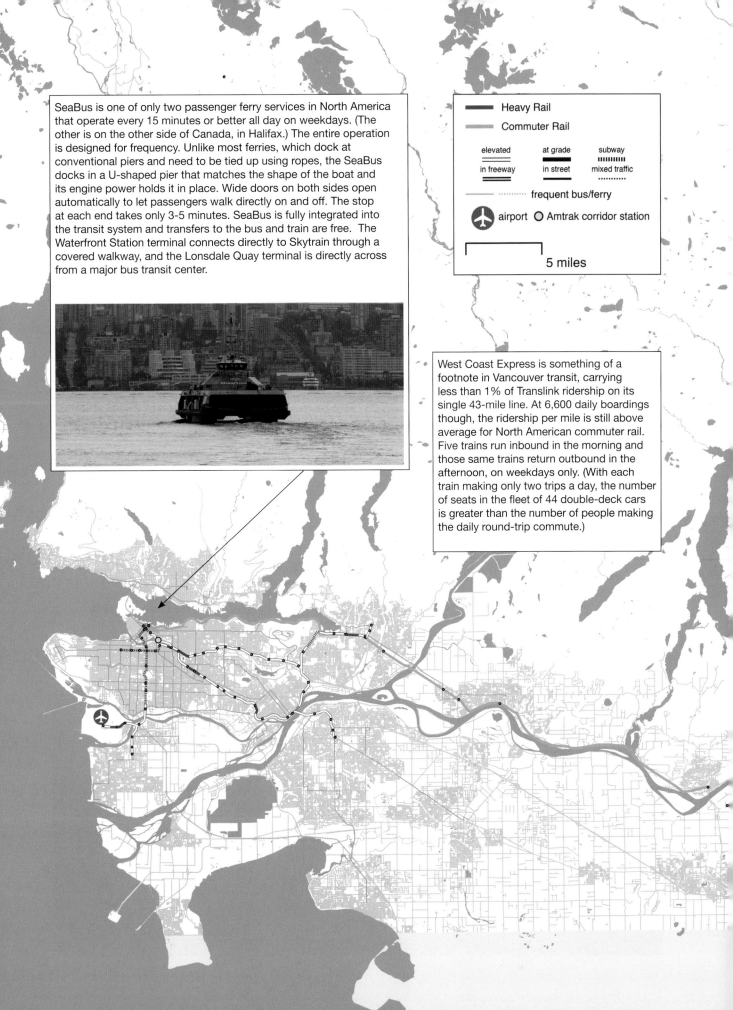

SeaBus is one of only two passenger ferry services in North America that operate every 15 minutes or better all day on weekdays. (The other is on the other side of Canada, in Halifax.) The entire operation is designed for frequency. Unlike most ferries, which dock at conventional piers and need to be tied up using ropes, the SeaBus docks in a U-shaped pier that matches the shape of the boat and its engine power holds it in place. Wide doors on both sides open automatically to let passengers walk directly on and off. The stop at each end takes only 3-5 minutes. SeaBus is fully integrated into the transit system and transfers to the bus and train are free. The Waterfront Station terminal connects directly to Skytrain through a covered walkway, and the Lonsdale Quay terminal is directly across from a major bus transit center.

Heavy Rail
Commuter Rail

| elevated | at grade | subway |
| in freeway | in street | mixed traffic |

frequent bus/ferry

✈ airport   ◯ Amtrak corridor station

5 miles

West Coast Express is something of a footnote in Vancouver transit, carrying less than 1% of Translink ridership on its single 43-mile line. At 6,600 daily boardings though, the ridership per mile is still above average for North American commuter rail. Five trains run inbound in the morning and those same trains return outbound in the afternoon, on weekdays only. (With each train making only two trips a day, the number of seats in the fleet of 44 double-deck cars is greater than the number of people making the daily round-trip commute.)

Heavy Rail (SkyTrain)
HIGH PERFORMER

Opened: 1985
Last Expanded: 2016
Length: 49.5 miles
Stations: 53
Frequency: 2-7 min peak and midday, 3-20 min evening and weekend
Avg weekday ridership: 512,400
Ridership per mile: 10,352

Commuter Rail (West Coast Express)
SMALL SYSTEM

Opened: 1995
Last Expanded: N/A
Length: 43 miles
Stations: 8
Frequency: 5 trains a day in each direction, rush hour only
Avg weekday ridership: 10,300
Ridership per mile: 240

Vancouver's bus network is as remarkable as Skytrain. The 99B bus on Broadway is the busiest bus route in North America, with 55,900 passengers on an average weekday. It's a limited-stop crosstown rapid-route anchored at one end by the campus of the University of British Columbia (below). At peak, 60-foot articulated express buses run every three minutes; in the middle of the day they run every 4-5 minutes, and even at 11:00 pm there's still a bus every 10 minutes, all in addition to the local buses that use the same street. But at that frequency the route is stretched beyond capacity. The city estimates that 2,000 people a day at Commercial/Broadway find no room on the first bus and have to wait for a second.

A half-mile stretch of Granville Street in downtown Vancouver (above), from the Waterfront through the heart of downtown, has been a bus-and-taxi-only transit mall since 1974. Granville is the busiest downtown retail street and the hub of nightlife. The mall was rebuilt between 2006 and 2010 with wider sidewalks and curbs that encourage pedestrians to cross the transit lanes anywhere, not just at crosswalks. At peak, there is a bus here every 80 seconds, and 82,700 riders use the transit mall on an average weekday.

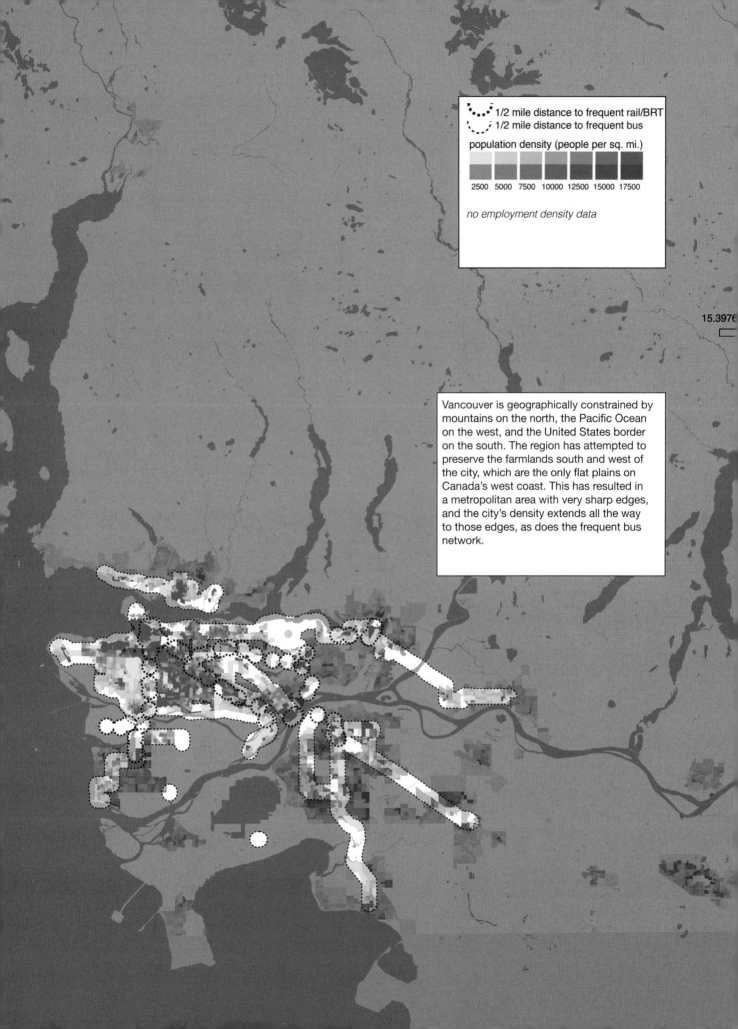

1/2 mile distance to frequent rail/BRT
1/2 mile distance to frequent bus

population density (people per sq. mi.)

2500 5000 7500 10000 12500 15000 17500

no employment density data

15.3976

Vancouver is geographically constrained by mountains on the north, the Pacific Ocean on the west, and the United States border on the south. The region has attempted to preserve the farmlands south and west of the city, which are the only flat plains on Canada's west coast. This has resulted in a metropolitan area with very sharp edges, and the city's density extends all the way to those edges, as does the frequent bus network.

Technologically, Skytrain is actually two networks. The Expo and Millennium Lines (center left), which opened in segments between 1985 and 2016, use unusual linear-induction technology, where a continuous wide metal strip between the rail acts as part of the motor, with the train pushing off it through magnetic force. This allows fast acceleration and steep grades and minimizes moving parts. The Canada Line (bottom left), which opened in 2009, uses more conventional electric third-rail technology like most heavy rail lines. All lines use relatively short trains (below, in front of a West Coast Express train at Waterfront) — 250-foot maximum on Expo/Millennium and 130 foot on the Canada Line. Capacity comes from frequency, not train length.

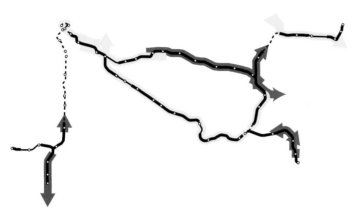

True to its name, most of Skytrain is elevated. The original Expo Line (center right) used an existing 0.9-mile railroad tunnel under downtown, with the two tracks stacked one above the other in the narrow-but-tall tunnel. For most of the way from Vancouver to New Westminster it follows an old interurban streetcar line. The remainder of the Expo Line and the Millennium Line follow highways (red, above; Lougheed Highway, bottom). Former rail lines that are still in use (yellow) are almost entirely elevated (thick black lines). The Skybridge (upper right) brings Skytrain across the Fraser River to Surrey. At 1,120 feet, it's the longest transit-only span in North America. The Canada Line has a much longer tunnel (below). It runs nearly six miles from Waterfront to just north of Marine Drive. South of there, it is largely elevated. The Richmond branch is above No. 3 Road.

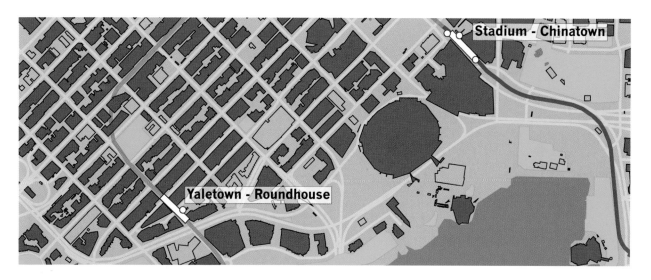

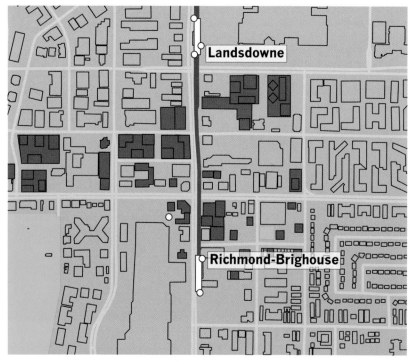

Skytrain has transformed the Vancouver skyline (below). Stations across the system— from the outer suburbs to the edges of downtown— are surrounded by clusters of residential high rises. This is the result of deliberate development policy across the region. These maps show examples from six different municipalities (Vancouver, Richmond, Burnaby, New Westminster, Coquitlam, and Surrey); all of which have their city hall within two blocks of a Skytrain station. Buildings in dark brown top out at over 20 meters (approximately five floors). This development has happened in many different kinds of places: former railyards at Yaletown; an old downtown at New Westminster; single-family neighborhoods at Joyce-Collingood; and suburban malls and strip malls at Richmond-Brighouse, Lincoln, Metrotown, and Surrey Central.

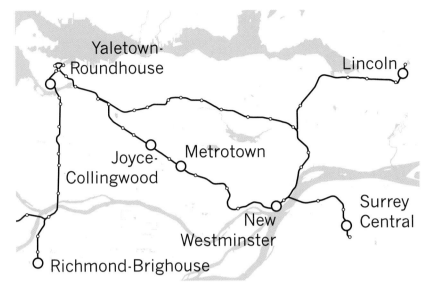

Yaletown-Roundhouse

Lincoln

Joyce-Collingwood

Metrotown

Surrey Central

New Westminster

Richmond-Brighouse

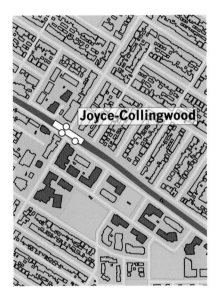

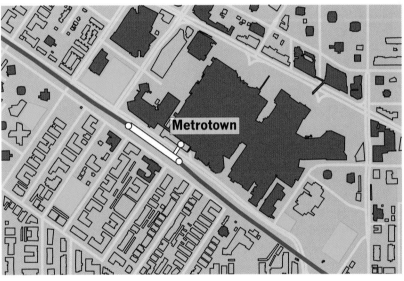

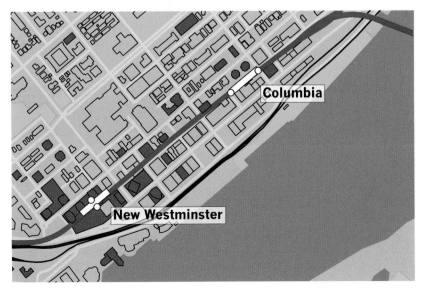

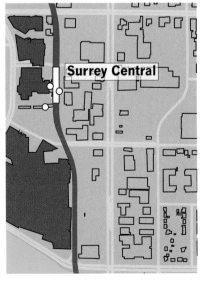

31. **INDIANAPOLIS**

Indianapolis-Carmel-Muncie, IN

population 2,457,286 (33rd)   **served by frequent transit** 8%   **daily trips per 1000** 12

IndyGo

Indygo
municipal
BRT
Frequent Bus

Indianapolis' BRT is notable for its ambition. The city's first BRT line, the Red Line, opened in 2019; the Purple Line is scheduled to follow in 2023, and the Purple Line in 2025. This adds up to nearly 50 miles of BRT, stretching to the edges of the city in five directions, 70% of which will have dedicated lanes. That is more street-running BRT than any other city in the United States and Canada, all of which would be built in seven years.

This scale and speed is made possible by a thrifty approach to BRT. The BRT stations are full-featured, with level boarding, full canopies, and heated platforms to melt snow. The electric buses are nice too, with custom left-hand doors to allow for center platforms. But the dedicated lanes are largely created by reallocating current street space, not by widening.

Fitting dedicated transit lanes into existing streets is not politically easy. Parking was removed, and general traffic lanes were converted to transit. There are compromises to transit—segments in mixed traffic, and some sections where a single lane serves buses on both directions—but Indianapolis has been willing to inconvenience drivers, and make the kinds of changes residents and business have opposed in other cities, to dramatically improve transit.

This is all the more remarkable in a city that doesn't have a strong transit history. Unlike Chicago, Cleveland, and Cincinnati, Indianapolis is largely a postwar city—Marion County had 460,000 people in 1940 and has 960,000 today. The city has been growing steadily as other Midwestern cities have shrunk. Indianapolis didn't have a strong bus system—service was cut, and ridership dropped for decades. In 2015, the metro area not only had far less transit ridership than its older neighborhoods, it had half the per-capita transit riders of similar-sized metros like Raleigh, Orlando, Tampa, and Sacramento. Indianapolis politics did not support transit. The state is solidly Republican; the consolidation of the city of Indianapolis with Marion County means that city politics are also more conservative than most, and the transit agency is a city department.

The new BRT lines are part of an overall expansion in the city's transit network, implemented with support from business leaders and Mayor Greg Ballard, who championed infrastructure and stood out from his fellow Republicans with his focus on sustainability. The 2014 Marion County Transit Plan formed the basis of an income tax adopted in 2017 to fund BRT and increase service on local routes. A new downtown transit center opened in 2016, and a system redesign was adopted in 2019 to move to a grid network and significantly increase frequent bus service. ■

BRT (Red Line)

Opened: 2019
Last Expanded: N/A
Length: 13 miles (7.3 miles guideway)
Stations: 19 (guideway only)
Frequency: 15 min
Avg weekday ridership: 6,518
Ridership per mile: 501

The typical Red Line lanes are separated with painted stripes (not physical barriers) and while the streets were repaved, they were not completely rebuilt. On College Avenue, a single lane serves buses in both directions. Schedules are coordinated but buses sometimes need to wait at stations for buses to pass in the opposite direction.

+ **Developing large BRT network extending to the edges of the city**
+ **Extensive dedicated BRT lanes implemented at low cost**

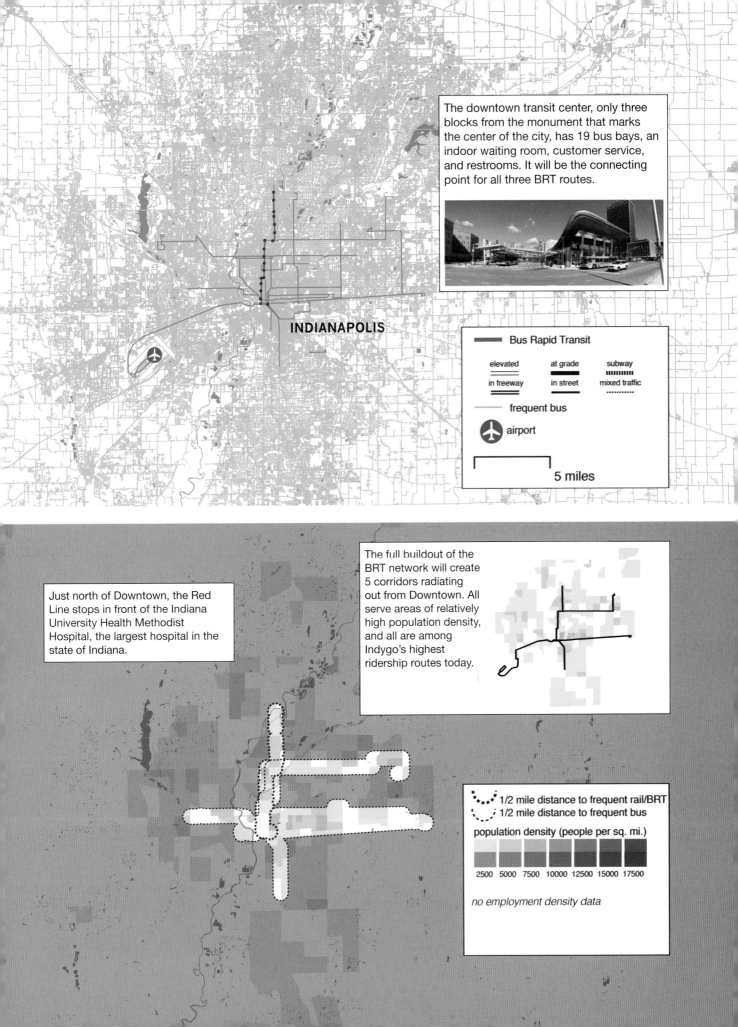

The downtown transit center, only three blocks from the monument that marks the center of the city, has 19 bus bays, an indoor waiting room, customer service, and restrooms. It will be the connecting point for all three BRT routes.

INDIANAPOLIS

Bus Rapid Transit

elevated	at grade	subway
in freeway	in street	mixed traffic

frequent bus

airport

5 miles

Just north of Downtown, the Red Line stops in front of the Indiana University Health Methodist Hospital, the largest hospital in the state of Indiana.

The full buildout of the BRT network will create 5 corridors radiating out from Downtown. All serve areas of relatively high population density, and all are among Indygo's highest ridership routes today.

1/2 mile distance to frequent rail/BRT
1/2 mile distance to frequent bus

population density (people per sq. mi.)

2500 5000 7500 10000 12500 15000 17500

no employment density data

32. LAS VEGAS

Las Vegas–Henderson–Paradise, NV

population 2,313,238 (34th)   **served by frequent transit** 23%   **daily trips per 1000** 76

RTC
independent agency
Frequent Bus
BRT

Las Vegas Monorail
independent agency
Monorail

Las Vegas does not look like a transit-friendly city, and the Las Vegas Strip doesn't look like a typical transit destination. But the Strip draws lots of visitors, and to serve them it has lots of employees. It has 12 of the world's 20 largest hotels. It is also the seventh-largest employment center in the United States. These are two big potential transit markets, with different needs, and Las Vegas has been trying to figure out for the past three decades how to serve both.

The Las Vegas monorail is designed for the tourists. Six stations are directly connected to casinos and the seventh is connected to the convention center. Tickets are targeted at visitors, at $5 for a one-way ride, as are the hours, which don't start until 7:00 a.m. but extend to midnight or 3:00 a.m. Service is frequent and reliable, with 17,000 riders on a typical day and an average of 67,000 daily during major trade shows. This system works for conventioneers and gamblers. The monorail was the only privately owned, unsubsidized rail transit line in the United States until it went bankrupt durng the COVID pandemic and was bought by the Las Vegas Convention and Visitors Authority.

But the monorail does not extend beyond the strip. Employees heading to the casinos depend on buses. Until 1993, Las Vegas actually had the last major privately owned, citywide bus system in the United Sates. Since then, the Regional Transit Commission has bought new buses and improved service. Las Vegas has multiple frequent routes, and is one of the few US systems that operates 24 hours a day.

Since the 1990s, the RTC has been trying to build upgraded transit corridors. The first tangible result was a semi-BRT line using 4.5 miles of shared transit/right-turn lanes from Downtown to Nellis Air Force Base. That route is operated as a regular local bus corridor.

The next project, SDX, built 2.5 miles of center-running dedicated bus lanes to serve an 11-mile route that connects the Strip (lower right) to Downtown. It is now operated as part of the Deuce, a local route from Downtown along the full length of the strip that uses double-decker buses. Stops on the guideway segment are distinctively branded with neon signs. The route runs every 15 minutes all day and offers 24-hour service. Single-ride tickets are priced at $6 for tourists, but the $65 monthly system-wide monthly pass makes the line work for employees as well.

Discussions of light rail have resumed. A 2016 long-range plan recommended light rail from Downtown down the Strip to the airport. Design is underway for curb-running "BRT" in the Maryland Parkway corridor from Downtown past UNLV to the airport, which is currently a frequent-bus route. ■

Monorail (Las Vegas Monorail)

Opened: 2004
Last Expanded: N/A
Length: 3.9 miles
Stations: 7
Frequency: 4-8 min
Avg weekday ridership: 13,151
Ridership per mile: 3,372

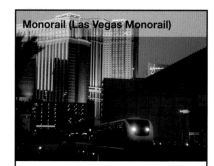

BRT (The Deuce)
SMALL SYSTEM

Opened: 2010
Last Expanded: N/A
Length: 9.3 miles (1 guideway miles)
Stations: 2 (guideway only)
Frequency: 15 min
Avg weekday ridership: 20,609
Ridership per mile: 2,212

+ **High-ridership, tourist-oriented monorail and BRT**
+ **Relatively large frequent network with some 24 hour service**

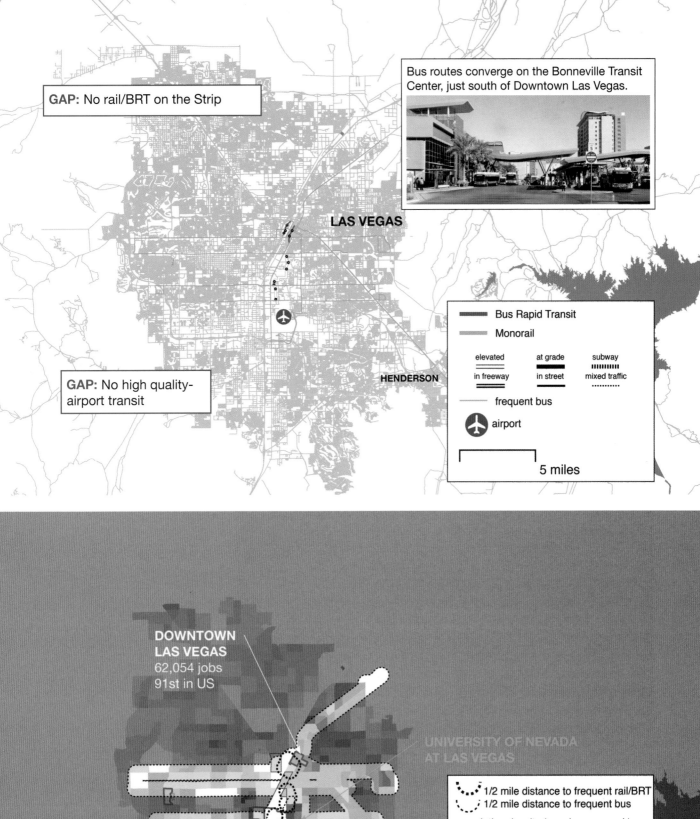

GAP: No rail/BRT on the Strip

Bus routes converge on the Bonneville Transit Center, just south of Downtown Las Vegas.

LAS VEGAS

GAP: No high quality-airport transit

HENDERSON

Bus Rapid Transit
Monorail

| elevated | at grade | subway |
| in freeway | in street | mixed traffic |

frequent bus

airport

5 miles

DOWNTOWN
LAS VEGAS
62,054 jobs
91st in US

UNIVERSITY OF NEVADA
AT LAS VEGAS

1/2 mile distance to frequent rail/BRT
1/2 mile distance to frequent bus

population density (people per sq. mi.)

2500 5000 7500 10000 12500 15000 17500

employment density (jobs per sq. mi.)

15000 30000 45000 60000

college campus (100 U.S. largest)

GAP: Frequent-bus network misses many dense neighborhoods

LAS VEGAS STRIP
312,785 jobs
7th in US

33. SAN JUAN

San Juan-Carolina, PR

population 2,297,875 (35th)   **served by frequent transit** 3%

Departamento de Transportación y Obras Públicas
state agency
Heavy Rail

The Caribbean island of Puerto Rico is one of the most urbanized places in the United States. Three point four million people live in the commonwealth and a third of them are in the six municipalities that make up the core of the San Juan metropolitan area. San Juan is fairly dense (the city itself has the population density of Los Angeles, Minneapolis, or Seattle), congested, and transit-dependent (25% of households in the city do not own a car). It is a place that needs a good transit system.

Tren Urbano, opened in 2004, is not that system. Its ridership is among the lowest of US heavy-rail systems. That is not a surprise—it is the only metropolitan area in the United States whose rail network does not reach downtown. And the bus network doesn't help much—not a single route in the city runs frequently. ■

At its northern terminus (below), Tren Urbano's stops just as it reaches the edge of Saturce, the densest part of the city."Phase 1A" of the project, which would extend rail into this area, is now indefinitely postponed due to lack of funds. There have been occasional proposals to build light rail instead.

- **Single line heavy-rail system that stops short of the densest part of the city**
- **No frequent buses**

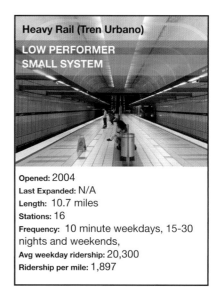

Heavy Rail (Tren Urbano)

LOW PERFORMER
SMALL SYSTEM

Opened: 2004
Last Expanded: N/A
Length: 10.7 miles
Stations: 16
Frequency: 10 minute weekdays, 15-30 nights and weekends,
Avg weekday ridership: 20,300
Ridership per mile: 1,897

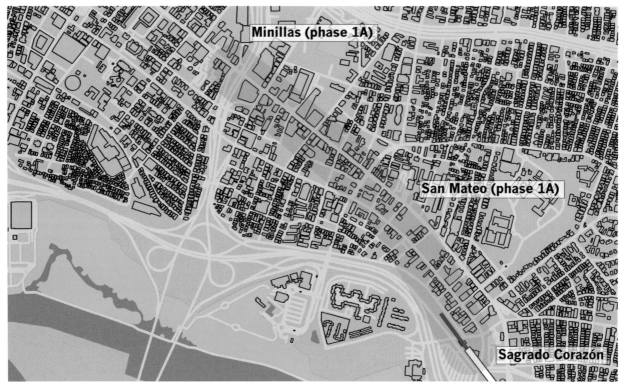

Minillas (phase 1A)

San Mateo (phase 1A)

Sagrado Corazón

Until the 1950s, Puerto Rico had a 310 mile rail system. Part of the route is now used by the Tren Urbano. The last miles and a half of rail into the passenger station in Old San Juan has been repurposed as a busway, carrying several routes into a transit center.

Heavy Rail

| elevated | at grade | subway |
| in freeway | in street | mixed traffic |

✈ airport

5 miles

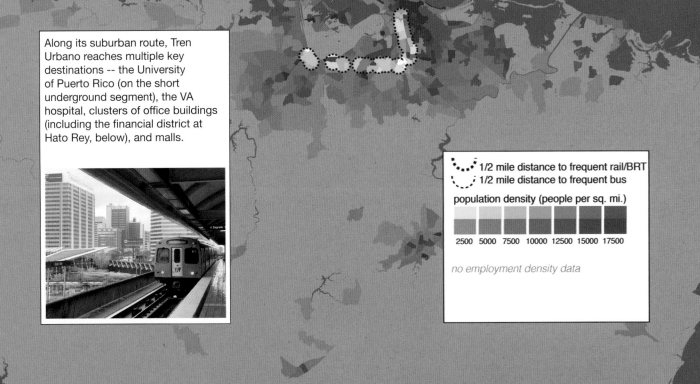

Along its suburban route, Tren Urbano reaches multiple key destinations -- the University of Puerto Rico (on the short underground segment), the VA hospital, clusters of office buildings (including the financial district at Hato Rey, below), and malls.

1/2 mile distance to frequent rail/BRT
1/2 mile distance to frequent bus

population density (people per sq. mi.)

2500 5000 7500 10000 12500 15000 17500

no employment density data

34. CINCINNATI

Cincinnati–Wilmington–Maysville, OH-KY-IN

population 2,280,246 (36th)   **served by frequent transit** 7%   **daily trips per 1000** 21

Cincinnati has an obvious primary transit corridor: from Covington, Kentucky, across the river through Downtown, and then up the hill to Uptown, the University of Cincinnati, and its medical center. Unfortunately, it has built only a third of that.

The Cincinnati streetcar, like many other recent streetcar systems, came out of a desire for economic development. The city's population peaked at 500,000 in 1950 and has been declining ever since, dropping below 300,000 by 2010. A 2013 presentation by the city manager identified "people," "businesses," and "development" as "what we need." A 2008 study concluded "the inadequate public transportation system puts Cincinnati and the region at a very serious competitive disadvantage" and recommended that "the City should aggressively pursue establishing a streetcar system, the first phase of which should link Downtown and Uptown, the city's two leading job-generation areas." A study forecast $1.48 billion in new development over 10 years. In 2008, Cincinnati City Council voted to move forward. The project was nearly stopped several times. Citywide referendums to block it failed in 2009 and 2011. In 2010, a new Republican governor canceled $52 million in state funds promised by his Democratic predecessor. In 2013, with construction underway, the city elected an anti-streetcar mayor.

Somehow, the streetcar project (right) survived and opened in 2016, but in much-reduced form. It extends a mile from the center of Downtown, stopping a mile and half—and a steep hill—short of Uptown, and it is on time only 40 percent of the time, compared to 85 percent for local buses. This was what the city could afford, and politics would allow, but it doesn't address the most significant transportation need in the corridor. Three months in, the streetcar was carrying barely more than 1,000 people on an average weekday instead of the projected 3,200.

Even with low ridership, the streetcar may still promote new development, which was its fundamental purpose. But that is not without its issues. The Agenda 360 visioning effort, launched in 2009, argued that "streetcars in other cities have been shown to bring new people to an area. Streetcars attract people who don't ride buses. They are popular with young professionals, who tend to live in and near urban areas." But the neighborhood the streetcar does serve—Over-the-Rhine—is 70 percent African American, with a median household income under $15,000. New development is more likely to displace these residents than serve them. The Cincinnati streetcar may turn out to be more effective at gentrification than at transportation. ∎

METRO
Southwest Ohio
Regional Transit
Authority
independent agency
Frequent Bus

TANK
TRANSIT AUTHORITY OF NORTHERN KENTUCKY

Transit Authority of
Northern Kentucky
independent agency
Frequent Bus

Cincinnati Bell connector
Cincinnati Streetcar
municipal
Streetcar

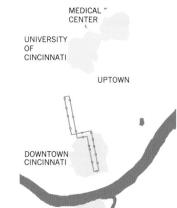

Streetcar (Cincinnati Bell Connector)
SMALL SYSTEM
LOW PERFORMER

Opened: 2016
Last Expanded: N/A
Length: 2 miles
Stations: 9
Frequency: 12–15 min
Avg weekday ridership: 1,454
Ridership per mile: 727

– **Short streetcar line designed for development, not transportation**

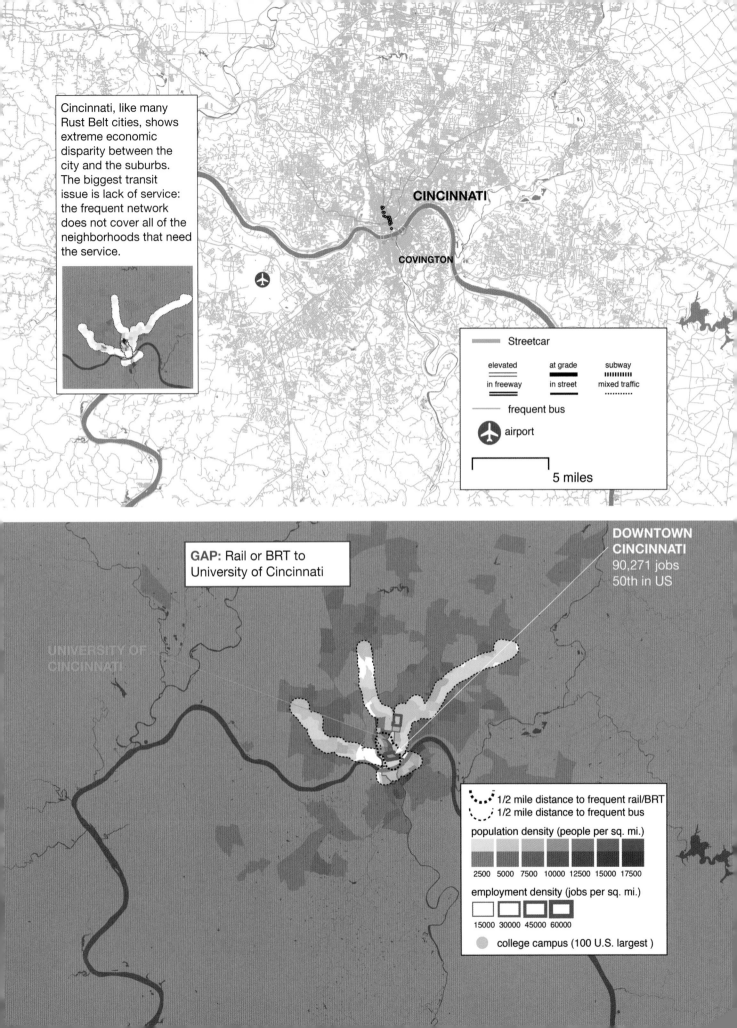

Cincinnati, like many Rust Belt cities, shows extreme economic disparity between the city and the suburbs. The biggest transit issue is lack of service: the frequent network does not cover all of the neighborhoods that need the service.

CINCINNATI

COVINGTON

Streetcar

elevated	at grade	subway
in freeway	in street	mixed traffic

frequent bus

airport

5 miles

GAP: Rail or BRT to University of Cincinnati

UNIVERSITY OF CINCINNATI

DOWNTOWN CINCINNATI
90,271 jobs
50th in US

1/2 mile distance to frequent rail/BRT
1/2 mile distance to frequent bus

population density (people per sq. mi.)

2500 5000 7500 10000 12500 15000 17500

employment density (jobs per sq. mi.)

15000 30000 45000 60000

college campus (100 U.S. largest)

35. AUSTIN

Austin–Round Rock, TX

population 2,227,083 (37th)   **served by frequent transit** 22%   **daily trips per 1000** 40

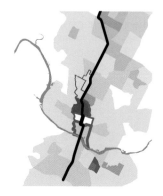

🏛 **METRO**

Capital Metro
independent agency
Frequent Bus
Commuter Rail

One might assume that Austin, the most environmentally minded city in Texas, and the only one that resisted wide-scale freeway construction, would be an early adopter of rail transit. Not so: Houston and Dallas built first, and, even now that Austin has a single line operating, it is less ambitious, less used, and ultimately less useful than either of the other systems. Dallas and Houston are both cited, in very different ways, as examples of how to do rail right. Austin became a cautionary tale. In 2021, though, Austin is embarking on a massive transit expansion and may become a national model for inclusive high-ridership transit.

Austin has long been a transit-friendly area, with higher per-capita transit use than any other Texas city. This level of ridership was achieved with dense, walkable, mixed-use neighborhoods; a well-run local bus network; and the University of Texas shuttle routes operated by Capital Metro, which have some 23,000 boardings a day. Austin has obvious corridors for major transit improvements. The city's population is strongly oriented in a north-south direction, along Congress and Guadalupe streets. Its three major activity centers—Downtown, the state capitol complex, and the University of Texas campus—are centered on that axis. That corridor has always been Austin's highest-ridership bus route, and current ridership alone is enough to support rail. However, while Austin's transit geography seems obvious, its politics are not. Capital Metro was created in 1985. Like DART in Dallas, or METRO in Houston, it had the explicit goal of building rail. Capital METRO put a plan on the ballot in 2000. It proposed 14.6 miles of light rail, running down streets from downtown, up Guadalupe past the capitol and the university to north Austin. A second phase would continue down South Congress.

Capital Metro, like most transit agencies, encompasses both urban and suburban areas. In Dallas, the suburban areas were the political key to enabling rail, and in Houston, urban neighborhoods played that role. In Austin, both constituencies ended up fighting rail. Suburban areas opposed spending dollars on rail that could go to roads. In central neighborhoods, the concerns were varied. Businesses on South Congress feared the impacts of rail construction. Activists in Hispanic East Austin wanted to see more money spent on buses. Light rail also triggered a fear of growth. In 1990, environmentalists concerned about the impact of new development on the natural pools of Barton Springs succeeded in blocking 4,000 acres of development. Ever since, environmental groups have been a driving force in Austin politics, and fear of runaway development has become one of the primary themes. Residents of urban neighborhoods like Hyde Park, with tree-lined streets of turn-of-the-century bungalows, feared that rail would bring big new apartment buildings, increase traffic congestion, and destroy trees. The 2000 referendum went down in a narrow defeat, with 49.6 percent in favor. Urban neighborhoods didn't provide enough support to balance out the suburban votes.

The failed 2000 light-rail plan (above) would have linked Austin's densest areas. The 2010 Red Line (below) avoided neighborhood conflict, but also missed the places people want to go. The 2020 Project Connect plan, by contrast focuses on density, serving not just the 2000 corridor but adding lines to the east and southeast.

+ **High-ridership bus network**
− **Politically planned commuter rail**
+ **Ambitous transit plan with strong support**

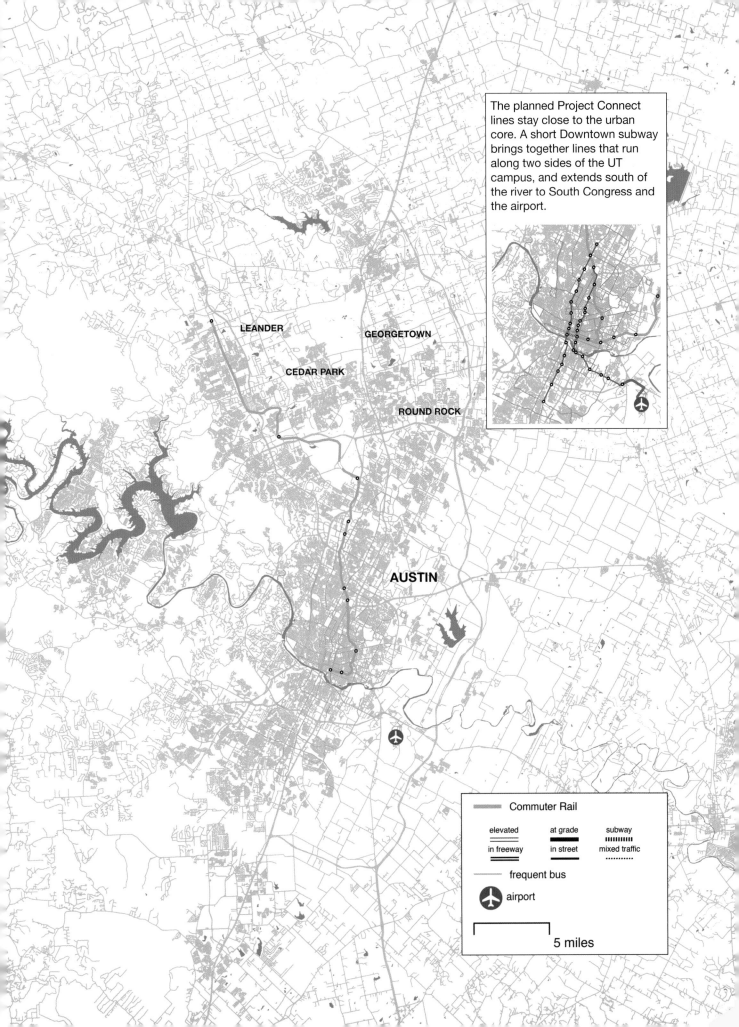

The planned Project Connect lines stay close to the urban core. A short Downtown subway brings together lines that run along two sides of the UT campus, and extends south of the river to South Congress and the airport.

LEANDER

GEORGETOWN

CEDAR PARK

ROUND ROCK

AUSTIN

Commuter Rail

elevated   at grade   subway

in freeway   in street   mixed traffic

frequent bus

airport

5 miles

DMU Commuter Rail (Capital MetroRail)

SMALL SYSTEM
LOW PERFORMER

Opened: 2010
Last Expanded: N/A
Length: 32 miles
Stations: 9
Frequency: every 30–60 min weekday, with additional peak srvice, Saturday afternoon/evening service (no Sunday service)
Avg weekday ridership: 2,200
Ridership per mile: 69

Local buses and MetroRapid go right into the heart of Downtown, the UT campus, and the capitol complex (above). Capital MetroRail, though, stops at the convention center (right), within view of downtown skyscrapers, but still a quarter mile away. Historically, this track actually continued. Mainline Southern Pacific passenger trains ran on city streets through the center of Downtown until the 1950s, and tracks were in place for decades afterward.

That loss stung Austin's political leaders, who decided that Austin had to get rail built somehow. They crafted a plan to avoid opposition. Rather than build down city streets, rail transit would follow a rail line that Capital Metro has purchased in 1986. That gave pro-rail voters something to vote for, but avoided neighborhood impacts and reduced costs to only $60 million. Sixty-two percent voted in favor, and Austin started building the new Red Line.

The same decisions that made the Red Line politically palatable ensured it would not be particularly useful. Because it follows existing rail, it makes it barely to the edge of Downtown and does not serve the capitol or UT at all. Curving to the east, it misses Austin's most densely populated areas. Because it is designed to minimize cost, it uses diesel trains on single track with passing sidings, limiting frequency to a train every half hour. Ridership is now only 2,900 on an average weekday—compared to an estimated 37,400 for the 2000 proposal—and that is still straining the line's capacity. By building a line to avoid conflict, Austin built a line that avoided people.

With no rail in the core, Capital Metro focused on improving buses, and in 2014, it launched MetroRapid, a branded network of limited-stop routes in mixed traffic, including one serving the 2000 rail corridor on Guadalupe. Capital Metro is now implementing a branded frequent network that connects to MetroRapid. MetroRapid 80 in the Guadalupe/Lamar corridor now carries over 6,000 people a day.

After another failed try at urban rail in 2014, Cap Metro launched an intensive planning process that resulted in a new plan. A new generation of activists that see transit as a part of a more sustainable, more equitable city pushed for years to create a good plan, and they campaigned for it. Transit advocates pushed for rail corridors through the dense core. Racial justice advocates pushed for protection against gentrification. The result was a plan that goes right where the people are, with light rail (largely street running, with a short downtown subway) in Austin's two most important corridors, Congress/Guadalupe/Lamar and Riverside, plus BRT (future rail) on the east side of UT. These rail lines—connecting to Downtown, the capitol complex, UT, and major hospitals—will link to Austin's redesigned bus network and rapid bus service, becoming the spines of the entire network. The $7.1 billion plan includes improvements to those routes too. This is also a political shift, a similar pattern to what we've seen in Houston and elsewhere: cities that were once split on support for transit are now strongly in favor, and more ambitious plans do better than small ones.

Austin is a city that believes deeply in public process. After 30 years, that process has resulted in a good plan. Now Austin has to implement it. ■

Austin's east side was traditionally the Hispanic and Black side of town; as areas near Downtown gentrified, low-income residents settled in the southwest and northeast. The 2018 bus-network redesign, "Cap Remap," significantly increased frequent service in these areas.

MEDICAL CENTER
65,568 jobs
86th in US

**DOWNTOWN
AUSTIN / UT**
214,865 jobs
13th in US

UNIVERSITY OF TEXAS
AT AUSTIN

GAP: Rail or BRT in Guadalupe / South Congress corridor

1/2 mile distance to frequent rail/BRT
1/2 mile distance to frequent bus

population density (people per sq. mi.)

2500 5000 7500 10000 12500 15000 17500

employment density (jobs per sq. mi.)

15000 30000 45000 60000

college campus (100 U.S. largest)

36. NASHVILLE

Nashville–Davidson–Murfreesboro, TN

population 2,062,547 (39th)   **served by frequent transit** 6%   **daily trips per 1000** 13

Nashville's Music City Star was the cheapest modern commuter-rail startup in the United States, using used locomotives, secondhand passenger cars, and track owned by a small, locally based freight railroad. It is a project born of opportunity, not need. It heads east where track was available, not northeast, southeast, or west, where the population is. Thus, Music City Star is also the lowest-ridership commuter-rail line in the country.

There are definitely corridors where Nashville needs better transit. One of most obvious is an east–west route through downtown, connecting dense inner neighborhoods and Vanderbilt University. In 2012, Mayor Karl Dean proposed a BRT line, AMP, in this corridor; studies showed it would speed up transit trips and reduce congestion. Well-funded local opposition and statewide conservative anti-transit politics (including a proposed bill to ban center-running transit lanes in state highways) killed that project in 2015 after $2.5 million in design funds had been spent. Instead, the regional transit authority implemented four rapid-bus corridors that, unlike the commuter train, align well with the city's density and greatly expand its frequent network. ■

WeGo
Public Transit

WeGO
independent agency
Frequent Bus
Commuter Rail

Commuter Rail (Music City Star)

LOW PERFORMER
SMALL SYSTEM

Opened: 2006
Last Expanded: N/A
Length: 32 miles
Stations: 6
Frequency: 4–6 trains a day in each direction weekday (no weekend service)
Avg weekday ridership: 1,200
Ridership per mile: 38

+ **Strong frequent-bus network**
− **Low-ridership commuter rail in low-population corridor**

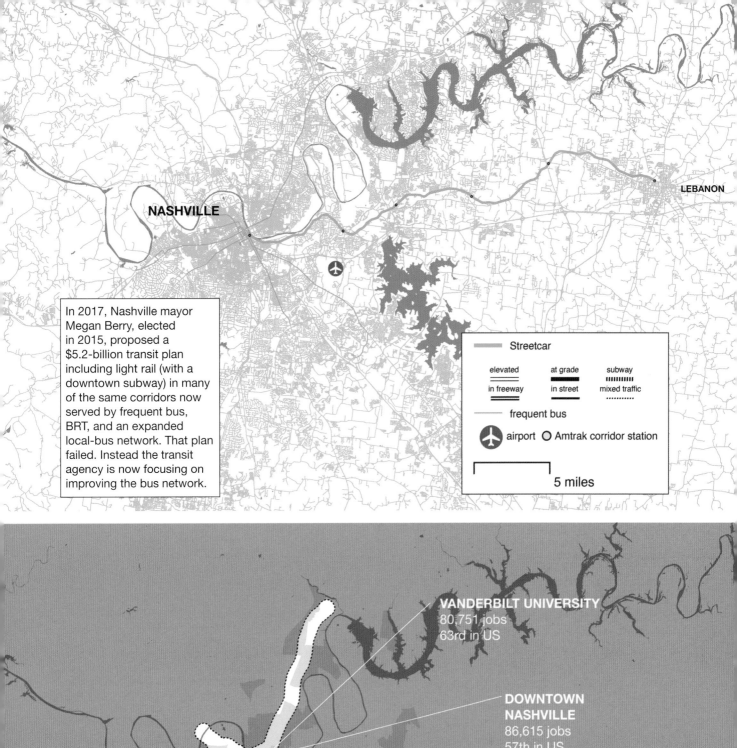

In 2017, Nashville mayor Megan Berry, elected in 2015, proposed a $5.2-billion transit plan including light rail (with a downtown subway) in many of the same corridors now served by frequent bus, BRT, and an expanded local-bus network. That plan failed. Instead the transit agency is now focusing on improving the bus network.

NASHVILLE

LEBANON

Streetcar

| elevated | at grade | subway |
| in freeway | in street | mixed traffic |

frequent bus

airport   ○ Amtrak corridor station

5 miles

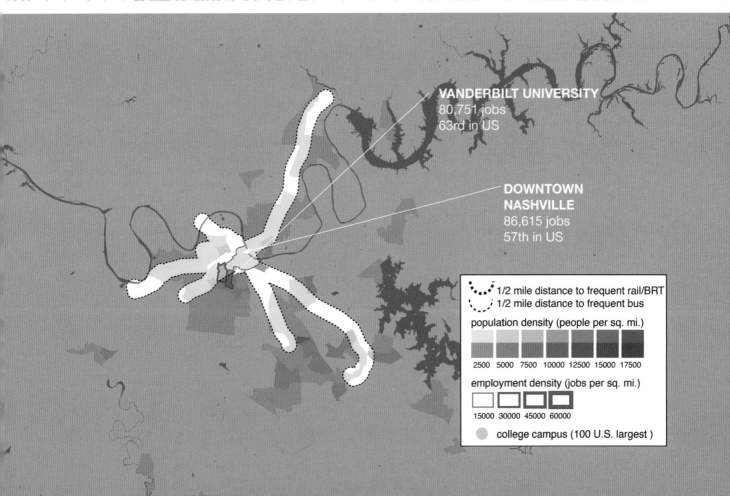

VANDERBILT UNIVERSITY
80,751 jobs
63rd in US

DOWNTOWN NASHVILLE
86,615 jobs
57th in US

1/2 mile distance to frequent rail/BRT
1/2 mile distance to frequent bus

population density (people per sq. mi.)

2500 5000 7500 10000 12500 15000 17500

employment density (jobs per sq. mi.)

15000 30000 45000 60000

○ college campus (100 U.S. largest)

37. MILWAUKEE

Milwaukee–Racine–Waukesha, WI

population 2,047,966 (40th)   served by frequent transit 16%   daily trips per 1000 43

City of Milwaukee
municipal
Streetcar

Milwaukee County Transit System
county
Frequent Bus

Milwaukee's streetcar is a sort of consolation project.

In the 1990s, under Mayor John Norquist, Milwaukee became a national model for urban revitalization, tearing down a freeway, creating pedestrian paths along the once industrial river, reconnecting Downtown with the lakefront, and building thousands of units of new Downtown housing. One of his priorities was a regional light-rail system. Studies began in 1990, and resulted in a state plan to build a line west from Downtown Milwaukee to suburban job centers in Waukesha.

But statewide politics killed light rail. Opposition from suburban areas and resistance to spending state tax dollars on transit first cut the project short, then killed it in 1997. Since then, the political climate has only gotten more difficult. In the 1990s, statewide Republicans like Tommy Thompson, an outspoken proponent of intercity rail, supported transit. Since 2010, Republican governor Scott Walker, elected on an anti-rail platform, has canceled the state's high-speed rail program (returning two trainsets after the state had already spent $50 million on them), and the legislature has tried to revise utility relocation laws to make it more expensive for the City of Milwaukee to build rail.

The loss of state and county support, though, did not end the city's desire for rail transit. In 2000, the federal government found that canceling light rail while funding highways discriminated against low-income, minority transit riders, and the state promised to spend remaining federal funds originally designated for light rail on transit in Milwaukee. Using those, as well as an additional federal TIGER Grant and local funds, the city moved ahead with a streetcar, the direct successor of the light-rail project.

Thus, instead of a 10- or 20-mile light-rail line, Milwaukee's desire for rail is expressed in a two-mile circulator. It connects the Amtrak station on the south and downtown residential on the north to the center of Downtown, but, unlike the light-rail plan, it does nothing to speed up the trips of current transit riders or link Milwaukee residents to suburban jobs.

The Milwaukee streetcar began as a plan for a larger system. Each leg is actually a short version of a much longer corridor that could be built in the future. That more extensive system could improve transit in many of the city's densest neighborhoods and serve important destinations like the University of Wisconsin–Milwaukee and Marquette University. Eventually, Milwaukee may get the more expansive system it was trying for all along. ∎

Streetcar (the Hop)

SMALL SYSTEM

Opened: 2018
Last Expanded: N/A
Length: 2 miles
Stations: 10
Frequency: 10 min weekday, 15 min weekend
Avg weekday ridership: 2109
Ridership per mile: 1055

This map from the Milwaukee streetcar-planning effort shows how the initial line (blue/green) is intended as the beginning of a citywide system. Even modest extensions, like a 2.5-mile line to the University of Wisconsin–Milwaukee (with nearly 30,000 students) would be very useful. But building the initial legs as a streetcar, with tracks in shared traffic and stations designed for one-car trains, will limit the reliability and capacity of any extensions.

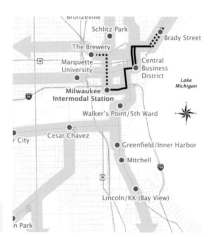

– **Short downtown streetcar that doesn't go far enough**

The rapid-bus Gold Line, initiated in 2015, follows the route of the light-rail line proposed in the 1990s.

The Milwaukee bus network focuses on the University of Wisconsin campus nearly as strongly as on Downtown.

MILWAUKEE

WAUKESHA

With 14 trains and 2,300 riders a day, Amtrak's Hiawatha corridor from Chicago to Milwaukee is its busiest outside of the Northeast and California. Under Governor Tony Evers, the state plans to fund more service.

The Hop suffers from the same problem as many other streetcars: it is too short. At Burns Commons, the tracks end, but buses keep going to the University of Wisconsin, two miles away. Rail doesn't go far enough to replace the bus route, so they operate alongside each other.

Streetcar

| elevated | at grade | subway |
| in freeway | in street | mixed traffic |

Frequent Bus

✈ airport ◯ Amtrak corridor station

5 miles

Suburban Waukesha is in a different county, which, unlike Democratic Milwaukee County, is dominated by Republicans. This was a hotbed of opposition to light rail, and today's service reflects that—riders on the frequent Milwaukee bus must transfer to a half-hourly Waukesha County bus near the county line.

GAP: Streetcar to University of Wisconsin

UNIVERSITY OF WISCONSIN – MILWAUKEE

DOWNTOWN MILWAUKEE
136,277 jobs
28th in US

⌐ 1/2 mile distance to frequent rail/BRT
⌐ 1/2 mile distance to frequent bus

population density (people per sq. mi.)

2500 5000 7500 10000 12500 15000 17500

employment density (jobs per sq. mi.)

15000 30000 45000 60000

● college campus (100 U.S. largest)

GAP: Frequent-bus network misses many dense neighborhoods

38. NORFOLK

Virginia Beach–Norfolk, VA-NC

population 1,857,626 (41st)   **served by frequent transit** 1%   **daily trips per 1000** 22

Hampton Roads
Transit
Independent agency
Light Rail

Hampton Roads is the second smallest metropolitan area to have a light-rail line (behind Buffalo), and it has the second-smallest light-rail system in the country (also behind Buffalo). The Tide light rail starts at Norfolk's medical center, runs along streets through the city's thriving downtown, and then runs due west along an abandoned freight-rail line to park-and-ride lots and bus connections. It is reasonably fast (18 mph average) and reasonably frequent (every 10–15 minutes until 9:00pm all day, seven days a week, though Sunday service doesn't start until noon), and it has been a modest success. The initial ridership estimate was 2,900 a day; in the first year it averaged 4,800.

The Tide, though, is only part of a bigger vision that has never been realized. At one time or another, all of Hampton Roads' major cities have made plans for light rail. The Tide terminus at Newtown Road, where the tracks end less than 100 feet from the city limit, was always intended to be temporary. Virginia Beach has acquired the rail corridor to the west. In 2012, its residents approved a non-binding referendum in support of that logical extension, and design proceeded. In 2016, though, a second election turned down city funds for that project. Thus, the Tide remains one of only two modern light-rail lines in the United States (the other, once again, is Buffalo) that has never been extended, though studies are underway for an eastern extension to Old Dominion University and Naval Station Norfolk, the region's largest employer.

Hampton Roads has geography that favors transit. It is a multi-centric region, with several pockets of concentrated employment, walkable downtowns, and relatively dense residential areas. It is divided by bays and rivers, creating transportation bottlenecks. But that same geography has worked against transit. Hampton Roads Transit is funded by its eight member cities; different levels of funding lead to dramatically different levels of transit service. Not a single bus route in the network is frequent, and light rail remains limited to only one city. The Tide is a good start, but it's not enough. ∎

Light Rail (The Tide)

LOW PERFORMER

SMALL SYSTEM

Opened: 2011
Last Expanded: N/A
Length: 7.4 miles
Stations: 11
Frequency: 10 min peak, 15 min off-peak
Avg weekday ridership: 4,200
Ridership per mile: 568

The Tide runs right through the center of Norfolk's Downtown, a hub of employment, shopping, and nightlife.

– **No frequent bus network**
– **Short rail line that doesn't go far enough on either end**

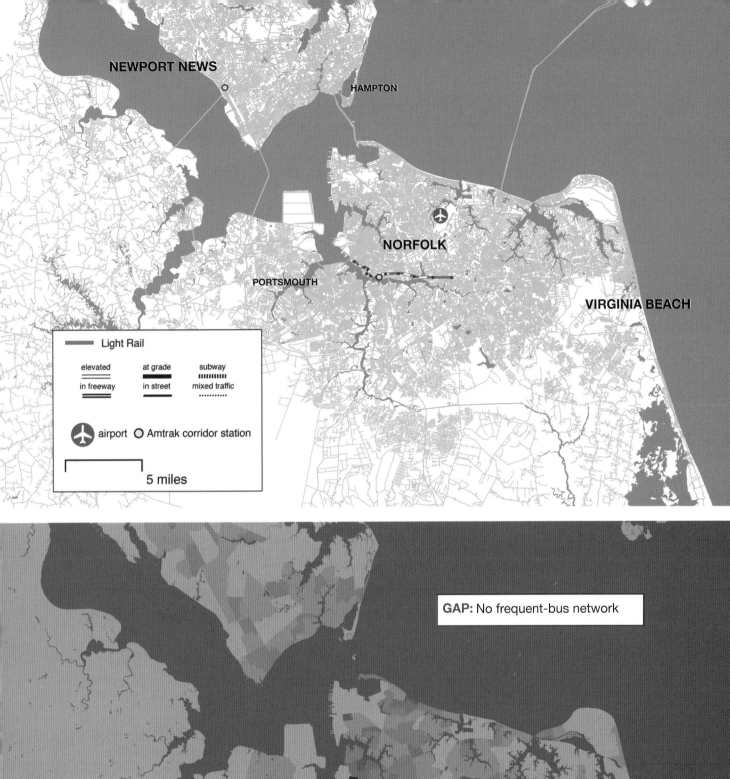

NEWPORT NEWS

HAMPTON

NORFOLK

PORTSMOUTH

VIRGINIA BEACH

Light Rail

elevated   at grade   subway

in freeway   in street   mixed traffic

✈ airport   ○ Amtrak corridor station

5 miles

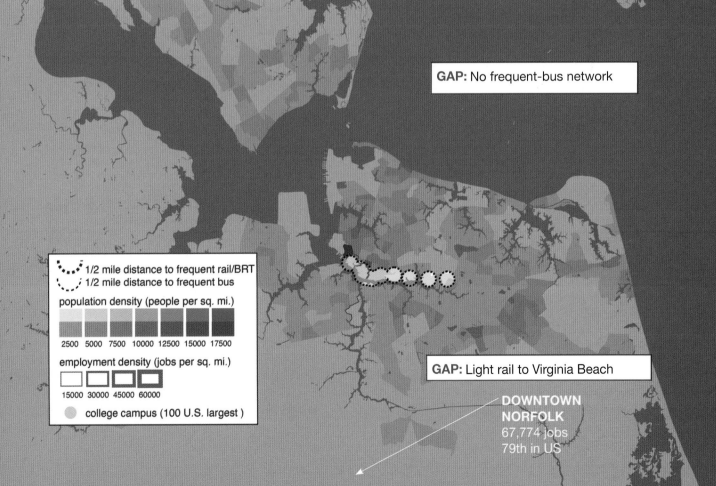

GAP: No frequent-bus network

◠ 1/2 mile distance to frequent rail/BRT
⌒ 1/2 mile distance to frequent bus

population density (people per sq. mi.)

2500 5000 7500 10000 12500 15000 17500

employment density (jobs per sq. mi.)

15000 30000 45000 60000

● college campus (100 U.S. largest)

GAP: Light rail to Virginia Beach

**DOWNTOWN
NORFOLK**
67,774 jobs
79th in US

39. JACKSONVILLE

Jacksonville–St. Marys-Palatka, FL-GA

population 1,688,701 (43rd)   **served by frequent transit** 8%   **daily trips per 1000** 19

JTA
independent agency
Frequent Bus
Peoplemover

Jacksonville spent the 1980s and 1990s building a 1970s vision of urban transit. Peoplemovers were seen as a key part of future transit, networks, circulating people through downtown in comfort above the congested streets. The federal program to develop automated urban peoplemover systems enrolled 11 cities in 1976 and 1977. Jacksonville was one of only three (along with Miami and Detroit) to actually build such a system; the first 0.7-mile segment finally opened in 1987. When construction was ready to start on the remainder of the system, the transit agency couldn't agree on a contract with Matra, the manufacturer of the proprietary trains and control systems for the initial lines, and thus has to rebuild the entire system with Bombardier technology. By 2000, the full 2.5-mile system was open.

The Skyway was to serve many of the purposes that streetcars are intended for today. Nearly 40 percent of riders would be bus riders transferring from bus routes terminated at the Skyway stations instead of extending downtown, Fifty percent would be circulating within downtown, and 10 percent would be downtown employees, shoppers, and visitors parking at the edge of downtown. But ridership never matched expectations. Office buildings continued to build more parking, downtown retail declined, and bus riders wanted to stay on the bus all the way to their destination. Instead of 10,000 daily riders, the initial segment had 1,200. The full system got less than 3,000; eliminating fares increased that to 5,000. In some ways, that is not bad. Similar-size streetcars built for the same purposes in Atlanta, Charlotte, Cincinnati, Tacoma, and Seattle are carrying fewer people. But neither the Skyway's ridership nor downtown's growth met 1970s expectations. With the trains aging, and the technology discontinued, JTA is now considering turning the elevated guideway into a path for automated vehicles, which would continue into the neighborhoods surrounding Downtown, replacing 1970s technology of the future with 2020s technology of the future.

Many more riders are benefitting from a different kind of innovation. In 2014, JTA redesigned its entire bus network, simplifying routes, reducing the number of stops, increasing evening and weekend service, and creating 10 frequent routes. Ridership increased by six percent in the first year at the same operating cost. Unlike the Skyway, the Route Optimization Initiative became a model for cities elsewhere. ■

Peoplemover (Skyway)

Opened:	1989
Last Expanded:	2000
Length:	2.5 miles
Stations:	8
Frequency:	3–6 min
Avg weekday ridership:	2,800
Ridership per mile:	1,120

The Skyway connects the center of downtown (below) to hotels and condos across the river, the community college and transit center to the north, and surface parking to the east.

+ **Extensive frequent-bus network**
- **Small and useless downtown peoplemover**

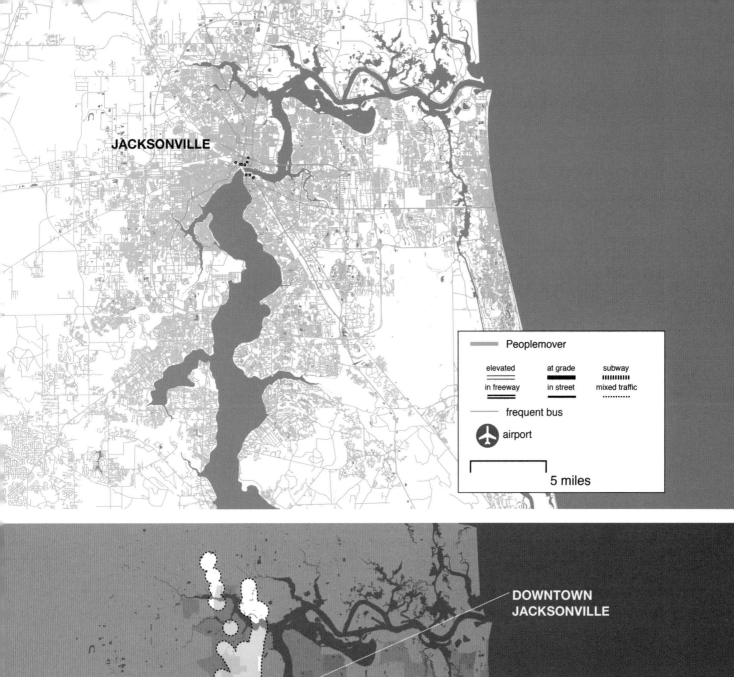

JACKSONVILLE

Peoplemover

| elevated | at grade | subway |
| in freeway | in street | mixed traffic |

frequent bus

✈ airport

5 miles

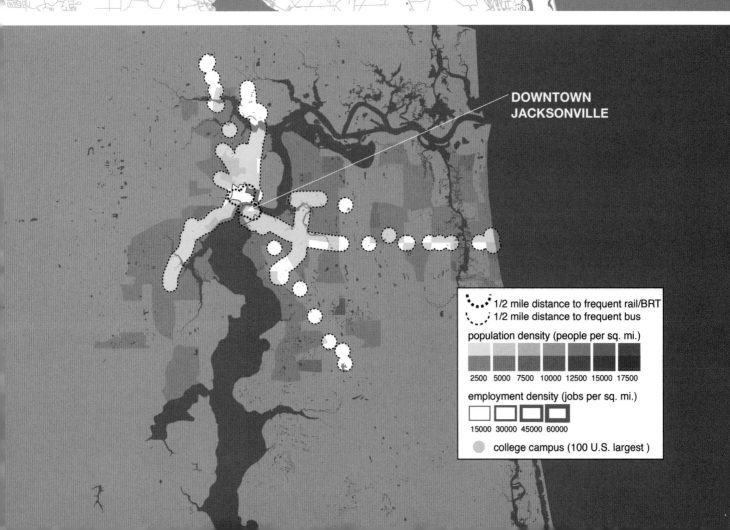

DOWNTOWN JACKSONVILLE

··· 1/2 mile distance to frequent rail/BRT
--- 1/2 mile distance to frequent bus

population density (people per sq. mi.)

2500 5000 7500 10000 12500 15000 17500

employment density (jobs per sq. mi.)

15000 30000 45000 60000

● college campus (100 U.S. largest)

40. NEW ORLEANS

New Orleans–Metairie–Hammond, LA-MS

population 1,507,017 (44th)   **served by frequent transit** 5%   **daily trips per 1000** 34

RTA
independent agency
Streetcar

In the early 2000s, New Orleans remained a sort of transit time capsule. A large portion of the city's residents lived in fairly dense, mixed-use, and walkable neighborhoods. A quarter of the city's households did not own cars. An extensive bus network carried more than 100,000 trips a day. The pattern of the city's transit was little changed in decades; bus routes still followed old streetcar lines, and one of those streetcar lines, on St. Charles, remained in operation with 1920s equipment, still carrying 10,000 people a day as the system's busiest route. New Orleans was one of the last US cities to take over its private transit system, which was operated by New Orleans Public Service, the local electric utility, until 1983. After the Regional Transit Authority took over, little changed.

Then came Hurricane Katrina in 2005. Nearly the city's entire transit fleet was flooded, its operating facilities were destroyed, and the neighborhoods where its riders lived were devastated. The city lost 30 percent of its population. No large US transit system had faced such a crisis in a century. It took a month for the first buses to start rolling again.

In its recovery, New Orleans' transit system took two radically different paths. The streetcar network became an immediate focus of rebuilding and then expansion. This continued an effort starting in the 1980s. The St. Charles Street line, saved because it was the highest-ridership line in the old network and because the neighborhood it ran through had the political clout to protect it, became one of the city's leading attractions as the economy shifted decisively toward tourism. In 1984, New Orleans hosted a World's Fair, and afterward the city developed the waterfront fair site into a new convention center and tourist-oriented mall. To link those to the French Quarter, a new streetcar line, the Waterfront Line, opened in 1988 along the city-owned freight-railroad tracks on the waterfront. With 1,800 trips a day, nearly all tourists, the line was considered a success, and was expanded and upgraded over the next decade. That

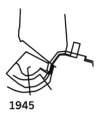

1945

1964

1988
Riverfront

1997

2004
Canal

2013
Loyola

2016
Rampart

- **Busy streetcar system limited by historic design and tourist orientation**
- **No frequent-bus network**

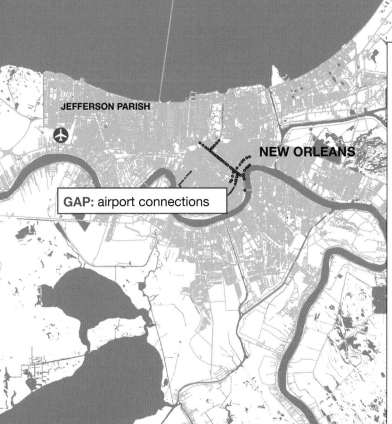

In a majority Black city where a small, white business community has traditionally held power and white neighborhoods had more political connections, New Orleans kept an existing streetcar line in a white neighborhood while tearing out those that served Black areas, then built new lines oriented to tourists. The Garden District, served by the St. Charles Line, is on high ground, which made it even more desirable after Katrina and further gentrified the surrounding areas.

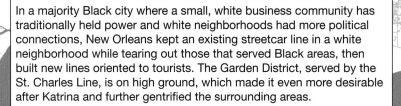

red dots: white residents
blue dots: Black residents

JEFFERSON PARISH

NEW ORLEANS

GAP: airport connections

Single-door boarding (above) and lack of signal priority (below) reduce the reliability of New Orleans streetcars.

inspired a much more ambitious next step: rebuilding the Canal Street streetcar, the city's second-busiest transit line behind St. Charles, which had been converted to bus in 1964. That involved four and a half miles of new route, and a fleet of streetcars elaborately designed to resemble 80-year old historic cars, albeit with air conditioning and wheelchair lifts. By the time that line opened in 2004, RTA was already planning the next new line, rebuilding the St. Claude streetcar 2.9 miles east from downtown, past the French Quarter through Marigny, Bywater, and St. Claude, to the edge of the Lower 9th Ward. RTA was still trying to get funding when Katrina hit. After the storm, it took two and a half years to get the streetcar lines restored. Then the push to expand the network continued. In 2010, a federal TIGER grant funded a new 0.8-mile east–west streetcar line from the Union Passenger Terminal to Canal Street which opened in 2013, and in 2016 a shorter one-and-a-half mile version of the St. Claude line opened. Today, the streetcar system has as much service, as many riders, and 15 percent more track than it did before Katrina.

The bus network has not recovered in the same way. Today RTA runs only 42 percent as much bus service as it did before the storm. Many routes operate less frequently; before Katrina, 17 bus routes had frequent service during rush hour; today only three do. A third of routes are gone altogether. Some neighborhoods have only 20 percent as much transit service as they did in 2005. As a result, today's New Orleans has 80 percent of its pre-Katrina population, but only 40 percent of its pre-Katrina ridership. While local leadership focused on new streetcars, the average New Orleans transit rider had significantly worse service than they did before the storm.

New Orleans streetcars are not merely tourist attractions or downtown circulators; they are critical transit routes. The St. Charles Street and Canal routes are the two busiest in the system, and they carry 40 percent of overall system ridership. Unlike other US streetcars, St. Charles and Canal link multiple important destinations and are long enough to serve many trips in their entirely. They are integrated into the bus network, with useful transfer points. They operate frequently all day, seven days a week. But they could be much better. Despite having reserved lanes for its entire length, the Canal streetcar averages only 6.5 miles per hour, taking over half an hour to cover three and a half miles. Frequent stops, lack of traffic signal priority, boarding-up steps, on-board fare payment, and the use of wheelchair lifts rather than level boarding slow down service dramatically. Streetcars are also notorious for bunching, increasing waits. Locals note that when buses get substituted for streetcars during track construction, their commutes get faster. The new lines built since Katrina are actually worse; the tracks are in the mixed traffic the whole way, the 2.4 mile crosstown is short and requires transfers to many key destinations, and streetcars run only every 20 minutes. Remarkably, the RTA actually advertises that streetcars and buses on Rampart street combine to offer frequent service, leaving passengers to peer down the street to see which is coming first and then scramble to the correct stop. It would not take much to dramatically improve the system, but nostalgia and a desire to attract tourists has led New Orleans to hobble streetcars and harm everyday riders.

Meanwhile, Katrina has only accelerated other trends. While the city itself has lost 20 percent of its population since Katrina, the metropolitan area as a whole has recovered to pre-storm levels. More jobs and more people have moved to suburban areas, which are not served well by transit. Jefferson Parish, immediately to the west of the city, has a higher population than New Orleans but less than 20 percent as much transit service, and anyone connecting between the two parish systems has to pay a separate fare on incompatible fare cards. The average New Orleans resident can reach only 44 percent the region's jobs in an hour by transit, but 98 percent by car.

Transit still plays an important role in New Orleans— seven percent of residents commute by transit—and rail plays an important role in the transit system. Forty percent of RTA riders use streetcars, a percentage that exceeds any other streetcar system in the United States and matches large light-rail systems in cities like Dallas, Denver, Portland, and San Diego. But in those cities rail offers higher capacity, speed, and reliability than bus; in New Orleans it merely looks more quaint. ■

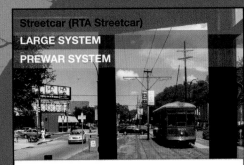

Streetcar (RTA Streetcar)

LARGE SYSTEM
PREWAR SYSTEM

Opened: 1893
Last Expanded: 2016
Length: 15.2 miles
Stations: 103.9
Frequency: 8–20 min, 20–40 min night (24 hour service on some lines)
Avg weekday ridership: 21,400
Ridership per mile: 1,408

Today RTA's frequent service (left)—limited to two streetcar lines—serves mainly Downtown and more affluent whiter neighborhoods. A proposed network redesign (right), released in draft form in 2020, would greatly increase frequent-bus service, especially in low-income predominantly Black neighborhoods like East New Orleans and the Lower Ninth Ward.

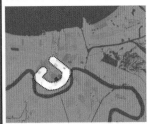
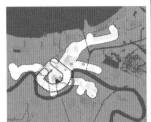

Large parts of Jefferson Parish are dense as New Orleans itself, but it has a separate transit system with much less service and uncoordinated fares. In 2018, both agencies revived the combined all-day pass that existed before Katrina.

DOWNTOWN NEW ORLEANS
84,566 jobs
60th in US

GAP: no frequent-bus network

⌣ 1/2 mile distance to frequent rail/BRT
⌣ 1/2 mile distance to frequent bus

population density (people per sq. mi.)

2500 5000 7500 10000 12500 15000 17500

employment density (jobs per sq. mi.)

15000 30000 45000 60000

● college campus (100 U.S. largest)

41. OKLAHOMA CITY

OKLAHOMA CITY
STREETCAR

OKC Streetcar
municipal
Streetcar

Oklahoma City–Shawnee, OK

population 1,481,542 (46th)   **served by frequent transit** 1%   **daily trips per 1000** 8

Oklahoma City is one of the great downtown revitalization success stories of the past two decades. In 1993, city voters approved MAPS ("Metropolitan Area Projects"), a five-and-a-half-year citywide sales tax that funded $350 million in projects including a ballpark, an urban canal, convention center upgrades, an arena, a concert hall renovation, a downtown library, and a new river park. This was followed by MAPS for Kids, using the same temporary sales tax for school projects, and then by MAPS 3, in 2009, including a new convention center, a downtown park, and sidewalk upgrades.

The results of MAPS, and other public projects coordinated with it, have been dramatic. Downtown Oklahoma City is now an all-day, seven-day-a-week destination. In Bricktown, restaurants, bars, and lofts overlook a man-made canal in what had been an abandoned industrial area. In Automobile Alley, former car dealerships are now white-tablecloth restaurants. The river is now the year-round training location for the US Olympic rowing and canoe/kayak team. The NBA Oklahoma City Thunder, lured by the new arena, bring fans downtown for 40 home games a year.

The Oklahoma City Streetcar is an integral part of this program. Funded in MAPS 3, it is seen as a way to tie together and cement the downtown revitalization. Mayor Nick Cornett calls it "a much more enjoyable way to investigate and explore downtown Oklahoma City." The streetcar also speaks to broader goals: as the mayor said, it came from "a generation which raised its hand and said, 'We want to move Oklahoma City forward, faster than it's ever moved before.'"

These same aspirations, though, handicap the streetcar. In trying to reach every downtown destination, it traces an irregular looping path. It does connect places that are too far apart to walk easily, but it doesn't connect them directly or quickly.

The streetcar hasn't changed the fact that Oklahoma City's transit network lags behind its peers. There is not a single frequent-bus route, and before 2019 there was no Sunday service at all. The streetcar may work for people out having fun, but it doesn't help commuters. It serves the downtown transit center, but only northbound; the southbound stop is two blocks away. The jobs it serves are already served by multiple local-bus routes. Oklahoma City needs better transit. But there is hope: MAPS 4, adopted in 2019, includes $87 million for transit, including bus-stop upgrades, new buses, and future "advanced transit options" which could include new BRT lines. ∎

+ **Long-term downtown revitalization strategy**
− **Roundabout streetcar**

Streetcar (OKC Streetcar)

HIGH PERFORMER
SMALL SYSTEM

Opened: 2019
Last Expanded: N/A
Length: 2.3 miles
Stations: 11
Frequency: 10 min
Avg weekday ridership: 3,943
Ridership per mile: 1714

The streetcar loop (below) connects the dots of downtown revitalistation names reflect the key destinations planners were trying to reach. The irregular loop, though, makes for long trips. Transit Center to Midtown, for example, is 0.4 miles as the crow flies, or 1.5 miles by streetcar. Trying to get the streetcar to the front door of everything actually makes it less useful.

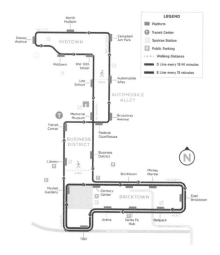

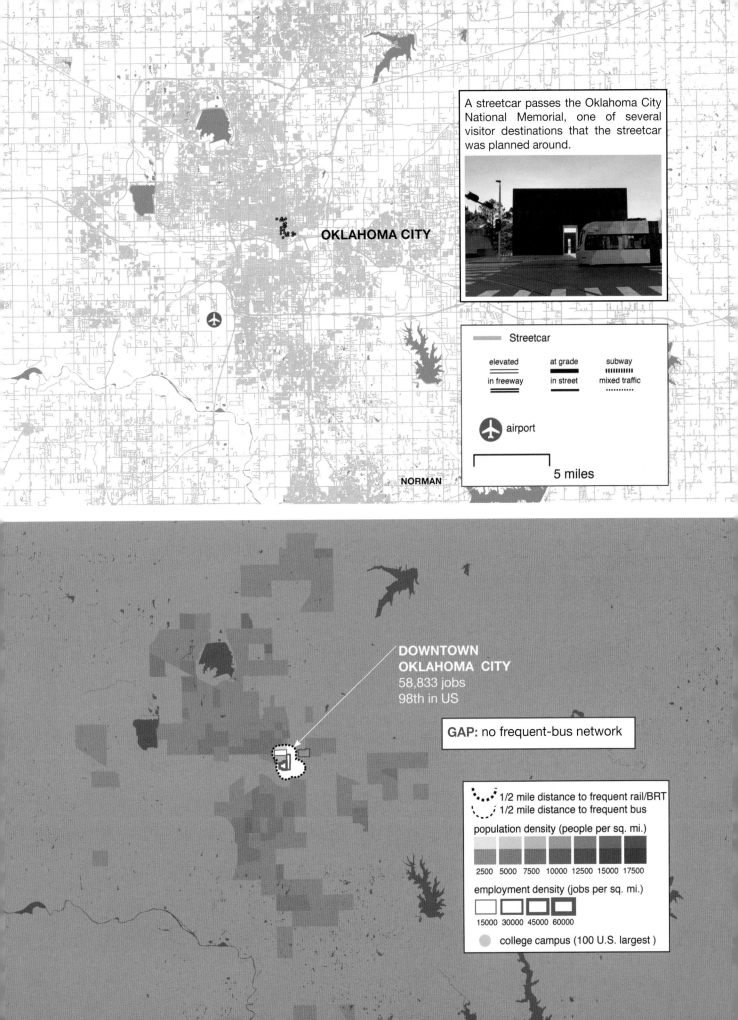

A streetcar passes the Oklahoma City National Memorial, one of several visitor destinations that the streetcar was planned around.

OKLAHOMA CITY

NORMAN

Streetcar

elevated | at grade | subway
in freeway | in street | mixed traffic

✈ airport

5 miles

DOWNTOWN
OKLAHOMA CITY
58,833 jobs
98th in US

GAP: no frequent-bus network

⟍⟋ 1/2 mile distance to frequent rail/BRT
⟍⟋ 1/2 mile distance to frequent bus

population density (people per sq. mi.)
2500 5000 7500 10000 12500 15000 17500

employment density (jobs per sq. mi.)
15000 30000 45000 60000

● college campus (100 U.S. largest)

42. HARTFORD

Hartford–West Hartford, CT

population 1,470,083 (48th)   **served by frequent transit** 7%

In the popular mind, Connecticut is leafy New York suburbs and quaint shore towns. Hartford doesn't fit that picture. It is a very urban place, with a downtown that has as many jobs as the downtowns of Cleveland and St. Louis, a significant industrial base, and row-house neighborhoods.

This disconnect is not accidental. Since World War II, Connecticut has deliberately weakened cities and minimized regional government to empower suburbs and small towns. County governments were eliminated in 1960, leaving the state divided into 169 towns as the largest units of local government. A quarter of the towns have fewer than 5,000 people, and the largest has only 144,000. Thus, decision making is either on a very local level (like land use) or statewide (like transit).

This governance model has led to dramatic disparities. Most of Connecticut's towns tightly regulate growth, limiting most development to single-family houses and setting minimum lot sizes, keeping out people who can't afford such homes. The Hartford metropolitan region, population 1,183,000, is one of the wealthiest in the country with a median household income of $52,000. The city itself, population 124,000, has a median income of only $20,000. In a state that is 71 percent non-Hispanic white, Hartford itself is 16 percent white, 43 percent Hispanic, and 39 percent African American.

Unsurprisingly, when transit comes up as a statewide political issue, it is usually about improving commuter rail, as when the state rebuilt and upgraded the rail line from New Haven through Hartford to Springfield, MA, or added another eight roundtrip trains to a route already served by nine Amtrak round trips a day.

But in 2012, the state broke ground on a very different project, building a busway along 9.4 miles of active and abandoned railroad right-of-way between New Britain and Hartford. CTfastrak is the first US example of a true "open" BRT system. Like the Los Angeles Orange Line, Eugene EmX, or the Cleveland HealthLine, CTfastrak has branded buses, high-quality stations, off-vehicle fare payment, and level all-door boarding. But unlike those systems, CTfastrak actually has seven different routes, of which six extend beyond the busway. Three make all stops along the busway, then continue as local routes beyond it, and three make only limited stops, then continue as express routes. CTfastrak improves commutes for downtown Hartford employees riding express buses from the suburbs, but it also dramatically improves the local bus network in Hartford, doubling its frequent coverage and connecting city residents to jobs around the region. ∎

CT transit
CT Transit
state agency
Frequent Bus
BRT
Commuter Rail

Commuter Rail (Hartford Line)
SMALL SYSTEM
LOW PERFORMER

Opened: 2018
Last Expanded: N/A
Length: 62 miles
Stations: 9
Frequency: 17 round trips a day
Avg weekday ridership: 2000
Ridership per mile: 32

BRT (CTfastrak)

Opened: 2015
Last Expanded: N/A
Length: Open BRT (9.4 guideway miles)
Stations: 10 (guideway only)
Frequency: 12 min weekday/Saturday, 20 min Sunday
Avg weekday ridership: N/A
Ridership per mile: N/A

+   **High quality "open" BRT with branching routes serving a wide area**

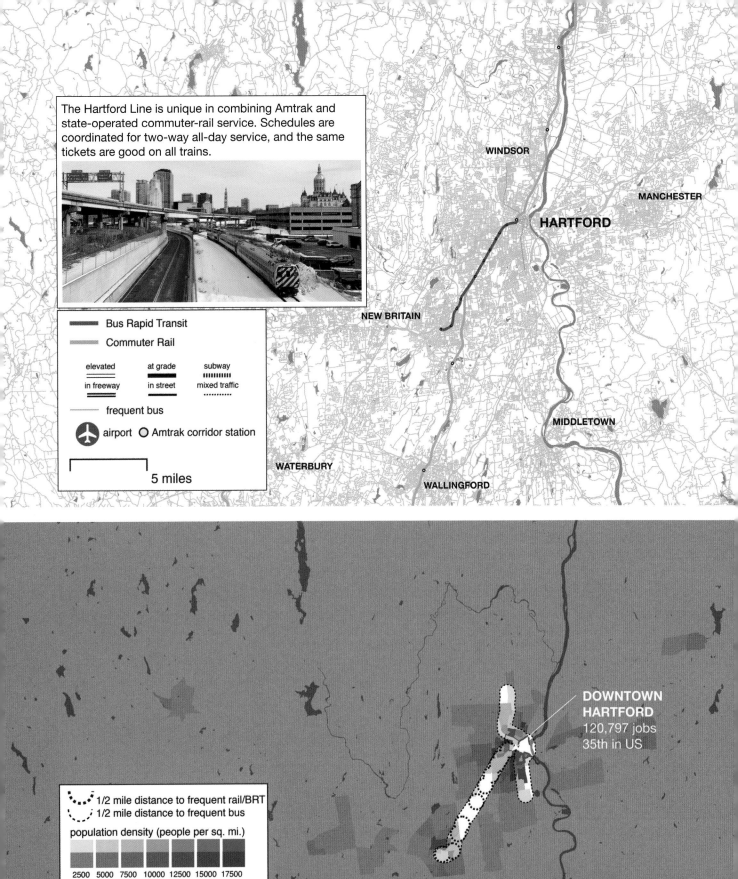

The Hartford Line is unique in combining Amtrak and state-operated commuter-rail service. Schedules are coordinated for two-way all-day service, and the same tickets are good on all trains.

WINDSOR

MANCHESTER

HARTFORD

NEW BRITAIN

MIDDLETOWN

WATERBURY

WALLINGFORD

Bus Rapid Transit
Commuter Rail

elevated | at grade | subway
in freeway | in street | mixed traffic
frequent bus

airport ○ Amtrak corridor station

5 miles

DOWNTOWN HARTFORD
120,797 jobs
35th in US

1/2 mile distance to frequent rail/BRT
1/2 mile distance to frequent bus

population density (people per sq. mi.)

2500 5000 7500 10000 12500 15000 17500

employment density (jobs per sq. mi.)

15000 30000 45000 60000

● college campus (100 U.S. largest)

43. CALGARY

Calgary, AB

population 1,392,609 (50th) **served by frequent transit** 20% **daily trips per 1000** 324

Calgary Transit
municipal
light rail
frequent bus

In many ways, Calgary's CTrain is one of the prototypes for North American light rail. It runs at street level through downtown (right), not in a subway like a 1970s metro system, or the Edmonton light rail, which opened three years earlier. Unlike San Diego, which opened the same year, it wasn't a bare-bones conversion of an existing rail line either—it has a mix of rights of way, some short tunnels, and large station structures (like Erlton Stampede, on the original line, below) not just simple shelters.

While its design feels quite familiar, Calgary stands out for its ridership levels and its comprehensive coverage. Four lines radiate out from downtown through the suburbs, almost to the edge of open countryside. Calgary is a medium-sized city dominated by suburban development and single-family homes. It resembles Oklahoma City or Austin much more than it does Los Angeles, Boston, or Vancouver. Forty-five percent of downtown employees use the train to get to work. It's the highest ridership rail system in the US and Canada, and not by a small margin—it has 50% more riders than Los Angeles, the second highest. Remarkably, it does that with less than 40 miles of rail, so it is also the top system in ridership per mile.

All of this is possible due to sustained planning and political support. The CTrain was built through 40 years of nearly continuous construction, often adding just one or two stations at a time. Calgary has also made major capacity upgrades, rebuilding stations and adding electric substations to support four-car trains. Other policies helped, too: the city put limits on the construction of downtown parking spaces even as new high rises were built and downtown employment increased. The result is some of the most expensive downtown parking in North America (higher than Boston or Chicago). Calgary is a transit city unlike any of its peers. ■

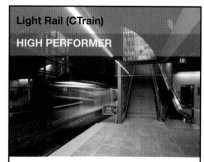

Light Rail (CTrain)

HIGH PERFORMER

Opened: 1981
Last Expanded: 2014
Length: 37.2 miles
Stations: 45
Frequency: 3-7 min peak, 10 midday, 10-15 evening and weekend
Avg weekday ridership: 313,800
Ridership per mile: 8,453

+ **Extremely high transit ridership in a modern, very suburban city**
+ **Sustained light-rail expansion over 40 years**
- **Low frequency bus network**

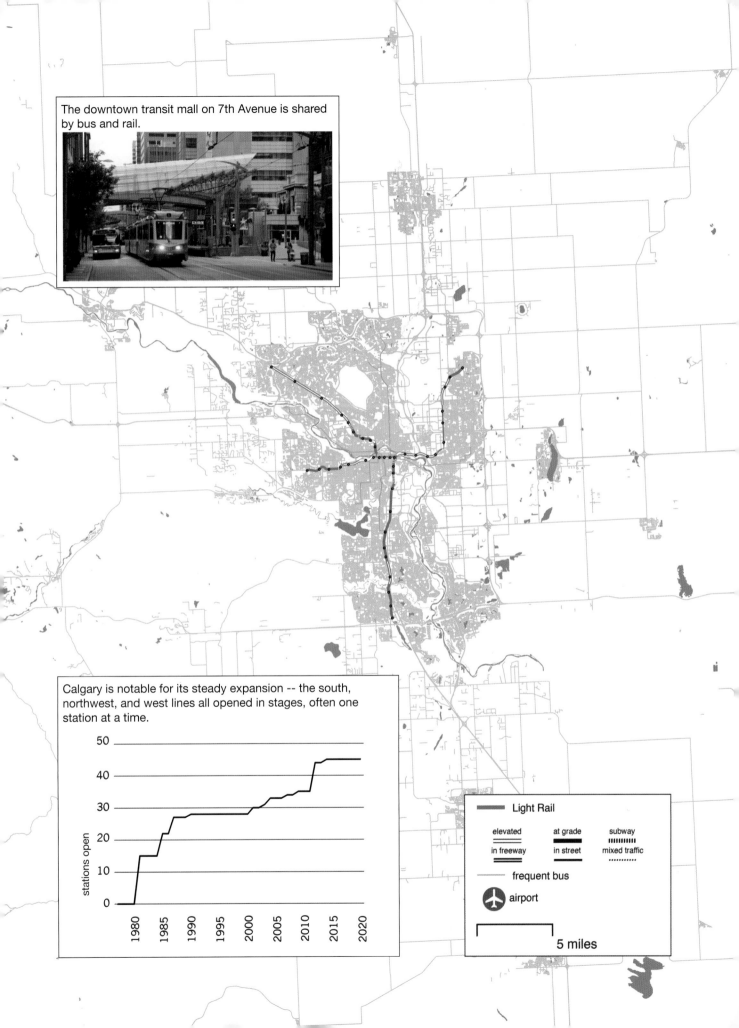

The downtown transit mall on 7th Avenue is shared by bus and rail.

Calgary is notable for its steady expansion -- the south, northwest, and west lines all opened in stages, often one station at a time.

stations open

50
40
30
20
10
0

1980 1985 1990 1995 2000 2005 2010 2015 2020

Light Rail

elevated   at grade   subway

in freeway   in street   mixed traffic

frequent bus

airport

5 miles

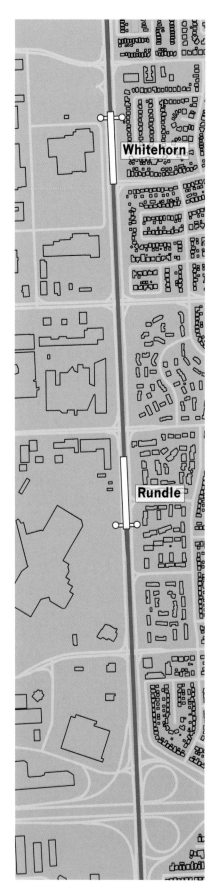

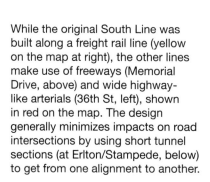

While the original South Line was built along a freight rail line (yellow on the map at right), the other lines make use of freeways (Memorial Drive, above) and wide highway-like arterials (36th St, left), shown in red on the map. The design generally minimizes impacts on road intersections by using short tunnel sections (at Erlton/Stampede, below) to get from one alignment to another.

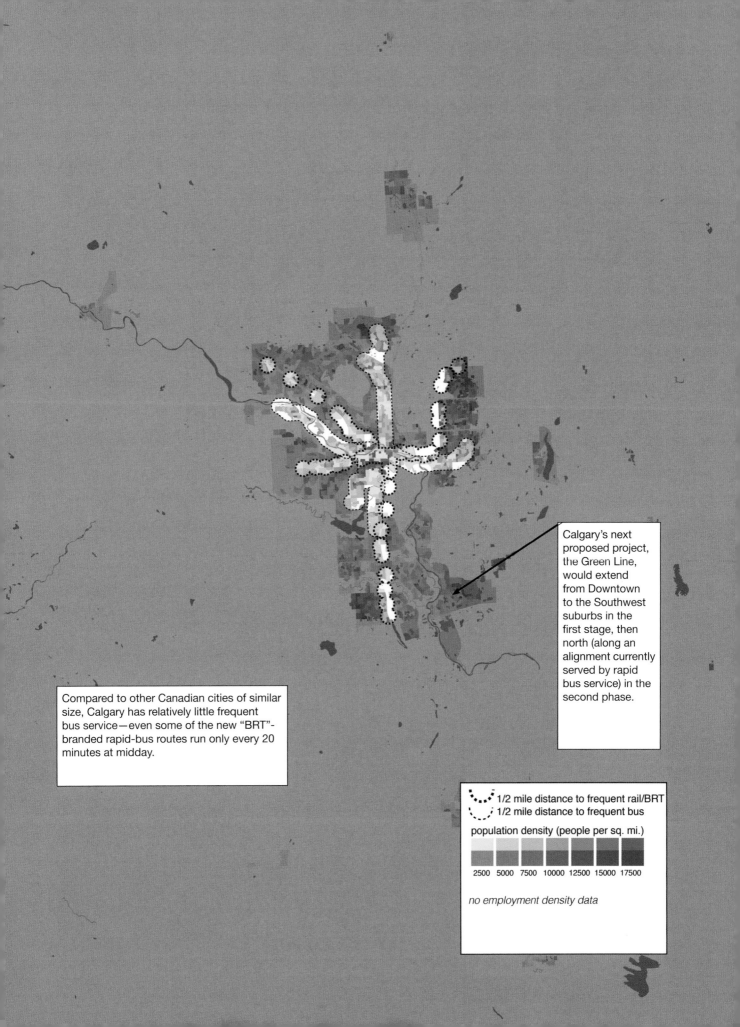

Calgary's next proposed project, the Green Line, would extend from Downtown to the Southwest suburbs in the first stage, then north (along an alignment currently served by rapid bus service) in the second phase.

Compared to other Canadian cities of similar size, Calgary has relatively little frequent bus service—even some of the new "BRT"-branded rapid-bus routes run only every 20 minutes at midday.

1/2 mile distance to frequent rail/BRT
1/2 mile distance to frequent bus

population density (people per sq. mi.)

2500 5000 7500 10000 12500 15000 17500

no employment density data

44. MEMPHIS

Memphis-Forrest City, TN-MS-AR

population 1,371,039 (51st)   **served by frequent transit** 1%   **daily trips per 1000** 12

MATA
municipal
Frequent Bus
Streetcar

Memphis was an early streetcar adopter. In 1978, trying to stem the loss of retail to the suburbs, the city had converted Main Street, the center of the downtown retail district, to a pedestrian mall, the grandly named "Mid-America Mall." By the 1990s, it was clear that this was failing, and vintage streetcars were seen as a way to draw more shoppers.

The streetcar was an immediate hit. Seven thousand people rode on the first day in 1993, and 1,300 on an average day in 1994. A 1994 survey found half of riders taking it for entertainment, and half for transportation. The route was simple—a two-and-a-half mile route straight down Main Street in both directions—easy to understand, frequent (five-minute headways), connected to the bus network, and useful for getting between the different parts of downtown. By 2001 15 percent of MATA's passenger trips were on the trolley. The streetcar was also credited with a boom in downtown development, including restaurants, lofts, and offices, both in restored historic buildings and new ones.

All this built political support, which led to expansion. A one-way riverfront loop, using an existing rail line, opened in 1997. Then came a major step outwards: a two-and-a-half-mile line in Madison Street to connect downtown the Medical Center with 21,000 jobs. It was seen as the first leg of an eventual light-rail system that would go to the suburbs and the airport.

But opening day for the Madison line in March of 2004 proved to be the high point for the system. Ridership on the medical center route never matched expectations. Total trolley ridership peaked at nearly 6,000 a day in 2004, and by 2014 at was at half that level. Then, in 2013 and 2014, two of the streetcars—both vintage cars from Australia—caught fire while operating. Investigations revealed serious maintenance shortcomings, and the entire system was suspended until 2018, when only the Main Street line reopened.

The lack of streetcars highlights the problems with Memphis' overall transit network. The metropolitan area is sprawling. Jobs are spread out. FedEx, the region's largest employer, is at the airport, surrounded by other distribution companies, adding up to 83,000 jobs. Downtown Memphis has only 47,000 jobs, but that is where the bus network is centered. That radial network is even less useful because downtown is actually at the western edge of the region, not in the center. That is one of the issues with the Madison line: most medical center employees are coming from the east, not the west as the streetcar does, and that streetcar route did not link to either of the downtown bus transit centers. The streetcar was the only frequent route on the system. Most buses run half hourly or hourly, even at peak, and half the routes don't run on Sunday. It is not surprising, then, that bus ridership is dropping. In 1992, the year before the streetcar opened, the bus carried 12.7 million rides, in 2015 it was only 7.8 million.

Memphis built a useful streetcar. It hasn't yet built a useful transit system. ■

A view down Main Street shows the original line's strength. From here, the downtown core is visible, but over half a mile away. The streetcar goes there in a straight line, and with a car every five minutes pre-2014 you would not wait long. It was easy to understand and convenient.

+ **Useful Main Street streetcar**
- **Inadequate bus network that underserves major job centers**

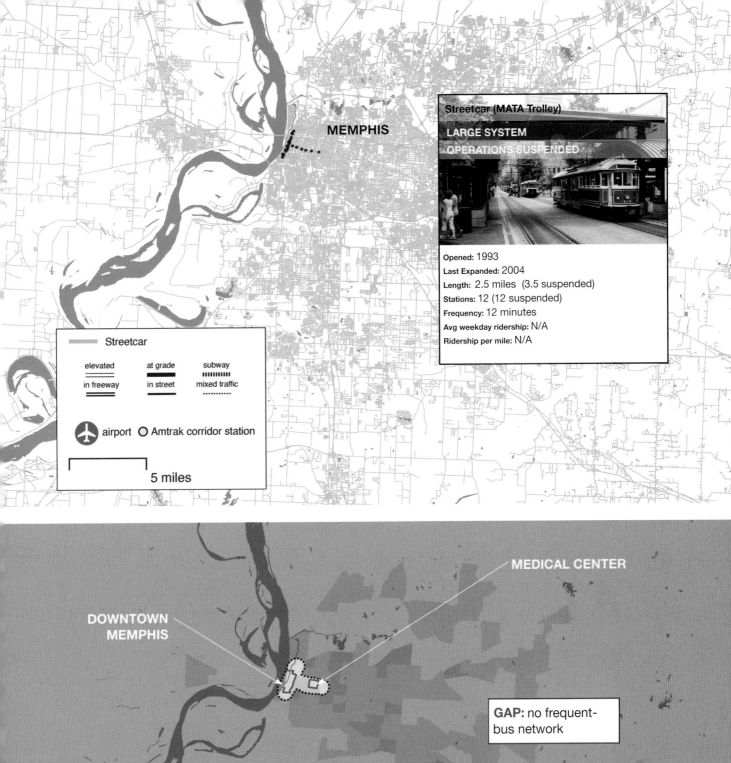

MEMPHIS

Streetcar

| elevated | at grade | subway |
| in freeway | in street | mixed traffic |

✈ airport ◯ Amtrak corridor station

5 miles

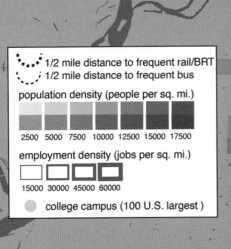

MEDICAL CENTER

DOWNTOWN MEMPHIS

GAP: no frequent-bus network

1/2 mile distance to frequent rail/BRT
1/2 mile distance to frequent bus

population density (people per sq. mi.)

2500 5000 7500 10000 12500 15000 17500

employment density (jobs per sq. mi.)

15000 30000 45000 60000

● college campus (100 U.S. largest)

45. OTTAWA

Ottawa - Gatineau, ON-QE

population 1,323,783 (52nd)   **served by frequent transit** 46%   **daily trips per 1000** 195

 OC Transpo

OC Transpo
municipal
light rail
commuter rail
BRT
frequent bus

◆ **STO**

Société de transport de l'Outaouais
independent agency
BRT
frequent bus

Ottawa has long been a transit innovator. It is world famous for its busways, one of the earliest examples of heavy-duty bus-rapidtransit infrastructure in the world when they first opened in the 1980s. It was one of the first North American cities to put lightweight European diesel commuter rail into service, and it operates the most frequent commuter-rail line in North America. It is also notable for being one of the few examples anywhere in the world of a busway being converted to rail.

Ottawa committed to rapid transit in the early 1970s. This was to meet a goal of increasing public transit ridership and also part of a regional land-use strategy. Downtown was redeveloped and joined by a series of suburban employment centers. The population of Ottawa more than doubled between 1950 and 1975. Suburban sprawl was allowed within the regional greenbelt created around the city in the 1950s.

In the 1970s Ottawa was still relatively small—roughly 500,000 people—and the cost of heavy rail seemed out of reach. The desire to accommodate suburban growth put a priority on developing a transit system that could cover a lot of area quickly. That resulted in using buses instead of rail and building "outside-in," investing in suburban busways (designed to allow rail conversion) rather than the more complex inner segments of the transit lines. In 1983, the first segments of busway opened. Over the next 30 years, the system was expanded east, southeast, west, and southwest.

From the beginning the busways had an unusually high level of service. Buses stopping at every station provided all-day frequent service. Additional routes radiated out from the stations into the suburbs. On many of these

The busways were notable for their infrastructure. They were largely grade separated, stations had passing lanes to allow express service and multiple buses stopping at once, and stations were large and well sheltered. The guideway infrastructure is now used for light rail; the stations (like Lees, below) are being rebuilt.

- **+ Extremely high ridership busway converted to light rail**
- **+ High frequency commuter rail line**
- **- Rail and BRT misses core neighborhoods**

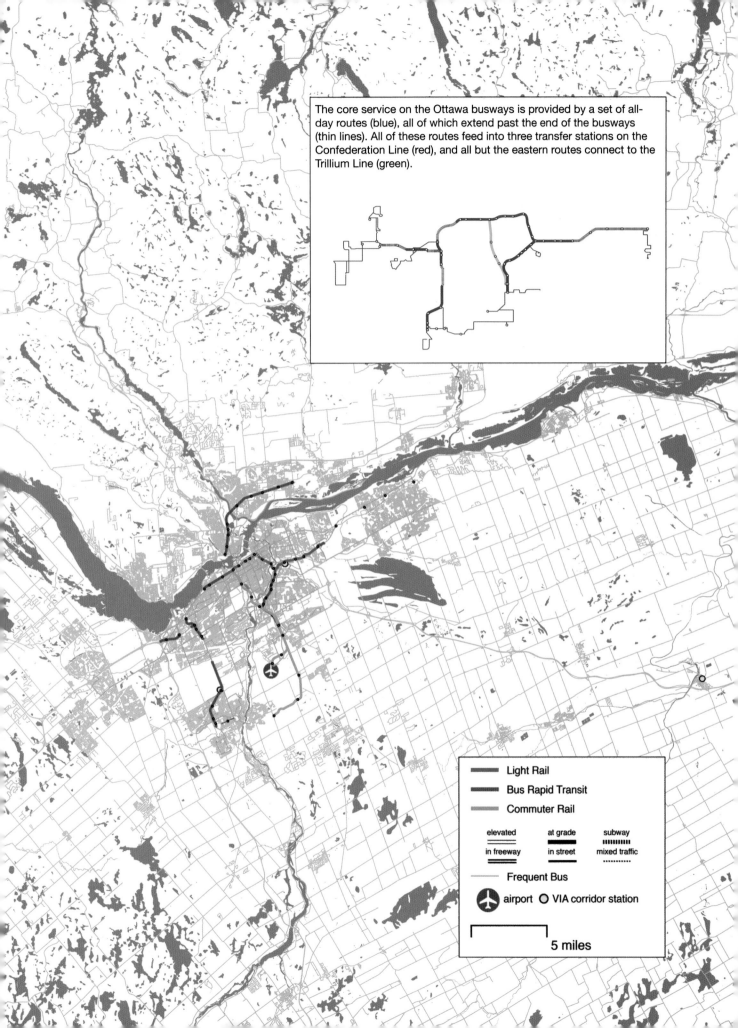

The core service on the Ottawa busways is provided by a set of all-day routes (blue), all of which extend past the end of the busways (thin lines). All of these routes feed into three transfer stations on the Confederation Line (red), and all but the eastern routes connect to the Trillium Line (green).

Light Rail

Bus Rapid Transit

Commuter Rail

| elevated | at grade | subway |
| in freeway | in street | mixed traffic |

Frequent Bus

airport   VIA corridor station

5 miles

BRT (TransitWau)

LARGE SYSTEM

Opened: 1983
Last Expanded: 2011
Length: Open busway (22 miles guideway at peak, being replaced by rail)
Stations: 57 (guideway only)
Frequency: varies
Avg weekday ridership: N/A
Ridership per mile: N/A

Light Rail (Confederation Line)

VERY HIGH PERFORMER

Opened: 2019
Last Expanded: N/A
Length: 7.8 miles (16.8 in construction)
Stations: 13 (16 in construction)
Frequency: 4-5 min peak, 10 min midday and weekend, 15 min night
Avg weekday ridership: 159,000
Ridership per mile: 20,385

DMU Commuter Rail (Trillium Line)

VERY HIGH PERFORMER

SMALL SYSTEM

Opened: 2001
Last Expanded: ongoing
Length: 5 miles (9.9 U/C)
Stations: 5 (6 U/C)
Frequency: 12 min
Avg weekday ridership: 16,900
Ridership per mile: 3,380

routes, buses ran express for faster trips. At peak, 180 buses per hour ran into downtown on the busway.

The busway system was a clear success. It carried 200,000 people on an average weekday. In 2016, Ottawa had a public-transit modal share of 19%—close to the 22% of Montreal and 24% of Toronto, despite the fact that those cities are much larger and much denser. Thanks to the broad outward reach of the transitway, nearly all of the city's population was within walking distance of a bus connection to downtown.

Rail remained an aspiration. There were multiple plans for rail, beginning in the 1990s. These finally took shape in the form of diesel railcars on a disused freight rail line that had transitway connections at both ends and a major university campus in the middle.

Meanwhile, the busway became a victim of its own success. At the core of the system, a bus every 20 seconds ran down ordinary bus lanes, separated from cars by onky paint and signs, hitting traffic lights every block, lining block faces end to end as passengers boarded. The streets could handle no more. A 1980s proposal to build a bus tunnel died based on cost. By 2010, planners had concluded that the solution was conversion to light rail, using the busway outside downtown and a subway within it, designed for 320-foot-long trains with the capacity for 1,200 passengers each at headways of four minutes during rush hour. That line opened in 2019, and the next stage of expansion, which will fully replace the east and west busways, is under construction.

Ottawa's busways did their job, and the success of the new rail line vindicates their planning. But the shortcomings of that thinking remain: the busways are fundamentally suburban. They skip the densest parts of the city, and there has been little effort to develop around stations. In some ways, Ottawa—shiny new trains aside—remains the embodiment of a 1970s vision of a transit city. ∎

1983-1986
Original transitway

1987-1989
East

1991-1995
Southeast

2001
Trillium Line, West

2005-2011
Southwest

2019
Confederation Line

2019
Rail Phase 2

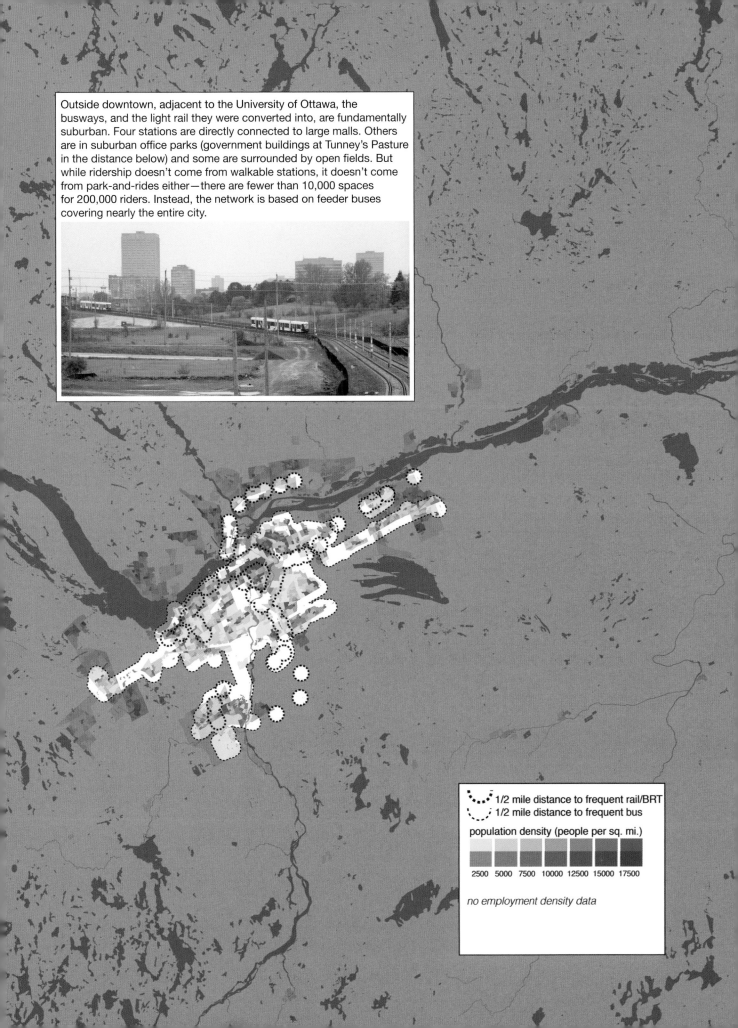

Outside downtown, adjacent to the University of Ottawa, the busways, and the light rail they were converted into, are fundamentally suburban. Four stations are directly connected to large malls. Others are in suburban office parks (government buildings at Tunney's Pasture in the distance below) and some are surrounded by open fields. But while ridership doesn't come from walkable stations, it doesn't come from park-and-rides either—there are fewer than 10,000 spaces for 200,000 riders. Instead, the network is based on feeder buses covering nearly the entire city.

----·-·: 1/2 mile distance to frequent rail/BRT
- - - -: 1/2 mile distance to frequent bus

population density (people per sq. mi.)

| 2500 | 5000 | 7500 | 10000 | 12500 | 15000 | 17500 |

no employment density data

Parliament

Lyon

Confederation Line

Pimsi

Bayview

Trillium Line

LeBreton

Transitway

In downtown, the busway (below) fed into bus lanes on Albert and Slater Streets. That has been replaced with the light-rail subway (above) connecting to the former busway right of way at both ends.

BRT (Rapibus)

Opened: 2013
Last Expanded: N/A
Length: Open BRT (7.5 miles guideway)
Stations: 10 (guideway only)
Frequency: every 30 in offpeak, more frequent peak
Avg weekday ridership: N/A
Ridership per mile: N/A

Ottawa's sister city of Gatineau, across the river in Quebec, has its own busway. It opened in 2013 along a freight-rail corridor, part of which is still active, alongside the bus corridor. Many of the routes that use it continue across the bridge into Ottawa. Compared to Ottawa, the infrastructure is relatively minimal, and service is less frequent.

The Trillium Line (above) had all the makings of a failure: a project driven by a political desire for rail (rather than a defined transport need), a demonstration of a new technology, a corridor picked because it existed, and a focus on getting something running quickly. But the former CP freight rail line was in the right location, running through the center of the Carleton University campus with transitway stations on both ends. Equally importantly, OC Transpo ran great service—every 15 minutes all day, now increased to every 12. That's the most frequent commuter-rail line in North America, and it is operating on a single-track line (right). That is remarkable: 90 trains a day serve the single-track termini at Bayview and Greenboro—many more than Caltrain handles in San Francisco on 12 tracks. The key is precise schedules, and efficient operating procedures. The line has three passing tracks (right) and the trains are precisely scheduled to meet there—at 12-minute headways each train meets three other trains on its 16-minute trip.

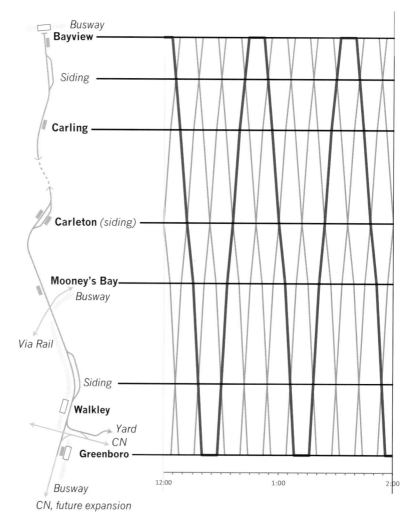

Ottawa's busways were built as two-lane roadways (above, at Lees). Since the busways are nearly completely grade separated, and the stations have long platforms, passing lanes, and pedestrian overpasses so many buses can pull in, stop, and pull out at once (top right, at Greenboro), they can handle several buses a minute. The bottleneck was downtown (right), where all those buses had to make it down a city street with a single painted bus lane, frequent traffic signals, and cars crossing the bus lane to pull in and out of curbside parking spots. The new light rail (below) replaces a bus every 20 seconds (a capacity of roughly 10,000 people an hour) with a tunnel that can handle a 600-passenger-light-rail train every two minutes (roughly 18,000 people an hour).

46. **EDMONTON**

Edmonton, AB

population 1,321,426 (53rd)   **served by frequent transit** 25%   **daily trips per 1000** 288

ETS

Edmonton Transit Service
municipal
light rail
frequent bus

In 1974, Edmonton started construction on a 4.5-mile light-rail line. That was an unexpected move—not only was this a brand new technology for North America (Calgary and San Diego did not start construction until 1977 and 1978), but Edmonton had a population of only 500,000, while the only other cities building transit were big metropolitan areas like Boston, Washington DC, and San Francisco.

That first line was built following a quite conventional template: tracks following a freight-rail right of way feeding into a short downtown tunnel. While the use of light rail allowed for a handful of at-grade crossings on the surface segment, the infrastructure resembled heavy rail: high platforms (not low platforms like in San Diego), stations built for five-car trains, and no street running. The stations even started out with turnstiles and station agents.

The system was an immediate success, with 18,000 weekday boardings in 1978, but the commitment to subway made expansion slow and expensive. The subway was extended under downtown streets by one station in 1981 and two stations in 1982, then by another in 1989. This brought the tunnel to the edge of the deep North Saskatchewan River valley. From here, a 1,700-foot-long bridge and another subway segment brought light rail to the University of Alberta campus in 1992.

After 18 years, Edmonton had 71.2 miles of light rail, and it took 14 years for the next opening, the start of a five-station extension southward that largely follows a highway-like street. With this, what is now known as the Capital Line was complete, 13 miles from northeast to southwest. It reflects a 1970s approach to transit planning: a tunnel in the core (downtown, the capital, and

Light Rail (ETS LRT)
HIGH PERFORMER

Opened: 1978
Last Expanded: ongoing
Length: 15.1 miles (8.1 miles under construction)
Stations: 18 (12 under construction)
Frequency: 5-10 min peak, 5-15 min offpeak
Avg weekday ridership: 110,768
Ridership per mile: 7336

The Dudley B. Menzies Bridge over the North Saskatchewan River (below) connects the subway beneath the University of Alberta (in the distance) to the subway beneath the provincial capitol and downtown. The lower level, suspended from the track structure, is part of the city's 100-mile-pedestrian-and-bike-trail network. Trains are typically three-to-five-cars long.

+ **First light-rail system in North America linked to a comprehensive bus network**
+ **High-capacity, largely grade-separated approach resembling heavy rail**

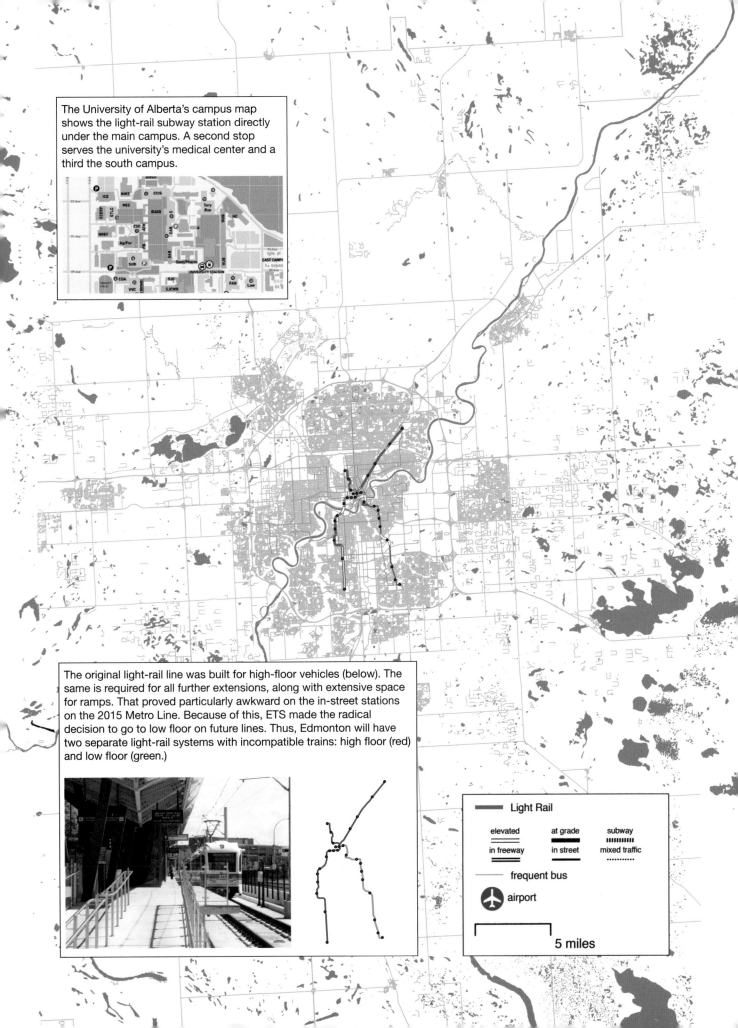

The University of Alberta's campus map shows the light-rail subway station directly under the main campus. A second stop serves the university's medical center and a third the south campus.

The original light-rail line was built for high-floor vehicles (below). The same is required for all further extensions, along with extensive space for ramps. That proved particularly awkward on the in-street stations on the 2015 Metro Line. Because of this, ETS made the radical decision to go to low floor on future lines. Thus, Edmonton will have two separate light-rail systems with incompatible trains: high floor (red) and low floor (green.)

Light Rail

| elevated | at grade | subway |
| in freeway | in street | mixed traffic |

frequent bus

✈ airport

5 miles

The first line combined a downtown subway (Bay/Enterprise Square station, top) with a rail corridor (Clareview, 2nd from top). The southern extension added a long segment in the median of a major arterial wide enough that stations (Century Park, 3rd from top) need to have skybridges for safe access. Newer lines, like the Metro Line (near Kingsway RAH Station, bottom) and the Valley Line now under construction, are designed to blend into the urban fabric in more walkable areas.

the university) linked to suburban corridors following rail and highway rights of way. Outside of that core, the stations are in sprawling, car-oriented places; the only major destination of note is a mall. The system depends on feeder buses, and to some extent park and ride, for access to the stations. That strategy has worked well for commuters headed to the core. Overall, 32% of commuters headed downtown, and 45% headed to the university use transit, and the transit-mode share is notably higher around the light-rail corridors (below) than in other similar suburban areas.

In the 2000s, the city started planning for significant expansion into a five-line system. While the new lines are also long radial routes into the suburbs, they reflect a different planning approach, which the city calls "urban LRT." Stations will be closer together, with more attention to pedestrian and bikeway connections and non-downtown activity centers. To accomplish this, the lines use much more street running, shorter trains, and, on the newest lines, low-floor cars. The 2.1-mile Metro Line, opened in 2015, branches off from the existing downtown subway and then immediately surfaces next to the Rogers Place hockey arena and McEwan University. From there, it largely follows city streets to stations at the Royal Alexandra Hospital and the Northern Alberta Institute of Technology community college. It's intended to be the inner segment of a longer line to the north. The next expansion project, a line into the southeastern suburbs, also uses street alignments, both in the outer areas and in downtown. ■

Like other Canadian cities, Edmonton has very high transit coverage. Of the 1.3 million people in the metro area, 70% live within 1/2 mile walk of a transit stop. In 2020, though, ETS is shifting more resources to frequent service in the core.

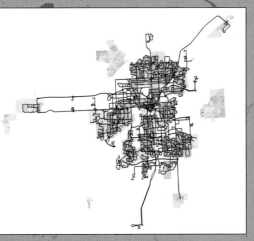

The Edmonton bus system is closely integrated with light rail. At Century Park, for example, 27 bus routes pull into a transit center with an enclosed waiting area linked to the station platform by a skybridge.

Transit-mode share is significantly higher around the light-rail corridors than elsewhere. Dark blue represents a mode share of over 20%.

```
‿‿‿   1/2 mile distance to frequent rail/BRT
⁝‿⁝   1/2 mile distance to frequent bus
```

population density (people per sq. mi.)

2500	5000	7500	10000	12500	15000	17500

no employment density data

47. RICHMOND

Richmond, VA

population 1,291,900 (56th)   **served by frequent transit** 10%   **daily trips per 1000** 19

GRTC
intergovernmental partnership
BRT
Frequent Bus

In 2010, Richmond began planning a new 7.6-mile BRT line in the Broad Street corridor, which was partially funded in 2014 with a federal TIGER grant and started construction in 2016. It follows the city's historic commercial main street and its densest corridor, past the State House, the business downtown, the convention center, Virginia Commonwealth University, museums, and historic townhouse neighborhoods.

Two things stand out about Richmond's BRT, called Pulse. One is that, unlike many systems branded as "BRT," it actually has significant dedicated lanes, extending 2.5 miles down the middle of Broad Street, along with curbside bus lanes in downtown. The second is that the BRT route was implemented as part of a complete transit-network redesign. Notably, the redesign is based on a study initiated not by the transit agency (GRTC) but by the City of Richmond, one of the three local jurisdictions that funded GRTC, in 2016. The new network has 10 frequent local-bus corridors extending out from downtown (compared to none in the old network) and simplified the network in general. This redesign allows Pulse to serve as a spine for the transit network as a whole.

Thus, in 2018, after years of ridership declines and reduced service, Richmond's transit system was fundamentally transformed through new infrastructure and new service. ∎

BRT (Pulse)

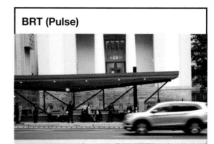

Opened: 2018
Last Expanded: N/A
Length: 7.6 miles (2.5 guideway miles)
Stations: 5 (guideway only)
Frequency: 10 min peak, 15 min off-peak
Avg weekday ridership: 6,349
Ridership per mile: 835

The new bus network (bottom right) was designed around the new BRT route (in black). Pulse runs every 10–15 minutes; red routes run every 15 minutes, blue routes every 30 minutes, and green routes once an hour. West of downtown, Pulse uses dedicated lanes in the street median (top right), with boarding platforms reached by cross-walks. One traffic lane in each is being converted to transit, and on-street parking spaces were eliminated at station locations.

Routes 2a, 2b, 2c combine to form Frequent Route 2 on Semmes.

- + **BRT on the city's strongest transit corridor**
- + **Legible frequent-bus network redesigned around BRT**

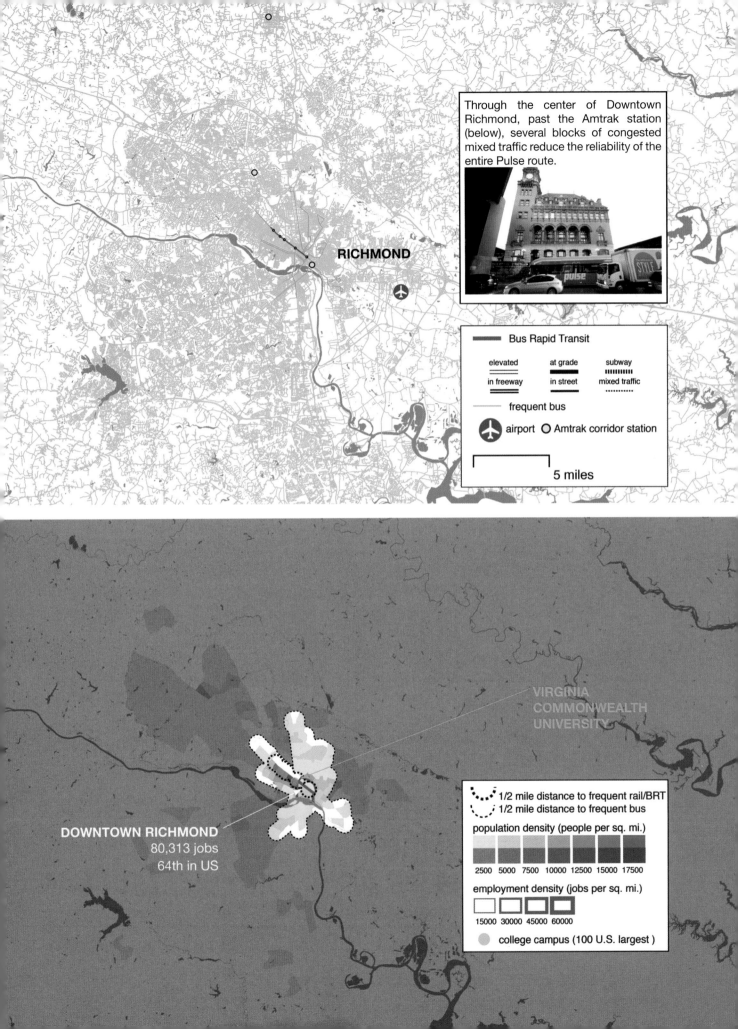

Through the center of Downtown Richmond, past the Amtrak station (below), several blocks of congested mixed traffic reduce the reliability of the entire Pulse route.

RICHMOND

Bus Rapid Transit

elevated	at grade	subway
in freeway	in street	mixed traffic

frequent bus

✈ airport ○ Amtrak corridor station

5 miles

VIRGINIA
COMMONWEALTH
UNIVERSITY

DOWNTOWN RICHMOND
80,313 jobs
64th in US

1/2 mile distance to frequent rail/BRT
1/2 mile distance to frequent bus

population density (people per sq. mi.)

2500 5000 7500 10000 12500 15000 17500

employment density (jobs per sq. mi.)

15000 30000 45000 60000

college campus (100 U.S. largest)

48. BUFFALO

Buffalo–Cheektowaga–Niagara Falls, NY

population 1,204,100 (58th)   **served by frequent transit** 19%   **daily trips per 1000** 36

NFTA
independent agency
Light Rail
Frequent Bus

Buffalo's light-rail line is often seen as failure. It is the shortest light-rail system in the United States, and one of only two that have never been expanded. (Norfolk is the other.) It also has an odd configuration that has never been repeated. It is on the surface in downtown and in a subway outside it. But the numbers tell a different story. With 17,000 riders on only 6.4 miles, Metro Rail outperforms most of the light-rail lines in the United States.

Buffalo is the smallest metropolitan area in the United States to have a full light-rail line, as opposed to a streetcar. But Buffalo does have one really strong transit corridor, and that is where the light rail is. At one end is downtown, where the line runs on Main Street, right in the center of activity (literally running through the middle of Buffalo's tallest building). The other side is the south campus of the University of Buffalo, with a station right on campus. The line traverses Buffalo's densest area and links to numerous bus routes. It is a straight line where transit demand is greatest. A further extension to the university's north campus—part of the original plans, and being studied again, with an environmental impact statement published in 2020 —would make sense, but otherwise this may be all the light rail Buffalo needs. ∎

Light Rail (Metro Rail)
SMALL SYSTEM

Opened: 1984
Last Expanded: 1986
Length: 6.4 miles
Stations: 14
Frequency: 10 min peak, 12 min midday, 15–20 min evening/weekend
Avg weekday ridership: 15,100
Ridership per mile: 2,359

Metro Rail connects two centers: downtown (below) and the University of Buffalo (bottom). University Station includes parking and a large, off-street bus transit center.

+ **High-ridership light-rail line that acts as spine for transit network**

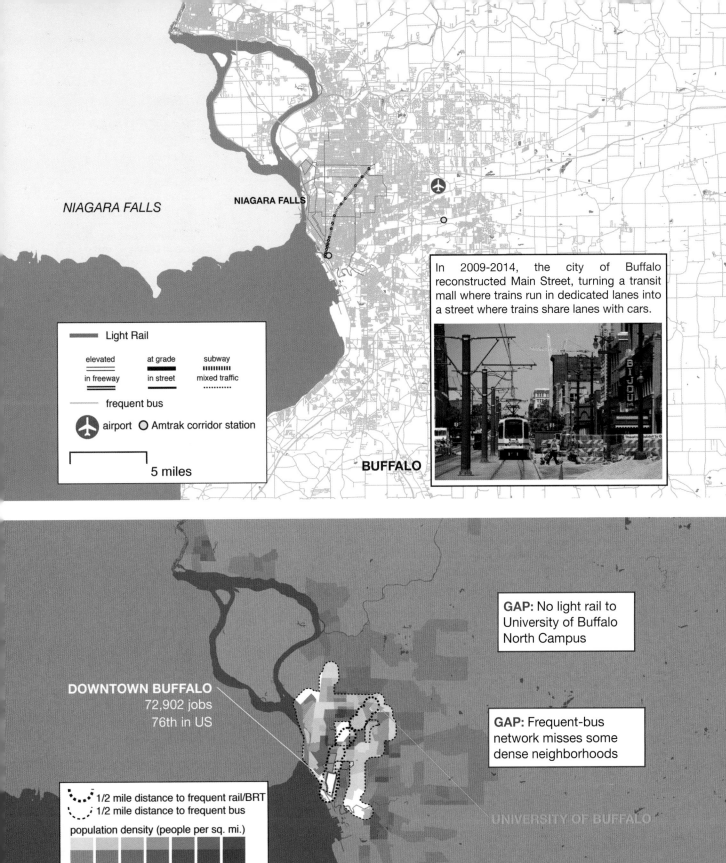

NIAGARA FALLS

NIAGARA FALLS

In 2009-2014, the city of Buffalo reconstructed Main Street, turning a transit mall where trains run in dedicated lanes into a street where trains share lanes with cars.

Light Rail

| elevated | at grade | subway |
| in freeway | in street | mixed traffic |

frequent bus

✈ airport ◯ Amtrak corridor station

5 miles

BUFFALO

DOWNTOWN BUFFALO
72,902 jobs
76th in US

GAP: No light rail to University of Buffalo North Campus

GAP: Frequent-bus network misses some dense neighborhoods

UNIVERSITY OF BUFFALO

1/2 mile distance to frequent rail/BRT
1/2 mile distance to frequent bus

population density (people per sq. mi.)

2500 5000 7500 10000 12500 15000 17500

employment density (jobs per sq. mi.)

15000 30000 45000 60000

● college campus (100 U.S. largest)

49. ALBUQUERQUE

Albuquerque–Santa Fe–Las Vegas, NM

population 1,158,464 (62nd)   **served by frequent transit** 7%   **daily trips per 1000** 6

ABQ Ride
municipal
Frequent Bus

Rio Metro Regional Transit District
independent agency
Commuter Rail

With only two million people, the entire state of New Mexico has fewer people than midsize metro areas like Portland or Sacramento. But half of those people live along Interstate 25 between Belen, Albuquerque, and Santa Fe. While much of the region is sprawling, both Albuquerque and Santa Fe have walkable mixed-use cores. This is a place that can support good transit.

In Albuquerque, the prime corridor is Central Avenue, which connects downtown, the medical center, and a series of neighborhoods. In 2004, that route got an upgraded local bus service, branded "Rapid Ride," with limited, branded stops and frequent service all day on weekdays. It has now been upgraded to full BRT, with off-board fare collection, level boarding, and extensive stretches of dedicated median lanes. Rapid Ride more than doubled corridor ridership, to more than 15,000 on an average weekday, a quarter of the total ridership in the system. The faster, more-reliable BRT service is projected to add another 3,000.

Beyond the cities, this is a land of long commutes. Growth restrictions in Santa Fe have made it a very expensive place to live, and Indian reservations restrict growth to the south. But, thanks to the state government, Santa Fe is a major employment center. That means a lot of people are commuting into Santa Fe from Albuquerque and its northern suburbs, 60 miles away. By 2025, freeway travel times are expected to be at two hours. This geography—a linear corridor, long commutes, and concentrated employment centers—is fertile ground for transit. In August of 2003, Governor Bill Richardson asked the department of transportation and the local council of governments to study commuter rail and the legislature to fund it; it took only five years to implement. The first trains ran to the southern suburbs of Albuquerque in 2006, and the line to Santa Fe opened in 2008. The key ingredient: an existing railroad line that carried relatively little freight traffic but had been maintained to 79-mph standards for Amtrak service. BNSF was willing to sell it to the state, along with the rest of the line all the way to the Colorado border, nearly 269 miles of mainline track in good condition with room for double track, for $75 million. But New Mexico also built more than 15 miles of brand-new railroad line, much of it in the median of I-25. That's a notable departure from the typical philosophy of "we'll run the trains where the tracks happen to be already." Trip time from Santa Fe to Albuquerque, 60 miles, is an hour and a half.

ART (above) had a rocky start. After a ceremonial opening under the outgoing mayor (and BRT supporter) in late 2017, the new mayor announced a series of design issues and major problems wth the range of the electric buses. After failing to resolve the bus issues, the city rejected the buses and ordered new ones. What was to be the first all electric BRT in the US opened 2 years late with diesel buses. But the other aspects of the project -- the alignment, the dedicated lanes, and the high quality stations -- have worked well.

Albuquerque is the 60th-largest metro area in the country, on par with Dayton and Omaha. Santa Fe is the 282nd, smaller than Muscle Shoals, AL. In that context, 18,000 riders a day in an urban bus corridor, and 4,000 riders a day on commuter rail, are remarkable achievements. ■

+ **Sucessful rapid-bus corridor converted to high-quality BRT**
+ **Commuter rail linking two downtowns**

SANTA FE

The North Central Regional Transit District operates a large network of rural routes in northern New Mexico, connecting small towns and Indian reservations to Taos and Santa Fe.

RIO RANCHO

ALBUQUERQUE

When the state of New Mexico bought the line that carries the Rail Runner, it inherited a curvy roundabout route into Santa Fe. Using the existing track would have resulted in unacceptably slow trips, so a new section was built (red in the map below), largely in the median of Interstate 35, to connect the existing lines (in black) to shorten the distance by 24 miles and trip times by 35 minutes. The difference between the routes reflects different goals. The old line was built to be as level as possible, allowing heavier trains at the cost of curves. The new line, designed only for light commuter trains, is much straighter, but with steeper hills.

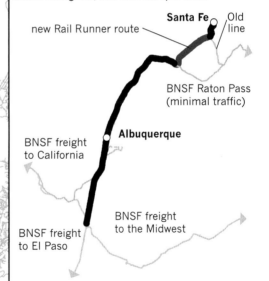

new Rail Runner route — **Santa Fe** — Old line

BNSF Raton Pass (minimal traffic)

BNSF freight to California — **Albuquerque**

BNSF freight to the Midwest

BNSF freight to El Paso

Bus Rapid Transit
Commuter Rail

| elevated | at grade | subway |
| in freeway | in street | mixed traffic |

frequent bus

✈ airport

5 miles

BRT (ART)

Opened: 2019
Last Expanded: N/A
Length: 14.6 miles (8 guideway miles)
Stations: 15 (guideway only)
Frequency: 7.5 min peak, 10–15 off-peak
Avg weekday ridership: 5,578
Ridership per mile: 382

Commuter rail (Rail Runner Express)

LOW PERFORMER

Opened: 2006
Last Expanded: 2010
Length: 97 miles
Stations: 13
Frequency: 7–8 trains each way daily weekday, 3–5 trains each way daily weekends
Avg weekday ridership: 2,400
Ridership per mile: 25

The Alvarado Transportation Center, (below) in downtown Albuquerque, brings together local and express buses, BRT, commuter rail, Amtrak, and Greyhound. It is centrally located within walking distance of downtown offices, the convention center, and new lofts. The Rail Runner website has schedules for connecting bus routes in Albuquerque and Santa Fe local buses, where Rail Runner riders get free transfers.

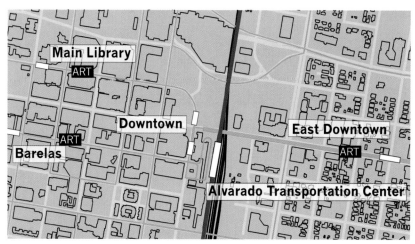

Central Avenue is the old Route 66, Albuquerque's traditional main street. ART stops directly in front of the University of New Mexico, the shops of Nob Hill (right), and Presbyterian Hospital (below). The distinctive signs and fabric canopies, lit up at night (above), make ART very visible.

Rail Runner's ridership can be attributed to a market of long commutes and conveniently located stations. Santa Fe, for example, has two stations. South Capitol (below), alongside a state government complex, is closer to the front door of one office building than most of the parking lot is. The other is in downtown, a third of a mile from the state capitol and half a mile from the Plaza. All of the major job concentrations in Santa Fe are within walking distance of commuter rail.

DOWNTOWN ALBUQUERQUE

The Central Avenue ART corridor runs through some of the city's low-income areas in addition to its major activity centers. But communities to the north and south have to depend on less frequent local bus service.

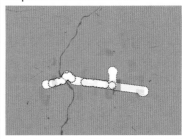

GAP: Frequent-bus network misses some dense neighborhoods

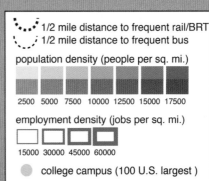

1/2 mile distance to frequent rail/BRT
1/2 mile distance to frequent bus

population density (people per sq. mi.)

2500 5000 7500 10000 12500 15000 17500

employment density (jobs per sq. mi.)

15000 30000 45000 60000

college campus (100 U.S. largest)

50. TUCSON

Tucson–Nogales, AZ

population 1,093,777 (65th)   **served by frequent transit** 22%   **daily trips per 1000** 30

sun tran

Sun Tran
municipal
Frequent Bus
Streetcar

Tucson, like many other US cities, set out to build a streetcar in the 2010s. But unlike Atlanta or Oklahoma City, it is not a downtown circulator. Unlike Seattle or Dallas, it doesn't feed into a larger rail system. Unlike Milwaukee or Cincinnati, it is not a tentative first line in a city that long tried to build rail. And unlike Tampa or Little Rock, it is not aimed at tourists. It is intended to be everyday transit on the most important corridor in the city.

Sun Link connects Tucson's key activity centers. It starts just southwest of downtown in the Mercado District, a 14-block new urbanist development stalled by the 2008 recession but now slowly developing. From there, it passes the convention center and the city and county government complexes on the way into the center of downtown. From there it continues past the bars and restaurants on 4th Avenue and to the front gate of the University of Arizona. It skirts the center of campus, then turns and ends at the university's medical school and hospital.

Along nearly the entire route, the streetcar is in the center of activity, and it serves a wide variety of destinations. It is not a straight line, but is effectively a diagonal route in a rectilinear street grid, and therefore has to make six right angle turns along the way. But it is as direct as it can be.

The streetcar is branded and operated as an integral part of the Tucson's transit network. Ticketing and fares are seamless between different parts of the network. It serves the downtown transit center in both directions, and connects with other bus routes along the way. Service is generally frequent—every 10–15 minutes—and runs 12–17 hours a day.

For a small metro area, Tucson has a remarkably strong transit system. Per capita transit ridership exceeds not only similar-size metro areas like Albany, Tulsa, or Knoxville, but doubles that of much bigger regions like Dallas, Orlando, and Charlotte. Ten frequent-bus routes cover a large portion of the city's densest neighborhoods, and less-frequent routes extend to the edge of the desert in every direction.

The streetcar is now a key route in that system. Three years after opening, the streetcar is carrying 3,000 riders on an average weekday. Along with Kansas City's, it is one of the success stories of the latest round of US streetcar systems. ∎

Streetcar (Sun Link)

Opened: 2014
Last Expanded: N/A
Length: 3.9 miles
Stations: 17
Frequency: 10 min midday, 15 min morning/evening, 15–30 min weekend
Avg weekday ridership: 3,100
Ridership per mile: 795

In the medical center (top), in downtown (bottom), and elsewhere along the route, Sun Link is in the center of activity.

+   **Streetcar serving everyday transit trips between downtown and university**

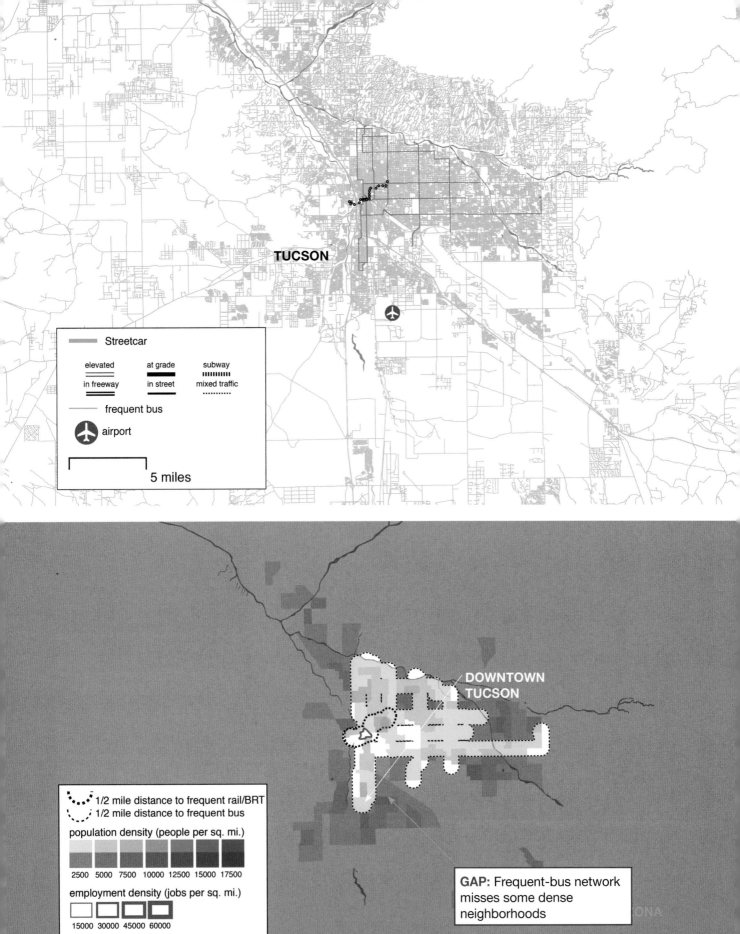

TUCSON

Streetcar

| elevated | at grade | subway |
| in freeway | in street | mixed traffic |

frequent bus

airport

5 miles

1/2 mile distance to frequent rail/BRT
1/2 mile distance to frequent bus

population density (people per sq. mi.)

2500 5000 7500 10000 12500 15000 17500

employment density (jobs per sq. mi.)

15000 30000 45000 60000

college campus (100 U.S. largest)

DOWNTOWN TUCSON

GAP: Frequent-bus network misses some dense neighborhoods

51. EL PASO

El Paso-Las Cruces, TX-NM

population 1,062,319 (68th)   **served by frequent transit** 13%   **daily trips per 1000** 10

Sun Metro
municipal
Frequent Bus
Streetcar

El Paso is constricted by natural and political borders. The Rio Grande squeezes though a narrow gap between mountain ranges and forms the border between the United States and Mexico. In downtown, the river and the mountains are only two miles apart, and the metropolitan area's one million people extend from there in three distinct directions. On the other side of the river, Ciudad Juarez has another 1.34 million people. Beyond that is open desert—the nearest major city in any direction is four hours' drive.

This geography creates a natural form for a transit system. Sun Metro is building four enhanced bus corridors radiating from downtown, with distinct "Brio" branding, limited stops, upgraded stop amenities, off-vehicle fare collection, and 14-hour-a-day frequent service on weekdays. At eight transfer centers, these corridors will connect to every local bus route in the Sun Metro network. When all four corridors are completed in 2020, Brio will be the most comprehensive rapid bus network in any US metropolitan area.

El Paso also has a new streetcar, though it is largely an exercise in nostalgia. Until 1973, streetcars ran through downtown El Paso and across the border to Ciudad Juarez. El Paso was the last US city to abandon its old streetcar system, and rather than being scrapped the cars were simply placed in a dirt field at the airport. Now, they've been pulled out and rehabilitated for service on a new line. The corridor is actually strong: a long straight line from the UTEP campus, with 24,000 students, through a dense mixed-use neighborhood to downtown. But the streetcar only starts running at 10:00 am, runs less frequently than the buses in the same corridor, and, thanks to closely spaced stops, riders paying as they board, shared lanes, and waits at traffic lights, takes 22 minutes to run two and a half miles. This could be a great line, but the way it's operated prevents that.

Amidst the empty desert, El Paso is a surprisingly urban place. Downtown, laid out in the 1850s, has a thriving retail district patronized by Americans and Mexicans walking across the border bridge, and the surrounding neighborhoods are dense and walkable. The city's master plan and revised zoning code encourage mixed-use development and complete streets. Transit ridership is already high, driven partially by a median household income of $13,421, one of the lowest in the US. El Paso, often forgotten, is building a stronger transit network than most US cities. ∎

Streetcar (El Paso Streetcar)

LOW PERFORMER
SMALL SYSTEM

Opened:	2018
Last Expanded:	N/A
Length:	2.4 miles
Stations:	14
Frequency:	15 min
Avg weekday ridership:	1600
Ridership per mile:	667

From a distance, it is impossible to recognize the border between El Paso (foreground, below) and Ciudad Juarez (background). Streetcars (above) once connected them; today private local bus service crosses the border every 30 minutes seven days a week.

+ **Rapid bus system covering much of the metro area**
+ **Useful streetcar linking university to downtown**

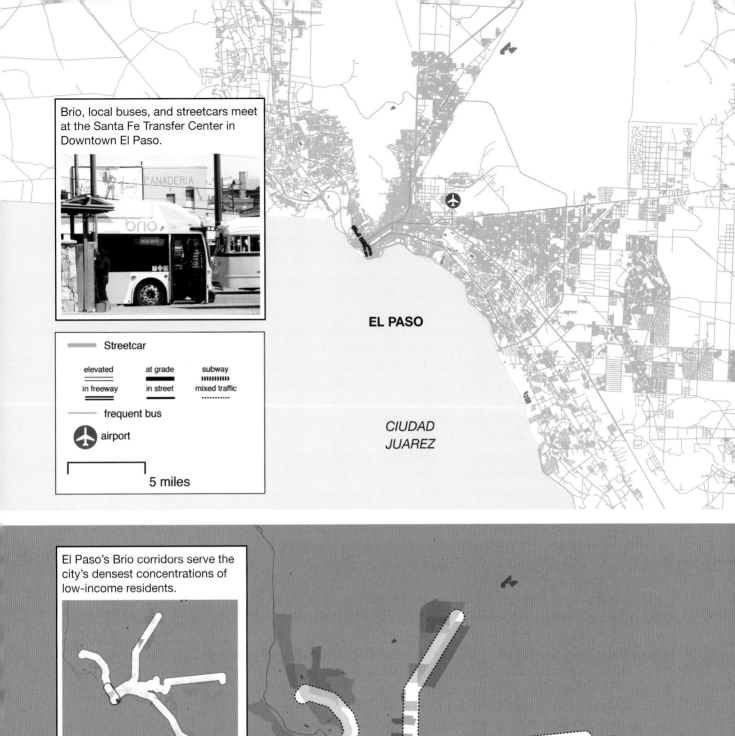

Brio, local buses, and streetcars meet at the Santa Fe Transfer Center in Downtown El Paso.

Streetcar

| elevated | at grade | subway |
| in freeway | in street | mixed traffic |

frequent bus

airport

5 miles

EL PASO

CIUDAD JUAREZ

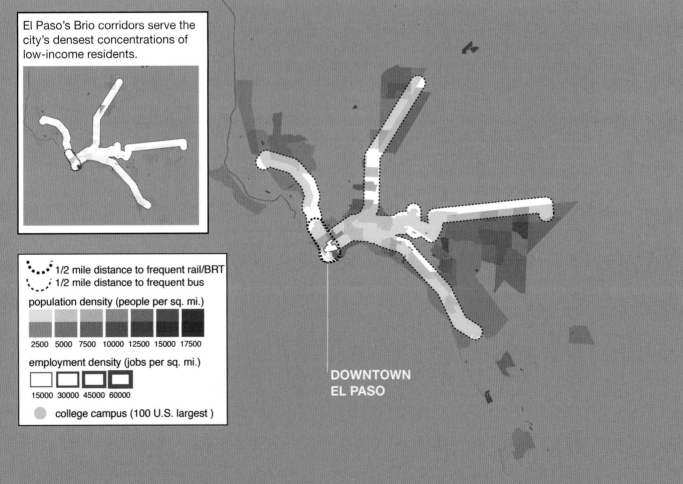

El Paso's Brio corridors serve the city's densest concentrations of low-income residents.

1/2 mile distance to frequent rail/BRT
1/2 mile distance to frequent bus

population density (people per sq. mi.)

2500 5000 7500 10000 12500 15000 17500

employment density (jobs per sq. mi.)

15000 30000 45000 60000

college campus (100 U.S. largest)

DOWNTOWN
EL PASO

52. HONOLULU

Honolulu, HI

population 974,563 (71st)   **served by frequent transit** 29%   **daily trips per 1000** 176

Hawaii is not only remote but tiny. The entire state is no bigger in land area than Maryland, and two thirds of the population is on the island of Oahu. Furthermore, the vast majority of that island in uninhabitable. The 800,000 residents of the urbanized area of Honolulu squeeze into a narrow strip between the Pacific and mountain slopes at 4,700 people per square mile, a density only 10 percent less than that of New York–Newark.

This density is ideal for transit. Nine percent of residents in the urbanized area travel to work by transit, low compared to the 32 percent in New York but similar to 12 percent in Chicago, and nine percent in Philadelphia. This high ridership has been achieved with conventional local and express-bus service, with minimal bus lanes, simple stops, and on-board fare payment. Because of the city's congested traffic, on-time performance is under 70 percent.

All of this makes a strong argument for rail, and that is what Honolulu is now building. A single 20-mile line will serve the majority of the metropolitan area, from the Alao Manoa shopping area near Waikiki Beach through Downtown and past the airport and naval base to the western suburbs. It promises all the elements of successful transit: stations in the middle of major activity areas, good connections and free transfers to bus service, speed (a 30-mph average, compared to 10 mph for the existing limited-stop bus service in the same corridor), frequency (every five minutes at peak and every 11 off-peak), and reliability, with entirely grade-separated (largely elevated) right-of-way.

However, Honolulu is also a cautionary tale. Rail planning actually started in the 1960s, and the current project was initiated in 2004. It became a major issue in the 2008 mayoral election, and a non-binding referendum that year got 53 percent support for the project. Since construction started in 2011 the cost estimate has increased from $5.3 billion to over $10 billion and the schedule has slipped by six years. In 2016, the Federal Transit Administration asked for a "recovery plan" that considered alternatives. Since construction started at the far suburban end of the line, a shorter version would leave off the densest areas and be much less useful. Currently, the outer section is scheduled to open in 2021 and the full line in 2026.

If all goes well, HART will carry 120,000 trips on an average weekday in 2023, a ridership per mile among the highest in the United States, on par with the Washington Metrorail. It will significantly improve transit in a city with already high transit use. But first it has to get built. ■

+ **State-of-the-art automated heavy-rail system serving unusually dense city between mountains and sea**

The Bus
City and County of Honolulu

The Bus
municipal
Frequent Bus

HART
independent agency
Heavy Rail

Heavy Rail (HART)
UNDER CONSTRUCTION

Opened: 2021
Last Expanded: N/A
Length: 0 miles (20 under construction)
Stations: 0 (20 under construction)
Frequency: 5 min peak, 11 min off-peak (proposed)
Avg weekday ridership: N/A
Ridership per mile: N/A

HART will be the first rail-transit system in the United States built to the standards of modern European and Asian metros, with automated trains and platform-edge doors (below) to prevent passengers from falling onto the tracks. The trains are manufactured by the same consortium that did the Copenhagen Metro.

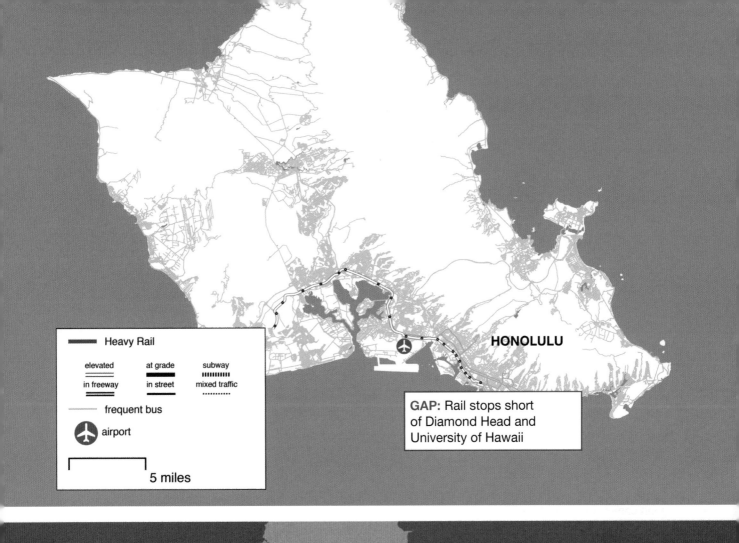

Legend

Heavy Rail		
elevated	at grade	subway
in freeway	in street	mixed traffic

frequent bus

✈ airport

5 miles

GAP: Rail stops short of Diamond Head and University of Hawaii

HONOLULU

HART's Phase 1 is scheduled to open in 2021—but Phase 2 (dashed) is required to make the system useful, and construction contracts have yet to be awarded for the most complex section, which is in Downtown. Without that, the system will miss the most important destinations.

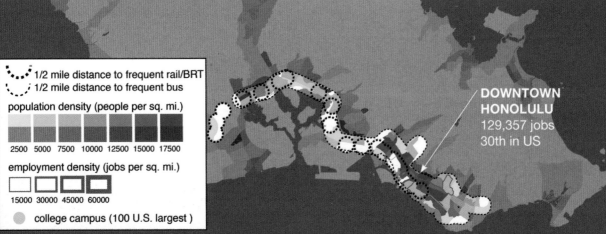

🌓 1/2 mile distance to frequent rail/BRT
⋮ 1/2 mile distance to frequent bus

population density (people per sq. mi.)

2500 5000 7500 10000 12500 15000 17500

employment density (jobs per sq. mi.)

15000 30000 45000 60000

● college campus (100 U.S. largest)

DOWNTOWN HONOLULU
129,357 jobs
30th in US

53. LITTLE ROCK

Little Rock–North Little Rock, AR

population 908,941 (74th) **served by frequent transit** 0% **daily trips per 1000** 19

Rock Region METRO
independent agency
Streetcar

Arkansas is still a rural state. Only 56 percent of the population lives in urbanized areas, compared to 80 percent nationwide. Little Rock, the capital, has twice as many residents as any other metropolitan area in the state, but that is still fewer than a million residents, and they are widely spread out. Four freeways radiating out from downtown encourage sprawl. Even compared to other small metro areas, the population density is remarkably low, with only one census tract exceeding 2,500 people per square mile.

Little Rock has the kind of transit system one would expect in such a place: 22 local bus routes, most hourly, five express routes, and three park-and-ride lots. Most of the routes radiate out from a transit center at the edge of downtown. It is a well-run system, recently rebranded, with relatively new buses and a real-time arrival app, but it is nothing remarkable. A 2016 ballot measure for a new sales tax to expand service and implement BRT failed.

What is unusual is that Little Rock is the smallest city in the United States to have a rail-transit system. The downtown streetcar line was opened in 2004, when only a handful of US cities were operating or even discussing streetcars, and was extended further in 2006.

The streetcar was designed for tourists. It connects the Bill Clinton Presidential Center, the convention center, the old state house, the Historic Arkansas Museum, the entertainment district around River Market, restaurants, hotels, and, across the river in North Little Rock, Verizon Arena, the maritime museum, and the minor league baseball stadium. Full service doesn't start until 9:00 a.m., the looping route makes for roundabout trips, and it doesn't even connect to the transit center. This works for visitors, for whom the ride on a replica historic trolley is part of the fun, but it doesn't do much for commuters or even downtown residents.

Rock Region Metro carries some 10,000 trips a day. The streetcar carries 230 of those trips. It is, in other words, a minor part of the transit system. It is better seen as part of an overall push for the revitalization of downtown Little Rock, and the restaurants and street life along the line suggest it is helping accomplish that purpose, even with its low ridership. ∎

Streetcar (METRO Streetcar)

LOW PERFORMER

Opened: 2004
Last Expanded: 2007
Length: 3.4 miles
Stations: 10
Frequency: 12.5–25 min; no Sunday service on one section
Avg weekday ridership: 348
Ridership per mile: 102

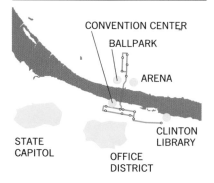

CONVENTION CENTER
BALLPARK
ARENA
STATE CAPITOL
OFFICE DISTRICT
CLINTON LIBRARY

The streetcar serves tourists by being the center of activity, but that also slows it down as it mixes with traffic, restaurant valets, and parking cars (below right). Trips are further slowed by the streetcar's loop, which serves tourist destinations but also takes riders out of their way (above). Notably, the route does not serve the high-rises of the central business district, the state capitol, or the main transit hub.

– **Low-ridership, tourist-oriented streetcar**

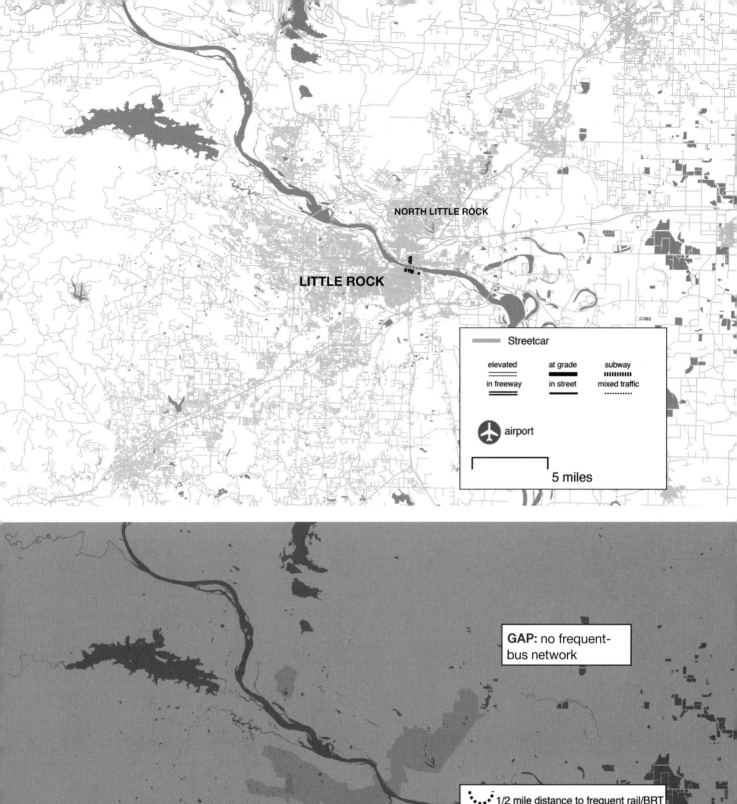

NORTH LITTLE ROCK

LITTLE ROCK

Streetcar

| elevated | at grade | subway |
| in freeway | in street | mixed traffic |

✈ airport

5 miles

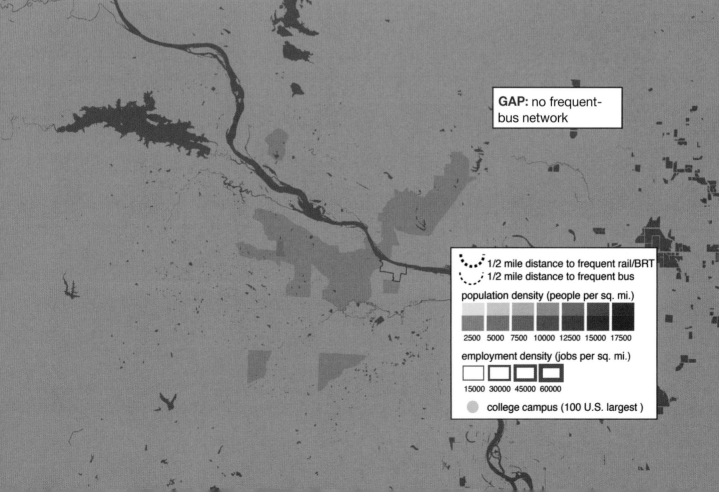

GAP: no frequent-bus network

⌒ 1/2 mile distance to frequent rail/BRT
⌒ 1/2 mile distance to frequent bus

population density (people per sq. mi.)
2500 5000 7500 10000 12500 15000 17500

employment density (jobs per sq. mi.)
15000 30000 45000 60000

● college campus (100 U.S. largest)

54. WINNIPEG

Winnipeg, MB

population 778,489 (86th)   **served by frequent transit** 24%   **daily trips per 1000** 170

Winnipeg Transit
Municipal
Frequent Bus
Light Rail

Winnipeg is small (the metro area has the population of Charleston, SC or Dayton, OH) and surrounded by open prairie, but still has typically Canadian high-ridership transit: 170,000 boardings a day, as many as Salt Lake City, which has three times as many people. Thirteen percent of the city's residents commute by transit. This is due to a fairly strong downtown employment core, the 30,000-student campus of the University of Manitoba, fairly dense suburban development patterns with clearly defined edges, and a comprehensive network that puts nearly every resident within walking distance of transit.

Winnipeg has been planning some sort of rapid transit since the 1950s, and identified the corridor from downtown to the University of Manitoba for bus rapid transit in the 1970s. Its wasn't until 2008, though, that there was a decision to build it, and that came with the mayoral caveat that it should be rail convertible.

In 2012, a 2.2-mile, four-station busway opened that follows the transcontinental railroad line southwest from downtown. The infrastructure is quite elaborate: the entire busway is grade separated including a short tunnel under the tracks. The Osborne Station (below), elevated where the busway crosses a major street, is fully enclosed. But, when they reach the edge of downtown, the buses run for three quarters of a mile in mixed traffic on city streets (left) to reach the downtown transit mall, opened in 1995. In 2020, the busway was extended southward to the university and the southern suburbs. ■

Bus Rapid Transit (RT)

Opened: 2012
Last Expanded: 2020
Length: Open BRT (6.8 miles guideway)
Stations: 13
Frequency: 4-15 min peak, 6-35 min offpeak
Avg weekday ridership: N/A
Ridership per mile: N/A

+ **Busway connecting downtown to university**
+ **High bus ridership**

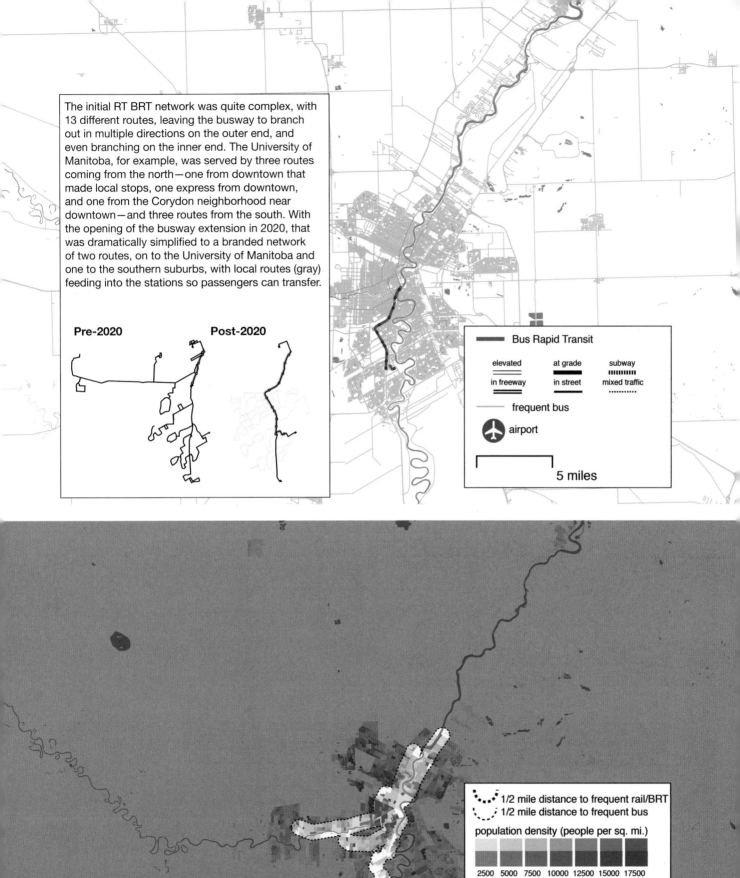

The initial RT BRT network was quite complex, with 13 different routes, leaving the busway to branch out in multiple directions on the outer end, and even branching on the inner end. The University of Manitoba, for example, was served by three routes coming from the north—one from downtown that made local stops, one express from downtown, and one from the Corydon neighborhood near downtown—and three routes from the south. With the opening of the busway extension in 2020, that was dramatically simplified to a branded network of two routes, on to the University of Manitoba and one to the southern suburbs, with local routes (gray) feeding into the stations so passengers can transfer.

Pre-2020

Post-2020

Bus Rapid Transit

| elevated | at grade | subway |
| in freeway | in street | mixed traffic |

frequent bus

airport

5 miles

1/2 mile distance to frequent rail/BRT
1/2 mile distance to frequent bus

population density (people per sq. mi.)

2500 5000 7500 10000 12500 15000 17500

no employment density data

55. WATERLOO

Cambridge - Kitchener - Waterloo, ON

population 523,894 (113th) **served by frequent transit** 43% **daily trips per 1000** 147

Grand River Transit
municipal
Frequent Bus
Light Rail

Metrolinx
independent agency
Commuter Rail
(see Toronto section)

The Cambridge–Kirchener–Waterloo area—three cities in a 15-mile corridor along the Grand River—is Canada's technology hub (it's where the once ubiquitous Blackberry was born) and home to one of the country's 10 biggest universities, but it's tiny. The metro area population is similar to Lancaster, PA, Corpus Christi, TX, or Kalamazoo, MI.

Thus, the Ion light-rail line is unique simply because Waterloo is the smallest metro area in North America with its own rail transit line. It is notable in that it is not an inexpensive line through an easy corridor. The entire line has dedicated lanes. It follows an existing rail corridor where that corridor runs right through the University of Waterloo campus, but follows streets to put it in the heart of downtown Waterloo (below), in front of a major hospital, and right through downtown Kitchener. The 100-foot-long vehicles, with four doors on each side, have significantly more capacity than a typical streetcar. Ridership per mile matches much bigger systems in larger cities like Denver and Salt Lake City.

Budget limited the first phase to Kitchener and Waterloo. Both ends of the line are at suburban malls (Fairway, right) that serve as transit hubs with frequent bus service. Future expansion, yet to be funded, will extend to downtown Cambridge, and a planned transit hub in Kitchener will simplify connections to VIA Rail corridor trains, GO regional buses, and the peak-only GO commuter rail to Toronto. ■

Light Rail (Ion)
SMALL SYSTEM

Opened: 2019
Last Expanded: N/A
Length: 11.8 miles
Stations: 16
Frequency: 8 min peak, 10-15 min offpeak
Avg weekday ridership: 17,166
Ridership per mile: 1,455

+ **Small city with a full-scale light-rail line**
+ **Strong corridor through two downtowns and a university**

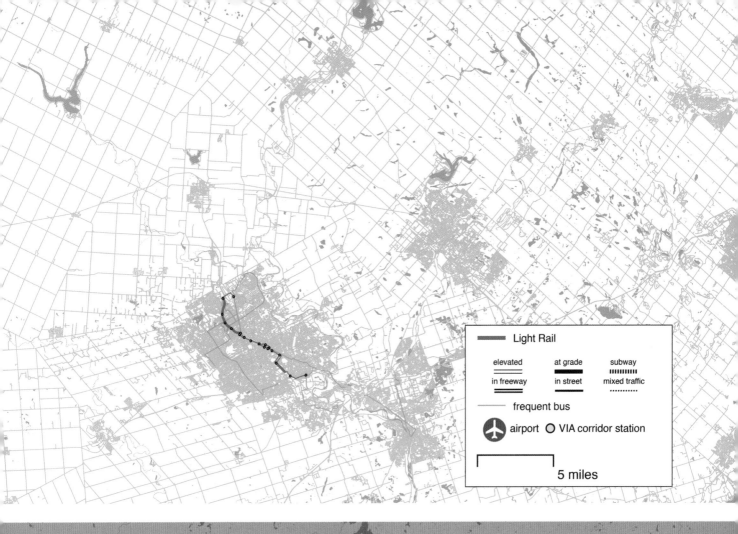

Light Rail

elevated	at grade	subway
in freeway	in street	mixed traffic

━━ frequent bus

✈ airport ◯ VIA corridor station

5 miles

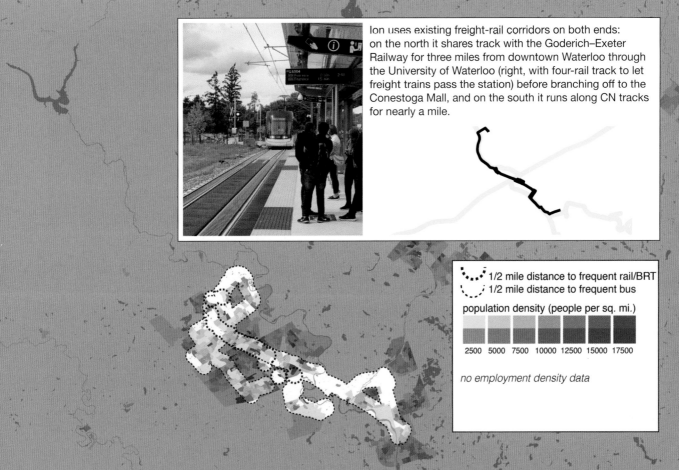

Ion uses existing freight-rail corridors on both ends: on the north it shares track with the Goderich–Exeter Railway for three miles from downtown Waterloo through the University of Waterloo (right, with four-rail track to let freight trains pass the station) before branching off to the Conestoga Mall, and on the south it runs along CN tracks for nearly a mile.

⸜⸝ 1/2 mile distance to frequent rail/BRT
⸜⸝ 1/2 mile distance to frequent bus

population density (people per sq. mi.)

2500 5000 7500 10000 12500 15000 17500

no employment density data

56. EUGENE

Eugene, OR

population 382,0677 (141st)   **served by frequent transit** 20%   **daily trips per 1000** 71

Lane Transit District
independent agency
BRT
Frequent Bus

College towns tend to have both high ridership and well-managed transit agencies. Transit systems in places like Madison, Wisconsin; Amherst, Massachusetts; East Lansing, Michigan; and Gainesville, Florida dramatically outperform their peers in similar-size cities. But few college town systems stand out as much as Eugene, Oregon's Lane Transit District, which serves the 18,000 students of the University of Oregon. It carries 35,000 trips on an average weekday, exceeding metropolitan areas like Nashville or Winston-Salem that are four or five times as big. And, in 2007, it opened EMX, the first long, street-running, reserved-lane BRT corridor in the United States, beating Cleveland's HealthLine by a year.

The first EMX line connected the downtown transit centers in Eugene and Springfield, stopping at the front entrance to the university campus in between. About 60 percent of the route has dedicated lanes in the street median, and every station has level boarding through all doors, with ticket vending machines on the platforms. Travel times were reduced by a quarter and ridership doubled in the first year.

In 2011, a northward extension opened from Springfield to a regional medical center and major retail and employment area. A four-mile extension east from Eugene opened in 2017 despite significant opposition from local businesses. This has created lines reaching the edge of the developed area in three directions, giving Eugene the most comprehensive BRT system in the nation. More lines are in LTD's long range plan, though it isn't clear that the political support is there: a recent study on the Main Street corridor in Springfield, LTD's most frequent local bus route, eliminated a new EMX line as an option, and the reconstruction of Franklin Boulevard on the original EMX line didn't include new transit lanes. ■

BRT (EMX)

Opened: 2007
Last Expanded: 2017
Length: 20.5 miles (2.8 guideway miles)
Stations: 15 (guideway only)
Frequency: 10 min weekday, 15 min weekend
Avg weekday ridership: 12,488
Ridership per mile: 609

Transit centers in Eugene and Springfield (right) connect EMX to Eugene's other bus routes.

Some of EMX's center-running guideways (right) have two concrete strips for the bus wheels with grass in between, making it clear to motorists that these are not traffic lanes. Buses have doors on both sides so they can stop at both single-platform stations in the median and curbside.

+ **High-quality regional BRT**

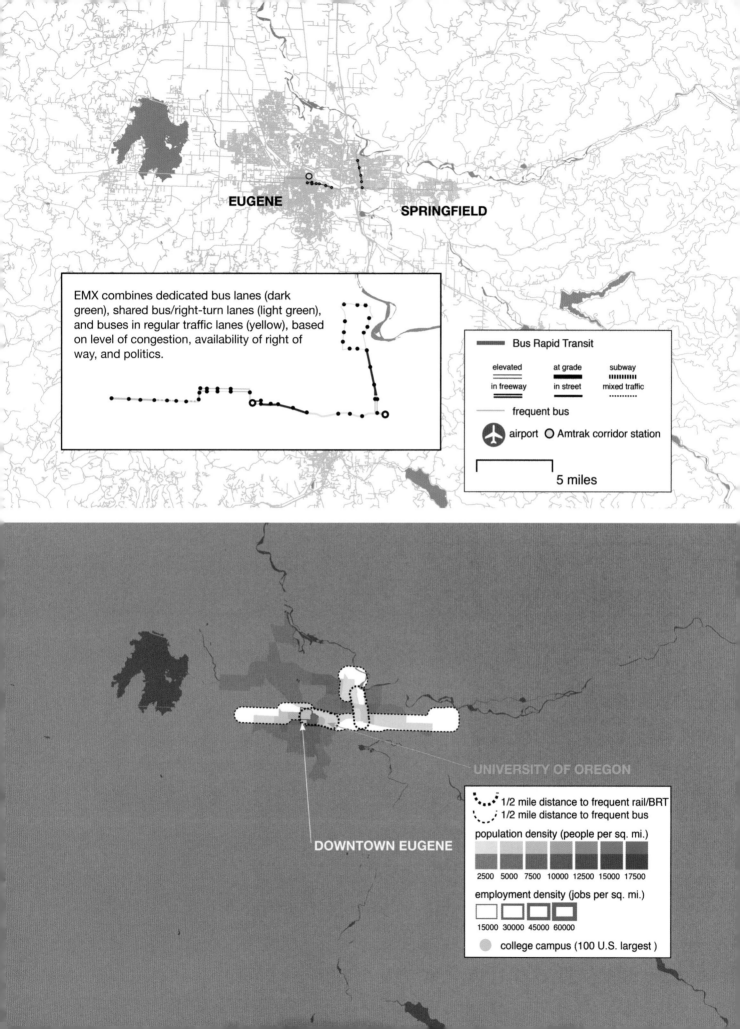

EMX combines dedicated bus lanes (dark green), shared bus/right-turn lanes (light green), and buses in regular traffic lanes (yellow), based on level of congestion, availability of right of way, and politics.

EUGENE

SPRINGFIELD

Bus Rapid Transit

elevated	at grade	subway
in freeway	in street	mixed traffic

frequent bus

airport ○ Amtrak corridor station

5 miles

UNIVERSITY OF OREGON

DOWNTOWN EUGENE

1/2 mile distance to frequent rail/BRT
1/2 mile distance to frequent bus

population density (people per sq. mi.)

2500 5000 7500 10000 12500 15000 17500

employment density (jobs per sq. mi.)

15000 30000 45000 60000

college campus (100 U.S. largest)

57. FORT COLLINS

Fort Collins, CO

population 356,899 (152nd) **served by frequent transit** 12% **daily trips per 1000** 35

TRANSFORT

TransFort
city department
BRT
Frequent bus

Fort Collins, like many Western cities, grew up around a railroad line. Every day, eight or so BNSF trains between Denver and Wyoming grind through the southern edge of town, across the Colorado State campus, and down through downtown on Mason Street, where, for nearly a mile, the tracks were simply laid in the pavement in the middle of a one-way arterial street.

In Fort Collins, as in many cities, the railroad is a nuisance, but here it also became a transit opportunity. BNSF wanted better separation for trains on Mason Street in the form of two-way traffic and concrete curbs to prevent cars from driving onto the track between intersections. The city asked for, and got, an agreement to acquire an easement to build a busway in BNSF's right-of-way south of downtown.

The result is MAX, a five-mile bus-rapid-transit line, about three miles of which is in a dedicated two-lane busway. Stations have level boarding and ticket machines; the branded buses run every 10 minutes during the day on weekends. With great service from residential areas to the university and downtown, and connections to every other Fort Collins Transfort bus route, it is carrying an impressive 4,600 passengers a day. ■

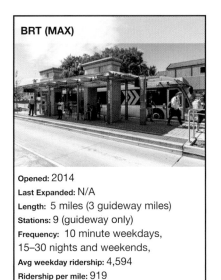

BRT (MAX)

Opened: 2014
Last Expanded: N/A
Length: 5 miles (3 guideway miles)
Stations: 9 (guideway only)
Frequency: 10 minute weekdays, 15–30 nights and weekends,
Avg weekday ridership: 4,594
Ridership per mile: 919

+ **High quality BRT linking neighborhoods, university, and downtown**
+ **Good frequent network**

The dedicated busway runs along the BNSF railroad tracks (below). Stations are center platforms, and buses cross over to the left side of the busway at stations so that the conventional right-side doors face the platforms. Gates keep cars and other vehicles out of the busway; a parallel trail serves bikes. After leaving the busway, buses run alongside freight trains through downtown (above).

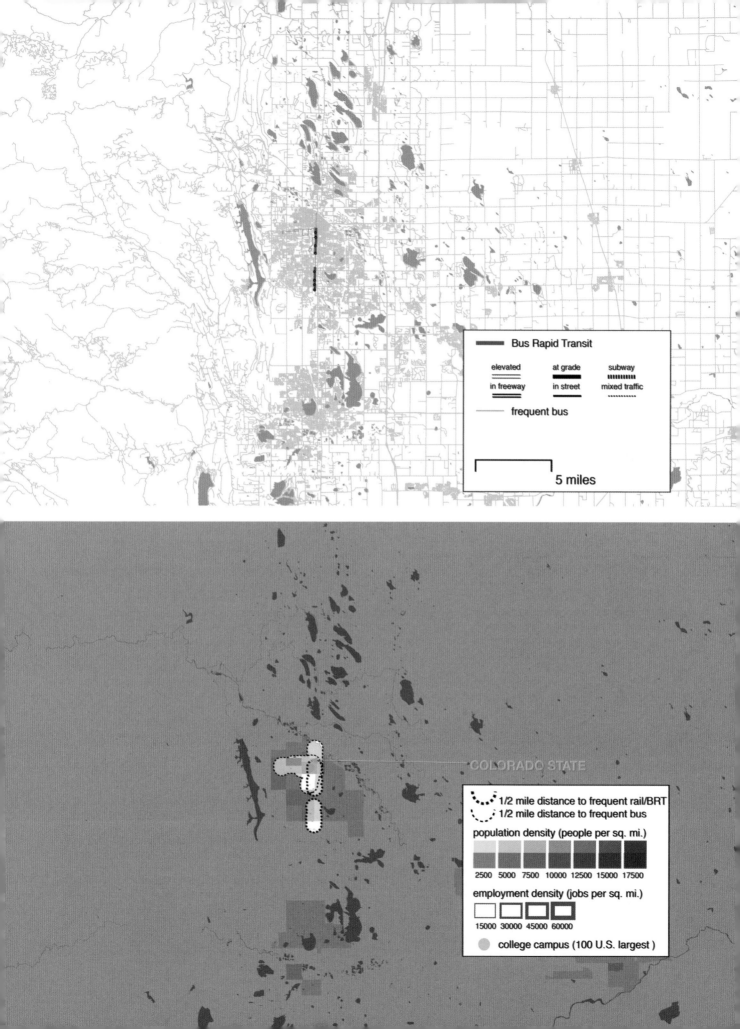

Bus Rapid Transit

elevated	at grade	subway

in freeway	in street	mixed traffic

frequent bus

5 miles

COLORADO STATE

1/2 mile distance to frequent rail/BRT
1/2 mile distance to frequent bus

population density (people per sq. mi.)

2500 5000 7500 10000 12500 15000 17500

employment density (jobs per sq. mi.)

15000 30000 45000 60000

college campus (100 U.S. largest)

CONCLUSION

A TRANSIT AGENDA

Across the United States and Canada, the public wants better transit. If agencies and elected officials really want to improve transit, what can they do? Here's a starting point. ■

We need to have smarter conversations about transit. We need to **define goals**, and to talk about **service, not mode**. We need to **acknowledge the racism** built into our transit networks. We need to focus on where the **demand is greatest**. And we need agency staff, consultants, board members, and elected officials to **ride transit**.

More homes, jobs, and services near existing transit makes that transit useful to more people. Building more next to transit—including **affordable housing**—can be fast and easy. Park-and-ride lots are a good place to start.

Many cities have **zoning** that prohibits dense development, often limiting buildings around rail stations to 3 or 4 stories. This drives up the cost of housing and prevent people from living near transit.

Minimum parking requirements come from an odd premise: that a government bureaucrat knows better than a resident or business owner how many parking spaces they need. Across the country, people who own no cars are still paying for empty parking spaces in their rent because cities force them to.

Government agencies, educational institutions, health-care, and social services need to locate on transit. The social security office, the community college, and the clinic are essential parts of life—they should be convenient for transit riders, not in a car-oriented neighborhood on a hourly bus route, or at the end of a shuttle bus.

We need **sidewalks and bikeways** leading to transit stops and **shelters** at the stops; every city, every county, every state and province, and the federal government can help make that happen.

Much of our transit is shaped by **roadway policy**. Every street project should include good sidewalks, regularly spaced crosswalks, and high quality bus stops. Many should include dedicated bus lanes. Every highway project should consider transit as an alternative. And, if we truly want to address global warming, we need to stop widening existing freeways and building new ones.

Riding transit in the US and Canada can be a confusing experience. That's easy to fix.

Most US rail networks have fairly easy to understand **maps**. Bus networks, though, don't. It's often hard to trace a route through a spaghetti of other routes, and it's almost always impossible to tell the difference between a route that runs frequently all day and a route that runs once or twice a day. Nearly every bus network needs a better map. Some just need a map. Amazingly, New Jersey Transit, an 11,000-employee agency operating in a developed country in the 21st century, doesn't even have a bus map.

Every **bus stop sign** in the United States should have the number of the bus, the name of the bus route, the destination of the bus, an indication of frequency, an indication of how what days and how late that bus runs, and a stop name. (It makes it easier to give directions, and easier for riders to get off at the right place and navigate.) This is all basic information, but most bus stops do not have it. Why not have a standard bus sign design like we have standard road sign designs?

Agencies need to make **fares** simpler. No transit rider should have to carry multiple farecards for multiple agencies, a first time rider shouldn't need cash, and transfers shouldn't be penalized. Fares shouldn't be enforced by police. And every agency should have fares that work for low income residents and families.

A frequent network lets transit riders can go where they want, when they want. Every metro area in this book should have a frequent network.

More cities need to r**edesign bus networks** to make routes simple and to focus resources on frequent routes.

Agencies need to **add midday and weekend service** to routes that are already frequent at rush hour.

Agencies need to **designate their frequent networks** on maps and at stops.

Some of the busiest and most useful transit systems are prewar and have never really been modernized.

The **New York subway** still has people in underground booths using 1930s technology to manually control trains. Only 23% of the city's subway stations have elevators.

San Francisco's **Muni Metro** trains glide under Downtown in a subway, but once they reach the surface they act like

1920s streetcars. Trains share lanes with cars, passengers board from traffic lanes, and intersections are controlled by stop signs. The city could put the lines into dedicated lanes, with traffic signal priority and real boarding platforms. The **SEPTA subway-surface lines** in Philadelphia need the same upgrades. **Toronto** also needs more dedicated lanes on its existing high ridership streetcar lines.

New Orleans streetcars actually have dedicated lanes, but go slower than buses because they have no traffic signal priority and boarding is so slow. Some new traffic signals, and carefully hidden transponders on the cars, would keep the historic ambiance but make streetcars much more useful for the locals who depend on them.

Some of the busiest transit corridors in North America are so crowded that there's no room for more people. It's worth investing just to make current riders' trips better, and to provide the capacity for more growth.

The **New York City Subway** needs more capacity. Paris built the RER to do this, improving suburban rail trips but also adding more capacity in the busiest part of the city to shift trips off existing metro lines. London is doing the same with the Elizabeth Line.

With 52,000 riders a day, **Geary Street** in San Francisco is one of the busiest bus corridors in the country. Buses run standing-room-only every 2.5 minutes at rush hour. MUNI is preparing to build BRT in that corridor, but it will be at capacity from day one. This level of ridership needs rail.

San Francisco's BART is out of capacity on its **Transbay Tube** under San Francisco Bay. It's one of the few ways for the 2.5 million people living in the East Bay to get to San Francisco. A second tunnel would add capacity and add redundancy in case of disruptions. The commuter-rail tunnel under the **Hudson River** has the same issues.

Los Angeles's **Wilshire Blvd.** carries over 80,000 people a day on buses. A subway extends under part of the street, and it's getting extended to UCLA by 2027, but ultimately it should go all the way to Santa Monica.

UBC, on the western edge of Vancouver by the Pacific Ocean, is already filling buses; it should have Skytrain service. Current construction will get only partway there.

DC's **Metrorail** is at capacity in the core, and the addition of the Silver Line—which means three lines have to share the same set of tracks—has reduced frequency and added scheduling quirks that make the system harder to understand. DC needs another subway under downtown.

The **Toronto Subway** is out of capacity. Some version of the endlessly rethought second downtown is needed now.

In **Boston**, getting from Back Bay to Harvard—2 miles—takes 26 minutes on an unreliable bus or an indirect rail trip. Boston needs north–south rail or BRT here.

Many cities are missing reliable transit—BRT or rail—in **key high ridership bus corridors**: Denver on Colfax, north-south in St. Louis, and the Strip in Las Vegas are three examples.

The United States has invested billions in commuter rail. But rather than being operated as all-purpose transit, that infrastructure is focused on 9-to-5 commuters, even when the surrounding areas have the density to justify all-day, two-way, frequent service.

Chicago's **Metra Electric** serves a dense area that doesn't have 'El' lines, with destinations like the University of Chicago, but service is infrequent and fares are expensive. It could be transferred from suburban-focused Metra to the city-focused CTA and integrated with local transit.

In New York City, densities along the inner portions of **New Jersey Transit, Long Island Railroad, and Metro-North** are greater than those that support heavy rail and light rail elsewhere in the country. At least 10 lines would justify all-day, 15-minute service, especially if off-peak fares matched local bus fare. **Boston** and **Philadelphia** could use similar upgrades; **Toronto** has already committed to all day frequent service on the core of its network but needs to follow through. Changing this will require a change in attitude, coupled with new ticketing systems and work rules that allow trains to be operated at lower cost with fewer crew members.

Trinity Railway Express connects Downtown Dallas to Downtown Fort Worth, with useful bus connections in between. Dallas runs trains every 20 minutes, 7 days a week, on every light-rail line, but the TRE is hourly at midday and runs only 6 days a week.

Airports do not provide nearly as much ridership as major activity centers, and the airport connection isn't useful to many unless the city already has a robust network. But in cities were economies depend on tourism or where many people don't own cars, investment in a good airport connection makes sense.

New York stands out among its peers for the lack of good transit connections to its airport. JFK has a decent connection, but Newark's Airtrain connects only to a commuter rail line that sometimes has nearly hour-long gaps between trains, and LaGuardia has only unreliable bus service. Unfortunately, the plans on the table are rather dumb—an overpriced PATH extension to Newark and a peoplemover from LaGuardia that would actually take people in the opposite direction from Manhattan.

The **Las Vegas** airport is only two miles from the world's largest concentration of hotel rooms. It needs rail or BRT to close that gap. **New Orleans** is another place where tourists don't need a car once they get into the city—but the airport bus is confusing, slow, and infrequent.

INDEX

Note: city names refer to metro regions rather than strict city limits.